KU-607-421

Economics and hermeneutics

Hermeneutics has become a major topic of debate throughout the scholarly community, in sociology and social theory, political and legal philosophy, the philosophy of art and literature, theology, the philosophy of history, anthropology, and the philosophy of science. What has been called the 'interpretive turn' has not only led to interesting new approaches in each of these disciplines, it has helped to forge an interdisciplinary language that is transforming the divided disciplines by bringing them closer together.

Yet one of the largest and most important social sciences, economics, has so far been almost completely left out of the transformation. A yawning gap continues to divide scholars in economics from the growing hermeneutics literature. *Economics and Hermeneutics* takes a significant step toward rectifying the situation, introducing scholars on both sides of the divide to ways that hermeneutics might help economists address some of their most important problems.

The essays are not philosophical commentaries from the outside of economics, but substantive contributions to economics. Among the topics addressed are entrepreneurship, price theory, rational expectations, monetary theory, welfare economics, and economic policy. The approaches to economics represented include the Austrian school, which has strong historical roots in continental philosophy, McCloskey's 'rhetoric' approach, Marxian critical theory and institutionalism.

Don Lavoie is editor of the journal *Market Process* and a member of the editorial board of *History of Political Economy*. His publications include *Rivalry and Central Planning: The Socialist Calculation Debate Reconsidered* (CUP 1985), and he is one of the leading contemporary contributors to the Austrian school of economics. His research interests include the history of Marxian and market-socialist theories of socialism and the methodology of economics.

Of related interest from Routledge:

The Philosophy of Economics   Subroto Roy
The History and Philosophy of the Social Sciences   Scott Gordon
The Methodology of Economic Model Building   Lawrence Boland
Social Theory as Science   Russell Keat and John Urry
The Idea of a Social Science and its Relation to Philosophy   Peter Winch

Economics and hermeneutics

Edited by Don Lavoie

London and New York

UNIVERSITY OF BRISTOL
Department of Philosophy

9 Woodland Road
Bristol
BS8 1TB

First published 1990
by Routledge
11 New Fetter Lane, London EC4P 4EE

Simultaneously published in the USA and Canada
by Routledge
a division of Routledge, Chapman and Hall, Inc.
29 West 35th Street, New York, NY10001

© 1991 Don Lavoie

Typeset in English Times
by Pat and Anne Murphy, Highcliffe-on-Sea, Dorset
Printed in Great Britain by
Mackays of Chatham PLC, Chatham, Kent

All rights reserved. No part of this book may be reprinted
or reproduced or utilized in any form or by any electronic,
mechanical, or other means, now known or hereafter
invented, including photocopying and recording, or in any
information storage or retrieval system, without permission
in writing from the publishers.

British Library Cataloguing in Publication Data
Economics and hermeneutics.
    1. Economics. Role of in hermeneutics
    I. Lavoie, Don *1951–*
330i

    ISBN 0–415–05950–X

Library of Congress Cataloging in Publication Data
Economics and hermeneutics / edited by Don Lavoie.
        p.   cm.
    Includes bibliographical references and index.
    ISBN 0–415–05950–X
    1. Economics—Philosophy.   2. Hermeneutics.   I. Lavoie, Don.
HB72.E268   1991   90–8818
330′.01—dc20   CIP

In memory of Ludwig M. Lachmann
1 February 1906–17 December 1990

Contents

Part III Alternative views of hermeneutics from a particular economic standpoint: the controversy in the Austrian school

Part IV Hermeneutical reason: applications in macro, micro, and public policy

Acknowledgements

On March 28, 1986 the Center for the Study of Market Processes, an Austrian-school oriented research and education centre in the George Mason University economics department, ran a conference at GMU on 'Interpretation, Human Agency and Economics'. The idea for this book was conceived at the conference, and first drafts of three of its essays, those of Lachmann, Ebeling, and Madison, were written for it. On the momentum of that occasion, I commissioned most of the other essays to fit together into an overview of the sorts of issues the conference had raised. Although I was listed as the conference's director, its success was as much due to a group of graduate's students I worked with: Ralph Rector, Dave Prychitko, Pete Boettke, and Steve Horwitz. Together we had just formed a readings group which we called the Society for Interpretive Economics, and weekly meetings were held to discuss the possibilities of applying hermeneutical philosophy to economics. The group has continued to meet every week ever since, with a growing participation of graduate students, and over the past two years has been co-directed by Arjo Klamer and me. Throughout its existence, the group has shaped and inspired my own thinking about interpretive economics, and all of the participants should be thanked.

I am deeply grateful to the late Professor Lachmann, one of my teachers at New York University, who had the most to do with my own intellectual development in general, and who turned my thinking in a hermeneutical direction. Richard Ebeling alerted me to the literature of contemporary hermeneutics, for which I will be forever in his debt. I thank Jack High, director of the Center for the Study of Market Processes, for supporting me in this project. It is Jack, as well as Rich Fink, the founder of the Center, to whom I owe the most thanks for having created an intellectual home for me where extraordinary projects, such as the Society for Interpretive Economics, could be launched. The atmosphere of enthusiasm and openness that has been cultivated at the Center is rare in the scholarly world, and is extremely difficult to create and maintain.

All but three of the essays have not been previously published. Donald N. McCloskey's contribution was published in a somewhat different form in Christopher Nash (ed.) (1989) *Narrative in Culture*, London: Routledge, pp. 5–22. Much of Philip Mirowski's chapter was previously published in the *Journal of Economic Issues* 3 (Sept. 1987): 1001–38. Lawrence A. Berger's chapter is a revised version of a paper entitled 'Economics and Hermeneutics' published in *Economics and Philosophy* 5 (1989): 209–33.

The book's publication has undergone an evolutionary history too complex to detail, but I should mention Thomas McCarthy and David Levin as having played a crucial role. Their support and encouragement for the project, as well as their specific advice on several aspects of its overall structure, made the final product possible. I also benefited greatly from comments on the manuscript from Donald McCloskey, Pete Boettke, Bob Coats, Greg Johnson, Dave Beers, and an anonymous reader. Dave Beers helped me with the final preparation of the manuscript, and prepared the index. I sincerely thank Alan Jarvis of Routledge for seeing the significance of this kind of work, and enabling it to see the light of day. Perhaps most of all I need to thank the contributors who put up with my urgent appeals to hurry with their drafts, and then were more patient with me than I had been with them.

Notes on contributors

Lawrence A. Berger is Assistant Professor of Insurance and Risk Management at the Wharton School of the University of Pennsylvania. Professor Berger has published papers on the economics of insurance markets, and his article 'Economics and Hermeneutics' appeared in *Economics and Philosophy* in October, 1989.

Tyler Cowen is Associate Professor of Economics at George Mason University. He is currently working on two books: *Exploration in the New Monetary Economics* and a book on the theoretical foundations of welfare economics. His *The Theory of Market Failure* was published in 1988.

Richard Ebeling is the Ludwig von Mises Professor of Economics at Hillsdale College in Michigan. He also serves as the Vice-President for Academic Affairs of The Future of Freedom Foundation in Denver, Colorado. He is the editor of the volume, *Money, Method and the Market Process: Essays by Ludwig von Mises*, and the author of 'Inflation and Controls in Revolutionary France: The Political Economy of the French Revolution' in *Reflections on the French Revolution: A Hillsdale Symposium*.

Arjo Klamer is Associate Professor of Economics at George Washington University. He is the author of *Conversations With Economists* and co-author with David Colander of *The Making of an Economist*. He is co-editor with Donald McCloskey and Robert Solow of *Consequences of Economic Rhetoric*.

Randall Kroszner is Assistant Professor of Business Economics at the University of Chicago's Graduate School of Business where he teaches money and banking. His 'The Development of the New Monetary Economics', co-authored with Tyler Cowen, was published in the *Journal of Political Economy* (June 1987). He served on the President's Council of Economic Advisers during 1987–88.

Ludwig M. Lachmann is Emeritus Professor at the University of Witwatersrand, Johannesburg, South Africa. He is the author of *Economics as a Social Science, Capital and Its Structure, The Legacy of Max Weber, Macro-*

economic Thinking and the Market Economy, *Capital, Expectations, and the Market Process*, and *The Market as an Economic Process*.

Don Lavoie is Associate Professor of Economics at the Center for the Study of Market Processes at George Mason University. He is the author of *Rivalry and Central Planning* and *National Economic Planning: What is Left?* He is co-editor with Arjo Klamer of a book series with Basil Blackwell Publishers on Interpretive Economics.

Donald N. McCloskey is John F. Murray Professor of Economics and Professor of History at the University of Iowa. He was a co-founder of the Cliometric Society, was co-editor for several years of the *Journal of Economic History*, and is the author of four books on British economic history. He is the co-director of the Project on Rhetoric of Inquiry, and the author of *The Rhetoric of Economics*.

G.B. Madison is Professor of Philosophy at McMaster University and in the Graduate Faculty of the University of Toronto. He is author of *The Phenomenology of Merleau-Ponty*, *Understanding: A Phenomenological-Pragmatic Analysis*, *The Logic of Liberty*, and *The Hermeneutics of Postmodernity: Figures and Themes*.

Uskali Mäki is Professor of Economics at the University of Helsinki and is currently a Fellow at the Swedish Collegium for Advanced Study in the Social Sciences in Upsala, Sweden. He has published papers on the methodology of economics, particularly on the issue of realism.

Philip Mirowski is Carl Koch Professor of Economics and History and Philosophy of Science at the University of Notre Dame. He is author of *More Heat than Light* and *Against Mechanism* and editor of *The Reconstruction of Economic Theory*. His *Who's Afraid of Random Trade?* is forthcoming from Princeton University Press.

Tom G. Palmer is Director of Student Affairs and Director of Eastern European Outreach Programmes at the Institute for Humane Studies at George Mason University. He has published widely on intellectual property rights and on economic policy.

Ralph A. Rector is a graduate student in economics at George Mason University and the recipient of a Bradley Fellowship. He is writing a doctoral dissertation on organizational culture and the decision-making process within business firms.

Jon D. Wisman is Professor of Economics at The American University in Washington, D.C. He has published widely in the history of economic thought, methodology, worker issues, and general topics in economics. His most recent work is the edited book, *Worker Empowerment: The Struggle for Workplace Democracy*.

1 Introduction

Don Lavoie

This book is an attempt to introduce to the reader two intellectual traditions which are at this time almost complete strangers: economics and hermeneutical philosophy. Indeed, it is probably fair to say that very few hermeneutical writers have more than a passing familiarity with economics, and that most economists have never even heard of hermeneutics.

Hermeneutics, or interpretive philosophy, is essentially a philosophy of understanding, which elucidates how it is that one person comes to understand the actions or words, or any other meaningful product, of another.[1] It takes the case of reading a text as paradigmatic of all forms of interpretation, throughout the arts and sciences, and in everyday life. It would treat a painting, for example, or a price, as a 'text' which needs to be 'read'.

The central point of hermeneutics might be summed up by clarifying the approach to understanding that it challenges, which might be called the 'copy' view. According to this view, when you read these words you are trying to reproduce as accurately as possible the original meaning I intended when I wrote them, you are trying to get an exact copy of my meaning. Human communication is implicitly treated as fundamentally similar to telecommunications. But if this was what actually happened when human beings tried to communicate with one another, then whenever there was a communication failure, our only recourse would be to send another copy, or otherwise build in some redundancy, as in computer communications. Instead, when we are misunderstood, we say it differently the next time, we explicate hidden assumptions, anticipate possible objections, deploy different examples. Our communicative process is not that of a fax machine sending a stream of bits in one direction only. Communicative partners engage with one another to discover a common understanding of a subject matter through a bidirectional, give-and-take process.

Against the copy approach, hermeneutics discusses the 'dialogical' process of interpretation, through which a meaning is developed out of a text by the reader's interaction with it. Especially in the version that has been developed by Hans-Georg Gadamer, it takes the process of spontaneous interplay which occurs in a good conversation to exemplify successful interpretation. The reader of a text reads it well when he both permits the author to speak and permits himself to listen. He allows the text to speak, in the sense that he does not merely subject it to his own examination but strives to be genuinely open to the challenges it may raise against him. He also actively listens, in the sense that he does not passively receive the text's message but needs to appropriate it for himself, relate it to what he already knows, see what it means *to him*.

The world is not understood by passive reception of sense data or by immediate access to objective reality in itself. It is only understood through the active participation of interpreters, who necessarily bring questions and 'prejudices' to the text that could not have pertained to its original context. We 'see' the world through our prejudices and questions, but these are best not considered distortions of an otherwise immediate reception of 'the world as it is in itself'. Our prejudices and questions are the only means by which we can understand, they are what Michael Polanyi called 'spectacles' through which we can come to see the world.[2] A better reading is not one that tries to reproduce the original, it is one that mediates between the horizons of the reader and the text, and integrates the text's message with the reader's own concerns. As Gadamer put the point, we understand differently when we understand at all.[3]

Hermeneutics would seem to apply to economics on two different levels: our understanding of the texts of economics; and our understanding of 'texts' of the economy – that is, the price movements, or monetary institutions, or industrial organization of economies, each of which is the meaningful product of human minds. We can ask how hermeneutics helps us to understand what economists are doing, and we can ask how it helps us to understand what economic agents are doing. Some of the earlier essays, in addressing the basic question of what hermeneutics is, pertain to the first level, but this book is primarily interested in the second.[4] The crucial question here, then, is how hermeneutical philosophy might help us to understand the economy.

For present purposes 'hermeneutics' may be understood in both a narrower and a wider sense. The narrower sense refers to the specific school of German philosophy, often called 'philosophical hermeneutics', with which the names of Gadamer and Paul Ricoeur are associated.[5] It can be traced back to the work of the German philosopher Wilhelm Dilthey, the father of twentieth-century hermeneutics, and was reshaped by the phenomenological tradition of Edmund Husserl and Martin Heidegger. In the narrower sense, hermeneutics stands for a radical philosophic position – challenging, and challenged by, the mainstream of the philosophical community.

In a wider sense, hermeneutics may be understood to refer to the many strands of 'interpretive' philosophy which share common ground with philosophical hermeneutics in their opposition to positivist-oriented philosophies. Such diverse writers as Thomas Kuhn, Charles Peirce, G.H. von Wright, Max Weber, E.D. Hirsch, Jacques Derrida, Charles Taylor, and Richard Rorty could all be intelligibly labelled 'interpretive', and, like philosophical hermeneutics, they raise radical philosophic challenges to mainstream philosophy, as well as to one another.[6] Although I happen to have a strong preference for hermeneutics in the narrower sense, I have deliberately tried to include in this book a broad sampling of essays that are hermeneutical in the wider sense. While the broader notion of interpretive philosophy admittedly ignores some important differences, it underscores the elements these philosophies share with one another, and do *not* share with most economists.

In this wider sense, all the contributors would support a more 'interpretive' approach to economics than is typically permitted in the profession. Most of them are in this sense radicals, challenging the way economics is done today. The interpretive approaches are as open to non-quantitative as they are to quantitative evidence, as open to verbal modes of expression as to mathematical ones, as open to 'close-up' empirical research in the form of individual case studies as to statistical and econometric research involving large sample sizes.

Interest in hermeneutics has grown over the past decade – in both the wider and narrower sense – among English-speaking scholars, in a wide variety of disciplines.[7] The rise of hermeneutics represents a shift of Anglo-American philosophy towards that of Europe. Translations from the German of Husserl's and Gadamer's works, and from the French of Ricoeur's, are having an impact on American philosophers. Phenomenology and hermeneutics are becoming an integral part of English-language philosophical curricula, and are not merely topics for European specialists. The 'interpretive turn' – as Richard Rorty dubs this transformation of philosophy – has already affected many of the human sciences such as sociology, anthropology, history, linguistics, and psychology. Much of the literature considers implications for the methodology of the human sciences in general, in a way that would seem to apply to economics. So far, however, very little of it has taken up economics explicitly. In its turn, contemporary economics has for the most part simply ignored the 'interpretive turn'.

It is important to realize that economics and hermeneutics have not always been such strangers. Most of the contributors to this volume would cite approvingly such interpretive sociologists as Max Weber and Georg Simmel, who were widely read in both the hermeneutical and economic literature of their day.[8] Only a few decades ago, two of the economics profession's leading figures were Fritz Machlup (a follower and friend of Weberian sociologist and phenomenologist Alfred Schütz and Frank Knight (who translated one of Weber's books), both of whom were familiar with the German philosophical literature and argued forcefully for an interpretive economics. Indeed, many economists can still be found who are interpretive in their overall orientations.[9] However, the rank and file of the profession – and most of its most respected leaders – are quite distant from the kind of economics which people like Machlup and Knight were engaged in. The technical training of modern economists leaves them more able than their teachers to talk to mathematicians, statisticians, and engineers, but less able to talk to interpretive historians, sociologists, anthropologists, or philosophers. Those economists who can talk to such people, and who have made explicit efforts to nudge economists in an interpretive direction, have often provoked a hostile reaction from their fellow economists.

Since economics and hermeneutics have by now grown so far apart, the questions each has about the other, at this stage, are apt to be fundamental. Each is still beginning to figure out what the other is all about, so that it is understandable that there have been few efforts yet to go very far into the details of the other's subject matter. For this reason, the essays in this book have a certain introductory flavour, but they also aspire to getting past the introductions, and moving on to the details of the economics and the philosophy.

It is often remarked by specialists in the philosophy of economics that most practising economists retain positivistic methodological beliefs which philosophers have long ago rejected. Recently there has been a resurgence of interest by economists in the philosophy of science, but so far most of this work has involved attacks on the profession's complacent espousal of outmoded positivistic ideas. It seems nowadays that few economists are willing to make a philosophical defence of their research on the basis of positivism (or for that matter, on any other basis), so that little is gained from another devastating critique of positivism. The case for tolerance of anti-positivistic methodological perspectives has already been made persuasively.[10] What we need now is a more constructive effort in alternative directions.

The interpretive turn in philosophy does not merely replace positivistic rules of 'proper method' with anti-positivistic ones. Rather, it questions the role of philosophical prescription in the practices of scientists. On the other hand, most interpretive philosophers certainly do not want to refrain altogether from making informed comment on scientific practices. Implications of these philosophical ideas may ultimately require economists to substantially alter the way they do their research. Such implications for economics are best revealed not by abstract reflection on the nature of knowledge in general but in the details of actual economic research. Thus, the essays in this volume address specific problems of interest to economists in the light of ideas that come from hermeneutical philosophy. Most of the contributors are professional economists, not philosophers, and all of them have a deep respect for the human sciences in general, and economics in particular. The essays are not prescriptions from outside of economics by philosophers who see themselves as distant experts in knowledge. On the contrary, they strive to be genuinely interdisciplinary efforts to re-examine economic questions from the standpoint of hermeneutics. The case for the usefulness of hermeneutics has already been made in other disciplines with respect to their own substantive issues. It needs to be made within the discourse of economists.

WHAT IS HERMENEUTICS?

The essays in Part I represent preliminary efforts to introduce hermeneutics to economists. The paper by Arjo Klamer starts the discussion off by reflecting on the current status of economic discourse. It is no easy task to start up a discussion among economists about philosophical topics. It is useful to begin by examining this very difficulty. What is it about economics as a discipline which makes its practitioners so reluctant to examine themselves philosophically? Klamer's paper reflects on the difficulty, suggesting that the economist's view of rational choice is a big part of the problem. His strategy for changing the economists' conversation about the economy is to reflect first on what economists are doing, and to observe that the rational-choice model provides at most only a very incomplete account of what is going on in the practices of economists.[11]

Klamer then turns to the study of the economy itself, and argues that we have let our professional attention drift away from what Clifford Geertz calls 'the native's point of view'. We pay little attention to the *meaning* which economic phenomena have for everyday people whose actions, after all, constitute the economy. We need to come to terms with the meaning which economic processes have for everyday businessmen, civil servants, consumers, and so forth. We can also learn, of course, from exercises in the pure logic of choice, but it seems reasonable to try once in a while to actually *talk* to economic agents.[12]

The essay by Gary B. Madison suggests some specific ways in which adopting the themes of hermeneutics could improve economics. Madison first describes hermeneutics in terms of Gadamer's work, as a matter of getting away from 'objectivistic' prejudices about the nature of science, and proceeds to find elements of commonality here with what the economists call the 'subjective' theory of value and 'methodological individualism'. He then uses Ricoeur's work on the hermeneutics of the subject to restate what it is economists should mean when they somewhat misleadingly call themselves subjectivists or individualists. Critics of hermeneutics often charge that it is only capable of helping our understanding of intended purposes, and cannot help us to *explain* unintended causal processes. Madison responds to this charge by deploying Ricoeur's work on narrative to show how hermeneutics has its own way of dealing with causal explanation and unintended consequences.

ALTERNATIVE VIEWS OF ECONOMICS FROM A PARTICULAR PHILOSOPHICAL STANDPOINT

Part II surveys some of the encouraging possibilities that the 'interpretive turn' suggests to economists from four diverse economic perspectives: neoclassicism; institutionalism; critical theory; and Austrian economics. Each supports the interpretive turn in the broad sense, though each reads its significance for economics quite differently in some respects. Despite their disagreements, these writers would all like to see their field take its own interpretive turn, to liberate this important (if dismal) social science from the inhibitions of positivism.

One of the main themes of philosophical hermeneutics is that there is, in general, more than one correct way to read a text. To understand something is to apply it to what one already knows, to make it one's own, to appropriate it. When an economist asks the question 'what is hermeneutics?', then the question has already become 'what is it *to an economist*?'. Understanding is a 'fusion of horizons' between the author and his or her reader, where what is understood is not simply copied but is integrated with what the reader already knows, and in the process changed. Moreover, the interpreter who truly wants to understand leaves himself open to being changed by his confrontation with what he is interpreting. Each of the four essays in Part II is an attempt to *apply* the meaning of hermeneutics to the writer's own understanding of the economy.

Of course, each of the four schools of economics here represented is itself capable of a variety of different readings. The authors make no claim of dogmatic allegiance to the schools, but neither do they make the pretence of being purely 'school-less', and unconnected to any particular perspective on the world. It is one of the central points of hermeneutics to stress that we are always shaped by the intellectual traditions we come from, and that such 'prejudices' are not a contamination of an otherwise pure and objective view. Our prejudices need not imprison us or distort, and in fact they are what enable us to see anything at all. All that we mortals have is a variety of perspectives on the world; none of us has access to some kind of God's-eye, objective view of the world.

Donald N. McCloskey, one of the leading contributors to the 'Chicago' branch of neoclassicism, elaborates on one of the central themes of hermeneutics which Madison had sketched – that is, its idea of 'narrative'. McCloskey sees hermeneutics as helping us to recognize that most of what modern economists are already doing – despite what most of them seem to think – is fundamentally a hermeneutical exercise. In spite of the official methodological rhetoric of neoclassicism, economists are really telling stories. Drawing on the work of such hermeneutical writers as Wolfgang Iser and Hayden White, McCloskey shows the extent to which the practices of contemporary economics are already implicated in the hermeneutical act of emplotment, of interpreting economic processes as meaningful stories.[13]

In contrast to McCloskey's effort to re-interpret what modern neo-classical economists are already doing as hermeneutical, Philip Mirowski emphasizes the extent to which such economists fail to be sufficiently hermeneutical – a point, by the way, with which McCloskey generally agrees. Economists, Mirowski argues, need to change not only their philosophical self-image, but many of their basic scholarly practices as well. He suggests that in the rich tradition of American institutionalism – which had been systematically squeezed out of the profession in the heyday of neoclassical positivism – can be found a far more hermeneutical approach to economics than is possible within the neoclassical mainstream. Based on hermeneutically-oriented American pragmatist philosophers, such as Charles Peirce, the institutionalists present a bold challenge to the mainstream, a challenge which the profession cannot afford to ignore. Especially in the work of John R. Commons, Mirowski shows, one can find an approach that is exemplary of the hermeneutical spirit lacking in modern economics.

Like institutionalism, the intellectual tradition of Marxian economics went into serious decline with the rise of positivism, and is now undergoing resurgency with positivism's decline. Although orthodox Marxism is at least as far from the spirit of hermeneutical thinking as positivistic neoclassicism is, several strands of western Marxism – especially the so-called Frankfurt school – have had important ties to the hermeneutics tradition for many years. Marx himself emerges out of the same general milieu of German philosophy from which hermeneutics arises, and Georg Lukács, often called the founder of western Marxism, was significantly influenced by Wilhelm Dilthey. The work of the Frankfurt school's leading contemporary social theorist, Jürgen Habermas, has been particularly concerned to address the issues of hermeneutics, and his classic debate from the 1960s with Hans-Georg Gadamer remains among the most interesting intellectual encounters of our time.[14] Unfortunately, although Habermas's work touches on economic issues in a number of different ways, it has not specifically discussed the issue of the nature of economics as a science, nor have economists for their part dealt with Habermas's social theory. Jon D. Wisman's essay opens up the discussion of such issues, and shows how economics looks from a Habermasian perspective. Here one of the central themes of hermeneutics, the critique of a narrowly 'instrumental' view of reason, is used to introduce economics and hermeneutics to each other. Wisman shows how hermeneutics could help economists to better understand the processes of human interaction and communication taking place in the economy.

Ludwig M. Lachmann offers a view of yet another school of thought which has found important common ground with hermeneutics, the Austrians. Like western Marxism, the Austrians came out of a continental, philosophical environment which had already been influenced by traditional hermeneutics. In particular, Ludwig von Mises was substantially influenced by Dilthey as well as the interpretive sociologists Weber and Schütz. Like the institutionalists and Marxists, the Austrians were crushed by the rise of a positivistic version of neoclassicism. Lachmann elaborates on Madison's point that the kind of 'subjectivist' economics which the Austrians have been trying to defend finds powerful support in hermeneutical philosophy.[15]

The purpose of identifying the authors by school is not to reinforce but ultimately to undermine the traditional separations among them. They obviously come from a wide variety of economic perspectives, but it is my belief that where they are going to is a largely shared destination. Standard Chicago-school economics is far distant from standard Austrian-school economics on the topic of methodology, and from standard institutionalism and western Marxism in nearly every respect, but the four essays in Part II that came from these four schools make them sound close. Here we find what Clifford Geertz (1983) calls a 'blurring of genres', as when Lachmann the Austrian endorses both Keynes of Cambridge and Knight of Chicago. Undoubtedly, important divisions exist in the profession, but the divisions need to be redrawn. The common 'interpretive' thread that unites the contributions is more important than the historical divisions between their separate schools. My point, then, is not to encourage the schools to fight about who is more interpretive than the other, but rather to recommend that they try to achieve a fusion of horizons on the basis of what seems to be a common, interpretive orientation.

ALTERNATIVE VIEWS OF HERMENEUTICS FROM A PARTICULAR ECONOMIC STANDPOINT

As hermeneutics itself argues, the communication that this book would like to initiate between philosophers and economists should be a two-way process of communication, a dialogue in which each side is fundamentally open to the claim the other makes on it. If we aspire to what Gadamer calls hermeneutical openness, then it will not be enough to pick out a few economists who are already sympathetic with hermeneutics in order to use it to judge economics. We will need to ask what economists further removed from hermeneutics think of it, too. Just as Part II tried to indicate ways in which economists can learn about their shortcomings by encountering hermeneutics, so Part III suggests ways in which the hermeneutical philosophers may more clearly see their own weaknesses – at least in the presentation of their case, if not in the content – by dealing with the fears and objections they arouse among economists.

Part III thus raises questions about whether there might be serious problems in hermeneutics that economists in particular would do well to avoid. One of the four schools of economics discussed in Part II, the Austrian school, has already been having a heated controversy over hermeneutics. A distinct faction of the school has emerged which we might call the hermeneutical Austrians, who have been enthusiastically embracing the philosophy, and recommending bold revisions to traditional Austrian economics on the basis of its themes.[16] In reaction to the efforts of this faction have come a number of critiques which are more addressed at perceived difficulties with hermeneutics than at economic questions as such.[17] The central theme raised by the critics (which of course is of interest to other economists besides the Austrians) is essentially a concern about getting at the real world. Economists, the worldly philosophers, tend to be suspicious of philosophy as something out of the world. They worry that philosophizing would distract them from concrete issues of causal explanation, or worse would entangle them in relativism.

Although there are some interesting issues in the criticisms that have been raised so far of the hermeneutical Austrians, the critics, by and large, have not shown a very sophisticated appreciation of hermeneutics. Uskali Mäki, in contrast to the other critics, has a firm command of issues in the philosophy of economics, and contributes an important challenge to the hermeneutical Austrians by examining Georg Henrik von Wright's theory of understanding. Von Wright is one of the most prominent philosophers in the analytic tradition to have been singled out as especially 'hermeneutical'. Mäki finds von Wright's hermeneutics a coherent and very important contribution to philosophy, but he contends that his hermeneutics suffers from a serious shortcoming that severely limits its usefulness for economists.[18] He interprets von Wright's theory of understanding as fundamentally acausal and thus concludes that it is inappropriate to deal with such causal theories as Israel Kirzner's theory of entrepreneurship and Carl Menger's of the origin of money. Since these theories are indeed central to the Austrian economists' whole research programme, Mäki concludes that contributors to this school have no choice but to reject at least von Wright's version of hermeneutics, and possibly others as well.

In his essay, Richard Ebeling picks up a theme from Paul Ricoeur's classic essay 'What is a text? Explanation and understanding', to suggest – as do Madison (Ch. 3) and McCloskey (Ch. 4) – that at least this version of hermeneutics can support a notion of causal explanation. Ebeling contends that, contrary to the fear which many economists have of philosophy, some immediate and reasonably down-to-earth applications of hermeneutics can be found for issues that lie at the heart of economics – in its theory of price. Hayek and other Austrian economists have contributed to our understanding of the causal processes by which prices communicate knowledge among market participants and co-ordinate their purposes. Ebeling argues that the Austrian school needs to grapple more directly with the process by which prices are interpreted. It should not treat them as data – or, as Hayek tends to put it, telecommunication signals. Ebeling provides an indirect answer to the argument which Mäki has raised. Hermeneutical understanding, at least in Ricoeur's version (if not perhaps in von Wright's), is not opposed to causal explanation but encompasses it. The causal process by which prices change is inextricably intertwined with the interpretations of the prices made by human minds. Explaining price changes and understanding them are two aspects of one integrated activity.

Even if it is allowed that Ricoeur's approach to hermeneutics (if not, perhaps, von Wright's) leaves room for causal explanation, there remain a number of serious charges against hermeneutics that the critics have raised, especially the charge of relativism. The critics wonder whether hermeneutics permits us to say that our theories are rational models corresponding in some sense to the real world. Does hermeneutics deny philosophic foundations to support the substantive studies of the economy? Does it impair the economist's most powerful tool of positive analysis, the otherwise clear-cut and objective model of rational choice? Does it introduce needless mysteries and ambiguities into the discipline? If such criticisms are not answered, the economists will have little incentive to pay attention.

Ralph Rector's essay turns the critique of the hermeneutical Austrians on its head. He argues that the danger of relativism is not something which the hermeneutical Austrians are now introducing into economics. On the contrary, it is a danger already present: for example, in the leading mainstream school of macroeconomics – the 'rational-expectations' school. Hermeneutics can be viewed not as a source of this serious danger but as an escape from it.

Most of the criticisms of 'rational expectations' have argued that it exaggerates the degree to which agents are rational. Rector's essay argues that the agents in these models in a sense are not rational enough. To the extent that we include in our notion of rationality an ability to *justify* one's beliefs, the agents in these models are not super-rational but rather sub-rational beings. The justifications to which economists usually appeal – based on 'correspondence' or 'coherence' theories of truth – lead to an infinite regress problem and thus the spectre of relativism. Philosophical hermeneutics, Rector argues, offers a more persuasive way out of the 'epistemic regress', and thereby points the way to a richer understanding of the nature of rationality.

HERMENEUTICAL REASON: APPLICATIONS IN MACRO, MICRO, AND PUBLIC POLICY

The essays in Part IV provide several different examples of how hermeneutics can address specific problems in economics. Hermeneutics, as Rector argued, is not against reason but against the objectivistic notion of reason that comes to us from Cartesian rationalism. It offers a way not to attack but to rescue reason from the rationalists who claim too much for it. Each of the concerns just mentioned – about theories 'corresponding' to the real world, and being given philosophical 'foundations', about hermeneutics undermining the 'objective' model of rational choice and crippling our ability to take up issues of policy – are deconstructed by the essays that follow. But the primary aim in each case is not simply to destroy objectivistic approaches but to be constructive about what a more interpretive approach can do instead. The purpose is to put hermeneutical insights to work on specific problems in contemporary economic research, especially those surrounding 'rationality'.

Underlying most of contemporary macroeconomics, including much of the enthusiasm for rational expectations theory, is the hope that 'macro' can be connected to its 'micro' foundations. To many economists this means extending the Walrasian/Paretian tradition, the formal theory of 'general equilibrium', from its home in micro to issues in macro. Randall Kroszner suggests that there is a kind of 'fetish for foundations' here, similar to the one Richard Rorty notes among philosophers. The standard general-equilibrium approach is wedded to a theory of rational choice as strict optimization. It leaves no room for time and uncertainty, and no room for anything deserving the name 'money'. General equilibrium may be useful in a limited theoretical capacity as a 'foil' for thought, but it cannot serve as the all-encompassing framework for the whole of economics. Succeeding in restricting macro to its Walrasian micro foundations would amount to the destruction of macro, precisely because time and money would cease to be taken seriously.

By moving away from the general-equilibrium thinking prevalent in micro, Kroszner argues, macroeconomists might be able to illuminate several important issues in monetary theory. In particular, the Mengerian theory of money – the same 'invisible-hand' theory which Mäki had discussed, is taken as an exemplar. Menger's disequilibrium theory of marketability is summarized and used to support the recent arguments by such writers as Neil Wallace, Robert L. Greenfield, Leland B. Yeager, and Robert E. Hall that a 'moneyless' economy is possible.

Kroszner argues that the new proposals to separate the unit-of-account and medium-of-exchange functions of money – as radical as they admittedly are – may be more justifiable than many monetary theorists seem to think. The arguments against these proposals for monetary reform often depend on a dubious claim about what the 'essential' features of money must be, exactly the kind of claim that Rorty makes one suspicious about. Kroszner thus puts an old theory of money to new uses with some assistance from Rorty's critiques of foundationalism and essentialism.

Beyond the question of whether the microeconomists' theory of general equilibrium can sustain the weight of being the foundation for the whole field of macroeconomics, is the question of whether it can serve in its own domain as the basis for microeconomics. Lawrence A. Berger takes up the standard model of rational choice and asks whether it is adequate to analyse human action even on the micro level. Berger argues that the work of the hermeneutical philosopher Charles Taylor offers economists a richer notion of human agency than the one they have been using. Human agency is misunderstood if it is treated as a mechanical optimization of given ends under known constraints. The question of what to pay attention to in the first place cannot itself be a matter of rational calculation. What one considers worthy of attention, Taylor shows, is shaped by one's language, by the orientation of the particular discourses one participates in. Both macro-economists and microeconomists need to escape the confines of the rational-choice model.

If the Walrasian bases of both macroeconomics and microeconomics were undermined, the standard Paretian approach to welfare economics would be as well. The basis for judging the performance of an economic system may need to be re-examined. Tyler Cowen asks what a different, non-Paretian welfare economics might be like. He suggests that welfare theorists need to turn their attention more to actual history in order to discover which kinds of policies have led to which particular results. He outlines an example of a welfare standard that might be developed on the basis of three criteria: complexity; discovery/innovation; and the provision of consumer goods. Cowen points out that the non-Paretian approach seems closer to the ordinary-language discussions we have about economic policy than to those we are used to in welfare economics. The hermeneutical view of reason is one that would reconnect scholarly reason with practical, everyday reasoning.

Tom G. Palmer concludes the book by considering what hermeneutics may have to do with economic policy. Gadamer uses the model of the conversation to elaborate his theory of how we understand a text; Habermas uses the conversation as a model for politics. Palmer argues that the market, like a conversation, is a 'forum for persusasion'. He draws implications from Gadamer's hermeneutics for certain central questions in economic policy – such as public goods, the regulation of advertising, and the design of property rights. The different ways in which such issues would be appropriated by Habermasian and Gadamerian perspectives suggest that economists could profit from holding their own version of that classic debate.

These diverse essays take the interpretive turn seriously, and begin exploring the question of what this philosophical shift implies for the practice of economics. It is hoped that they will serve to open the economics profession to a broader set of philosophical perspectives than is typically considered.

NOTES

1 One of the best summaries of hermeneutical philosophy is Warnke (1987). Other works that provide useful interpretations of the philosophy include Bernstein (1983), Dallmayr and McCarthy (1977), Linge (1976), Mueller-Vollmer (1985), Weinsheimer (1985), and Winograd and Flores (1986).
2 For what is essentially a hermeneutic approach to the natural sciences see Polanyi (1958; 1959; 1969). For the argument that Polanyi's approach is similar to Gadamer's, see Weinsheimer (1985).
3 I have elaborated on Gadamer's point about understanding differently, and

related it to Hayek's work on the communicative processes of markets and culture in Lavoie (1987; 1990b).

4 The interpretation of the texts of economics raises no special problems not already encountered in any effort of intellectual history, and in any case it is what historians of economics are already doing. I do think such research would benefit from a dose of hermeneutics. A good place to start for economists might be Samuels (1990).

5 Among the main writings of Gadamer and Ricoeur which develop the main outlines of philosophical hermeneutics are Gadamer (1976; 1982; [1960] 1989) and Ricoeur (1981a; 1981b; 1984; 1985).

6 Some of the important contributions by writers who are hermeneutical in this wider sense, and which are of interest to anyone who would like to consider the relevance of the approach for the human sciences, include Geertz (1973; 1984), Rorty (1979), and Taylor (1971; 1980).

7 For an interesting collection of social-science essays that productively deploy hermeneutical insights, see Rabinow and Sullivan (1979; 1987), where economics is conspicuous by its absence.

8 Weber's magnum opus was entitled *Economy and Society: An Outline of Interpretive Sociology* (1978). Georg Simmel's *The Philosophy of Money* ([1907] 1978) is a neglected classic of monetary theory.

9 Among my own favourite books, written from a variety of perspectives, that articulate what is wrong with economics today, and point in the direction of what a more interpretive approach to economics might be like, are Hodgson (1988), Leijonhufvud (1981), O'Driscoll and Rizzo (1985), and Shackle (1972). Arjo Klamer and I have recently launched a book series in 'interpretive economics' with Basil Blackwell (publishers) to try to encourage more work of this kind in the profession.

10 For example, by Caldwell (1982).

11 Klamer's book of interviews with economists (1983) exposes some of the problems which economists have engaging with one another in productive dialogue, problems which an attention to hermeneutics might help them to overcome.

12 My own attempt to argue this point is in Lavoie (1990a).

13 McCloskey's work on 'rhetoric' (1983; 1985) has gone the furthest of any economist to bring interpretive themes to the attention of the mainstream of the profession.

14 An excellent summary of Habermas's complex social theory and his debate with Gadamer can be found in McCarthy (1985).

15 Lachmann's neglected book on Max Weber (1971) can be called the first explicitly hermeneutical contribution to Austrian economics.

16 The two economists who provoked the debate by beginning to use hermeneutics to revise Austrian economics are Ebeling (1985; 1986) who has mainly referred to Schütz and Ricoeur, and Lavoie (1986; 1990b), who has mainly referred to Gadamer.

17 Among the more strident critics of the hermeneutical Austrians have been Albert (1988) and Rothbard (1988). A counter-argument was written by G.B. Madison (1988), and a rejoinder by David Gordon (1990).

18 Mäki makes what many of the other critics of the hermeneutical Austrians would consider an important concession when he admits the ubiquitousness of hermeneutics in all scholarship.

14   *Introduction*

REFERENCES

Albert, Hans (1988) 'Hermeneutics and economics: a criticism of hermeneutical thinking in the social sciences', *KYKLOS* 41: 573–602.
Bernstein, Richard, J. (1983) *Beyond Objectivism and Relativism: Science, Hermeneutics, and Praxis*, Philadelphia: University of Pennsylvania Press.
Caldwell, Bruce (1982) *Beyond Positivism: Economic Methodology in the Twentieth Century*, Boston: Allen & Unwin.
Dallmayr, Fred R. and McCarthy, Thomas A. (eds) (1977) *Understanding and Social Inquiry*, Notre Dame, Indiana: University of Notre Dame Press.
Ebeling, Richard M. (1985) 'Hermeneutics and the interpretive element in the analysis of the market process', *Center for the Study of Market Processes Working Paper* no. 16, George Mason University.
—— (1986) 'Toward a hermeneutical economics: expectations, prices, and the role of interpretation in a theory of the market process', in Israel M. Kirzner (ed.) *Subjectivism, Intelligibility, and Economic Understanding: Essays in Honor of Ludwig M. Lachmann on his Eightieth Birthday*, New York: New York University Press.
Gadamer, Hans-Georg (1976) *Philosophical Hermeneutics*, translated and edited by David E. Linge, Berkeley: University of California Press.
—— (1982) *Reason in the Age of Science*, translated by F.G. Lawrence, Cambridge, Mass.: MIT Press.
—— ([1960] 1989) *Truth and Method*, revised translation of *Wahrheit und Methode: Grundzuge Einer Philosophischen Hermeneutik*, by J. Weinsheimer and D. Marshall, New York: Crossroad.
Geertz, Clifford (1973) *The Interpretation of Cultures*, New York: Basic Books.
—— (1983) *Local Knowledge: Further Essays in Interpretive Anthropology*, New York: Basic Books.
—— (1984) 'Distinguished lecture: anti anti-relativism', *American Anthropologist*, 86 (2): 263–78.
Gordon, David (1990) 'Review of G.B. Madison, *Understanding: A Phenomenological-Pragmatic Analysis*', *The Review of Austrian Economics* 4: 215–22.
Hodgson, Geoffrey M. (1988) *Economics and Institutions: A Manifesto for Modern Institutional Economics*, Philadelphia: University of Pennsylvania Press.
Klamer, Arjo (1983) *Conversations With Economists*, Totowa, N.J.: Rowman & Allenheld.
Lachmann, Ludwig M. (1971) *The Legacy of Max Weber*, Berkeley: Glendessary Press.
Lavoie, Don (1986) 'Euclideanism versus hermeneutics: a re-interpretation of Misesian apriorism', in Israel M. Kirzner (ed.) *Subjectivism, Intelligibility, and Economic Understanding: Essays in Honor of Ludwig M. Lachmann on his Eightieth Birthday*, New York: New York University Press.
—— (1987) 'The accounting of interpretations and the interpretation of accounts: the communicative function of "The Language of Business"', *Accounting, Organizations and Society* 12: 579–604.
—— (1990a) 'Hermeneutics, subjectivity, and the Lester/Machlup debate: toward a more anthropological approach to empirical economics', in Warren Samuels (ed.) *Economics As Discourse*, Boston: Kluwer Academic Publishing.
—— (1990b) 'Understanding differently: hermeneutics and the spontaneous order of communicative processes', *History of Political Economy* 22A (Special Issue): forthcoming.
Leijonhufvud, Axel (1981) *Information and Coordination: Essays in Macroeconomic Theory*, New York: Oxford University Press.

Linge, David E. (1976) 'Editor's introduction', in Hans-Georg Gadamer, *Philosophical Hermeneutics*, translated and edited by David E. Linge, Berkeley: University of California Press.
McCarthy, Thomas (1985) *The Critical Theory of Jürgen Habermas*, Cambridge: MIT Press.
McCloskey, Donald M. (1983) 'The rhetoric of economics', *Journal of Economic Literature* 21 (June): 481–517.
—— (1985) *The Rhetoric of Economics*, Madison, Wisconsin: University of Wisconsin Press.
Madison, G.B. (1988) 'Hermeneutical integrity: a guide for the perplexed', *Market Process* 6 (1): 2–8.
Mueller-Vollmer, Kurt (1985) *The Hermeneutics Reader*, New York: Continuum.
O'Driscoll, Gerald P. (Jun.), and Rizzo, M.J. (1985) *The Economics of Time and Ignorance*, New York: Columbia University Press.
Polanyi, Michael (1958) *Personal Knowledge: Towards a Post-Critical Philosophy*, Chicago: University of Chicago Press.
—— (1959) *The Study of Man*, Chicago: University of Chicago Press.
—— (1969) *Knowing and Being*, edited by Marjorie Grene, Chicago: University of Chicago Press.
Rabinow, Paul and Sullivan, W.M. (eds) (1979) *Interpretive Social Science: A Reader*, Berkeley: University of California Press.
—— (1987) *Interpretive Social Science: A Second Look*, Berkeley: University of California Press.
Ricoeur, Paul (1981a) 'The model of the text: meaningful action considered as a text', in P. Ricoeur, *Hermeneutics and the Human Sciences*, edited and translated by J.B. Thompson, New York: Cambridge University Press.
—— (1981b) *Hermeneutics and the Human Sciences*, edited and translated by J.B. Thompson, New York: Cambridge University Press.
—— (1984) *Time and Narrative*, vol. 1, Chicago: University of Chicago Press.
—— (1985) *Time and Narrative*, vol. 2, Chicago: University of Chicago Press.
Rorty, Richard (1979) *Philosophy and the Mirror of Nature*, Princeton, N.J.: Princeton University Press.
Rothbard, Murray N. (1988) 'The hermeneutical invasion of philosophy and economics', *The Review of Austrian Economics* 3: 45–59.
Samuels, Warren (ed.) (1990) *Economics As Discourse*, Boston: Kluwer Academic Publishing.
Shackle, G.L.S. (1972) *Epistemics and Economics: A Critique of Economic Doctrines*, Cambridge: Cambridge University Press.
Simmel, Georg ([1907] 1978) *The Philosophy of Money*, Boston: Routledge & Kegan Paul.
Taylor, Charles (1971) 'Interpretation and the sciences of man', *Review of Metaphysics* 25 (Sept.): 3–51.
—— (1980) 'Understanding in human science', *Review of Metaphysics* 34 (Sept.).
Warnke, Georgia (1987) *Gadamer: Hermeneutics, Tradition and Reason*, Cambridge: Polity Press.
Weber, Max (1978) *Economy and Society: An Outline of Interpretive Sociology*, Berkeley: University of California Press.
Weinsheimer, Joel C. (1985) *Gadamer's Hermeneutics: A Reading of Truth and Method*, New Haven: Yale University Press.
Winograd, Terry and Flores, F. (1986) *Understanding Computers and Cognition*, Norwood, N.J.: Ablex.

Part I

What is hermeneutics?

2 Towards the native's point of view
The difficulty of changing the conversation

Arjo Klamer

PRELUDE

Three economists are talking about economic development during lunch. The conversation is smooth until one of them tries to call attention to the 'native's point of view'.

Economist 1: We have been discussing economic development for a while, and all we have been talking about are resources and incentives. Shouldn't we also think of the influences of the cultural factor of economic development? The beliefs people hold, their perceptions and their aspirations could very well constrain their actions.
Economist 2: [?]
Economist 3: You mean that we should discuss people's preferences? I doubt if that will get us anywhere. The neoclassical model appears to be doing pretty well. At any rate, if we were to follow your suggestion we would do sociology.
Economist 2: Yeah. [He mumbles something about 'vagueness', 'science' and 'the road to madness'.]
Economist 1: But Amartya Sen points us in that direction.
Economist 2: [?]
Economist 3: Didn't he go to Harvard recently?
Economist 1: Clifford Geertz, an anthropologist, has done work on economic development in which he pays attention to the native's point of view. He . . .
Economist 3: Never heard of him.
Economist 1: Some economists are advocating a hermeneutic position. To them Geertz could . . .
Economists 2 and 3: [?]
Economist 2: Listen, I am having this problem with solving an iterative process that I get in my growth model. The computer program that I am using works all right for the first steps but then something goes wrong. Could it be that . . . ?

Like any conversation, a conversation among economists is constrained. 'Anything' does not 'go' in economics; in this case talk about the native's point of view (i.e., the meaning of economic phenomena to the agents whose actions constitute those phenomena) goes nowhere. The question that I want to press here is, simply, why that is. More specifically, what is the nature of the difficulty that the three economists have?

The temptation here is great to declare those who do not understand or do not make sense, 'obtuse', 'dogmatic', 'stupid', or, worse, 'unscientific' and 'not serious'. But such judgements will generally misrepresent the nature of the difficulty. To answer the question why the difficulty occurs, we need to go back to the source of the problem. Before I do so, we should be convinced that there is a problem.

IS THERE A PROBLEM?

I am willing to accept a lot that a physicist tells me. Quarks and strings do not play a critical role in my intellectual and emotional lives, and a discussion about them will meet little resistance from me unless it is for lack of interest or incomprehension. This is true for discussions in physics, chemistry, music theory, cricket, molecular biology and other disciplines of which I have acquired little knowledge. I have little to say and fail to see their problems as interesting.

This is not always true: some ideas that emanate from these disciplines intrigue me and can even bother me. When a physicist poses the possibility of time going backwards I am confused. I want to know more; I want to know what this means. What makes a difference here is that whereas I know little about quarks and strings, I have clear conceptions of time, and its going backwards is not one of them. I do not only not comprehend – how could I? – but I also resist. The possibility of time going backwards does not occur in the world as I understand it. I might be merely curious or intrigued if Carlos de Castaneda were the inventor of this idea, but since these are respectable physicists at well-known universities who utter the theory, I have a problem.

I have a similar problem when I listen to neoclassical economists discussing human behaviour. The talk about optimizing strategies and individual choice does not mesh with human behaviour as I understand it.[1] This is a problem. Because I am not a physicist I can ignore the talk about quarks and time going backwards. That I cannot do when neoclassicals present their models. Being an economist myself I am interested, and I have to deal with the discrepancy between those models and my partly tacit and partly articulated understanding of human processes.

AMPLIFICATION: RUMBLINGS IN THE MARGIN AND OUTSIDE OF ECONOMICS

The problem, which might be labelled a problem of cognitive dissonance, has hardly been noticed within the world of economics itself. Whether the issue is the buying of laundry detergent or economic development, a constrained maximization model is the way to go. Any other sound is doomed to be drowned out in conversations among economists.

There is, however, some rumbling in the margins. Amartya Sen (1977) perceives in the neoclassical characterization of individuals a 'rational fool'; Albert O. Hirschman (1985) adopts Sen's notion of metapreferences to express the possibility that people evaluate and change their preferences; George Akerlof (1984) introduces sociological variables into the model; Herbert Simon (1985) makes connections with cognitive psychology. Nothing too revolutionary here, but such rumbling heightens and amplifies the sensation of a problem.

The problem becomes loud and clear when one looks at economics from the outside, and begins reading the works of Clifford Geertz, Michael Foucault, Marshall Sahlins, Mary Douglas, Alasdair MacIntyre and their like. Take, for example, Geertz's *Peddlers and Princes* (1963): it deals with a subject that belongs to the economic domain – namely, economic development in Indonesia. But one seeks in vain for rational choice or formulations of optimizing strategies in Geertz's account. Instead there is much about symbolic actions of Javanese and Balinese villagers, the subjects in the book. The account is interesting. Even Harry Johnson, a neoclassical economist who reviewed the book for the *Journal of Political Economy* (1964) thought so.[2] Geertz's account seduces and persuades yet it does not 'go' in economic discourse. That makes for a problem.

The writings of MacIntyre and Foucault do not transgress directly into the domain of economists, but the effects on the economist reader are similar. Their historical and rhetorical ways of writing about ethics and knowledge add to the sense of a problem in the neoclassical accounts. They generate a discursive situation in which the concept of a rational individual solving constrained-optimization puzzles seems absurdly limited. We experience a problem. Can we go beyond its mere observation?

A ROUNDABOUT WAY OF GETTING TO THE PROBLEM

Practising economists hint at the problem when they complain about the unrealism of assumptions. Yet their criticisms do not seem to hold much water. Alternative assumptions, such as cost-mark-up pricing, seem *ad hoc*. Without being able to say precisely why, I suspected that the critics were caught up in the same language game as the neoclassicists. They did not help towards an understanding of the problem.

I began to reflect upon what economists do. Popper and Lakatos were the philosophers to which one turned at the time, but they did not help much either. Were they, too, speaking the same language as neoclassicals? Michael Polanyi showed new possibilities and the realm of argumentation and rhetorics opened up. That is where Foucault, MacIntyre, and also Aristotle came in.

Seeing economics as a discourse and exploring its rhetorical dimensions, to which their works inspire, seems to bring new life to the conversation *about* economics. It breaks the grip that a narrow logic had on methodological thinking and stimulates one to see beyond epistemology (the points of departure in conventional methodology), and to watch the behaviour of economists more directly.

But many economists, and especially the economic methodologists among them, hear in this conversation different sounds from those intended. They hear the denial of standards that can discriminate between strong and weak arguments, and advocacy of an 'anything goes' position. 'Rhetorics debunks science', they say. Extensive communication does not appear to get us much closer.[3] These reactions, which are quite common, were irritating at first. And then they began to intrigue me, because they seemed symptomatic of a problem. This problem is, namely, the Cartesian tendency to divide the world in twos. If a statement is not objective, many will almost automatically relegate it to the realm of the subjective; if someone denies the existence of fixed standards, they will see in this the denial of all standards and the embracement of relativism.

I now think that this problem in discussions on methodology is related to the problem that I am having with neoclassical economics. Thinking about the behaviour of economists, therefore, might offer insights into the behaviour of economic subjects. This is a roundabout way of getting to the problem, but it is one that I have found useful and pursue here.

A note of clarification

It is easy to confuse the discourse about economics and economists with the discourse about the economy and economic subjects. The discourse about economics and economists is a *meta*discourse; it takes us on to a metalevel from which we reflect on our activities as economists. The relationships are as follows:

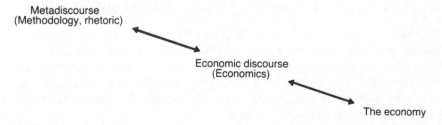

Metadiscourse
(Methodology, rhetoric)

Economic discourse
(Economics)

The economy

I argue in this essay that the metadiscourse in economics is analogous to economic discourse. The implied assertion is that economic discourse be thought of as a metadiscourse as well, in the sense that it reflects on our lives as economic agents.

THREE WAYS OF DEALING WITH A PROBLEM[4]

To understand the nature of this particular problem in conversations about economics, I propose to retreat as far back as possible to uncover the most fundamental reasons for human actions. This path leads to the strategies that are available to humans for dealing with any problem. Thus we will now come to recognize the source for the problem at hand.

We humans act because we experience a *tension*. We have a vague feeling of dissatisfaction (the stomach does not feel as we like it or we feel restless) and we walk to the refrigerator. We read or hear something that does not fit in with what we already know and we begin to think.[5]

Consider the action of thinking (which is presumably most relevant among the activities of economists). The action can imply the ignoring of the tension. Hearing about time going backwards creates a tension which I subsequently try to forget. Ignoring tensions is what we do all the time in our scholarly activities. The problem can also cause subversion of, or liberation from, all we know. That tends to happen when we experience something out of the ordinary, such as the death of someone close, chaotic behaviour of a physical system, a plunging stock market, or maybe the reading of Geertz, MacIntyre, or others. Another way of dealing with a tension is to recognize it as a problem and seek its solution within what we know already. This is what the normal scientist does with selected problems.

We ignore the majority of the tensions we experience and only rarely change our way of thinking because of a perceived tension.[6] But the third way of dealing with a tension usually draws our attention: identification of a tension as a problem and its subsequent subsumption into what we already know – possibly with minor changes – is the activity that constitutes most recognizable human action. We shall consider the thought strategies for subsuming problems into what is already known.

FOUR SUCH STRATEGIES FOR SUBSUMING PROBLEMS

One strategy is the solution of the problem by showing *identity* within a structure or a series of instances. (It may be better to speak here of an anomaly instead of a problem.) The subsumption of the anomaly in a structure of concepts and relationships is *deduction*. (An example is stagflation being deduced from a Phillips curve plus expectations.) The method of *induction* attempts to establish identity between the instance at hand with other instances – e.g., 'When the money supply goes up inflation goes up because it did so in other cases'. Both methods employ the language of necessity; the solution is a matter of logical consistency (logical identity) and empirical inference (phenomenal identity).[7]

The next strategy to consider is the reference to, or exercise of, *will*. Side-stepping the implementation of deductive and inductive strategies we can will a particular solution to the given problem – e.g., 'I, Milton Friedman, tell you that when the money supply goes up inflation goes up; the relationship is not immediate, as in the middle 1980s, but it has to be true over a longer period of time'. In discussions among philosophers of science, the operation of will is acknowledged through concepts such as subjectivity, convention, passion, emotion, and ideology. We also exercise our will when we ignore a problem by declaring it to be an invention of pseudo-science, a ploy of the ruling class, a piece of religious nonsense or, simply, a matter of personal taste.

Whereas the first strategy seeks identity (logical or empirical), the second strategy brings out *difference*. Will derives its significance from contrast: I will, in contradistinction to what is customary, prescribed, or willed by others – my will necessarily excludes another. Yet the two strategies have the focus on necessity in common: like the language of logic and fact the language of will expresses necessary connections.

The combination of these two strategies of dealing with problems cover the domain of conventional methodological inquiry. It is a domain divided in twos. The first strategy represents the 'objective', the positive, reason (rationality), science; the second the 'subjective', the normative, emotion (non-rationality or irrationality), the humanities. The first strategy is privileged within the world of conventional science (economics): the intention there is to reduce the exercise of will to a minimum. Partly in response to this privileged status of science in contemporary culture some people (some, but certainly not all, poets and artists, and many people in their personal sphere) assert the privilege of the subjective.

A third, usually ignored, strategy of dealing with problems is that of *irony*. The classical form of irony is to ridicule one solution to affirm one's own. Another form, the one that is relevant in this context, is that of critical reflection which calls into question the necessity expressed in the previous two strategies. Without offering an alternative, the ironic moment undermines foundations, interrupts continuity and coherence, and casts doubt on claims to privileged status, authenticity, truth, objectivity and so on; in other words, it deconstructs (see Booth 1974). In irony any solution to a problem becomes uncertain. The strategy of irony is parasitic. It has no method of its own. It may borrow from logic the method to deconstruct logic (cf. Gödel's theorem, the Duhem–Quine thesis). It also may borrow from the language of the fourth strategy.

The fourth strategy covers the realm of the *possible*, of the *contingent*. Aristotle called this strategy rhetoric in juxtaposition to dialectic, which is the strategy of deduction and induction. Its methods are those of hypothesis, metaphor, analogy, story, enthymeme (and incomplete syllogism), allegory and so on. Its characteristic reasoning is *abductive* – inferences are not based on necessary connections as in deduction and induction, but on analysis by analogy. Physicists practise abduction when they derive properties of atomic structures from the analogy with the solar system or a string; economists do it when a market analogy guides their speculations on the changes in car prices or unemployment. When we reason through analogy, metaphor, story, and so on, we allude to possible connections; we point at possibilities. Reasoning in this way is like covering a terrain with moving signs and boundaries: nothing appears fixed, given absolute, objective, strictly factual. Boundaries appear to be 'fuzzy'; ambiguous concepts are a fact of life.

Further (sub)divisions of strategies are conceivable. In particular the fourth strategy is too broad and rough as described here. But these divisions are sufficient for the initial task at hand, namely the unravelling of knots in the communication about economics (that is, in economic methodology).

To illuminate the distinctions I call in the help of a few cartoons to picture each strategy. In Picture Ia the square represents the realm of identity. Deduction and induction are its strategies. The circle represents the realm in which the will operates. Necessity prevails, either in form or through the imposition of will. The circle is small; the formal structures of economic theories, which pertain to the square, are privileged.

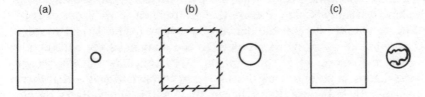

Picture Ia The world of economics according to conventional methodologists
Picture Ib The world of economics as 'seen' with the application of the ironic move
Picture Ic How people who are accustomed to (a) – i.e., just the square and the circle – 'see' Picture II

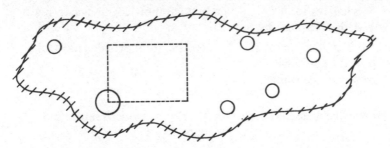

Picture II The world of economics according to rhetoricians

During the last decades, irony has become a dominant mode in methodological discourse. Klant (1984) and others have shown the logical limitations of economics as a science (in particular the logical constraints on falsification) and Friedman has convinced many that the reasoning within the square is 'as if' reasoning. Lucas, a pupil of Friedman, speaks of analogies. With the application of the ironic move, the picture changes, to become Picture Ib. The boundaries become blurred but no discourse is imagined outside of the square and the circle. The circle is a little larger to accommodate those who, frustrated by the blurriness of the square's boundaries, award more space to the operation of social and conventional factors (which they conceive as expressions of will).

In Picture II the square is subsumed in a larger whole which we could call rhetoric, or discourse. (Aristotle's distinction between dialectic and rhetoric is thus erased.) The space is curved to suggest its fluidity. Economics in this picture is discourse, or conversation, covering the realm of possibilities. Irony affects the boundaries, which are therefore blurred, and much else within. I am not sure what space to draw for the sphere of will, because I am not sure what position to award to an autonomous will. Here I have followed Don Lavoie's proposal to draw many circles of will throughout the picture to indicate its elusive but pervasive influence. Picture II also reflects the hermeneutic perspective on economics.

As Picture Ic shows, people who are used to seeing only squares and circles have difficulty 'seeing' Picture II. Because their world is one of twos (see Picture I) they interpret the denial of privilege to the formal strategy *necessarily* as the awarding of privilege to the domain of the will (or the subjective, the emotional, the normative). They conclude that knowledge from the rhetorical point of view must be 'purely conventional' – that there are no standards in Picture II and, hence, that anything goes. Barry Barnes (1987) has collected some of these translations:

Stated in Picture II	*As understood by those in Picture I*
to identify causes of belief in what is true/rational	to show that what seems true/ rational isn't 'really' true/rational
to show that there are 'rationally defensible' alternatives to our accepted knowledge/science/maths	to criticize/expose/debunk our accepted knowledge/science/maths
to show that the application of a body of empirical knowledge cannot be fixed and determined 'logically'	scientists are illogical/irrational
scientific knowledge is accepted on authority	authority overrides reason and experience

The tendency of the 'square' critics is to fit Picture II into the square and circle of Picture I. Enthymemes are squeezed into syllogistic forms;

abductive reasoning becomes deductive and what does not fit is speculative, ruled by will. The point of Picture II, however, is to imagine a realm beyond those two spaces, a realm of fluidity, possibility, and ambiguity. Picture II shows that the square does not cover much and that we do not necessarily step into the circle of subjectivity when we get outside the square.

So far, explorations of the rhetorical domain have focused on discourse analysis. The result is that now we are able to perceive a great variety of rhetorical devices that economists use in their discourse. Another part of the project has been the interpretation of what these rhetorical devices signify, which meanings they allow and which they exclude. This approach compels us to consider the 'native's point of view'. Given the fluidity and possible variety of meanings of a metaphor like the rational individual, the perceptions and beliefs of economists themselves become important. Thus the researcher becomes an anthropologist investigating the customs and rituals of a tribe. Unlike the conventional methodologist who can construct 'square' interpretations in isolation amidst the books of Popper, Hempel and possibly Lakatos, the rhetorician needs to mingle in order to find out the life and blood of academic interactions. Clearly the picture for this 'new conversation' about economics is different.

These are cartoons and should be read as such. They clearly indicate why people who are accustomed to seeing squares and circles can hardly be expected to 'understand' the fluid mass of Picture II. The problem of communication may be compounded, since those who inhabit Picture II have so far failed to make clear what the proper dimensions of the square are. After all, subsumption need not imply dissolution.

ECONOMICS ACCORDING TO PICTURE I

We can now pursue the analogy between the situation in metadiscourse and economic discourse. In other words, the same pictures fit the contrasting perspectives in economics. Picture I, with the square and circle only, represents the analytical division that neoclassical economists impose on their discourse. With Picture II in mind we are led to suspect that Picture I distorts and blocks our view of the richness and intricacies of economic actions.

Picture I, as a picture of economic discourse, divides the discourse in twos – that is, into the realm of the 'objective' (where establishment of identity is the goal) and that of the 'subjective' (where difference reigns). More specifically, according to this picture, preferences or utility refer to the circle and economic and environmental constraints define the square. All discursive activity is confined to the square; the circle is the realm of that which cannot be discussed. The objective is the deduction of hypotheses from a few axioms (such as constant preferences) plus the given constraints. The resulting model specifies the *logic* of choice.

IRONY IN PICTURE I

Naturally, those who practise economic discourse as framed by Picture I reflect on what they do. Usually, neoclassicists reflect with the same picture in mind; holding up what we could call the meta-square they perceive straight and strong lines that separate the scientific from the non-scientific, the positive from the normative, the objective from the subjective and so on. An increasing number of neoclassicists, however, are drawn to the ironic strategy in their reflections. They put the meta-square under erasure, questioning the sharpness or even validity of the lines drawn. Some insert elements of Picture II when they imagine the square model of choice as an analogy.[8] This irony is limited to the meta level; it does not transfer to economic discourse itself. Most contemporary neoclassical economics is very square.

But not all neoclassical economics is very square. Irony enters the picture – for example, when Robert Solow questions the general applicability of the logic of choice, or when Amartya Sen undercuts its structure through persistent questioning of the fundamental assumptions. Sen's irony is evident in the title of one of his (1977) essays: 'Rational fools'.

Sen is highly respected in the economics profession. Given his harsh criticism of the foundations on which neoclassical economics rests, such respect is puzzling. The explanation might be that Sen's rhetoric and argumentative strategy conform with Picture I. Sen operates within the square employing the analytical knife in his careful deconstruction of the neoclassical square. Sen alludes to a realm beyond the square when he posits, for example, the influence of ethics on individual preferences. He does that, however, while standing within the square (cf. Sen 1987 and 1988). Sen casts doubts on the significance of Picture I but does not alter it in any fundamental way. To imagine the path to which Sen's ironic intervention seems to point us we need to have Picture II in front of us.

PICTURE II FOR ECONOMIC DISCOURSE

When we want to investigate the ethical beliefs which people hold, their formation and their effects, we need to move outside the square and move into terrain where the ground shifts and the signs change. At least, that is what Alasdair MacIntyre concludes after years of taking apart analytical (or square) interpretations of ethics. Referring to Hegel, Collingwood, and Vico, he argues that morality is embodied in the way people live their lives and therefore can only be detected when we take people's lives seriously (see MacIntyre 1984, p. 266). The philosopher who operates within the square will be ill-equipped for this task; according to MacIntyre, the student of moral conduct has to become a historian.

The basic insight is that we do not live our lives within the square. If we think of our lives as sequences of actions which we take to deal with problems (or differences), the four strategies which I distinguished earlier become relevant again. Naturally, many differences that we perceive each day we ignore; some day we may experience a difference that brings about a revolution in our perspective, our beliefs and values. But when we deal with a difference – a low price, rising demand, the loss of a job – we have to rely on the four strategies. We can seek identity with what we already know (deduction or induction), affirm difference (will), reflect (irony), or entertain possibilities and allow the ambiguities of history.

The fourth strategy is clearly significant when we do economics (see McCloskey 1986; Klamer 1983; and Klamer, McCloskey and Solow 1988). When we communicate our thoughts about economics we cannot say all; we rely on metaphors and stories among other devices pertaining to the fourth strategy. I am saying nothing new here: throughout the literature people have pointed at the open (or, what we may call, curved) characteristic of discourse. Square concepts appear inadequate to capture curves in our intellectual lives.[9]

People have noticed the same difficulty in the discourse about social and economic actions. Concepts such as freedom, justice, and happiness cannot be pinned down with square definitions. William Connolly (1983) calls them *essentially contested concepts*, Nicholas Georgescu-Roegen (1971) *dialectical concepts*; in terms of Picture II we could call them curved concepts. All labels point out the same feature – namely, that the meanings of certain concepts with which we try to make sense of our world, are subject to continuous negotiation. The fluidity of certain meanings mirrors the fluidity of certain life's experiences. This small analogical step is all it takes to transfer insights gained in the reflection upon intellectual activities to the interpretation of other activities – such as buying and selling.

Think of our own expectations as buyers and sellers. Knowing what is ahead of us is a problem. We may seek solutions in the square, seeking identity with what we already know, respect convention, or reflect on what we know. It is just as likely that we will: figure out our beliefs and alter them in the light of what happens; reason by analogy; communicate with other human beings; and interpret our values (all of which are activities which constitute the fourth strategy and invoke Picture II).[10]

THE NATIVE'S POINT OF VIEW

We could follow the advice of neoclassical economists and ignore this fourth dimension in economic actions. But is it possible to be *serious* about our interpretation of economic actions and include the fourth dimension?[11] Of course it is. Many have done so. They have studied the history of economic actions, their psychology, and the social and cultural environment in which they take place. (Economists, however, in perceiving their discourse through Picture I, easily overlook these activities in the context of Picture II.)

Study of the actions of economists has suggested other possibilities. We discovered the promise of discourse analysis – that is, the careful reading of the texts economists produce – and of close observations. We have come to appreciate the significance of the beliefs economists hold, the meanings of the concepts that they recognize or dismiss, and their perceptions of other economists and their arguments. To those who are used to square reasoning these studies may seem ambiguous and undisciplined but they provide us with a different and, I think, better understanding of what economists do. They get us to the native's point of view.[12]

The native's point of view is the subject in ethnography. It is the view that Clifford Geertz tries to uncover in 'thick descriptions' of the life in specific communities. He elects to enter the 'life-worlds' of Indonesian and Moroccan villages, but we could follow his example and enter the 'life-worlds' of the Chicago trade-floor, IBM's boardroom, General Motors' shop floor, Iowa city's households, or Boston's fishmarket. (Nobody says that such research is easy; learning Arabic is certainly not easy and living in the midst of and finding out about a foreign culture is not easy either. Some may find mathematics easy in comparison.) By doing so, one is bound to discover worlds that are as yet unknown in the world of economists.

Take savings behaviour as an example. The neoclassical model has told us much about the constraining role of current and future income in decisions to save. But it tells all but nothing about attitudes towards saving and variations in such attitudes across cultures and through times. Mary Douglas and Baron Isherwood (1979) argue that, in their decision to save more (or less), people communicate not only their time-preference but also certain beliefs and values. In Puritan families, thriftiness was equated with prudent behaviour; in some communities it has the stigma of anti-social behaviour.[13] The neoclassical economist could retort that it is all in the preferences. However, to understand savings behaviour in a *serious* way we need to go beyond the model of logical choice and the statistics, and take a close-up look.

In another close-up look Michael Buroway (1979) offers surprising insights in the life-world of the shop floor. Researches generally emphasize either harmony or conflict on the shop floor, depending on their political affiliation. Buroway places himself in the Marxist camp, but rejects the deterministic theories of conflict and exploitation (cf. Braverman 1974). Having been a machine worker himself, he presents the native's point of view. His interpretation tells about the game that workers play on the shop floor, the game of *making out*. In order to make their quotas, machine workers enter into intricate arrangements with the truck drivers who supply the materials, and develop strategies for getting the most profitable assignments. These games get the workers deeply involved, compel them to work hard, and account for their consent with the process and resistance against union efforts for change. His ethnographic description exposes the squareness of the deterministic analysis of the labour process and ventures into the area beyond the square.

Likewise, Geertz (1963) goes beyond the square models of economic growth and development and shows a world in which rituals, myths, beliefs and economic constraints interact to produce a rich and dynamic reality.

These anthropological studies are not the final answer; they are also not the only vehicle for traversing the shifting grounds beyond the square. But they appear to get on to a track that promises new vistas on the economic life-world.

CONCLUSION

This essay does not conclude. It constitutes a beginning with a proposal for further exploration. The proposal is based on experience; it is a proposal, too, which cuts across disciplines.

The reason for writing is a problem which anyone in economics who pursues the proposal and becomes interested in the native's point of view is likely to encounter. The problem emerges in the communication with the established economic point of view. It shows in comments such as 'What you do is unscientific', or 'You cannot trust what people say they do', or 'Where is your model? – I can't understand what you mean if you don't write some constrained-optimization model'.

I have pointed out as the source of the problem the change in mental pictures that this proposal entails. In order to perceive the native's point of view we need to perceive space beyond the square and the circle. This is not a proposal to erase the square from the picture. As a matter of fact, the reasoning in this paper is to a great extent square reasoning. Starting from a few premises we deduce four strategies for dealing with problems. But there is more to all this. After all, this essay proposes more than it concludes.

During the final days of work on this essay, chance did its work. Seeking distraction, I read through some notecards and discovered that a citation from Francis Bacon's *Novum Organum* which I had copied a while back because it sounded good, now sounded most appropriate. Bacon noted:

> Those who have treated the sciences were either empiricists or rationalists. The empiricists, like ants, lay up stones and use them; the rationalists, like spiders, spin webs out of themselves, but the bee takes a middle course, gathering up her matter from the flowers of the field and garden, and digesting and preparing it by her native powers.
>
> (Bacon 1900) [1620]

NOTES

1 The term 'neoclassical' can cause confusion. I refer to the type of neoclassical economics that one finds in Varian's *Microeconomic Analysis*.
2 Harry Johnson considered the book 'fascinating' because it related the anthropological findings to 'questions of central concern to the economist'.

3 One case in point was a conference on economic rhetoric. See the evaluative papers of Klamer and McCloskey in the conference volume (Klamer, McCloskey, and Solow 1988). See also the exchange between Rosenberg and McCloskey in *Economics and Philosophy* (forthcoming).

4 A series of conversations with Barend van Heusden, a semiotician, were decisive in seeing the problem and finding a way out. Unfortunately, there are no writings of his to which I can refer.

5 How we are able to perceive a tension? If something does not fit what I already know, how do I know?

6 The distinction of the three ways of dealing with a tension and the following distinction of four strategies of subsuming the problem took much sorting out and is still far from settled in my own mind. I am relying in this very much on van Heusden's research and my interpretations thereof.

7 This does not imply the necessity of truth. The truth of inference through induction is obviously a matter of probability.

8 As I stated earlier, I do not think that the square covers what neoclassical economists do. Lucas is right when he speaks of models as analogies; the new conversation only expands the picture further as it pictures not only analogies, but also arguments, stories, and a plethora of other rhetorical devices.

9 One victim is the model of logical choice which is all but abandoned in rhetorical interpretations of discursive actions. There is no model of maximizing behaviour, no algorithm for rational choice in McCloskey's *Rhetoric of Economics*. Implicit in the text of McCloskey's essay is the proposal that we focus on human *action* instead of choice. A good articulation of such a proposal can be found in Harré *et al.* (1985).

10 Neoclassical economics casts the analysis of 'expectations' in the square terms of information and mathematical probabilities. The resolution of the problem of expectations is sought within the context of Picture I with an emphasis on the deductive strategy.

11 One defence of neoclassicists is the 'false-consciousness' argument: economic agents do not know what they do and hence we need to rely on economic models to understand what they do. The common sense of agents is irrelevant. Such a position cannot be dismissed outright but I try to show here how unpersuasive this way of thinking is.

12 We have noticed, for example, that Picture I features in the official justification of what economists do, but that Picture II prevails in informal discussions among economists (cf. Gilbert and Mulkay, 1984; and Klamer, in Klamer *et al.*, 1988).

13 They refer to a study of a mineworkers' community in England where the men expect from each other that extra money would be spent on beer for their mates.

REFERENCES

Akerlof, George (1984) 'Gift echange and efficiency-wage theory: four views', *American Economic Review* 74 (May): 79–83.

Bacon, Francis ([1620]) *Novum Organum*, New York: Collier and Son (1900).

Booth, Wayne (1974) *A Rhetoric of Irony*, Chicago: University of Chicago Press.

Buroway, Michael (1979) *Manufacturing Consent*, Chicago: University of Chicago Press.

Braverman, Harry (1974) *Labour and Monopoly Capital*, New York: Monthly Review Press.

Connolly, William E. (1983) *The Terms of Political Discourse*, Princeton, N.J.: Princeton University Press.

Douglas, Mary and Isherwood, Baron (1979) *The World of Goods*, New York: Basic Books.

Geertz, Clifford (1963) *Peddlers and Princes: Social Development and Economic Change in Two Indonesian Towns*, Chicago: University of Chicago Press.

Georgescu-Roegen, Nicholas (1971) *The Entropy Law and the Economic Process*, Cambridge: Cambridge University Press.

Harré, Rom, Clarke, David, and de Carlo, Nicola (1985) *Motives and Mechanisms: An Introduction to the Psychology of Action*, New York: Methuen Inc.

Helm, Dieter (ed.) (1984) *The Economics of John Hicks*, Oxford: Basil Blackwell.

Hirschman, Albert O. (1985) 'Against parsimony: three ways of complicating some categories of economic discourse', *Economics and Philosophy* I (April): 7–21.

Johnson, Harry (1964) 'Review of *Peddlers and Princes*', *Journal of Political Economy* 72 (Feb.): 104–5.

Klamer, Arjo (1983) *Conversations with Economists*, Totowa: Rowman and Allanheld.

—— (1987a) 'The advent of modernism in economics', unpublished manuscript.

—— (1987b) 'New classical economics: a manifestation of late modernism', unpublished manuscript.

—— McCloskey, Donald, and Solow, Robert M. (1988) *Consequences of Economic Rhetoric*, New York: Cambridge University Press.

Klant, Johannes J. (1984) *The Rules of the Game*, Cambridge: Cambridge University Press.

Lucas, Robert E. (Jnr.) (1980) 'Methods and problems in business cycle theory', *Journal of Money, Credit and Banking* 12 (Nov.): 696–715.

McCloskey, Donald (1985) *The Rhetoric of Economics*, Madison: University of Wisconsin Press.

—— (1988) 'Two replies and a dialogue on the rhetoric of Economics: Mäki, Rappaport, and Rosenberg', *Economics and Philosophy* 4 (April): 150–66.

MacIntyre, Alasdair (1984) *After Virtue*, 2nd edn, Notre Dame, Indiana: University of Notre Dame Press.

Mulkay, Richard (1985) *The World and the Word: Explorations in the Form of Social Analysis*, London: Allen & Unwin.

Rosenberg, Allan (1976) *Microeconomic Laws: A Philosophical Analysis*, Pittsburgh: University of Pittsburgh Press.

Sen, Amartya K. (1977) 'Rational fools: a critique of the behavioral foundations of economic theory', *Philosophy and Public Affairs* 6: 317–44.

—— (1987) *On Ethics and Economics*, Oxford: Basil Blackwell.

Simon, Herbert (1985) *Sciences of the Artificial*, Cambridge, Mass.: MIT Press.

Varian, Hal (1984) *Microeconomic Analysis*, New York: W.W. Norton & Co.

3 Getting beyond objectivism
The philosophical hermeneutics of Gadamer and Ricoeur

G.B. Madison

INTRODUCTION

The most significant development in the philosophy of the human sciences in the last two decades or so has been the movement away from the previously dominant positivistic or objectivistic approach.[1] This post-positivist turn is one which an increasing number of authors have come to be concerned with and have described in various ways. Richard Rorty (1979) has labelled it the move from 'epistemology' to 'hermeneutics'. In a useful collection of essays on the subject, Rabinow and Sullivan have referred to it as 'the interpretive turn'.[2] What 'the interpretive or hermeneutic approach' (Rabinow and Sullivan 1979, p. 1) stands for is a rejection of what Lewis White Beck (1971 [1949]) referred to as 'the Natural Science Ideal' – the idea espoused by the logical positivists of a 'unified science' embracing both the natural and the human sciences. The interpretive approach rejects this sort of methodological imperialism; it rejects the idea that the human sciences can or ought to be modelled on the natural sciences. It rejects the very idea that the purpose of the human sciences is to *explain* (in the customary scientistic sense) and *predict* human phenomena. Because the principal goal of the human sciences is not to *explain* human affairs but to understand them, formal scientific methodology and quantification techniques are ill-suited to these disciplines, having at best a strictly limited usefulness. What, above all, is called into question is the applicability to human affairs of the sub-human reductionist models (such as those borrowed from genetics or cybernetics) that objectivistic scientists are so fond of. The two leading exponents of the hermeneutical approach have been Hans-Georg Gadamer and Paul Ricoeur.

HERMENEUTICS

In this essay I would like to explore some of the implications of the hermeneutical critique of objectivism as they pertain to economics, which has traditionally been held to be the 'queen' of the social sciences, the one most approximating to the exactitude which is thought to characterize the 'hard'

sciences. The prime area where one might discern some significance of hermeneutics for economics is that of methodology. The issue of methodology
is in the forefront of a great deal of discussion in all of the human sciences
today,[3] and it is one which is increasingly occupying the attention of
economists. As a consequence of what appears to be something of a loss of
confidence in mainstream neoclassical economics, economists are once again
reflecting on the status of their discipline: on what in their intellectual praxis
they have been doing; on what they ought to be doing; and on the significance of what as economists they are and ought to be doing. The emergence
of some new economic journals that stress methodology is a case in point.

Symptomatic of this concern – but also of economists' inability to free
themselves from positivism's grip – is a *New York Times* article by John M.
Culbertson, professor of economics at the University of Wisconsin,
'American economics: 100 years in a rut'. This author laments the present
state of economics, which he sees as not being 'scientific' enough. What he
would like to see is the institution of 'a realistic, scientific economics', an
economics which, he says, 'underlay the anti-*laissez-faire* economic reforms
of the 1930s, which were a foundation of the era of great success of the
United States economy'. The trouble with present-day economics, it
appears, is its 'unscientific' commitment to the philosophy of the free
market – to what Culbertson refers to as 'the pre-scientific doctrines of
Adam Smith'. Implicitly raising the question, 'What Should Economists
Do?' (to quote the title of a noteworthy book by James Buchanan, which I
rather doubt Culbertson has read), our author says in effect that they
should firmly hitch their economic cart to 'empirical, objective, post-
Darwinian science'.[4]

Whatever might be said of Culbertson's article in other respects, it is in
any event symptomatic of a growing concern on the part of economists as to
the status of their discipline – an expression of the awareness that, as
Ludwig M. Lachmann would say, 'a crisis of the method of economic
thinking is taking shape' and that economics is entering 'a tempestuous
season' (Lachmann 1986). Culbertson is also fully representative of a
standard response to concerns over what might be called the 'epistemological' status of economics, one which we find repeated *ad nauseum* not
only in past economic literature but also in that of the other social sciences.
Economics could be put on a solid scientific footing if only it were made
somehow to imitate the natural sciences. In other words, Culbertson's
article is yet another restatement of the Natural Science Ideal, the idea that
the natural sciences exemplify knowledge in the truest sense and that all
other disciplines can achieve intellectual rigour only to the degree that they
can successfully transpose the methods of the natural sciences into their
own domains. Let us simply label this the Positivist Ideal.

The trouble with this kind of call for intellectual rigour is that it is not
nearly rigorous enough. On the one hand it naïvely accepts positivistic myths
as to what natural science is (such as the 'empirical' status of scientific

statements; the notion that scientific theories are accepted because they are or can be tested or verified; and so on). On the other hand, it does not raise any critical questions as to what the object of economics is or ought to be. I will not pursue the first difficulty, since, in the philosophy of science itself, we have now moved into a post-positivistic period – thanks to Thomas Kuhn's hermeneutical researches into science and the growth of knowledge literature – and now are able to see through the positivist myths about science. The real trouble with the natural-science-ideal position, as regards economics, is that it does not even pause to ask what would seem to me to be the crucial (indeed, the absolutely basic) question, if we are concerned with methodology in economics. The question is, quite simply: What is the nature of economic understanding?

To raise this question is to raise a properly hermeneutical question. For hermeneutics is concerned with the nature and scope of human understanding, in all its different modes. For the purposes of the present discussion I will define philosophical hermeneutics as that reflective discipline which is concerned with, in Gadamer's words, 'our entire understanding of the world and thus . . . all the various forms in which this understanding manifests itself' (Gadamer 1975, p. xviii). Defined thus, it follows logically that hermeneutics does indeed have implications for economics. Although Gadamer has repeatedly insisted that it was not his aim to lay down methodological criteria, his general theory of human understanding does have definite methodological implications;[5] and Ricoeur, for one, has deliberately sought to address some of the methodological problems in the human disciplines.

Before attempting to discern some of the implications of hermeneutics for economics, let us pause to take note of some of Gadamer's main contributions to overall hermeneutical theory.

GADAMER'S CRITIQUE OF OBJECTIVISM

Let us begin by noting Gadamer's most basic and decisive contribution. Hermeneutics, in one form or another, is a very ancient discipline, also one which was always more or less marginal in that it was concerned with an apparently very specialized topic: the right reading of texts. Thus there is a long tradition of biblical and juridical hermeneutics. Around the turn of the century Wilhelm Dilthey widened the scope of hermeneutics considerably when he proclaimed that the hermeneutical method of *understanding* (*Verstehen*) – as opposed to the scientific method of *explanation* (*Erklärung*) – should be the method of all the human or social sciences (*Geisteswissenschaften*). What Gadamer did, building on insights of the early Heidegger, was to completely de-regionalize, so to speak, hermeneutics. That is, with Gadamer hermeneutics ceased to be simply a method to be practised by this or that discipline and became a discipline in its own right. It became an all-inclusive discipline because its object became, as I indicated above, human understanding itself, in all its forms. In other words, Gadamerian hermeneutics does not advocate any particular method of understanding and does not itself fall under the rubric of 'methodology'.[6] It is, rather, a discipline having universal scope in that it is concerned with 'all human experience of the world and human living' (Gadamer 1975, p. xviii). Gadamer's goal was 'to discover what is common to all modes of understanding' (1975, p. xix). The question he sought to raise was a genuinely philosophical one: 'How is understanding possible?' (1975, p. xviii). Or, in a less Kantian fashion: What exactly is it that has happened whenever we claim to have arrived at an understanding of things, the world, our products, ourselves?

Gadamer thus inaugurated a wholly new form of hermeneutics – one which could be labelled 'philosophical' or 'phenomenological' – and which stands opposed, by reason of its philosophic universality, to the older, romantic version of hermeneutics running from Schleiermacher and Dilthey up through Betti and Hirsch.[7] What makes a decisive difference between these two forms of hermeneutics is that Gadamerian hermeneutics is not just another kind of *epistemological* theory. What is decisive about Gadamerian hermeneutics is that it abandons epistemology and traditional epistemological and foundationalist concerns altogether. It does not, for instance, seek to come up with new answers to the old epistemological questions, 'How can we be sure that our ideas are an adequate copy of objective reality?', 'What must, or can we do, to achieve this result?'. It seeks rather to deconstruct these and similar theory-laden questions. Hermeneutics is a discipline which completely displaces traditional, foundationalist epistemology. As Rorty (1979, p. 357) has quite rightly observed, hermeneutics, 'as a polemical term in contemporary philosophy', is a name for the attempt to set aside epistemologically centred philosophy.

The consequences of this basic shift in perspective are extremely numerous and extremely far-reaching. I will allude to just a few, in very summary form, and will then focus in on more specifically economic concerns.

Understanding, in whatever form (including the forms in which it occurs in the natural sciences), is not a matter of conforming to, copying, or mirroring a supposedly 'objective' nature which simply is what it is 'in itself' apart from our having anything to do with it (the conception of reality operative in objectivistic, foundationalist thinking). Understanding is not representational but transformative. To understand is to interpret.

Objectivism is a methodological naïvety. Objectivism could be defined as the attempt to achieve 'science' through the elimination of all 'subjective' factors (it thus presupposes the mirror conception of human understanding – the 'scientist' is he who seeks to have a very polished, non-distorting mirror for a mind). It presupposes (as in Hirsch's brand of hermeneutics) that the 'truth' is something 'out there', atemporal, invariant, which merely has to be 'discovered'. When applied to what is specifically human (such as consciousness, self-identity, economic transactions), it is the reductionist attempt to explain the human in purely 'objective', 'natural', physicalistic terms (as in Skinnerian behavioural psychology or cybernetic accounts of the 'mind').

There are no 'facts in themselves' (as we have now come to realize in the philosophy of science, all facts are 'theory-laden'). Facts are products of interpretation.

Whether it is texts or actions of people that we are trying to understand, there is no such thing as a 'correct' or best interpretation of them (no 'validation', in Hirsch's positivistic sense). Which is not to say that some interpretations may not be better (more persusasive, rational) than others (the hermeneutical rejection of objectivism and foundationalism does not entail relativism).

All understanding or knowledge is inter-subjective (it is not something purely individual and 'subjective'). The 'objective' is the inter-subjectively agreed upon, the result of agreement reached through conversation and dialogue on the part of a community of historically formed and culturally embedded subjects.

SUBJECTIVISM AND METHODOLOGICAL INDIVIDUALISM

Let us now focus our hermeneutical attention on economics. If as her-meneuticists our prime concern is the nature of economic understanding, we must make clear to ourselves just exactly *what*, in economics, we are trying to understand with our various methodological constructs. This is a most important methodological point which Aristotle made long ago when in his *Nicomachean Ethics* (see 1094a25 and elsewhere), he said that every science should adapt its method to its object, that the object under study should determine the method of studying it. Unfortunately, this bit of sound advice often goes unheeded. It is very likely to be ignored when in a precipitous attempt to make economics a 'positive science' one casts about for a suitable natural science model. Physics is not a very good model, since economic phenomena do not readily lend themselves to experimentation. But one can always appeal to astronomy, which is unquestionably a science even though it too cannot make use of experiments.[8] The manipulation of statistics (by means now of sophisticated computer-simulation models) would seem to be the answer to the would-be scientific economist. Do not statistics provide the economist with the hard-core, 'value-free', 'objective' data he needs if he is to be a positive scientist? And do not computer models furnish him with a rigorous method of attaining mathematical exactitude, and thus the means of 'predicting and controlling' events?

But what are statistics? Are they objective, natural data, as in the case of meteorological phenomena? Certainly not. They are not natural givens but are rather the result of classifying and organizing the results of *human action*. They are not 'facts' at all; they are interpretations of facts, facts having to do not with the 'objective' (nature) but with the 'subjective' (human action).[9] The real object of economics is human reality, human interactions, transactions, market processes. Humans, hermeneutics insists, are not objects but subjects, purposive beings – which is to say that they are not properly understood if they are understood merely objectivistically. The implication of hermeneutics for economics would be that, whatever use it might make of objective measuring techniques, if it is to do justice to its object economics must understand 'explanation' as fundamentally a matter of 'interpretation'.

Even though present-day economics relies heavily on the mathematical manipulation of supposedly objective statistics and continues to aspire to the status of a 'positive' science of 'objective' reality, economics was, ironically enough, one of the first of the social sciences to make an important break with objectivism. I am referring to the subjective theory of value based on the principle of marginal utility which presides over the birth of neoclassical economics. As early as 1871, Carl Menger, simultaneously with Leon Walras and William Stanley Jevons, rejected the classical notion that the value of a thing is something 'objective', an intrinsic property of the good itself; in doing so they established the basis of modern value theory. Value is the expression of preferences on the part of individual subjects, of the satisfaction they expect to derive from the incremental use of goods.

Menger's 'subjectivist' approach has become a distinguishing mark of the Austrian school. As further developed by one of Menger's most famous followers, Ludwig von Mises, subjectivism furnishes additional points of convergence between economics and hermeneutics. The gist of Mises's approach is that economic phenomena, such as interest rates, cannot be explained in terms of mere objective, physical conditions or factors. Under the influence of one of Gadamer's own teachers and the founder of phenomenology, Edmund Husserl, Mises understood time, the key element in interest, not in empirical terms but, non-objectivistically, as a dimension of human action, in terms of time-consciousness (see Mises 1963, pp. 488 ff). What is important for economic understanding is not Böhm-Bawerk's notion of the 'average period of production' which Mises said, is 'an empty concept' but the time-preference of individuals; economic phenomena must be understood in terms of forward-looking decisions on the part of individual producers and consumers. This approach to economics, like phenomenological hermeneutics, is thus thoroughly anti-reductionistic; economics has to do not with the natural but with the human, and what is human cannot be understood in terms of mere physical, objective processes.[10]

For his part, Lachmann provides us with an alternative to the usual mechanistic neoclassical models or what he calls 'late classical formalism' by suggesting that the goal of economic inquiry is *intelligibility* rather than causal explanation. This is a properly hermeneutical move. It suggests to me that what distinguishes economics from other disciplines, such as history, is not its object *per se*, since, viewed hermeneutically, the goal of all of these sciences would be the attempt to discern *meaningful* patterns of relations in human endeavours and action. The specificity of economics is that it focuses in on those meaningful modes of behaviour termed 'economic' – that is, those having to do with the production and exchange of goods and services.

The subjective theory of value has, in the economic literature, tended to be joined with the notion of 'methodological individualism'. This latter notion is a highly vague and ambiguous one, serving different methodological purposes in different Austrian thinkers, in non-Austrian neoclassical economics, and in the Popperian theory of the social sciences. All in all, it is a somewhat unfortunate term since it tends to imply that the proper way of understanding various social 'wholes' (to use Hayek's term) is to view them simply as a resultant of the conscious intentions of individual subjects, atomistically conceived (Hayek, for his part, never attempted to do such a thing). The attempt to make sense of social 'wholes', such as a particular economy or a particular polity – in terms of the subjective intentions of individual, isolated agents ('Robinson Crusoes') – is one aspect of what phenomenological hermeneutics refers to as 'subjectivism', and which it sees as being simply the obverse (indeed, the perverse) side of modern, mechanistic objectivism.

RICOEUR'S CRITIQUE OF SUBJECTIVISM

One useful function that hermeneutics could possibly serve in this regard would be to caution us against equating human purposive action in the realm of the 'economic' with *conscious* decisions and intentions. This seems to me to be a possible danger in the 'subjectivist' approach – on a par with the danger of conceiving of human action in purely individualist terms. 'Intentions', hermeneutics tells us, are often not open to introspection but must be *interpreted*. This is one of, if not the main theme in the hermeneutical theory of Paul Ricoeur. He would maintain, for instance, that there is more in human praxis than filters through to explicit consciousness, such that *the goal of understanding human action cannot be reduced to grasping the self-conscious meaning-intentions of the human actors*. In the case of textual interpretation, for instance, the hermeneutical goal is not, as an objectivist like Hirsch would maintain, getting at the intention of the author; for Ricoeur the meaning of a text, at least a good one, always surpasses the meaning intended by the author.[11]

For phenomenological hermeneutics, meaning itself is something that must be 'de-subjectivized'. Perhaps 'subjectivism' is not the best term for economists to use. It seems to me that in fact one of the main thrusts of the work of Mises's most famous student, F.A. Hayek, which emphasizes the role of social institutions and the kind of unarticulated knowledge embedded in social practices, was to effect a kind of Ricoeurian decentring or *désaissisement* of the conscious ego (the same 'ego') of which Mises (1963, p. 44) speaks.[12] The object of economics may, like all the other human sciences, be meaning, but meaning is not reducible to subjective intentions. Meaning is always the meaning of human action, but, as Hayek himself strenuously insisted, it often is not the result of human design.

One consequence of this is that the distinction between knowledge 'from the outside' and knowledge 'from the inside' – which in the older, pre-Gadamerian hermeneutical tradition paralleled the distinction between the natural sciences and the human sciences – may be somewhat misleading and inappropriate.[13] It would certainly be such if Ricoeur is right, and it is indeed the case that meaning-intentions are not always open to direct inspection, and thus cannot simply be described 'from within', but must be deciphered and interpreted, as it were, 'from without'.

Understanding or 'knowledge', hermeneutics maintains, is always inter-subjective.[14] The implication of this for economics would be that the meaningful patterns of human action it studies are not to be made intel-ligible in terms merely of the action on the part of isolated individuals. The notion of 'methodological individualism', while it does have some methodological usefulness,[15] stands in need of refinement. I have never understood why it is that economists show such a penchant for explaining social 'wholes' in Robinson Crusoe terms – as if somehow this strange, pitiful character epitomized the essence of mankind and embodied in himself alone the essence of society, as if the 'economic' were to be found in a society consisting of only one member (that is, a society which is a non-society). As a hermeneuticist, I feel very uneasy when an economist friend of mine says: 'institutions are merely complexes and patterns of individual acts, *no more* [my italics], there is nothing over and above the actions of individual people. . . . [I]nstitution[s] consist *solely* of a complex pattern of individual actions' (Block 1980, p. 405).

As was mentioned, the notion of methodological individualism is widely shared by economists. However, it is perhaps worth noting that Hayek employs it in a distinctly non-empiricist and non-Popperian way. In fact, in his case, it served a properly hermeneutical purpose in that it had for its effect to reinstate the inter-subjective as an irreducible realm. Only in the light of the inter-subjective does methodological individualism make good sense. Consider for instance these words of Hayek:

> One curious aspect of this problem which is rarely appreciated is that it is only by the individualist or compositive method that we can give a definite meaning to the much abused phrases about the social processes and formations being in any sense 'more' than 'merely the sum' of their

parts, and that we are enabled to understand how structures of interpersonal relationships emerge, which make it possible for the joint efforts
of individuals to achieve desirable results which no individual could have
planned or foreseen.

(Hayek 1972, pp. 151–2)

Thus, far from standing for some kind of atomistic individualism (as it does
in the case of many economists), Hayek's *methodological* individualism is,
in effect, a defence of what might be called the *hermeneutical* priority of the
'social'. This is fully apparent when one considers that for Hayek the
'compositive' approach of methodological individualism is to be *contrasted*
to the 'resolutive', analytical approach which according to him characterizes the natural sciences. The latter approach is one which, in accordance
with the traditional mechanistic–empiricist–positivist way of proceeding,
decomposes complex wholes into simple parts and which seeks to explain
the whole (e.g., an organism, an economy) in terms solely of the interactions between its (supposed) constituent parts – the ontological prejudice
at work here being that the 'parts' are more real than the whole. From a hermeneutical point of view, it could be said that the whole point of methodological individualism is, or should be, not to reduce the whole to the sum of
its parts but to remind us that these irreducible 'wholes' are nevertheless not
things – to be explained causally – but are, rather, *interpreted* objects and
are not understandable apart from the categories of human understanding
and agency (it goes without saying, of course, that only individuals understand and act).

One thing that the interpretive approach has emphasized is that human
action cannot properly be understood if the trans-subjective dimension of
human existence is not also recognized; if, in other words, we do not
recognize a 'category' beyond those of the merely 'objective' and
'subjective'. Charles Taylor, a prominent hermeneutical writer and
associate of Ricoeur, has spoken out persuasively on this score:

> what we are dealing with here is not subjective meaning . . . but rather
> intersubjective meanings. It is not just that of the people in our society all
> or most have a given set of ideas in their heads and subscribe to a given set
> of goals. The meanings and norms implicit in these practices are not just
> in the minds of the actors but are out there in the practices themselves,
> practices which cannot be conceived as a set of individual actions, but
> which are essentially modes of social relation, of mutual action.
>
> (Taylor 1979, p. 48)

Thus it seems to me that posing the methodological problem in terms of
individualism versus collectivism or universalism, as Mises does (1963,
pp. 41–2), may give rise to unnecessary difficulties. To ask: 'Which is
prior, the individual or society?' may be to ask a misleading question – even
if the question is not posed in a merely temporal sense (which Mises does

not do) but in an ontological-epistemological sense (which he does appear to do). A properly dialectical approach might well be more fruitful. It is quite true, as Mises says, that 'The life of a collective is lived in the actions of the individuals constituting its body' (Mises 1963, p. 42). Even Ricoeur (with the Marxians particularly in mind) said that: 'The only reality, in the end, are individuals who do things' (Ricoeur 1985, p. 216). And yet it is equally true that the individual achieves meaning in his own life and an understanding of himself only through his practical preflective engagement with others and his participation (on a level before any self-conscious awareness) in society. The question, 'Which is prior, and which is to be explained in terms of the other, the individual or society?' is an epistemological-foundationalist question which we, in a post-foundational age, would perhaps be best not to raise in the first place.

In Mises the question of methodological individualism is tied up with the question of the individual's relation to the meaning of his own action. When discussing methodological individualism he also says: 'It is the meaning which the acting individuals and all those who are touched by their action attribute to an action, that determines its character (Mises 1963, p. 42). What Ricoeur has termed the 'hermeneutics of suspicion' – the deconstructive work of Marx, Nietzsche, and Freud – has taught us to be suspicious of the accounts that individuals may give of their own actions. In fact, as Ricoeur concedes to the hermeneutics of suspicion, 'consciousness is first of all false consciousness, and it is always necessary to rise by means of a corrective critique from misunderstanding to understanding' (Ricoeur 1974, p. 18).[16] If we have legitimate reasons to be suspicious of statements of intention (in the interpretation of either actions or texts), there are also good reasons for doubting that, as Mises puts it: 'If we scrutinize the meaning of the various actions performed by individuals we must necessarily learn everything about the actions of collective wholes' (Mises 1963, p. 34).

If economics is indeed a *social* science, it ought to avoid overprivileging the individual (the 'subjective'); its object is not so much subjective meaning and intention as it is *inter*subjective patterns of action. In this context, Mises can once again serve as an example. It seems to me that Mises's discussion of the 'I and We' in his *magnum opus* is an unfortunate weak point in his overall philosophy. Mises simply assumes that the *I* is something given and indubitable. In a sense, of course, it is. Descartes was right: No one can legitimately doubt their existence. Mises's version of Descartes' *cogito*, posed in terms of the praxeological *Ego*, would run: 'I act, therefore I am'. The trouble with the *I* which is open to direct introspection ('from the inside') is, as Ricoeur would say, that it is a completely empty *I*. In other words, I exist, no doubt about it, but who or what exactly am I? This question, Ricoeur maintains, cannot be answered descriptively (the *I* is not something 'observable') but only through a roundabout process of deciphering *interpretation*. He writes:

the celebrated Cartesian *cogito*, which grasps itself directly in the experience of doubt, is a truth as vain as it is invincible. . . . [T]his truth is a vain
truth; it is like a first step which cannot be followed by any other, so long
as the *ego* of the *ego cogito* has not been recaptured in the mirror of its
objects, of its works, and, finally, of its acts. . . . Thus reflection is a
critique . . . in the sense that the *cogito* can be recovered only by the
detour of a decipherment of the documents of its life.

(Ricoeur 1974, pp. 17–18)

Heidegger, who fathered phenomenological hermeneutics, had already
insisted that 'if we posit an ''I'' or subject as that which is proximally given,
we shall completely miss the phenomenal content of Dasein [human
existence]' (Heidegger 1962, p. 72).

Mises was clearly being overly sanguine when he said that: 'The
endeavors of psychology to dissolve the *Ego* and to unmask it as an illusion
are idle' (Mises 1963, p. 44). Anti-humanism, the 'demise of subjectivity',
and the 'death of man' are themes which have never been so alive and
flourishing as they are today on the postmodern, poststructuralist, deconstructive philosophical scene.[17]

EXPLANATION/UNDERSTANDING

If economics is to make an effective move beyond objectivism, it must
abandon subjectivism as well, taking this term in its phenomenological
sense. One of Gadamer's contributions to hermeneutics in this connection is
the way he has called into question Dilthey's dichotomy between the *Naturwissenschaften* and the *Geisteswissenschaften*. To Gadamer's mind,
Dilthey's dichotomizing distinction is simply a relic of Cartesian dichoto-
mous dualism (mind/matter, man/nature, subjective/objective) which has
infected all of modern thought and which needs to be overcome.[18] Thus,
from the point of view of phenomenological hermeneutics, one would not
want to say, with Dilthey, that while the natural sciences aim at universal
patterns and adopt a view 'from the outside' ('explanation', in Dilthey's
terminology), the social sciences seek to understand individual events,
'from the inside' ('understanding'), as if the goal here were merely to
penetrate empathetically into the minds of individual human actors. There
are undoubtedly implications in this for economics. I wonder for instance if
there is not perhaps an element of Diltheyian methodological dualism in
some neoclassical thinking (reflected in the very adoption of the contrary
term to 'objectivism' – namely, 'subjectivism') which economics might do
well to divest itself of.

Economics has long been looked upon as one of, if not the most, 'exact'
of the human sciences. This is because the phenomena it deals with readily
lend themselves to treatment by means of explanatory, 'objective' techniques – statistical, arithmetic calculation. While some schools such as the

Post-Keynesian, Institutionalist, Marxist, and Austrian have shunned the mathematical approach, this has not prevented others from making the utmost use of it − and from being rewarded with Nobel prizes for their efforts. And yet the 'explanatory' approach − the Natural Science Ideal − would seem to be inappropriate if economics, by reason of its subject matter, is not a natural but a human science. We seem to be confronted with a dilemma here: *either* economics is an 'objective', 'positive' science dealing with quantitative magnitudes by means of statistical techniques which give rise to testable hypotheses (in which case there is no need for 'interpretation'); *or*, economics, dealing as it does with meaningful action on the part of human beings, is a hermeneutical, interpretive discipline and should thus renounce the use of formal, quantitative models and the attempt to construct 'objective', causal explanations. Is there anything to be found in philosophical hermeneutics which might suggest a way out of this dilemma? I believe there is.

The explanation-versus-understanding debate has been going on for numerous decades. It is an issue which Ricoeur has greatly concerned himself with, and what he has sought to do is to overcome the dichotomy by situating 'explanation' within the wider compass of 'understanding'. This, it seems to me, is the tactic that must be followed if, on the one hand, one wishes to allow for the legitimacy of purely objective, explanatory techniques in the human sciences (and there is every reason to do so, since they do enable us to make social phenomena somewhat more intelligible − though nothing to the degree that some of their more outspoken advocates would have us believe) but if one also, on the other hand, wishes to safeguard the specificity of what is human and resist the reductionistic, dehumanizing results which invariably ensue when the explanatory approach is accorded either a methodological monopoly or a methodological priority.

In the case of textual interpretation − the paradigmatic instance of hermeneutical understanding − the ultimate goal is understanding, appropriating for ourselves the meaning of the text, explicating the understanding of what it means to be in the world that is unfolded in and through the text. Purely explanatory techniques do have their legitimate place in the overall interpretive process; they form one segment of what Ricoeur calls the *hermeneutical arc* (see Ricoeur 1981b). For instance, in the initial stage of textual interpretation one may find it very useful to analyse the text in terms of its formal organization, its internal relations, its structure. Structural and semiological analyses as well as computer analysis of word distribution here play a role analogous to that of statistics and algorithmic procedures in economics. Explanatory techniques are a hindrance to an understanding of the 'deep meaning' of a text − its existential significance − only if we allow ourselves to believe that they are an adequate substitute for 'interpretation'. (In addition, it must not be forgotten that explanatory, 'empirical' data are not neutral and 'value-free'; they are themselves products of interpretation. For example, one must first program the computer to ask the 'right' questions – a crucial phase in the interpretive-understanding process which is usually never explicitly thematized as to its hermeneutical significance by the practitioners of objectivistic explanation.)

If, to speak like Ricoeur, we were to view meaningful action on the model of the text,[19] it seems to me that there might well be significant implications in the explanation/interpretation problematic for economics. As this problematic applies to economics, one might be tempted to adopt the following position: saying that the usual mechanistic models are sufficient for dealing with most of the classic economic issues and that they need simply to be *supplemented* by a more 'interpretive' approach in other areas, such as entrepreneurship, where their limitations are painfully obvious. One might say, for instance, that an interpretive economics does not oblige us to reconsider traditional, orthodox, quantitative economics; that the important things it has to say about, for instance, entrepreneurship can simply be incorporated into the general body of existing economic 'knowledge'. I think that one of the implications of hermeneutics for economics is that this would not be a satisfactory tactic to adopt.

If, as I have argued, the important thing from a hermeneutical point of view is to situate purely explanatory techniques within the wider compass of interpretive understanding (so as to avoid unacceptable methodological dualism), then we should not view the limits of the explanatory approach as merely, somehow, *external* but rather as essentially *internal*. In other words, we need to recognize that, even in regard to those phenomena to which purely explanatory techniques can be legitimately applied, and in regard to which they have a certain explanatory usefulness, the *intelligibility* that they provide is none the less essentially partial and one-sided. The phenomena themselves cannot properly be understood, in the last analysis, until the results of the explanatory approach are integrated into a wider, interpretive understanding.

A suitable example could perhaps be found in monetary theory. Milton Friedman has criticized the monetary policy of the US government and the Federal Reserve for its 'erratic' approach to the control and manipulation of the money supply. The solution to the problem of inflation, he has argued, would be to mandate a fixed rate for monetary growth, one which would be implemented automatically and which could not be altered arbitrarily by government or by the Federal Reserve Board. The logical implication would seem to be that we should dismiss those human beings who constitute the Board of Governors of the Federal Reserve and install in their place a pre-programmed computer.[20] From what I have said above, it follows that a purely objectivist approach such as this is open to criticism. The criticism of Friedman's position that has in fact been voiced by Henry Hazlitt is of a properly hermeneutical sort. In answer to the question, 'Why don't you consider the type of monetarism espoused by Friedman and Meltzer to be an adequate response to Keynesianism?' Hazlitt replied:

The monetarist outlook, as proposed by Milton Friedman is, in fact, a mechanical quantity theory of money. He assumes that 'the' price level – that is to say, an average of prices – will rise proportionately to the amount of paper money that is issued. That *can* happen for a certain period, but the value of money is not determined mechanically and proportionately with the amount issued. It is determined by public psychological forces. A panic can break out when people suddenly expect the value of money to collapse. That was illustrated by the German inflation of 1920 to 1923. Prices rose for a time roughly proportional with the amount of money issued. But suddenly prices soared far faster than the money supply because the public got panicky. It is psychologic forces that determine the value of money as of other commodities, although influenced, of course, by quantitative considerations.

(Hazlitt 1984, p. 4)

Money seems to be one of the most concrete, 'objective', mundane of things – the ideal object for an exact, quantitative science on the Natural Science Model – and yet it is one of the most specific and irreducible of *human* things. Only man engages in economic activity, and only man makes use of that thing called 'money'. The epitome of money, *gold* (whose sole use as an 'objective' measure or 'standard' of value some economists advocate today as the solution to all our problems), has absolutely no objective value in itself (except within strictly delimited areas – such as for the maker of large-scale, glittering church icons who wants to depict symbolically the radiant glory and splendour of the divine; or for the engineer designing a new computer who finds gold to be a superb conductor of electricity). As a measure of value, however, gold is not natural but 'artefactual', purely human and 'subjective'. From an *economic* point of view, there is no 'objective' difference whatsoever between gold and glass beads, where both are used as general media of exchange. Money is not an 'objective' entity and cannot be controlled in a merely 'objective' fashion.

I have said that human phenomena cannot properly be understood until the results of the explanatory approach are integrated into a wider, interpretive understanding. In his latest work culminating in his three-volume study, *Temps et récit*, Ricoeur has argued that the attempt to understand what is specifically human (and economics, let us not forget, is nothing if it is not a study of what is specifically and irreducibly human) *necessarily* assumes, in the final analysis, the form of a *narrative* account, a *récit* (Ricoeur 1984 and 1985). 'Objective data' (that is, the data that are produced as a result of the application of objective measuring techniques) achieve their maximum intelligibility not when, as is the goal of the natural sciences, they have been subsumed under (supposedly) universally binding and timeless 'covering laws' (whose putative purpose is that of 'explanation' and 'prediction') but when – only when – as in history or psychotherapy, they have been interrelated and integrated into a narrative account, one which, precisely, confers meaning on them through narrative emplotment. The most primordial of all forms of understanding is indeed that of *storytelling*. Ricoeur writes:

> to follow a story is to understand the successive actions, thoughts and feelings as displaying a particular *directedness*. By this I mean that we are pushed along by the development and that we respond to this thrust with expectations concerning the outcome and culmination of the process. In this sense, the 'conclusion' of the story is the pole of attraction of the whole process. But a narrative conclusion can be neither deduced nor predicted. There is no story unless our attention is held in suspense by a thousand contingencies. Hence we must follow the story to its conclusion. So rather than being *predictable*, a conclusion must be *acceptable*. Looking back from the conclusion towards the episodes which led up to it, we must be able to say that this end required those events and that chain of action. But this retrospective glance is made possible by the teleologically guided movement of our expectations when we follow the story. Such is the paradox of the contingency, 'acceptable after all', which characterises the understanding of any story.
>
> (Ricoeur 1981a, p. 277)

All of this has direct and important implications for economic 'explanation' (i.e., understanding). The interpretive economist Don Lavoie has taken note of some of these implications. After remarking that:

> History is in this view not an attempt to find quantitative covering laws that fully determine a sequence of events, but an attempt to supply a qualitative interpretation of some part of mankind's 'story'. The whole purpose of the theoretical social sciences (including economics and accounting research) is to equip people with the capacity better to distinguish acceptable from unacceptable historical narratives.

Lavoie goes on to say:

> What we find ourselves doing in the social sciences is not so much the testing of *ex ante* predictions but is more of the nature of what the Austrian economist F.A. Hayek calls an *ex post* explanation of principles. The only 'test' any theory can receive is in the form of a qualitative judgment of the plausibility of the sequence of events that has been strung together by narrative. Theoretical sciences can supply the principles of explanation but only the historical narrative can put these principles to work and establish their applicability and significance in the specific concrete circumstances under investigation.
>
> (Lavoie 1987, pp. 595–6)

It is interesting to note as well that the 'method of methodological individualism', as Lachmann describes it, displays the characteristic form of storytelling Ricoeur describes. The method, Lachmann says, has two aspects to it, a 'forward-looking' one and a 'backward-looking' one. On the forward-looking side, which is what Hayek called the 'Compositive Method', one seeks to show how a 'general equilibrium' (Lachmann himself is careful to place this term within quotation marks) results from the interaction of the plans and purposes of many individuals – or fails to so result. Here one seeks to determine what are the implications of a number of plans simultaneously carried out. It is important to note, however, that although one appeals to principles here and seeks to determine what is the likely outcome of a course of action, the compositive method most definitely eschews any attempt at making *predictions* in the usual scientist sense. The goal is most definitely not that of elaborating 'laws' which will enable us to 'predict' specific outcomes. The outcome, as Ricoeur would say, 'can be neither deduced nor predicted'. 'Explanation' here is thus not explanation in the scientistic, causalistic sense – one couched in terms of so-called 'behavior variables', to use Lachmann's term. It is, instead, an attempt to make events *intelligible* in a hermeneutical sense.

When the method is employed in reverse order, Lachmann says, one seeks to determine what constellation of plans has given rise to an existing situation. This is storytelling in the most proper, Ricoeurian sense of the term. As Lachmann himself says:

This is the real meaning of the method of *Verstehen*, which is also, of course, the historical method. There appears to be no reason why the theoretical social sciences, when they pursue their enquiries into the typical causes of typical social phenomena, should not make use of it.

(Lachmann 1984 [1969], p. 307)

The method of methodological individualism, as Lachmann portrays it, is thus also perfectly described in Ricoeur's words: 'Looking back from the conclusion towards the episodes which led up to it, we must be able to say that this end required those events and that chain of action.' Or, as Lavoie says: 'The only "test" . . . [is] the plausibility of the sequence of events that has been strung together by narrative.' What truly counts in economic 'explanation' is not empirical *verification* (or falsification) but narrative *acceptability*.

CONCLUSION

In economics one is never dealing with 'brute facts'. Statistics, as I said before, are themselves interpretations. 'Economic facts' are interpretations on the part of the economist; they are interpretations of the actual behaviour of a myriad of acting human beings *which is itself interpretive* (for an individual's economic behaviour cannot be adequately understood in merely objective terms, as a kind of automatic reaction to objective stimuli; it must be understood in terms of his or her *reading* of prices, opportunities, relative costs, and so on). One could say of the economist what Roy Schafer says of the psychoanalyst: 'The psychoanalyst interprets not raw experience, but interpretations' (Schafer 1978, p. 24). Or again, the economist could say with the interpretive anthropologist Clifford Geertz: 'what we call our data are really our own constructions of other people's constructions of what they and their compatriots are up to' (Geertz 1973, p. 9). If, like the culture the anthropologist studies, the economic order, which is the sphere of purposeful behaviour on the part of human agents, is not a realm of mechanical action and reaction but is a semiotic web of significance that they themselves have spun, it would follow, to use Geertz's words, that 'the analysis of it [is] therefore not an experimental science in search of law but an interpretive one in search of meaning' (Geertz 1973, p. 5).

Interestingly enough, this is a point that Hayek in effect argued in the early 1940s, in the heyday of objectivistic positivism, in a series of articles subsequently published in book form (1972) under the title *The Counter-Revolution of Science*. In this book, which is an attack on what he aptly referred to as 'scientism' or 'the scientific prejudice', Hayek, like Geertz later on, said that, unlike the situation in the physical sciences, 'in the social sciences our data or "facts" are themselves ideas or concepts' (Hayek 1972, p. 61). A purely explanatory, causalistic, physicalistic type of approach will not enable us to grasp these meanings; in the social sciences 'the relations between men . . . cannot be defined in the objective terms of the physical sciences but only in terms of human beliefs' (Hayek 1972, p. 52). Although Hayek expressed himself to a large extent in the dualistic language of modernist, Cartesian–Kantian epistemology and spoke, for instance, in terms of the mental versus the physical, the point he was seeking to make by means of his 'anti-physicalist' thesis is of genuine hermeneutical interest. We can, as the positivist would say, 'observe and describe' physical objects, but in order properly to understand things 'mental' we must *interpret* them. As Hayek remarked 'wherever we speak of mind we interpret what we observe in terms of categories which we know only because they are the categories in which our own mind operates' (Hayek 1972, p. 136). As Gadamer has pointed out, understanding the humanly other involves a 'fusion of horizons'. Where such a 'fusion' is not possible, neither, says Hayek, is an understanding possible (see Hayek 1972, pp. 136 ff.). Interpretation, Hayek says, 'is the only basis on which we ever understand what we call other people's intentions, or the meaning of their actions; and certainly the only basis of all our historical knowledge since this is all derived from the understanding of signs or documents' (Hayek 1972, p. 135). To speak of 'interpretation' is to speak of a situation where (as Heidegger would say) understanding is possible only because, in virtue of our *being* human subjects, we already have a pre-theoretical understanding of that which is to be understood and of what it means to be a human subject.

Perhaps the ultimate implication of hermeneutics for economics is that 'economic reality' is not itself something fixed and objective that can be fully or even adequately grasped by means of objective, formalistic techniques and constructs – however sophisticated these might be made to be by having recourse to cybernetics, systems theory, organization theory, 'economic data', computer simulation models, or artificial intelligence. The acting human being, the proper object of economics, is not *homo economicus*, a mere economizing, calculating entity, for the latter is an interpretive abstraction, and while, like the purely objective body, he can be thought and has his uses, he does not, to speak like Merleau-Ponty, exist.[21] 'Economic reality', similarly, does not exist, in any purely objective sense of the term (if it did there would be no need or place for entrepreneurship). It is dependent on, is the expression of, is the way in which a community of human agents interpret and arrange their collective being – in the same way that what counts as an economic 'good' is dependent upon how people interpret their lives and the priorities they set for themselves. Different cultures do this differently, and thus it would not be surprising if the 'laws' of economics were to vary from culture to culture. People everywhere can be said to want always to maximize their utility (this, I gather, is one of the fundamental 'laws' of economic science) only if one recognizes that they will always interpret 'utility' to mean what they want it to mean.[22] Man is the speaking animal, the interpretive being, who is constantly telling stories and interpreting himself to himself, and he can properly be understood only in a storytelling fashion, interpretively.[23]

In his major work, *Being and Time*, Heidegger introduced a new twist into the 'hermeneutical circle'. In traditional, pre-phenomenological hermeneutics, this notion expressed the fact that in textual interpretation our understanding of the 'whole' is built up as we read from our understanding of the meaning of the 'parts', however, the way we understand the parts is itself a function of the meaning of the whole that we project at the outset. The reading or interpretive process is thus one wherein the meaning of the whole and of the parts is constantly being modified through a kind of dialectical interchange. Geertz has shown that the hermeneutical circle applies as much to anthropology as it does to 'literary, historical, philological, psychoanalytic, or biblical interpretation or for that matter . . . everyday experience'. What is called for in an understanding of men and their institutions is 'a continuous dialectical tacking between the most local of local detail and the most global of global structures in such a way as to bring both into view simultaneously' (see Geertz 1979, pp. 239–40).

The new twist that Heidegger introduced was that of maintaining that *all* understanding is basically of a circular nature. In opposition to empiricist positivism (for which the mind is a kind of *tabula rasa* or neutral mirror), Heidegger argued that we would never arrive at an explicit understanding of anything if we did not already have a kind of implicit understanding of that which is to be understood; if, that is, we did not bring to our encounter with the object in question certain interpretive presuppositions or 'forestructures' (Heidegger 1962, p. 195). Because understanding is *essentially* circular in this way, it makes no sense to say, as a logical positivist would, that the interpretive process involves a 'vicious' circle.

The simple phenomenological fact of the matter is that there is no way out of the hermeneutical circle; there is no disengaged subject. The attempt to get out of the circle – an attempt which serves to characterize modern objectivism – can only result in what Sartre would have called 'bad faith'. If, *per impossibile*, we were able, in accordance with the objectivistic ideal, to divest ourselves of all of our culturally inherited presuppositions, we would find ourselves without anything at all to understand! Thus, the important thing, as Heidegger said, 'is not to get out of the circle but to get into it in the right way'. It is meaningless and absurd to want to rid ourselves of all presuppositions, but what can we do, Heidegger says, is to try to see to it that they are not determined for us by mere 'fancies and popular conceptions'. What economists need to get out of is their Cartesian anxiety – to use Richard Bernstein's nice term (1983) – their epistemological hangups over absolute starting-points, self-contained certainties, and presuppositionless foundations – the great, culturally inherited 'popular conception' of scientistic modernity.[25]

NOTES

1 Milton Friedman's famous article, 'The methodology of positive economics', is probably the best argued case for economics as a positive science.
2 See their joint introductory essay, 'The interpretive turn: emergence of an approach' in Rabinow and Sullivan (1979).
3 See, for instance, Polkinghourne (1983).
4 Speaking of the nineteenth-century founders of the American Economic Association, Culbertson says:

> The founders would be struck by the powerful new tools that now could be used to build an evolutionary, empirical, scientific economics: the ideas of cybernetics, systems theory, organization theory, the wealth of data on economies, the new ways to think realistically about complex, interactive systems with computer simulation models, the new possibilities of applying empirical knowledge to economic policy with computer based expert systems and artificial intelligence.

5 See, in this regard, my essay 'Method in interpretation', in Madison (1988).
6 The work of hermeneutics, Gadamer (1975, p. 263) says, 'is not to develop a procedure of understanding, but to clarify the conditions in which understanding takes place'.
7 For a Gadamerian hermeneutical critique of Hirsch's hermeneutical theory, see my essay 'A critique of Hirsch's *validity*', in Madison (1988).
8 Unfortunately, Gwartney and Stroup in their finely written (1980) textbook, *Economics: Private and Public Choice*, take over unquestioningly the orthodox, objectivistic view of science and presuppose an objectivistic, mirror view of knowledge as 'consistency with events in the real world' when they write:

> *The Test of a Theory Is Its Ability to Predict. Economic Thinking Is Scientific Thinking.* The proof of the pudding is in the eating. The usefulness of an economic theory is revealed by its ability to predict the future consequences of

economic action. Economists develop economic theory from the analysis of how incentives will affect decision-makers. The theory is then tested against the events in the real world. Through testing, we either confirm the theory or recognize the need for amending or rejecting it. If the events of the real world are consistent with a theory, we say that it has predictive value. In contrast, theories that are inconsistent with real-world data must be rejected.

If it is impossible to test the theoretical relationships of a discipline, the discipline does not qualify as a science . . .

How can one test economic theory since, for the most part, controlled experiments are not feasible? Although this does impose limitations, economics is no different from astronomy in this respect. The astronomer also must deal with the world as it is. He cannot change the course of the stars or planets to see what impact the changes would have on the gravitational pull of the earth.

So it is with the economist. He cannot arbitrarily institute changes in the price of cars or unskilled labor services just to observe the effect on quantity purchased or level of employment. However, this does not mean that economic theory cannot be tested. Economic conditions (for example, prices, production costs, technology, transportation cost, etc.), like the location of the planets, do change from time to time. As actual conditions change, economic theory can be tested by analyzing its consistency with the real world. The real world is the laboratory of the economist, just as the universe is the laboratory of the astronomer.

9 See Gadamer's remarks on the subject in 'The universality of the hermeneutical problem', in *Philosophical Hermeneutics*:

> Statistics provide us with a useful example of how the hermeneutical dimension encompasses the entire procedure of science. It is an extreme example, but it shows us that science always stands under definite conditions of methodological abstraction and that the successes of modern sciences rest on the fact that other possibilities for questioning are concealed by abstraction. This fact comes out clearly in the case of statistics, for the antici-patory character of the questions statistics answer make it particularly suitable for propaganda purposes. . . . what is established by statistics seems to be a language of facts, but which questions these facts answer and which facts would begin to speak if other questions were asked are hermeneutical questions. Only a hermeneutical inquiry would legitimate the meaning of these facts and thus the consequences that follow from them.
>
> (Gadamer 1976, p. 11)

10 In his article, 'On Robert Nozick's "On Austrian methodology" ', Walter Block writes:

> The reason we may object to the explanation of human action in terms of the movement of subatomic particles or electrical impulses across neurons is because there is simply no *equivalence* between the thoughts, feelings, pains, purposes, and plans which make up the reality of acting individuals, on the one hand, and the constructs of physics and neurophysiology, on the other. And this is completely apart from the question of whether these sciences will ever succeed in correlating the two, or explaining human decision-making in these terms. . . .
>
> Purposeful, future- and forward-looking behaviour is the essence of human action. People act because they envision a future that is preferable to one that does not include their present action. The explanation, then, of why people act is *teleological*; they act because they have *purposes* which they think can be

accomplished if they act. But such a mode is completely at variance with that which prevails in the natural sciences. There, causality or correlation is all, and teleology is dismissed as a suspect and illegitimate kind of anthropomorphism.

Austrians reject the reduction of economics to physics on the grounds of the incompatibility of the subject-matters of the two disciplines.

(Block 1980, p. 398)

11 This has to do with the conception of understanding as essentially transformative that I mentioned above. Compare Gadamer, *Truth and Method*, p. 264: 'Not occasionally only, but always, the meaning of a text goes beyond its author. This is why understanding is not merely a reproductive, but always a productive attitude as well. . . . It is enough to say that we understand in a different way, if we understand at all.' On this theme (the linking of understanding with interpretation and 'application'), see also: pp. 275, 278, 289, 293, 297, 304, 346, 350, 357, 359, 364, 428, 430, 432, 497.

12 Typical of Hayek's position are the following remarks:

We flatter ourselves undeservedly if we represent human civilization as entirely the product of conscious reason or as the product of human design, or when we assume that it is necessarily in our power deliberately to re-create or to maintain what we have built without knowing what we were doing. Though our civilization is the result of a cumulation of individual knowledge, it is not by the explicit or conscious combination of all this knowledge in any individual brain, but by its embodiment in symbols which we use without understanding them, in habits and institutions, tools and concepts, that man in society is constantly able to profit from a body of knowledge neither he nor any other man completely possesses. Many of the greatest things man has achieved are the result not of consciously directed thought, and still less the product of a deliberately co-ordinated effort of many individuals, but of a process in which the individual plays a part which he can never fully understand.

(Hayek 1972, pp. 149–50)

Speaking of the actions of people in response to changing prices, Hayek says: 'their decisions have significance far beyond their immediate aim' (see Hayek 1948, p. 47).

13 On this issue I am at odds with some of the remarks expressed by Don Lavoie in his (1985) paper, 'The interpretive dimension of economics: science, hermeneutics and praxeology'. In subsequent writings of his, Lavoie is careful to note the misleading characteristic of speaking of 'knowledge from the inside'.

14 Compare Frank H. Knight (1956, p. 156): 'A conscious, critical social consensus is of the essence of the idea of objectivity or truth'.

15 With reference to Hayek's notion of methodological individualism, Ricoeur remarks:

One can indeed ask whether, to understand 'we', it is not first of all necessary to know the meaning of 'I'. But such a derivation of 'we' from 'I', as sketched by Husserl in his fifth *Cartesian Meditation*, is not a scientific hypothesis: it concerns the origin of meaning though it is in no way empirical; it consists in saying that one cannot understand the meaning of an institution, a group belief or a collective symbolism unless these phenomena are related to a 'we'. But one can speak of a 'we' only if every member of it can say 'I'; thus meaning proceeds from 'I' to 'we' and thence to the group, the beliefs, the institutions. In this sense Hayek's and Popper's thesis might be justified, but it would no longer be the thesis of a *methodological* individualism.

Human phenomena can accordingly be regarded as irreducibly social for the purposes of description and explanation; their reduction into terms of an 'I' is relevant to an analysis of a different sort, which has nothing to do with the construction of a theory of social phenomena.

(Ricoeur 1979b, p. 138)

16 See also my essay, 'Ricoeur and the hermeneutics of the subject', in Madison (1988).
17 That the *We* is merely 'the result of a summing up which puts together two or more *Egos*' (Mises 1963, p. 44) is highly dubious. There may be some worthwhile implications for economics in recent hermeneutical research into the nature of subjectivity and the relationship between the *I* and the *We*. See, for instance, my essay 'The hermeneutics of (inter)subjectivity, or: the mind/body problem deconstructed', in Madison (1988); and also Schrag (1986).
18 See Gadamer, 'The problem of historical consciousness', in Rabinow and Sullivan (1979). See also my essay, 'Husserl's contribution to the explanation/ understanding debate', in Madison (1988).
19 See Ricoeur, 'The model of the text: meaningful action considered as a text', in Rabinow and Sullivan (1979).
20 See, for instance, Friedman's writings on the subject in *Bright Promises, Dismal Performances: An Economist's Protest* and, more recently, the paper he presented to the 1983 Regional Meeting of The Mont Pelerin Society, 'What could reasonably have been expected from monetarism: the United States'.
21 I am here paraphrasing from my study of the philosophy of Merleau-Ponty: 'The body of which science and objectivistic philosophy speak, is a secondary, thematized body, and that body does not *exist*; it is but a thought body' (Madison 1981, pp. 23–4). Merleau-Ponty was one of the first people to direct a sustained, explicit attack against objectivistic thinking – what he called 'la pensée objective' – and his work remains, in this regard, a classic. Anyone who is seriously concerned with the status of the social sciences should, at least one time in their lives, have made a serious study of Merleau-Ponty's *Phenomenology of Perception*.
Unlike some of his many students, Frank H. Knight was fully aware of the artificiality of *homo economicus*, of the fact that it is a theoretical construct useful for certain purposes but that it in no way designates a reality or tells us what man *is* (to think so would be to fall into what Knight would have called 'naïve economism'), and this awareness has been inherited by one of his students, James Buchanan (for numerous remarks on the subject, see Buchanan, *What Should Economists Do?*). Israel Kirzner, quoting William Jaffe, maintains that Menger, too, was not a victim of economism in his conception of man. Kirzner writes:

In Menger, man is not depicted as a hedonistic 'lightning calculator of pleasures and pains'. Man, as Menger saw him, far from being a 'lightning calculator' is a 'bumbling, erring, ill-informed creature, plagued with uncertainty, forever hovering between alluring hopes and haunting fears, and congenitally incapable of making finely calibrated decisions in pursuit of satisfactions'.

(Kirzner 1979, p. 61)

22 This freedom of interpretation poses problems for scientific prediction and led Knight (1956, pp. 175–6) to say: 'This trait of human beings, in contrast with physical things . . . is admittedly embarrassing to the economist as a scientist, but there does not seem to be anything that he can do about it.'
23 See, in this regard, the remarks of Charles Taylor:

Man is a self-interpreting animal. He is necessarily so, for there is no such thing as the structure of meanings for him independently of his interpretation of them; for one is woven into the other. But then the text of our interpretation is not that heterogeneous from what is interpreted; for what is interpreted is itself an interpretation: a self-interpretation which is embodied in a stream of action. It is an interpretation of experiential meaning which contributes to the constitution of this meaning. Or to put it another way, that of which we are trying to find the coherence is itself partly constituted by self-interpretation.

(Interpretation and the sciences of man, Taylor 1979, pp. 37–8)

See also the remarks of James Buchanan:

[Man is] an artifactual animal bounded by natural constraints. We are, and will be, at least in part, that which we make ourselves to be. We construct our own beings, again within limits. We are artifactual, as much like the pottery sherds that the archaeologists dig up as like the animals whose fossils they also find.

(Buchanan 1979, pp. 94–5)

Mises himself knew full well that what determines human history is not 'facts' but ideas, the ideas that human beings make of their own existence.

24 Geertz writes: 'Hopping back and forth between the whole conceived through the parts which motivates them, we seek to turn them, by a sort of intellectual perpetual motion, into explications of one another' (Geertz 1979, p. 239).

25 In this paper I have not been able to deal with one of Gadamer's most important contributions to philosophy, which is surely of the utmost relevance to economics. This is his reconceptualization of *rationality*, and it forms a dominant motif in his writings subsequent to *Truth and Method*. In opposition to the traditional and still dominant view of reason as essentially theoretical-instrumental (scientific-technological), Gadamer defends (not as a substitute for the former but as something more basic than it) what could be called a communi-cative-critical conception of reason or rational praxis. I have sought to spell out the political implications of this view of rationality in my (1986) book, *The Logic of Liberty*. I have also shown how this alternative conception of rationality is fully present, long before it was dealt with in philosophy, in the work of Frank H. Knight.

For his part, Kirzner has argued that the rationality of entrepreneurial activity cannot be understood as a mere 'economizing' one (reason in the usual, instrumental sense), as *calculative* rationality. Entrepreneurial decision-making is most definitely not irrational, but *neither is it rational in the usual, scientific sense of the term* (see, for instance, Kirzner 1979, pp. 109, 226ff). Here is a good instance where work on a particular economic topic – entrepreneurship – calls for a non-traditional concept of rationality; one, precisely, which is Gadamer's great merit to have attempted to articulate philosophically. Formalistic economics is radically called into question when it is realized that choice, the central phenomenon in economic analysis, does not have to do with solving a maximization problem (as Kirzner maintains that it does not), and that, as Lachmann maintains, the traditional economic view of decision, as Kirzner (1979, p. 227) says: 'abstracts from elements that are crucial to the true character of human choice'.

This is one area where the convergence between certain strands of thinking in economics, on the one hand, and the position explored and defined in pheno-menology and hermeneutics, on the other, is truly amazing.

REFERENCES

Beck, Lewis White (1971 [1949]) 'The "Natural Science Ideal" in the social services', in R.A. Manners and D. Kaplan (eds) *Theory in Anthropology: A Sourcebook*, Chicago: Aldine Publishing Co. (originally published in *Scientific Monthly* 68 [1949].

Bernstein, Richard (1983) *Beyond Objectivism and Relativism: Science, Hermeneutics and Praxis*, Philadelphia: University of Pennsylvania Press.

Block, Walter (1980) 'On Robert Nozick's "On Austrian methodology"', *Inquiry* 23, pp. 397–444.

Buchanan, James (1977) *What Should Economists Do?*, Indianapolis: Liberty Press.

Culbertson, John M. (1986) 'American economics: 100 years in a rut', *New York Times*, Jan. 12.

Friedman, Milton (1953) 'The methodology of positive economics', Chicago: University of Chicago Press.

—— (1972) *Bright Promises, Dismal Performances: An Economist's Protest*, San Diego: Harcourt Brace Jovanovich.

—— (1983) 'What could reasonably have been expected from monetarism: the United States' (paper presented to the Mont Pelerin Society) *Focus* no. 6, 'Challenging complacency', Vancouver: The Fraser Institute.

Gadamer, Hans-Georg (1975) *Truth and Method*, New York: Seabury Press.

—— (1976) 'On the scope and function of hermeneutical reflection', in Gadamer, *Philosophical Hermeneutics*, trans. and ed. by David E. Linge, Berkeley: University of California Press.

—— (1979) 'The problem of historical consciousness', in P. Rabinow and W.M. Sullivan (eds) *Interpretive Social Sciences: A Reader*, Berkeley: University of California Press.

Geertz, Clifford (1973) *The Interpretation of Cultures*, New York: Basic Books.

—— (1979) 'From the native's point of view: on the nature of anthropological understanding', in P. Rabinow and W.M. Sullivan (eds) *Interpretive Social Science: A Reader*, Berkeley: University of California Press.

Gwartney, James D. and Stroup, Richard (1980) *Economics: Private and Public Choice*, 2nd edn, New York: Academic Press.

Hayek, F.A. von (1948) 'The use of knowledge in society', in Hayek, *Individualism and Economic Order*, Chicago: University of Chicago Press.

—— (1972) *The Counter-Revolution of Science: Studies on the Abuse of Reason*, 2nd edn, Indianapolis: Liberty Press.

Hazlitt, Henry (1984) 'An interview with Henry Hazlitt', *Austrian Economics Newsletter*, Spring, Auburn, Al.: The Ludwig von Mises Institute of Auburn University.

Heidegger, Martin (1962) *Being and Time*, trans. by J. Macquarrie and E. Robinson, New York: Harper & Row.

Kirzner, Israel (1979) *Perception, Opportunity, and Profit*, Chicago: University of Chicago Press.

Knight, Frank H. (1956) 'A conscious, critical social consensus is of the essence of the idea of objectivity of truth', in Knight, *On the History and Method of Economics*, Chicago: University of Chicago Press.

Lachmann, Ludwig M. (1984 [1969]) 'Methodological individualism and the market economy', in D.M. Hausman (ed.) *The Philosophy of Economics: An Anthology*, Cambridge: Cambridge University Press.

—— (1986) 'Economic theory in tempestuous season', in Lachmann, *The Market as an Economic Process*, New York: Basil Blackwell.

Lavoie, Don (1985) 'The interpretive dimension of economics: science, hermeneutics and praxeology', Working Paper Series no. 15, Fairfax, Va.: Center for the Study of Market Processes, George Mason University.

—— (1987) 'The accounting of interpretations and the interpretation of accounts: the communicative function of "the language of business"', *Accounting, Organizations and Society*, 12, no. 6, pp. 579–604.

Madison, G.B. (1981) *The Phenomenology of Merleau-Ponty* (preface by Paul Ricoeur), Athens: Ohio University Press.

—— (1986) *The Logic of Liberty*, Westport, Conn.: Greenwood Press.

—— (1988) *The Hermeneutics of Postmodernity: Figures and Themes*, Bloomington: Indiana University Press.

Merleau-Ponty, Maurice (1962) trans. Colin Smith, *Phenomenology of Perception*, London: Routledge & Kegan Paul.

Mises, Ludwig von (1963) *Human Action*, 3rd rev. edn, Chicago: Contemporary Books.

Polkinghorne, Donald (1983) *Methodology for the Human Sciences: Systems of Inquiry*, Albany: University of New York Press.

Rabinow, P. and Sullivan, W.M. (eds) (1979) *Interpretive Social Science: A Reader*, Berkeley: University of California Press.

Ricoeur, Paul (1974) *The Conflict of Interpretations: Essays in Hermeneutics*, ed. by Don Ihde, Evanston, Ill.: Northwestern University Press.

—— (1979a [1971]) 'The model of the text: meaningful action considered as a text', in P. Rabinow and W.M. Sullivan (eds) *Interpretive Social Sciences: A Reader*, Berkeley: University of California Press (originally published in *Social Research* 38 (3) Fall, 1971).

—— (1979b) *Main Trends in Philosophy*, New York: Holmes & Meier.

—— (1981a) 'The narrative function', in Ricoeur, *Hermeneutics and the Human Sciences*, trans. and ed. by J.B. Thompson, Cambridge: Cambridge University Press.

—— (1981b) 'What is a text? Explanation and understanding', in Ricoeur, *Hermeneutics and the Human Sciences*, by J.B. Thompson, Cambridge: Cambridge University Press.

——(1984/5) *Time and Narrative*, trans. by K. McLaughlin and D. Pellauer, Chicago: University of Chicago Press.

—— (1985) 'History as narrative and practice' (Paul Ricoeur interviewed by Peter Kemp), *Philosophy Today*, Fall.

Rorty, Richard (1979) *Philosophy and the Mirror of Nature*, Princeton: Princeton University Press.

Schafer, Roy (1978) *Language and Insight*, New Haven, Conn.: Yale University Press.

Schrag, Calvin O. (1986) *Communicative Praxis and the Space of Subjectivity*, Bloomington: Indiana University Press.

Taylor, Charles (1979) 'Interpretation and the sciences of man', in P. Rabinow and W.M. Sullivan (eds) *Interpretive Social Science: A Reader*, Berkeley: University of California Press.

Part II

Alternative views of economics from a particular philosophical standpoint: hermeneutics 'appropriated' by neoclassicism, institutionalism, critical theory, and Austrian economics

4 Storytelling in economics[1]

Donald N. McCloskey

It is good to tell the story of science and art, economics and the nineteenth-century novel, the marginal-productivity theory of distribution and the tradition of the Horatian ode as similarly as possible. I intend to do so. Economists are tellers of stories and makers of poems, and from recognizing this we will know better what economists do.

There seem to be two ways of understanding things: either by way of a metaphor or by way of a story, through something like a poem or through something like a novel. When a biologist is asked to explain why the moulting glands of a crab are located just as they are he has two possibilities. Either he can call on a model – a metaphor – of rationality inside the crab, explaining that locating them just *there* will maximize the efficiency of the glands in operation; or he can tell a story, of how crabs with badly located glands will fail to survive. If he is lucky with the modelling he will discover a mathematical model with analytic solutions. If he is lucky with the storytelling he will discover a true history of some maladapted variety of crabs, showing that it is dying out. Metaphors and stories, models and histories, are the two ways of answering 'why'.

It has doubtless been noticed before that the metaphorical and the narrative explanations answer to each other. Suppose the biologist happens first to offer his metaphor, his hypothetical individual crab moving bits of its body from here to there in search of the optimal location for moulting glands. The listener asks: 'But why?' The biologist will answer with a story: he says, 'The reason why the glands must be located optimally is that if crabs did a poor job of locating their glands they would die off as time passed.' A story answers a model. Likewise, a model answers a story. If the biologist gives the evolutionary story first, and the listener then asks 'But why?', the biologist will answer with a metaphor: 'The reason why the crabs will die off is that poorly located glands would serve poorly in the emergencies of crabby life.' The glands would not be optimally located: that's why.

Among what speakers of English call the sciences, metaphors dominate physics and stories dominate biology. The modes, of course, can mix; that we humans regard metaphors and stories as antiphonal guarantees they will.

Mendel's thinking about genetics is a rare case in biology of pure modelling, answered after a long while by the more usual storytelling. In 1902 W.S. Sutton observed homologous pairs of chromosomes in grasshoppers. Sutton answered the question put to a metaphor – '*Why* does the Mendelian model of genes work?' – with a story: 'Because, to begin with, the genes are arranged along pairs of chromosomes, which I have seen, one half from each parent.'

The modes of explanation are more closely balanced in economics. An economist can explain the success of cotton farming in the *ante bellum* South indifferently in static, modelling terms (i.e., the South in 1860 had a comparative advantage in cotton) or in dynamic, storytelling terms (i.e., the situation in 1860 was an evolution from earlier successes). The best economics, indeed, combines the two. Ludwig von Mises' famous paper of 1920 on the impossibility of economic calculation under socialism was both a story of the failures of central planning during the recently concluded war and a model of the ignorance that would plague any attempt whatever to replace the market (Lavoie 1985, p. 49).

The metaphors are best adapted – one could use here either an evolutionary story from the history of science or a maximizing model from the sociology or philosophy of science – to making predictions of tides in the sea or of shortages in markets, simulating out into a counterfactual world. Seventeenth-century physics abandoned stories in favour of models, giving up the claim to tell in a narrative sense how the gravity reached up and pulled things down; it just did, according to such-and-such an equation – let me show you the model. Similarly, a price control on apartments will yield shortages: don't ask how it will in sequence; it just will, according to such-and-such an equation – let me show you the model.

On the other hand, storytelling is best adapted to explaining something that has already happened – such as the evolution of crabs or the development of modern corporation. The Darwinian story was notably lacking in models, and in predictions. Mendel's model, on the other hand, which offered to explain the descent of man by a metaphor rather than by a story, was neglected for 34 years, while evolution was in the telling.

The contrast carries over to the failures of the two modes. When a metaphor is used too boldly in narrating history it becomes snared in logical contradictions, such as those surrounding counterfactuals (McCloskey 1987). If a model of an economy is to be used to imagine what would have happened to Britain without the industrial revolution, then the contradiction is that an economy of the British sort did in fact experience an industrial revolution. A world in which the Britain of 1780 did not yield up an industrial revolution would be a very different one before and after 1780. The model wants to eat the cake and have all the ingredients, too. It contradicts the story. Likewise, when a mere story attempts to predict something, by extrapolating the story into the future, it contradicts some persuasive model. The story of business cycles can organize the past, but contradicts itself when offered as a prediction of the future. If the models of business cycles could predict the future there would be no surprises, and by that fact no business cycles.

The point is that economists are like other human beings in that they use metaphors and tell stories. They are concerned both to explain and to understand, *erklären* and *verstehen*. I am going to concentrate here on storytelling, having written elsewhere about the metaphorical side of the tale (McCloskey 1985). What might be called the poetics or stylistics of economics is worth talking about. But here the subject is the rhetoric of fiction in economics.

I propose to take seriously as assertion by Peter Brooks, in his *Reading for the Plot*: 'Our lives are ceaselessly intertwined with narrative, with the stories that we tell, all of which are reworked in that story of our own lives that we narrate to ourselves. . . . We are immersed in narrative.' (Brooks 1985, p. 3). As the historian J.H. Hexter put it, storytelling is 'a sort of knowledge we cannot live without' (Hexter 1986, p. 8). Economists have not lived without it, not ever. It is no accident that the novel and economic science were born at the same time. We live in an age insatiated with plot.

Tell me a story, Dr Smith. Why, of course.

A pension scheme is proposed for the nation, in which 'the employer will pay half'. It will say in the law and on the worker's salary cheque that the worker contributes 5 per cent of his wages to the pension fund but that the employer contributes the other 5 per cent. The example is a leading case in the old debate between lawyers and economists. A law is passed 'designed' (as they say) to have such-and-such an effect. The lawyerly mind goes this far, urging us therefore to limit the hours of women workers or to subsidize American shipping. The women, he thinks, will be made better off; as will the American ships. According to the lawyer, the workers under the pension scheme will on balance be 5 per cent better off, getting half of their pension free.

No economist, however, will want leave the story of the pension plan in the first act – the lawyer's and legislator's act of laws 'designed' to split the costs. She will want to go further in the drama. She will say: 'At the higher cost of labour the employers will hire fewer workers. In the second act the situation created by the law will begin to dissolve. At the old terms more workers will want to work than the employers wish to hire. Jostling queues will form outside the factory gates. The competition of the workers will drive down wages. By the third and final act a part of the "employer's" share – maybe even all of it – will come to the workers themselves, in the form of lower wages. The intent of the law will have been frustrated.'

Thus, in Chicago, when a tax on employment was proposed, the reporters asked who would bear the tax. Alderman Thomas Keane (who subsequently went to jail, though not for misappropriation of economics) declared that the city had been careful to draft the law so that only the employers paid it. 'The City of Chicago,' said Keane, 'will never tax the working man.'

Thus, in 1987, when Senator Kennedy proposed a plan for workers and employers to share the cost of health insurance, newspapers reported Kennedy as estimating: 'the overall cost at $25 billion – $20 billion paid by employers and $5 billion by workers'. (In other words, Senator Kennedy will never tax the working man.) The manager of employee relations at the US Chamber of Commerce (who opposed Senator Kennedy's plan) apparently disagreed with his economic analysis of where the tax should fall, and said: 'It is ridiculous to believe that every company . . . can afford to provide such a generous array of health care benefits.' (In other words, the US Chamber of Commerce will never tax the company.)

The latter case illustrates a number of points about economic stories. It illustrates the delight that economists take in unforeseen consequences – a delight shared with other social scientists. It illustrates the selection of certain consequences for special attention: an accountant or political scientist would want to hear how the pension was funded, because the manner of funding would affect business or political behaviour in the future; but economists usually set such consequences to one side. It also illustrates the way in which economists draw on typical scenes (e.g., the queues in front of the factory) and typical metaphors (e.g., workers as commodities to be bought and sold). Especially, it illustrates the way in which stories support economic argument. Since Adam Smith and David Ricardo, economists have been addicted to little analytic stories – the Ricardian vice. The economist says, 'Yes, I know how the story starts; but I see dramatic possibilities here. I see how events will develop from the situation given in the first act.'

It is not controversial that an economist is a storyteller when telling the story of the Federal Reserve Board or of the industrial revolution. Plainly and routinely, 90 per cent of what economists do is such storytelling. Yet even in the other 10 per cent, in the part more obviously dominated by models and metaphors, the economist tells stories. The applied economist can be viewed as a realistic novelist or a realistic playwright – a Thomas Hardy or a George Bernard Shaw. The theorist, too, may be viewed as a teller of stories, though a non-realist – whose plots and characters have the same relation to truth as those in *Gulliver's Travels* or *A Midsummer Night's Dream*. Most economics is saturated with narration.

On the face of it, the analogy seems apt. Economics is a sort of social history. For all the brave talk about being the physicists of the social sciences, economists do their best work when looking backwards, the way a biologist or geologist or historian does. Journalists and politicians demand that economists be seers, forecasting the social weather. Sometimes, unhappily, the economists will take money for trying. But it is not their chief skill, any more than earthquake forecasting is the chief skill of seismologists or election forecasting the chief skill of political historians. Economists cannot predict much, and certainly cannot predict profitably. If they were so smart they would be rich (McCloskey 1988). Economists are mainly tellers of stories.

Well, so what? What is to be gained by thinking this way about economics? One answer can be given at once, and illustrates the uses of the literary analogy – namely, storytelling makes it clearer why economists disagree.

Disagreement among scientists is as suggestive for the rhetoric of science as simultaneous discovery is for its sociology. The lay person does not appreciate how much economists agree, but he is not entirely wrong in thinking that they also disagree a lot. Economists have long-lasting schools, more typical of the humanities than the sciences. Why then do they disagree?

When economists themselves try to answer the question they become sociological or philosophical, though in ways that a sociologist or philosopher would find uncongenial. When in a sociological mood they will smile knowingly and explain that what drives monetarists or Keynesians to 'differentiate their product' (as they delight in putting it) is self-interest. Economists are nature's Marxists, and enjoy uncovering and then snickering at self-interest. When in a more elevated and philosophic mood they will speak sagely of 'successive approximations' or 'treating a theory merely *as if* it were true'. Some have read a bit of Popper or Kuhn, and reckon they know a thing or two about the Methodology of Science. The stories that result from these ventures into ersatz sociology and sophomore philosophy are not entirely convincing. The economists do not know why they disagree.

Storytelling offers a richer model of how economists talk and a more plausible story of their disagreements than an economics of ideas or a philosophy of science. From a literary perspective, in other words, the disagreement can be understood in more helpful ways than by saying that one economist has a divergent material interest from another, or a different 'crucial experiment', or another 'paradigm'.

It is first of all the theory of reading as held by scientists that permits them to disagree, and with such ill temper. The over-simple theory of reading adopted officially by economists and other scientists is that scientific texts are: transparent; a matter of 'mere communication'; 'just style'; simply 'writing up' the 'theoretical results' and 'empirical findings'. If reading is so free from difficulties, then naturally the only way our readers could possibly fail to agree with us is on account of their dimness or their ill will. (But let us leave aside the disappearingly unlikely event of our own dimness!) It's right there in black and white. Don't be a dunce.

A better theory of reading – one that admits that scientific prose, like literary prose, is complicated and allusive, drawing on a richer rhetoric than mere demonstration – might soothe this ill temper. The better theory, after all, is the one that a good teacher uses with students. She knows well enough that the text is not transparent to the students, and does not get angry when they misunderstand. God, likewise, does not get angry when his students misunderstand His text. In fact, like scientists and scholars, God 'writes' obscurely – to snare us. As Gerald Bruns has noted, St Augustine viewed the obscurity of the Bible has having, as Bruns put it: 'a pragmatic function in the art of winning over an alienated and even contemptuous audience' (Bruns 1984, p. 157). Bruns quotes a remark from St Augustine about the difficulty of reading the Bible, that might as well be about the latest proof in mathematical economics: 'I do not doubt that this situation was provided by God to conquer pride by work and to combat disdain in our minds, to which those things which are easily discovered seem frequently to be worthless.'

One source of disagreement then, is a naïve theory of reading – the theory that would ask naïvely for the 'message' in a poem, as though poems were riddles in rhyme. Another source of disagreement is, similarly, a source of disagreement about literature: compression, a lack of explicitness. Partly, this is economic. Had she but world enough and time, the writer could make everything explicit. In a world of scarcity, however, she cannot. Yet explicitness is no guarantee of agreement; even if the writer has all the time in the world, the reader does not. I cannot pay attention long enough to understand some of my Marxist friends (though I urge them to keep trying). Similarly, mathematicians in economics have an expository style based on explicitness and a zero valuation of time. Everything will be clear, they promise earnestly, if the readers will but attend carefully to the axioms. The readers grow weary. They cannot remember all the axioms and anyway cannot see why one would wish to doubt them. They do not have the toleration for such language that the mathematician has. The point involves more than the economic scarcity of journal space and the leisure time to read. It involves the anthropology of science, the customs of its inhabitants and their ability to read a language. A scientist convinced of what she writes will come from a certain background, supplied with a language. Unless her reader knows roughly the same language – that is unless he has been raised on approximately the same conversation, or is a cosmopolitan – he will misunderstand and will be unpersuaded. This is an unforgivable failure only if it is an unforgivable failure to be, say, non-Balinese or non-French. The reader comes from another culture, with a different tongue. The training in reading English that a Ph.D. in English provides, or the training in reading economics that a Ph.D. in economics provides, are trainings in rapid reading – filling in the blanks.

A third and final source of disagreement in literature and in economics, beyond the naïve theory of reading and the limits on understanding foreign speech, is an inability of the reader to assume the point of view demanded by the author. A foolishly sentimental poem has the same irritating effect on a reader as does a foolishly libertarian piece of economics. The reader refuses to enter the author's imaginative world, or is unable to. A literary critic has said: 'A bad book, then, is a book in whose mock reader we discover a person we refuse to become, a mask we refuse to put on, a role we will not play' (Gibson 1980 [1950], p. 5). The reader, therefore, will naturally misread the text – at least in the sense of violating the author's intentions. We do not submit to the authorial intentions of a badly written greetings card. In a well-written novel or a well-written scientific paper we agree to submit to the authorial intentions, so far as we can make them out. The entire game in a science such as biology or chemistry or economics is this matter of submission to authorial intentions. Linus Pauling commands attention, and his readers submit to his intentions (at least outside of vitamin C); Paul Samuelson likewise (at least outside of monetary policy).

The argument can be pushed further. An economist expositing a result creates both an 'authorial audience' (an imagined group of readers who know this is fiction) and a 'narrative audience' (a group who do not). As Peter Rabinowitz (1980 [1968], p. 245) explains: 'the narrative audience of "Goldilocks" believes in talking bears'. In other words, the authorial audience knows it is a fiction. The split between the two audiences created by the author seems weaker in economic science than in explicit fiction, probably because we all know that bears do not talk but we do not all know that marginal productivity is a metaphor. The 'narrative audience' in science, as in 'Goldilocks', is properly taken in by the fiction. In science, too, the authorial audience is taken in (and so, incidentally, is the literal audience – the actual readers as against the ideal readers the author appears to want to have). Michael Mulkay (1985) has shown how important is the choice of authorial audience in the scholarly correspondence of bio-chemists. The biochemists, like other scientists and scholars, are largely unaware of their literary devices, and become puzzled and angry when their literal audience refuses to believe in talking bears. Little wonder that scientists and scholars disagree, even though their rhetoric of 'what the facts say' would appear to make disagreement impossible.

Taking economics as a kind of writing, then, explains some of the dis-agreements of economists. Economists go on disagreeing after the 'theoretical results and empirical findings' have been laid out for inspection; not merely because they are differentiating their product or suffering from inflamation of the paradigm but because they read a story or a scientific paper written in an unfamiliar language inexpertly, yet do not realize it. They are like the tourist in Florence who believes firmly that Italians really do understand English, and can be made to admit it if he speaks slowly and very loudly.

Telling the stories in economics as matters of beginnings, middles, and ends has many attractions. One can start with pure plot, breaking 100 economic stories down into their components – as Vladmir Propp did in 1928 for 100 Russian folk tales (pp. 19–24). For example, the capitalization of Iowa corn prices tale, the exit from and entry to computer selling in the 1980s tale, the correct incidence of the Kennedy health insurance tale, and so forth. The tales can then be analysed into 'functions' (Propp's word for actions). And, to Proppize it entirely, one can ask whether the sequences of functions prove to be constant, as they are in Russia.

The task sounds bizarre. But in a way economics is too easy a case.

Economics is already structural, as the linguist Ferdinand de Saussure suggested (1983 [1916] pp. 79 and 113). The actions of an economistic folk-lore are few: entry; exit; price setting; orders within a firm; purchase; sale; valuation; and a few more. It is indeed this self-consciously structural element that makes economics so irritating to outsiders. Economists say over and over again: 'action X is *just like* action Y' – labour is just like a commodity, slavery is just like capitalization, children are just like refrigerators, and so forth. The economist's favourite phrase – 'underneath it all' – would please Claude Levi Strauss. Underneath it all, international trade among nations is trade among individuals, and can be modelled in the same way. Underneath it all, an inflated price is earned by someone as an inflation wage, leaving average welfare unchanged. Underneath it all, we owe the national debt to ourselves. In such a highly structured field, whose principles of storytelling are so well known by the main storytellers, it would be surprising to find as many as thirty-one distinct actions, as Propp (1968 [1928]) found in his 100 Russian folk tales (p. 64). He found seven characteristics (p. 80). That seems more likely: in his economic tales David Ricardo got along with three.

Tale-telling in economics follows the looser constraints of fiction, too. The most important is the sense of an ending, as in the story of the pension scheme. Let us go straight to the third act. The 5 per cent pension gained by the worker is 'not an equilibrium', as economists say when they do not like the ending proposed by some unsophisticated person. Any descendant of Adam Smith, whether by way of Marx or Marshall or Menger, will be happy to tell you that there is more to the story.

Many of the disagreements inside economics turn also on this sense of an ending. To an eclectic Keynesian the story idea 'Oil prices went up, which cased inflation' is full of meaning, having the merits that stories are supposed to have. But to a monetarist it seems incomplete, no story at all, a flop. As A.C. Harberger says, it does not make the economics 'sing'. It ends too soon, half-way through the second act: a rise in oil prices without some corresponding fall elsewhere is 'not an equilibrium'. From the other side, the criticism of monetarism by Keynesians is likewise a criticism of the plot line, complaining of an ill-motivated beginning rather than a premature ending: where on earth does the money *come* from, and why?

There is more than prettiness in such matters of plot. There is moral weight. The historian Hayden White (1981, p. 20) has written that: 'The demand for closure in the historical story is a demand . . . for moral reasoning.' The economist's ending to the pension story says: 'Look: you're getting fooled by the politicians and lawyers if you think that specifying the 50–50 share in the law will get the workers a 50 per cent cheaper pension. Wake up; act your age; look beneath the surface; recognize the dismal ironies of life.' Stories impart meaning, which is to say worth. A *New Yorker* cartoon shows a woman looking up worried from the TV, asking her husband, 'Henry, is there a moral to *our* story?' A monetarist is not morally satisfied until she has pinned the blame on the Federal Reserve.

The sense of adequacy in storytelling works in the most abstract theory, too. In seminars on mathematical economics a question nearly as common as 'Haven't you left out the second subscript?' is 'What's your story?' The story of the pension scheme can be put entirely mathematically and metaphorically, as an assertion about the incidence of a tax on a system of supply-and-demand curves in equilibrium:

$$w^* = -[Ed/(Ed + Es)]T^*.$$

The mathematics here is so familiar to an economist that he will not require explanation beyond the metaphor. But in less familiar cases he will. Like the man who is listening to the biologist explaining about moulting glands in crabs, at the end of all the modelling the economist will insistently ask *why*. 'What's your story?' His question is an appeal to move to a lower level of abstraction, closer to the episodes of human life. It asks for more realism, in a fictional sense, more illusion of direct experience. It asks to step closer to a nineteenth-century short story, with its powerful and unironic sense of 'being there'.

Even the most static and abstract argument in economics, by refusing to become storylike, and by insisting on remaining poetic and metaphorical, is part of 'that story of our own lives which we narrate to ourselves'. A scholar has a story in which the work in question is an episode: this is why seminars so often begin with 'how I came to this subject', because such a fragment of autobiography gives meaning to it all. You will hear mathematicians complain if a seminar has not been 'motivated'. The motivation is a story, frequently a mythic history about this part of mathematics or about the speaker. The audience wishes to know why the argument might matter to the speaker, or to the audience itself. The story will then have a moral, as all good stories do.

'Economics as story' gives a number of places from which to see the plot of economics. To repeat, the author is either a storyteller or an explainer, telling either the experience in the happening or an explanation by way of metaphor. But the reader, too, figures in economic thought. A distinction has been drawn by Louise Rosenblatt between *aesthetic* and *efferent* (from Latin *effero*, carry off) reading. In efferent reading the reader focuses on what she will carry off from the reading. Efferent reading is supposed to characterize model-building and science. In aesthetic reading the reader focuses on her experience at the time of reading, which is supposed to characterize storytelling and art. Yet an aesthetic reading on a scientific text commonly carries the argument. The feeling 'Yes: this is right' in the last stanza of 'Among School Children' resembles the feeling in ancient proof that the square root of 2 cannot be expressed as the ratio of two whole numbers. Rosenblatt (1978, p. 34) supposes that 'To adopt an aesthetic stance . . . toward the directions for constructing a radio, is possible, but would usually be very unrewarding.' Well, usually. Yet the computer repairman takes the aesthetic attitude toward the schematics for a Murrow computer: 'A nice little machine,' he says, and smiles, and is brought to this or that solution. The physicist Steven Weinberg argues that aesthetic readings govern the spending of millions of dollars in research money. The pleasure of the text is sometimes its meaning, even in science.

Rosenblatt anticipates such an argument, noting that theories of literature that do not stress the reader's role are left puzzled by pleasurable non-fiction, such as Gibbon's *Decline and Fall of the Roman Empire*, or, one might add, the best applied economics. The reader's response gives a way of keeping track of the aesthetic readings when they matter. The usual theory of scientific reading claims that they never do.

The telling of artful stories has its customs, and these may be brought to economics, too. Take, for instance, the bare notion of genre – that is, types of literary production, with their histories and their interrelations. The scientific report is itself a genre, whose conventions have changed from time to time. Kepler wrote in an autobiographical style, spilling his laboratory notes with all their errors and dead-ends out on to the page, Galileo wrote urbane little dramas. It was Newton who insisted on the cramping literary conventions of the scientific paper (Medawar 1964). An economist should be aware that he adopts more than a 'mere' style when he adopts the conventions.

Pure theory in economics is similar to the literary genre of fantasy. Like fantasy it violates the rules of 'reality' for the convenience of the tale; and, of course, amazing results become commonplace in a world of hypothesis. That animals exhibit the foibles of human beings is unsurprising in a world in which animals talk. No blame attaches. The task of pure theory is to make up fantasies that have a point, in the way that Orwell's *Animal Farm* has a point. Pure theory confronts reality by disputing whether this or that assumption drives the result, and whether the assumption is realistic. The literary analogy puts the debate about the realism of economic assumptions in a strange light. Is it the talking animals or the flying carpets that makes *The Arabian Nights* 'unrealistic'?

To speak of pure theory as fantasy, I repeat, is not to put it at a low value. Swift's *Gulliver's Travels* is fantasy, too, but pointed, instructive, useful fantasy for all that. Theorists usually know in what genre they are writing. Their awareness reveals itself in their little jokes, of 'turnpikes' along the way to economic growth and 'islands' of labour in the economy. Yet the Ricardian vice characteristic of economics is most characteristic of high theory: allowing fancy too free a rein. Auden remarks, 'What makes it difficult for a poet not to tell lies is that, in poetry, all facts and all beliefs cease to be true or false and become interesting possibilities' (quoted in Ruthven 1979, p. 175). The hundredth possible world of international trade gives the impression of a poetry gone whacko. Economists would do well to know in what genre they are reading or writing, to avoid misclassifying the fantasy and to do the fantasy well.

Good empirical work in economics, on the other hand, is like realist fiction. Unlike fantasy, it claims to follow all the rules of the world (well . . . all the *important* ones). But of course it is fictional. That analogy is worth reflecting on, too.

The modernist schoolmaster so long in charge of our intellectual life would reply crossly that it is my analysis that is the fantasy and fiction. He will complain that the proper scientist *finds* the story. No fiction about it.

The answer to such an assertion has long been understood. The storyteller cloaks himself in Truth – which is what annoyed Plato about alleged imitations of life in sculpture or poetry. Just 'telling the story as it happened' evades the responsibility to examine the point of view. Realistic fiction does this habitually – which shows another use for the literary analogy, to note that realistic 'fiction' in science can also evade declaring a point of view. Michael Mulkay notes in the epistolary arguments of biologists a Rule 11: 'Use the personal format of a letter . . . but withdraw from the text yourself as often as possible so that the other party continually finds himself engaged in an unequal dialogue with the experiments, data, observations and facts' (1985: 66). The evasion is similar in history: 'the plot of a historical narrative is always an embarrassment and has to be pre-sented as "found" in the events rather than put there by narrative techniques' (White 1981, p. 20).

Admitting that the Battle of Waterloo has more promising material than the story of breakfast, it is nevertheless true that nothing is given to us by the world in story form already. *We* tell the stories. John Keegan has nicely illustrated the point in reference to Waterloo in his book, *The Face of Battle*. He speaks of the 'rhetoric of battle history' (p. 36) as demanding that one cavalry regiment be portrayed as 'crashing' into another, a case of 'shock' tactics. Yet an observant witness of such an encounter at Waterloo reported that 'we fully expected to have seen a horrid crash – no such thing! Each, as if by mutual consent, opened their files on coming near, and passed rapidly through each other' (p. 149). A story is something told to each other by human beings, not something existing ready-told in the very rocks or cavalry regiments or mute facts themselves. Niels Bohr once remarked that physics is not about the world but about what we as human beings can say about the world.

Stories, in other words, are selective. In this they are similar to metaphors and models, which must select, too. We cannot portray anything literally completely, as another Niels Bohr story illustrates. He asked his graduate class to *fully* describe a piece of chalk, to give *every* fact about it. As the students found, the task is impossible unless radically selective. We cannot know about the history of every atom in the chalk, or the location of every atom that bears any relation to the atoms in the chalk. We decide what matters, for *our* purposes, not God's or Nature's.

The fictional writer selects like the scientist, and invites the reader to fill in the blanks. Stories or articles can give only a small sample of experience, because actual experience is overwhelmed with irrelevance: taking out the garbage, bumping the table, scratching the back of one's head, seeing the title of the book one was not looking for. It is a sense of pointedness that distinguishes the good storyteller and the good scientific thinker from the bad.

The vaunted parsimony of scientific stories is not the result of some philosophy of science that says that parsimony is a Good Thing. It is a result of the way we read science, our ability to fill the blanks, telling stories in our culture. The economist can read the most unreadable and compressed production of his fellow economist, but only if both participate in the same community of speech. Wholly fictional stories are parsimonious in the same way.

Skilful fiction, whether taking the form of *Emma* or *The Origin of Species*, 'stimulates us to supply what is not there'. As Virginia Woolf (1953 [1925]) remarked of Jane Austen: 'What she offers is, apparently, a trifle, yet is composed of something that expands in the reader's mind and endows with the most enduring form of life scenes which are outwardly trivial' (p. 142). Remarking on Woolf in turn, Wolfgang Iser put it this way:

> What is missing from the apparently trivial scenes, the gaps arising out of the dialogue – this is what stimulates the reader into filling the blanks with projections [he has an image of the reader running a motion picture inside his head, which is of course why novels can still compete with television]. . . . The 'enduring form of life' which Virginia Woolf speaks of is not manifested on the printed page; it is a product arising out of the interaction between text and reader.
>
> (Iser 1980, pp. 110–11)

Scientific persuasion, too, is like that, as Arjo Klamer (1987) has shown for the economic postulate of rationality. Persuasion of the most rigorous kind must none the less have blanks to be filled at every other step if it is about a serious problem – about a difficult murder case, for example, or a difficult mathematical theorem or a difficult piece of economic history recently concluded. What is unsaid – but not unread – is often more important to the text as perceived by the reader than what is there on the page. And, as Klamer (1987, p. 175) says: 'The student of the rhetoric of economics faces the challenge of speaking about the unspoken, filling in the "missing text" in economic discourse.'

The running of different motion pictures inside each person's head is going to produce different texts as perceived. The story here returns to disagreement, that key to the literary character of economic and other science. Tzvetan Todorov makes the point: 'How do we explain this diversity [of literary readings]? By the fact that these accounts describe, not the universe of the book itself, but this universe as it is transformed by the psyche of each individual reader' (Todorov 1980 [1975], p. 72). And elsewhere: 'Only by subjecting the text to a particular type of reading do we construct, from our reading, an imaginary universe. Novels do not imitate reality; they create it' (pp. 67ff). The reader enters into the making of an economic text, too. This is why obscure texts are often influential. Keynes left many opportunities for readers to run their own internal motion pictures, filling in the blanks.

What, then, is to be done? Should economists go on pretending that scientific texts are transparent? If economists read texts differently, and know that they do, is economics left in chaos? Will admitting that economics like other sciences depends on storytelling lead to the war of all against all and low wages?

No. Much of the chaos that might be possible in fact already exists, in the grim little wars of misreading across the field. A literary turn might bring a peace of toleration and mutual trade. A community of readers is built the way a community of listeners to music or a community of businesspeople is built, by making them sophisticated readers and listeners and business-people, willing to try other ways of reading or listening or dealing.

Perhaps there is something, then, in treating economics as the telling of stories. The advantage to economic science in thinking this way is self-consciousness. A good thing, too. Much talk against self-consciousness comes from economists trying to manipulate the rules of conversation, but economists would do better to know what they are talking about. Looking on economics as poetry or fiction – or for that matter, as history – gives an economist a place to stand outside the field, from which to look in. It is a better place to stand than is provided by the usual philosophies of science, and is a great deal better than the homespun sociologies and philosophies that economists more commonly use.

There is another advantage to the larger culture. Economics should come back into the conversation of mankind. It is an extraordinarily clever way of speaking, and can do a lot of good. The way to bring it back is to persuade economists that they are not so very different from poets and novelists. For a long time now they have been standing aside, believing they have only the mathematical sciences as models, and practising a physics-worship that misunderstands both physics and themselves. Economists could get their gods from poetry or history or philology and still do much the same job of work, with a better temper.

Reunifying the conversation of mankind is most challenging with hard cases. Economics – standing alone on its hill, wrapped in its prideful self-image as Science – is a hard case. If even economics can be shown to be fictional and poetical and historical, then its story will be a better one. Technically speaking, it will be of the genre of comedy, with much wit in its lines, a charming array of types, an amused tolerance for human folly, and most characteristically a happy ending.

NOTE

1 Drafts of this essay were delivered as lectures to: Swarthmore College; the Centre for Research in Philosophy and Literature, University of Warwick, in the series 'Narrative as an Instrument of Culture'; the Political Economy Club at Harvard University; the Midwest Economics Association meetings for 1987 in St Louis, as the C. Woody Thompson Lecture; the Program on Social Theory and Comparative History, University of California, Davis, April 1987; the Conference on Methods, New School for Social Research, May 1987; and the University of Illinois, May 1987, as a Miller Committee Lecture. I thank the organizers for much good advice, and for indulging my stories.

REFERENCES

Brooks, Peter (1985) *Reading for the Plot: Design and Intention in Narrative*, New York: Vintage Books.

Bruns, Gerald L. (1984) 'The problem of figuration in antiquity', pp. 147–64, in G. Shapiro and A. Sica (eds) *Hermeneutics: Questions and Prospects*, Amherst: University of Massachusetts Press.

de Saussure, F. (1983 [1916]) *Course in General Linguistics*, trans. R. Harris, London: Duckworth.

Gibson, Walker (1980 [1950]) 'Authors, speakers, and mock readers', *College English* 11 (Febuary 1950), reprinted in Jane P. Tompkins (ed.) *Reader–Response Criticism*, pp. 1–6, Baltimore: Johns Hopkins University Press.

Hexter, J.H. (1986) 'The problem of historical knowledge', unpublished MS, Washington University, St Louis.

Keegan, John (1977) *The Face of Battle*, New York: Vintage Books.

Klamer, Arjo (1987) 'As if economists and their subjects were rational', in John Nelson, Allan Megill, and D.N. McCloskey (eds) *The Rhetoric of the Human Sciences*, Madison: University of Wisconsin Press, pp. 163–83.

Iser, Wolfgang (1980) 'The interaction between text and reader', in Susan R. Suleiman and Inge Crosman (eds) *The Reader in the Text: Essays on Audience and Interpretation*, Princeton: Princeton University Press, pp. 106–19.

Lavoie, Don (1985) *Rivalry and Central Planning: The Socialist Calculation Debate Reconsidered*, Cambridge: Cambridge University Press.

McCloskey, D.N. (1985) *The Rhetoric of Economics*, Madison: University of Wisconsin Press (in the series on the 'Rhetoric of the Human Sciences').

—— (1987) 'Counterfactuals', article in *The New Palgrave: A Dictionary of Economic Theory and Doctrine*, London: Macmillan.

—— (1988) 'The limits of expertise: if you're so smart, why ain't you rich?', *The American Scholar*, Summer, pp. 393–406.

Medawar, Peter (1964) 'Is the scientific paper fraudulent?' *Saturday Review*, August 1, pp. 42–3.

Mulkay, Michael (1985) *The Word and the World: Explorations in the Form of Sociological Analysis*, Winchester, Massachusetts: Allen & Unwin.

Propp, V. (1968 [1928]) *Morphology of the Folktale*, 2nd edn, trans. L. Scott and L.A. Wagner, American Folklore Society, Austin: University of Texas Press.

Rabinowitz, Peter J. (1980 [1968]) ' "What's Hecuba to Us?" The Audience's Experience of Literary Borrowing', in Susan R. Suleiman and Inge Crosman (eds) *The Reader in the Text: Essays on Audience and Interpretation*, pp. 241–63, Princeton: Princeton University Press.

Rosenblatt, Louise M. (1978) *The Reader, the Text, the Poem: The Transactional Theory of the Literary Work*, Carbondale: Southern Illinois University Press.

Ruthven, K.K. (1979) *Critical Assumptions*, Cambridge: Cambridge University Press.

Todorov, Tzvetan (1980 [1975]) 'Reading as construction', in Suleiman and Crosman (eds) *op. cit.*, pp. 67–82.

White, Hayden (1981) 'The value of narrativity in the representation of reality', in W.J.T. Mitchell (ed.) *On Narrative*, pp. 1–24, Chicago: University of Chicago Press.

Woolf, Virginia (1953 [1925]) *The Common Reader, First Series*, New York and London: Harcourt Brace Jovanovich.

5 The philosophical bases of institutionalist economics

Philip Mirowski

The precise nature of the relationship between the disciplines of economics and philosophy has yet to be explicated in detail. Certain family resemblances can be readily verified, and traced to a common lineage. Many of the precursors of western economic theory, such as John Locke and Adam Smith, were self-identified moral philosophers; many other inhabitants of the pantheon of economic theory, such as Karl Marx and John Maynard Keynes, are recognized as having made substantial contributions to philosophy. Nevertheless, in the modern era, ontogeny does not recapitulate phylogeny and the average economist in the late twentieth century would deny any neccessary or close links between the two fields.

In economics, the facade of the repudiation of philosophical preconceptions is propped up by the widespread conviction that modern economics has successfully adopted the character and attributes of a *science*. This invocation of science is intended to settle all arguments once and for all and to expiate all sins. Of course, this has been a vain hope. Disputes over method, epistemology and ontology have not been banished, because an invocation of science merely impounds controversy under the rubric of 'the philosophy of science', without really answering any of the hard questions. Once we can get beyond the lab coats and the particle accelerators and the rest of the clanking machinery, it is not at all clear that 'science' is inextricably committed to any particular programme or method, or to ontological construction. Indeed, once we get beyond the homiletic nostrums of Physics I, some exposure to the history of science demonstrates that there is no such thing as a single 'scientific method'. Science may at various junctures be realist or it may be idealist; it may be rationalist or it may be empiricist; it may be monistic or it may be dualistic; it may be naturalist or operationalist, or it may be instrumentalist; or, most bluntly, it may be true or it may be false. Nothing is substantially illuminated by the mere invocation of science by economists, although it has in the past proved useful in cowing certain critics.

A survey of the philosophical presuppositions of modern economics is made doubly difficult by the necessity of confronting the role of 'science' in both revealing and obscuring the main points of contention. Thorstein

Veblen, who first trained as a philosopher, once began one of his articles with the deadpan sentence: 'A discussion of the scientific point of view which avowedly proceeds from this point of view itself has necessarily the appearance of an argument in a circle; and such in great part is the character of what here follows' (Veblen 1969, p. 32). Veblen's predicament is particularly poignant for the issues at hand, because he was philosophically literate, he was the acknowledged progenitor of the Institutionalist school of economics, and he chose to raise the issue of the philosophical preconceptions of the economics of his day by attacking its credentials as a science. Ever since that time, the Institutionalist school has been distinguished from the general run of orthodoxy by a concern with the philosophical aspects of economic issues, especially in its role as a critic of neoclassical economics.

Nevertheless, things get stickier when one tries to briefly characterize the philosophical bases of Institutionalist economics, either as it is presently practised, or else as an ideal projection. (For some recent attempts, see Dyer 1986; Ramstaad 1986; Wilbur and Harrison 1978.) In this article, the reader should be prepared for one very individual and idiosyncratic reading of the philosophical underpinnings of Institutionalist theory: namely, that it has not yet found a way to break out of Veblen's ironic circle. The problem, as we shall argue in this chapter, is a failure to comprehend the fact that institutionalist economics was the offspring of an entirely distinct hermeneutical tradition from that which gave rise to neoclassical economics. These two traditions have a profound conflict over their respective images of a 'science', and therefore profoundly incompatible images of 'economic man' and 'rationality'.

The first urgent issue in the philosophy of economics is the question of the intelligibility of a separate discipline devoted exclusively to the explication of an abstract concept called 'the economy', separate from other categories of social phenomena, and separate from the relationships which we attribute to the physical or non-human world. This is not a new question, but one that has been broached throughout the history of economics. The debate over this issue was markedly heated around the turn of the century, with the Austrians and the German historical school bitterly disputing the feasibility of the unity of the *Geisteswissenschaften* and the *Naturwissenschaften*. Those impatient with philosophical discussions have since cited the 'Methodenstreit' as a prime example of the futility of methodological discourse; but such expressions of petulance do obscure the fact that most modern economists have no conception of the bounds which demarcate their discipline. There is the flippant imperialist response, that 'economics is what economists do', but that response misses the whole point of raising the question. Without some notion of what makes a discipline coherent, questions concerning the efficacy of methods of inquiry flounder aimlessly without a point of reference.

In the case of economics, the issue of the relationship of the 'economy' to other potential objects of inquiry already appropriated by other disciplines – say, the 'mind' of an actor, or the 'technology' of a society – has been a persistent sore point for economists. There has always existed the threat that an external intellectual discipline will contradict or falsify some crucial tenet of the abstraction designated by 'the economy'; or, conversely, that the external discipline will co-opt and absorb economics by reducing the economy to its own elemental abstractions. An example of the former was Karl Polanyi's attempt to redefine the meaning of the 'economy' from the vantage point of the anthropologist and economic historian (Polanyi 1968); an example of the latter would be the reduction of economic behaviour to psychology, and subsequently to biochemistry. It is a fact of life that all schools of economics must be buffeted and jostled by psychology, sociology, anthropology, biochemistry, genetics, physics, and mathematics, and that they must constitute their object of inquiry as justifiably separate, irrespective of the fact of life that experience is a seamless web. The immediate implication of this thesis is that the object of inquiry cannot be simply or easily disentangled from the method of inquiry, and that both cannot be dictated by some inert and independent subject matter. One plausible role for philosophy is to analyse the forces which jointly shape the theoretical object and the method of inquiry.

The second fundamental issue in the philosophy of economics is one which does not trouble the physical scientist. It has often been observed that, when addressed, people generally talk back, but atoms are silent. The economist confronts the thorny problem that he or she is imbedded inextricably in any social process under investigation; and, further, that the actors involved are free to disagree with the conclusions of the economist, challenging theories as well as interpretations of the events which are imputed to them. While Nature might be portrayed as recalcitrant, it has never revolted; but people have done so. Attempts to confront this issue often surface as statements about presence or absence of controlled experiments, or mastery of the phenomenon, or the putative success of the science in question. Philosophy also has an important function in unpacking this presupposition of the equation of scientific success with control, and showing how it shapes inquiry.

These are the fundamental issues which any coherent discipline of economic theory must address: it must carve up reality, and have some claim to have carved artfully 'at the joints'; it must have some resources to adjudicate boundary disputes with other disciplines, which requires a clear conception of its own theoretical object; it must nurture some epistemological conception of the economic actor and the economist, and presumably reconcile them one with the other; and it must build bridges to the conceptions of power and efficacy within the context of the culture in which it is to subsist. Although it is not inevitable, in the past these requirements have been satisfied to a greater or lesser degree by positing a curious symmetry between the portrait of the economic scientist and the theoretical portrait of 'rational economic man' in the particular school of economic thought. This symmetry exists on many levels, both formal and informal. It is the thesis of this chapter that once the pattern of this symmetry is understood, then the philosophical distinctions which divide and demarcate institutionalist economic theory from neoclassical economic theory become transparent; and, further, one can go quite a distance in explaining the evolution of institutionalist thought in the twentieth century.

THE DURKHEIM/MAUSS/DOUGLAS THESIS

In order to organize the various themes in the philosophy of economics, and to explain my symmetry thesis, I shall have recourse to a very important generalization about human behaviour – which was generated not in economics, but in anthropology. In 1903 the anthropologists Emile Durkheim and Marcel Mauss proposed an hypothesis which has become one of the core tenets of research programmes in the sociology of knowledge. They asserted that, in all primitive cultures, the classification of things reproduces the classifications of men (Durkheim and Mauss 1903). Although the Durkheim/Mauss thesis was only intended to apply to primitive societies, and the original empirical ethnographic evidence which they offered in its support was widely challenged and criticized, the thesis has been taken up and revised by the Edinburgh school of the sociology of science and applied to the history of western science (Bloor 1982; Barnes and Shapin 1979). Recently, the anthropologist Mary Douglas (1970, 1975, 1986) has further elaborated the hypothesis by asserting its antithesis: the social classification of men is often a mirror image of a culture's classifications of the natural world. To quote her own words:

> the logical patterning in which social relations are ordered affords a bias in the classification of nature, and that in this bias is to be found the confident intuition of self-evident truth. And here, in this intuition, is the most hidden and most inaccessible implicit assumption on which all other knowledge is grounded. It is the ultimate instrument of domination, protected from inspection by every warm emotion that commits the knower to the social system in which his knowledge is guaranteed. Only one who feels coolly towards that society can question its self-evident propositions.

> (Douglas 1975, p. 209)

For purposes of brevity, we can summarize the complete Durkheim/Mauss/Douglas (DMD) thesis in the format of the 'vortex model of the sociology of science' as shown in Figure 5.1. Societies differ tremendously in their sources of inspiration and sources of validation of their social and natural concepts, but they resemble one another quite dramatically in the way in which social and natural concepts are interlinked and the manner in

Figure 5.1   The 'vortex model' of the sociology of science: the DMD thesis

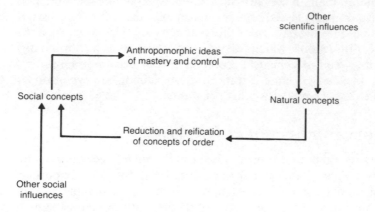

which belief in one reinforces belief in the other. Theories of the physical world are shaped by the social relations within the culture which generates them, and these are used in turn to express in reified format the essence of that culture's ideal of order. This ideal of order consequently moulds the expression of social concepts and classifications, eventually transforming the original notions of mastery and control in the social sphere. The circuit is completed by the persistent projection of anthropomorphic concepts on to 'Nature', and the intended demonstration of the efficacy and legitimacy of structures in the social sphere through its purported success in the mastery of personified nature.

While this 'vortex model' is a cornucopia of suggestions for the analysis of social life, the history of science and various controversies in epistemology, it is its effectiveness in helping to understand the preconceptions of institutional economics which concerns us here. Divergent assumptions about the relationship of social concepts to natural concepts, and the relationship of the possibility of mastery and control to the reified concept of order are the fundamental distinguishing hallmarks of institutional and neoclassical economic theory. The controversies around the turn of the century concerning the vexed issue of the unity or duality of the *Geisteswissenschaften* and the *Naturwissenschaften* were implicitly about the relative legitimacy of two views of science, and, by implication, two views of economics. Those economists were at loggerheads over two distinct versions of the DMD 'vortex', even though the various disputes were not argued out explicitly in those terms.

The discipline of economics in the western world has always been caught in the thrall of the contemporaneous western understanding of the physical world, particularly with respect to the concept of value.[1] It has been an even more recent phenomenon (say, since the early nineteenth century) that the idealized image of the method of natural science has played the predominant role in shaping the image of the economic actor in economic theory. However, at this juncture, the cultural diversity of various western societies has come into play: because there have been multiple variations on the theme of the correct scientific method, there have been equally numerous corresponding images of the 'economy' and the economic actor. Economic praxeology may recapitulate epistemology, but it can only do so within a specific cultural setting. Schools of economic thought may subsequently interpenetrate and cross-fertilize, but their initial integrity and specificity are due to their origins in a particular construct of our knowledge of the world and hence of ourselves and other actors.

Rather than discuss the interplay suggested by the DMD thesis of the reigning scientific epistemology and the ontology of the economic actor at an extremely rarified level, it will be more efficient to demonstrate the thesis through the display of two relevant examples: that of Cartesian analytic philosophy and neoclassical economic theory; and the American variant of the Continental hermeneutic tradition in philosophy and Institutionalist economics.

THE CARTESIAN TRADITION AND NEOCLASSICAL ECONOMIC THEORY

The Cartesian tradition in philosophy has made its appearance in the British and American contexts as a penchant for 'analytical philosophy', especially in the twentieth century. Although many of the modern tenets are not intended to be faithful representations of Descartes' original concerns, the 'Cartesian tradition' does serve as a shorthand for a certain sequence of canonical texts and attitudes (see Kuklick in Rorty *et al.* 1984). We shall characterize (yet hopefully not caricature) this tradition by the following seven tenets (cf. Tiles, 1984; Bernstein, 1983).

1 Analytical Cartesian philosophy is not overly concerned with the thought processes of the individual scientist, nor indeed, any group of scientists. Above all, it demands that science is mechanical and impersonal, and quarantines the context of discovery from the context of justification.
2 The process of inquiry is divided into 'deduction' and 'induction'. Philosophy analyses the former as a discrete set of logical statements, with concepts investigated only via their functions in isolated abstract statements. Philosophy is relatively helpless in analysing induction, because there is no guaranteed logic of induction.
3 'Logic' is interpreted to mean mathematical axiomatization.
4 There is an unbridgeable gulf between the philosophy of science and the history of science. The best one can do is construct a *post hoc* 'rational reconstruction' of what is, at best, a mess. Science reconstitutes itself perennially, and therefore has no real need of history.

5 The role of philosophy is to prescribe and defend the right rules of scientific method. The *summum bonum* would be an automaton to which all disputes would be submitted and hence would guarantee the validity of scientific work.
6 The separation of mind and body dictates that we know our own thought better than we can know the world. Hence all verification is the assuagement of personal doubt. This comes about by means of repeated personal contact with a stable external world, independent of any mediation by others as well as independent of the signs used to express such knowledge.
7 Knowledge, once attained, is passed along intact to other researchers. Knowledge is fully cumulative, the accretion of past individual researches.

One important corollary of the DMD thesis would be that the social theories which were prevalent in the culture dominated by the portrait of science consisting of the above seven points would project that image on to their understanding of their own social relations. If we look at the orthodox economics of Britain and America in the twentieth century, we discover that the neoclassical portrait of the 'rational economics man' conforms to the DMD outline, very nearly point for point, as follows:

1 Neoclassical economics is not concerned with the actual thought processes of the individual economic actors. The actors are subject to an ideal of rationality which is mechanical and impersonal, in the dual senses that constrained optimization imitates the 'behaviour' of the inert mechanical world in physical theory (Mirowski 1984a and 1989), and that interpersonal influences and processes of interpretation are ruled out by assumption (Mirowski 1986a). One must separate the context of socialization from the context of choice.
2 Rational choice is divided up into rational choice rules and independently given endowments. Neoclassical economics takes as its primary subject the logic of the former, and is relatively silent about the latter, because there is no logic of endowments which claims the allegiance of neo-classicists in general.
3 'Logic' is interpreted to mean mathematical axiomatization.
4 There is an unbridgeable gulf between neoclassical economics and the history of any particular economy. The market is always presumed efficient, and therefore exhibits no hysteresis (Mirowski 1987b).
5 Neoclassical economics prescribes and defends the right rules of market organization. The *summum bonum* is an automatic mechanism which co-ordinates the economy and guarantees its legitimacy.
6 The mind/body separation dictates that we know our own thought better than we know the world. Hence economic theory must be cast in the format of self-sufficient individual mental valuations brought in contact with a stable external world of commodities, independent of any mediation or dependence upon signs.

7 Capital accumulation is treated as analogous to knowledge accumulation: an incremental aggregation of discrete units. Indeed, the former should be reduced to the latter, in the guise of an inexplicable 'technological change'.

Our purpose here is not to put the DMD thesis through all its paces; nor is it our intention to discuss neoclassical theory in the detail warranted to illustrate seriously the above parallels.[2] All we wish to suggest for present purposes is that there exists a close correlation between the Cartesian epistemology and the structure of neoclassical economic theory: a familial resemblance which serves to fuse the natural world and the social world into a single coherent entity for the analytic Anglo-American mind. The social order of the economic world is reflected in the scientific order of the natural world: it hence comes as no surprise that Karl Popper has admitted that certain inspirations for his philosophy of science came from his particularly western understanding of economics (Hands 1985).

If we accept this thesis as a provisional working hypothesis, the question of interest then becomes: how to account for the existence of heterodox schools of economic theory? Most germane to our present task, how can we understand the existence of the only school of economic thought indigenous to the United States, which is in many respects incommensurable with neoclassical economic theory – that is, Institutionalist economics?

PRAGMATISM AND PEIRCE

Prompted by the DMD thesis, our answer shall be to search for its philosophical foundations elsewhere than in the Cartesian analytic tradition. The origins of this phenomenon must be traced back a century to the situation extant in philosophy and science in the America of the 'Gilded Age'. In the late nineteenth century, the predominant understanding of science in the United States was not that of the Cartesian tradition. Indeed, as Kuklick put it: 'In the late nineteenth-century American philosophical circles there were more Hegelians of various sorts than you could shake a stick at' (Kuklick 1984, p. 132). The main influences on the idea of science in the Gilded Age came not from Britain or France, but rather from the Germany of the research universities. The philosophy of science had not grown as separate and detached from social theory as it had elsewhere, and this was manifest in the three great movements in German philosophy: the dialectical idealism of Hegel, the historicist hermeneutics of Dilthey, and a revival of neo-Kantianism. These traditions took root in the US, and by a very convoluted route, sprouted an indigenous school of philosophy in America called 'Pragmatism'. It is my thesis that it was this Pragmatic conception of scientific endeavour and epistemology which later induced a novel reinterpretation of the economy and the economic actor, and that this conception was consolidated into an institutionalist school of economic theory in the first three decades of the twentieth century.

Bernstein (1966, p. 168) has written that: 'It is still a popular myth, even among philosophers, that positivism was a tough-minded variety of the more tender-minded and fuzzy pragmatism'. Judging by the *Dictionary of the History of Science*, the myth is still popular, since that source defines 'pragmatism' as: 'A variant of empiricism . . . foreshadowing both operationalism and the verifiability principle of logical positivism.' These impressions are unfortunate, because they obscure the fact that it was the project of the pragmatists to provide a systematic alternative to the Cartesian analytical tradition, as well as to the naturalist doctrines characteristic of positivism. (We shall see that this confusion has subsequently spilled over into economic controversies, to the extent that, in some quarters, institutionalist economics is misperceived as a sort of naïve empiricism.) The situation is further muddied by the fact that the founder of pragmatism, Charles Sanders Peirce left no synoptic account of his philosophical system. In this respect (as in some others as well: see Thayer 1981, p. 79), he resembles that other towering figure of twentieth-century philosophy, Ludwig Wittgenstein, in that he only bequeathed to us a disorganized sheaf of disconnected, epigrammatic and oracular accounts of his mature philosophy, which had to await publication until after his death (see Peirce 1934, 1935, 1958a and b).

Reading Peirce is no fun; and therefore, most who have a passing acquaintance with pragmatism base their knowledge on the more accessible but less reliable versions to be found in John Dewey or William James, or worse, simply upon their own understandings of the colloquial connotations of 'pragmatism'. It is frankly impossible to do justice to Peirce's writings in the space allotted in this essay; there is no reasonable substitute for reading his *Collected Papers* and the best of the commentaries upon them (such as Apel 1981). Both because Peirce was the only pragmatist philosopher trained in mathematics and the physical sciences, and because it is our intention to connect Peirce (through the DMD thesis) to the institutionalist conception of the economic actor, this discussion focuses predominantly on Peirce's philosophy of science.[3]

Because the Peircian corpus is so fragmented, it has been argued that certain of his texts – especially those concerned with induction – might be read as anticipatory of later neopositivist writings and some aspects of Popper (Rescher 1978, p. 52; Radnitzky 1973, pp. xxv–xxvii). Contrary to these suggestions, a survey of his entire work reveals that he was openly hostile to the Cartesian analytical tradition, and may be better understood as a sophisticated advocate of a hermeneutics of science and a semiotics of scientific practice. In highlighting Peirce's concern with the social aspects of science, we follow the lead of numerous modern commentators (Commons 1934, p. 102; Dyer 1986; Apel 1981; Bernstein 1983; Rorty 1979) who have seen in Peirce a third alternative to the conventional rationalist/empiricist dichotomies.

The mainstream tradition of the philosophy of science in the twentieth century has found itself driven from pillar to post, searching for the appropriate entity in which to ground the certainty of scientific knowledge. Early analytic philosophy began by touting the single linguistic term as the primary epistemic unit, but was fairly rapidly forced to retreat to the entire sentence, or proposition, as the lowest common denominator of scientific intelligibility. Complaints about the incoherence of an independent object language and the indeterminate consequences of scientific tests forced a further retreat to an entire conceptual scheme as the appropriate epistemic unit, but then careful historical critiques combined with scepticism about the notion of a self-contained theory have prompted some philosophers to insist that only a research tradition in all its complex historical development can do justice to the various forms of knowledge claims of a working scientist. One amazing aspect of this progressive erosion of logical atomism in the philosophy of science is that Peirce essentially anticipated its form and consequences a century ago. His definition of 'science' seems particularly relevant after the breakdown of logical atomism:

> What is Science? We cannot define the word with the precision and concision with which we define *Circle*, or *Equation*, any more than we can so define *Money, Government, Stone, Life*. The idea, like these, and more than some of them, is too vastly complex and diversified. It embodies the epitome of man's intellectual development . . . a particular branch of science, such as Physical Chemistry or Mediterranean Archeology, is no mere word, manufactured by the arbitrary definition of some academic pedant, but a real object, being the very concrete life of a social group constituted by real facts of inter-relation.
>
> (Peirce 1958a, pp. 37–9)

Peirce's insistence that 'the very origin of the conception of reality shows that this conception essentially involves the notion of a *community*' (Peirce 1934, p. 186) could be read as being founded on the thesis that scientific research is irreducibly hermeneutic, and therefore recourse to an independent law-abiding world or to some innate preconception of truth is impotent to account for the *process* of scientific inquiry. Because the word 'hermeneutics' is bandied about in a careless manner these days by literary critics, it might prove prudent to provide a brief working definition for the present audience.

Hermeneutics is the theory of the process of interpretation, be it of a text, a doctrine or a phenomenon, by a self-identified community of inquiry. Indeed, all coherent philosophies must possess some such theory of interpretation, be it explicit or implicit; however, this theory concentrates on the role of shared tradition as the locus of continuity and quality control in the interpretative process: it therefore follows that the discipline of *history* is an indispensable accessory of hermeneutics.

Hermeneutics is a response to the gridlock of communication that often results when strongly disparate perspectives confront one another. The doctrine of hermeneutics arose from the experience of trying to 'get into the other person's head', leading to a realization that comprehending an alien perspective often meant trying to grasp the whole of the other's experience. As Bernstein (1983) puts it, this 'hermeneutical circle' allows us to steer a course between objectivism and relativism. Rickman states:

> Put negatively this principle means that there are no absolute starting points, no self-evident, self-contained certainties on which we can build, because we always find ourselves in the middle of complex situations which we try to disentangle by making, then revising, provisional assumptions. This circularity – or perhaps one might call it a spiral approximation towards greater accuracy and knowledge – pervades our whole intellectual life.
>
> (Rickman 1976, p. 11)

Hermeneutical philosophies freely admit that rival interpretative communities may harbour incommensurable readings of some text or phenomenon; but it also recognizes that there will be pressure to attempt comparisons as long as the communities are rivals, and that posterity may decide that traditions were eventually rendered commensurable. Hermeneutics reinstates the importance of diversity in the process of understanding, to the extent of advocating the examination of alien or pariah traditions in the course of interpretation. Hermeneutics is also concerned to acknowledge the anthropomorphic element in human knowledge, viewing it as a fruitful and necessary aspect rather than an embarrassing and regrettable anachronism (Peirce 1934, p. 35fn.). Finally, hermeneutics is generally hostile to the Cartesian tradition of analytic philosophy, especially the presumption of the mind/body dichotomy and the programme of mechanical reduction (Peirce 1935, pp. 15–16). Peirce was himself particularly scathing about the plausibility of the Cartesian programme of radical self-doubt, which he termed a sham, merely formal, and incapable of altering any seriously held belief (Scheffler 1974, p. 20; Apel 1981, pp. 62–3).

It is important to understand that what one might call Peirce's brand of hermeneutics underwent revision and transformation over the course of his life, in part as a reaction to versions promulgated by William James and John Dewey. His disaffection with their readings and embellishments provoked him in 1905 to insist that he was not at all one of these 'pragmatists', but rather a 'pragmaticist', a label so contrivedly ugly that no one would be tempted to 'kidnap' it (Apel 1981, p. 82). Some of the fault for such a repudiation can be laid at Peirce's own door, if only because his early statements, and in particular his 'pragmatic maxim', were phrased in such a way as to foster the impression of a transparent and banal common-sense philosophy of science. The pragmatic maxim of 1878 was stated as: 'Consider what effects, that might conceivably have practical bearings, we conceive the object of our conception to have. Then, our conception of these effects is the whole of our conception of the object' (Peirce 1934, p. 1).

William James read the pragmatic maxim as equating those 'practical implications' with the psychological responses of the user of the concept, and therefore misrepresented pragmatism as a species of individual psychological behaviouralism, thus entirely neutralizing the hermeneutic aspects of the community of inquiry. John Dewey read the maxim as dictating that there was no such thing as an end or goal of inquiry, a position that Peirce explicitly repudiated (Apel 1981, p. 88). Others, less sophisticated, read the maxim as a celebration of a particularly American stereotype of a hard-nosed, no-nonsense man of action, heedless of hesitation or tergiversation over fine points of reasoning. It must be admitted that some of Peirce's early writings seemed to encourage a crude know-nothingism: 'pragmatism is generally practiced by successful men' (Peirce 1934, p. 21), or 'each of us is an insurance company' (Peirce 1934, p. 220). However, in the face of others' attempts to portray pragmatism as a kind of crypto-capitalism in the sphere of science, Peirce went out of his way to insist that, 'the meaning of [pragmatism] does not lie in individual reactions at all'.

Peirce divided the process of scientific inquiry into the three categories of deduction, induction, and what he termed 'abduction'. He had very little of any substance to say about deduction, although he did point out that no actual novelty, and therefore no progress, could be attained by deduction *mutatis mutandis* (Peirce 1958a, p. 47). Induction plays a much more substantial role in his system, and here Peirce brought into play both his extensive experience as an experimentalist and an interest in probability theory, in his discussions of empirical research. One important stabilizing influence on Peirce's community of inquiry was his postulate that *quantitative* induction was automatically self-correcting, albeit in the longest of long runs (Peirce 1935, p. 80; Rescher 1978).[4] However, nothing in these writings gave any aid or comfort to naïve empiricism. He commented upon the limited role that experiment occupied in the rise of modern mechanics (Peirce 1935, p. 13). He also observed that an hypothesis should not be abandoned immediately when contravened by empirical results, and that all good theories are always surrounded by a field of contradictory facts (Peirce 1958a, pp. 54 and 60). In these respects he appears to share contemporary concerns with the problem of the underdetermination of theory acceptance by the 'facts', and the Duhem/Quine thesis, which states that no hypothesis is definitively falsified, because it can always be immunized to adverse tests by some adjustment in the ever-present auxiliary hypotheses which accompany it (Harding 1976).

Most significantly, Peirce stated that induction and deduction, either jointly or severally, could not account for the progress of scientific inquiry. That effectively was reserved for the third mode – abduction:

Abduction is the process of forming an explanatory hypothesis. It is the only logical operation which introduces any new idea; for induction does nothing but determine a value, and deduction merely evolves the necessary consequences of a pure hypothesis.

(Peirce 1934, p. 106)

Of the three modalities of method, it is abduction which explicitly assumes a hermeneutic demeanour, because it is the method responsible for creativity, interpretation, and innovation which is an historical process made manifest in language and social behaviour, subject to the self-discipline of a normative logic. This is why 'the question of pragmatism . . . is nothing else than the question of the logic of abduction' (Peirce 1934, p. 121).

In order to discuss abduction Peirce often employed the language of 'instincts', or evolutionary talents, and these metaphors were often carried over into the works of Dewey, Veblen, and others influenced by pragmatism. Peirce's equation of abduction with instinct, and meaning with habit (Apel 1981, p. 71) probably strikes the modern reader as odd; but Peirce's unrelenting hostility to mechanical reductionism should signal that these passages are not to be read as anticipations of sociobiology. Instead, they seem to posit the existence of a naïve common sense metaphysics which provided physics with its early fundamental hypotheses about natural law. Given Peirce's further thesis that natural laws themselves evolve (Peirce 1935, p. 84), it follows that he would likewise expect the sources of inspiration for scientific hypotheses to evolve also. Peirce expressly asserted that *physical* laws evolve over time because laws of homogeneity could only be discerned against the backdrop of stochastic phenomena, from which they would be emergent. One can only marvel at his prescience in this respect, since only well after his lines were written did physicists begin to plumb their significance in quantum mechanics, cosmology, and elsewhere.[5]

No summary of Peirce's philosophy could be complete without some acknowledgement of his role as the founder of semiotics, the theory of the interpretations of signs and their interrelations. Peirce saw the sign relation as fundamentally triadic, a relation between the denotation of a word, the designated object, and the interpreter. The importance of this triad for Peirce lay in his conviction that previous philosophers had attempted to understand language by concentrating attention on only one or two aspects in isolation, a practice which he claimed served to quarantine the hermeneutic aspects of human inquiry. An important corollary of the triad was that it is impossible to discern the rules of sign-mediated behaviour by simple external observation; in other words, there is no such thing as the passive observation of rule structures (Mirowski 1986a). Not only did this anticipate the mature Wittgenstein's critique of rules and language games, but it also has profound relevance for the positivist attempt to explain rule structures by mechanistic models.

Finally, for a philosopher so concerned to explore the links between social processes and scientific inquiry, it should come as no surprise to discover that he also had a reasonable familiarity with the social theories of his day. It has not often been noted, however, that Peirce was hostile to orthodox economic doctrines, and downright livid when it came to hedonism and utilitarian doctrines (Peirce 1958a, p. 43; 1934, p. 59–60). He wrote:

> Bentham may be a shallow logician; but such truths as he saw, he saw most nobly. As for the vulgar utilitarian, his fault does not lie in pressing too much the question of what should be the good of this or that. On the contrary, his fault is that he never presses the question half far enough, or rather he never really raises the question at all. He simply rests in his present desires as if desire were beyond all dialectic.
>
> (Peirce 1934, p. 98)

This single passage captures much of the gist of Dewey's subsequent and much more verbose and pedantic disquisition upon the role of values in the process of inquiry.

In a few essays, Peirce trained his sights on American political economy, accusing it of 'an exaggeration of the beneficial effects of greed' (Peirce 1935, p. 193), and complaining of a tendency to want their 'mammon flavored with a soupçon of God' (Peirce 1935, p. 194). These indictments were directed not only at the more vulgar apologists of political economy, but also at some of its more illustrious writers. (Peirce's sophistication in this respect might be illustrated by his correspondence with Simon Newcomb, which includes, among other interesting titbits, an early discussion of the role of mathematics in the theory of supply and demand (Eisele 1957, p. 414).) The presuppositions of utilitarianism offended his hermeneutic view of science in a number of ways: it denied the role of tradition in human understanding; it blithely ignored the incommensurability of valuations; it gave short shrift to the dependence of behaviour on community interaction and semantic processes; it was incompatible with the idea of evolutionary change, and with abduction; and it smacked of Cartesian mechanical reduction. Although Peirce was not concerned to sketch out an alternative political economy, in retrospect it would seem obvious that anyone deeply influenced by his thought would certainly be sceptical of the encroaching tradition of neoclassical economics.

The modernity of Peirce's package of concerns – or, as he put it, his 'architectonic' – is striking. With some generosity of exegesis, one could credit him with the anticipation of the DMD thesis in certain respects, because he saw that one of the most fruitful sources of abduction in science was the transfer of metaphor from one sphere of inquiry to another.[6] Nevertheless, Peirce was definitely out of synchronicity with the 'ragtime era' of American culture. It is tragic that the theorist of the infinite community of science was himself expelled from that community in 1884, never to hold another academic position. He repaired to Milford, Pennsylvania, in 1887 –

to reside in almost total isolation, scribbling away at manuscripts that remained unread and unpublished during his lifetime. Peirce did not exert himself to make his thought readily accessible. As Thayer has written:

> In attempting to get at Peirce's philosophic thought in these volumes [i.e., Peirce's *Collected Papers*] of ambitious but incomplete writings, one is often in a position not unlike Peirce's creditors who came to the Milford house to collect on their bills.
>
> (Thayer 1981, p. 71)

In part because of this exile, it was generally either through William James or John Dewey that many learned about Pragmatism.

JOHN DEWEY

Dewey was the conduit through which many of the precepts of pragmatism migrated over to American social theory in the early twentieth century. From a certain point of view this was unfortunate, because the quality of his thought was not often up to the standard of Peirce; nevertheless, he managed to achieve much greater influence and renown than Peirce. Peirce himself once rebuked Dewey for a lack of logical subtlety, despite the fact that Dewey (along with Veblen) was one of the few illustrious students during his stint at Johns Hopkins University (Apel 1981, p. 5).

Richard Hofstadter was basically on the mark when he wrote of Dewey: 'His style is suggestive of the commanding of distant armies: one concludes that something portentous is going on at a remote and inaccessible distance, but one cannot determine just what it is' (in Cahn 1977, p. 9). Even an enthusiastic supporter such as Richard Bernstein was forced to admit: 'imagination and insight must be explicated and modified in detailed analyses, and this is what Dewey failed to do for us. Insofar as philosophy requires the funding of fertile imagination with systematic elaboration, his philosophy fails' (Bernstein 1966, pp. 171–2).

Dewey insisted that, for philosophy:

> the central problem is the relation that exists between the beliefs about the nature of things *due to natural science* to beliefs about values – using that word to designate whatever is taken to have rightful authority in the direction of conduct.
>
> (quoted in Thayer 1981, p. 166)

One can observe a familial resemblance to the concerns of Peirce here, but already, in contrast to Peirce's wide-ranging attempt to synthesize specific aspects of scientific practice to the social nature of inquiry, we discover exceptionally vague references to a monolithic 'science' and a premature reduction of the social sphere to an ill-defined phenomenon of 'values'. For Dewey, as for Peirce, inquiry is pre-eminently a *process* whereby doubtful or unsettled situations become settled. Yet Dewey's definition of inquiry is surprisingly impersonal and pedantic in the Germanic style: it is defined as 'the controlled or directed transformation of an indeterminate situation into one that is so determinate in its constituent distinctions and relations as to convert the elements of the original situation into a unified whole' (Dewey 1938, pp. 104–5). In this marriage of Hegel and Peirce, Thought comes perilously close to Thinking Itself, but is wrenched back from the Idealist precipice with the help of Peirce's pragmatic maxim of 1878. Dewey called this interpretation of reasoning 'Instrumentalism', and defined it as follows:

> Instrumentalism is an attempt to constitute a precise logical theory of concepts, of judgements and inferences in their various forms, by considering primarily how thought functions in the experimental determinations of future consequences. . . . It attempts to establish universally recognized distinctions and rules of logic by deriving them from the reconstructive or meditative function ascribed to reason.
>
> (quoted in Thayer 1981, p. 169)

Unfortunately, Dewey spent much more time talking about this attempt to establish universally recognized distinctions, etc. than actually suggesting a few concrete rules and exposing them to criticism, but this is precisely the remote and inaccessible distance which Hofstadter pointed to. In effect, Dewey extended some of the hermeneutic themes found in Peirce to explicit application in social theory, especially generalizing the concept of habit into the broader concept of social custom. Many have observed that Dewey equated pragmatism with social psychology (Apel 1981, p. 87; Thayer 1981, pp. 183–90), and indeed, he seemed to approach philosophy as if it were a branch of a more encompassing instrumentalist social science. Perhaps he felt that 'values' were discrete empirical entities, the description of which could be left to the social scientist. He often wrote in that way. For example:

> Valuations are empirically observable patterns of behavior and may be studied as such. The propositions that result are *about* valuations but are not themselves value-propositions in any sense marking them off from other matter-of-fact propositions.
>
> (Dewey 1939b, p. 51)

In retrospect, Dewey's numerous appeals to the scientific method appear awkward and strained. This reification of an abstract 'Science' would have serious consequences for the later evolution of pragmatism. In place of actual training in any specific science or in the history of one of the sciences, Dewey's favoured sources of inspiration were Hegel and Greek philosophy. The path of his intellectual evolution can be traced from the psychologistic idealism of his early career to a vague and politicized pragmatism towards the end of his life.

Dewey's crusade was to argue against the idea of truth as accuracy of representation, which took the form in his later life of an insistence that reality could not exist prior to and independent of the process of inquiry (Dewey 1939a, p. 308). The idea of 'warranted assertability' was as close as he ever got to Peirce's richer notion of the complex interaction of the interpretative commuity and the object of inquiry; in Dewey, this assumed the rather more prosaic cast of a comparison of scientific inquiry with a jury trial (Dewey 1939a, pp. 898–900). Dewey followed Peirce in his scepticism concerning the Cartesian analytic tradition, but as was his inclination, he tended to reinterpret philosophical problems as amenable to reduction to problems in psychology: 'the older dualism of body and soul finds a distinct echo in the current dualism of stimulus and response' (Dewey 1931, p. 233). Dewey also imitated Peirce in viewing human inquiry as an evolutionary process, but diluted this legacy by transmuting the sweeping portrayal of the evolution of natural law itself into the diminished banality that 'tool and material are adapted to each other in the process of reaching a valid conclusion' (Dewey 1939a, p. 929).

Whatever one's opinion about Dewey's conception of science, it is demonstrably true that his work in social theory found a sympathetic audience in an America that had previously associated evolutionary theory either with atheism or with social Darwinism. Although it had remained a familiar idea in the Continental tradition of philosophy, it was a jolt to find an American arguing that:

> History is the record of the development of freedom through the development of institutions . . . Here we have instead an anticipatory criticism and challenge of the classical liberal notion of freedom, a deliberate reflective and reactionary one. Freedom is a growth, an attainment, not an original possession, and it is attained by the idealization of institutions and law.
>
> (Dewey 1931, p. 285)

As a consequence, Dewey also maintained Peirce's hostility to utilitarianism, although his objections appeared to spring primarily from an aversion to the idea of given and immutable tastes:

> Not even the most devoted adherents of the notion that enjoyment and value are equivalent facts would venture to assent that because we once liked a thing we should go on liking it. . . . Desire and purpose, and hence action are left without guidance, although the question of the regulation of their formation is the supreme problem of practical life. Values (to sum up) may be connected inherently with liking, and not yet with *every* liking but only with those that judgment has approved.
>
> (Dewey 1939a, p. 786)

As a champion of the importance of the process of change over static notions of optimality, Dewey became associated with groups opposed to economic *laissez-faire* notions; he was a vocal advocate of the position that classical Liberalism had avoided all the hard questions of co-ordination and the definition of order by surreptitiously postulating that each citizen came naturally equipped with an innate complement of rights, desires and powers that were sufficient to do the job (Dewey 1931, p. 281). It is relevant to later developments in economics that he saw this flawed predisposition as part and parcel of the larger western predisposition to yearn for natural laws (Dewey 1939a, p. 745), which qualifies as a limited appreciation of the DMD thesis. As he put it 'the existing limitations of "social science" are due mainly to unreasoning devotion to the physical sciences as a model, and to a misconception of physical science at that' (Dewey 1939a, p. 949). Unfortunately, here Dewey became tangled in his own lack of system, for not only was he incapable of describing the actual historical instances of practices within the physical sciences, but he was also bereft of any coherent description of the promulgation of social order. This led him in later life to compound these weaknesses by proposing the *non sequitur* that the natural sciences would themselves provide the progressive ideals of social order (Dewey 1939a, p. 791). We suggest that Dewey's appreciation of the DMD thesis must have been limited, because this latter prescription clashes with his earlier warnings about the 'unreasoning devotion to the physical sciences as a model'. Democracy was said to be a pronounced improvement over previous modes of political organization because it deployed the same techniques as science to mediate freedom and authority (Dewey 1939a, pp. 358–60). All social problems would be thus purportedly solved (or dissolved?) by the scientific method, because democracy was the analogue of the scientific method in the political arena. Dewey may simply have meant that 'democracy' was another name for the trial-and-error process which he thought characterized all inquiry, but if so, it would portend a rather sloppy use of political terminology, and moreover, it was only an innocuous step to equate instrumentalism with social engineering, a fact noted by many soon afterwards. For example, White says:

Pragmatism, instrumentalism, institutionalism, economic determinism and legal realism exhibit striking philosophical kinships. They are all suspicious of approaches which are excessively formal; they all protest their anxiety to come to grips with reality . . . Veblen, interested in unmasking the effects of absentee ownership upon industry, and the role of the leisure class in American life, was brought face to face with the pattern of exploitation. Dewey met it when he examined the touchy relations of science, morality, and society and urged the scrapping of outworn theological and metaphysical creeds.

(White 1949, pp. 6–7)

THE PRAGAMATIC TRADITION AND INSTITUTIONALIST ECONOMIC THEORY

We now return to the DMD thesis in order to ask whether the alternative philosophical programme of pragmatism did provide an alternative template for rational economic man. In what follows, the essence of Peirce will rather dominate the musk of Dewey, for reasons already broached above: it is specifically philosophies of *science* which set the tone for the ensuing portraits of man. As we did for the Cartesian tradition, we can generate a brief bill of particulars which characterize the pragmatic philosophy of science:

1 Science is primarily a process of inquiry by a self-identified community, and not a mechanical legitimation procedure of some pre-existent goal or end-state. Science has conformed to no set of ahistorical decision rules, and for this reason history and science are inseparable. Most of this would come under the rubric of Dewey's 'instrumentalism'.
2 Possible methods of inquiry consist of deduction, induction, and abduction. No one method is self-sufficient without the other two as complements. Abduction is the explicit source of novelty, whereas induction and deduction provide the checks and balances.
3 There is no single logic, but rather a logic of abduction, a logic of deduction, and a logic of induction.
4 Because there are no foolproof impersonal rules of scientific method, decisions concerning the validity of scientific statements reside within the community of inquiry. The community of inquiry is the basic epistemological unit.
5 Without a strict mind/body duality, science has an irreducible anthropomorphic character. This is not inherently a dangerous phenomenon. Natural laws themselves evolved, as do the members of the community of inquiry. Social and natural concepts interpenetrate; therefore hermeneutic techniques are a necessary component of scientific inquiry, on the same epistemic level as mathematical techniques.
6 The study of semiotics and the interrelation of signs constitutes an integral part of the philosophy of science.
7 Because pragmatism must ultimately depend upon the community of inquiry, the Scylla and Charybdis it most frequently must negotiate between are a defence of the *status quo* and an advocacy of a technocratic utopia.

Just as with our previous experience with the connection between the Cartesian tradition and neoclassical economic theory, here too the conception of the rational economic actor in Institutionalist economics can be 'read' from the pragmatic programme. This reading is not nearly so easy as in the neoclassical case, however. This is because the neoclassicists have, by and large, practised what they preached: their research praxis depends upon a close imitation of their colleagues, the natural scientists, many of whom hew to the Cartesian ideas as self-evident. Adherents to the Institutionalist school, on the other hand, have confronted the quandary that 'Pragmatism' has not generally been a popular epistemology amongst the physicists, and therefore they possess no obvious role models. In practice, the research praxis of Institutional economics in the twentieth century displays little of the homogeneity and internal coherence across researchers of neoclassical economics, and therefore most of our characterization of Institutionalism will be drawn from programmatic statements. In our drawing of parallels, we shall concentrate upon the first generation of institutionalist economists, roughly from Thorstein Veblen to John R. Commons. Proceeding point by point:

1 The economy is primarily a process of learning, negotiation, and co-ordination, and not a ratification of some pre-existent goals or end-state. Economic rationality is socially and culturally determined, and therefore history, anthropology, and economics are different perspectives upon the same inquiry. The economy itself may be conceptualized as the prosecution of inquiry by material means, with the community both constructing and discovering its values.

2 Economic actors are defined by their habits, customs, and 'instincts', the physical or material relations which impinge upon them, and the expedients developed in order to adapt one to the other (Veblen 1934, p. 189). This portrayal seeks to find a middle way between 'nature' and 'nurture'. As Veblen put it: ' "instinct" being not a neurological or physiological concept, is not statable in neurological or physiological terms. The instinct of workmanship no more than any other instinctive proclivity is an isolable, discrete neural function' (Veblen 1914, p. 28fn.).

3 There is no unique logic of choice.

> Passion and enjoyment of goods passes insensibly and inevitably into appraisal. . . . Enjoyment ceases to be a datum and becomes a problem. As a problem, it implies intelligent inquiry into the conditions and consequences of the value-object; that is, criticism.
>
> (Dewey 1939, pp. 260–1)

4 Because there exist no innate rules of rational economic behaviour, the only gauge of the validity of such behaviour resides in the particular economic community. Laws are made by people, not nature. The appropriate epistemological unit is the institution. Institutions are trans-personal rules which endow individual economic actors with the ability to cope with interpretation of action and with change, or, as Commons put it: 'collective action controlling, liberating and expanding individual action' (Commons 1934, p. 70).

5 Acceptance of the thesis that science embodies anthropomorphic concepts prompts the social theorist to incorporate hermeneutics or a sociology-of-knowledge approach when comparing incommensurable interpretations

of the behaviour of economic actors. Diversity of interpretations are as important for the viability of social structures as are simpler economic indices – such as profit or growth.

6 Because rule structures cannot be comprehended by external detached observation, economists must self-consciously engage in participant obervation. Economics is based upon a theory of the semiotics of trade, production and consumption – which serves to explain how actors interpret the significance of transactions. (Examples are Veblen's 'conspicuous consumption' and Commons' typology of transactions.)

7 Institutional economics has displayed a certain tergiversation between a defence of the *status quo* and an advocacy of a technocratic regime which reifies science as a unique principle of rationality.

These seven points do not capture the whole of Institutionalist theory, but they do give some indication of the divergence of the conception of economic rationality from that characteristic of neoclassical theory. As previously noted, the first generation of institutionalists generally derived their pragmatism from William James, John Dewey, and other sources more accessible than Peirce. This path of influence made a mark on their writings; among other more subtle effects, it induced an image of science which was excessively vague. This weakness, especially in Veblen and Ayres, resulted in a vulnerability to neoclassical complaints that their appeals to science were less legitimate than those of the neoclassicists. Somewhat later, John Commons made more explicit reference to Peirce's philosophy of science, and consequently built upon a more robust philosophical foundation. Nevertheless, Commons' book *Institutional Economics* signals the end of the first phase of the development of institutionalist economic theory. This watershed was not so much due to the merits or demerits of Commons' work as it was to the rapid decline of the pragmatist philosophy of science in the US and its supersession by a Cartesian logical positivism.[7]

THORSTEIN VEBLEN

It has been observed that Veblen owed a number of debts to the Pragmatist tradition (Dyer 1986). What has not been noticed is that Veblen's conception of science and economic rationality owes more to Dewey and James than Peirce, with its stress that science is a process which has no goal or end; and that much of his initial ideas grew out of a struggle with Kantian antinomies. In his famous essay *The Place of Science in Modern Civilization* Veblen wrote:

> modern science is becoming substantially a theory of the process of cumulative change, which is taken as a sequence of cumulative change, realized to be self-continuing or self-propagating and to have no final term. . . . Modern science is ceasing to occupy itself with natural laws – the codified rules of the game of causation – and is concerning itself wholly with what

has taken place and what is taking place. . . . A scientific point of view is a consensus of habits of thought current in the community.

(Veblen 1969, pp. 37–8)

The influence of Dewey and Darwin here is fairly self-evident, but the key to understanding Veblen's use of the term 'natural law' derives from his first paper on Kant's *Critique of Judgement* (Veblen 1934, pp. 175–93). Veblen was absorbed by Kant's problem of the conflict of freedom and determinism, and thought that he had struck upon a new solution to the problem, making use of the notions of 'adaptation' and evolution. Veblen (1934) noted that: 'The principle of adaptation, in its logical use, is accordingly the principle of inductive reasoning.' (Curiously enough for a student of Peirce, Veblen chose the term 'adaptation' rather than Peirce's 'abduction'.) As Veblen became acquainted with economic theory, it dawned on him that neoclassical theory was beset with the very same Kantian conundrum – namely, it purported to be a mechanistically deterministic theory predicated upon teleological principles. In his famous article on the 'Limitations of marginal utility' he declared:

[neoclassical] theory is confined to the ground of sufficient reason instead of proceeding on the ground of efficient cause. The contrary is true of modern science, generally (except mathematics). . . . The two methods of inference – from sufficient reason and from efficient cause – are out of touch with one another and there is no transition from one to the other. . . . The relation of sufficient reason runs only from the (apprehended) future into the present, and it is solely of an intellectual, subjective, personal, teleological character and force; while the relation of cause and effect runs only in the contrary direction, and it is solely of an objective, impersonal, materialistic character and force. The modern scheme of knowledge, on the whole, rests, for its definitive ground, on the relation of cause and effect; the relation of sufficient reason being admitted only provisionally.

(Veblen 1969, pp. 237–8)

One might have expected a student of Peirce to see a third, transcendent, option: sufficient reason and efficient cause could have been united by recourse to an evolutionary epistemology and ontology, where both laws and our understanding of them jointly were altered by the activity of inquiry. In the sphere of the economy, institutions, defined as habits of thought and action, could serve as the connecting link between efficient cause and sufficient reason (McFarland 1986, p. 621). Yet this was not the road taken by Veblen's subsequent intellectual career. Instead, he tended towards an increasingly pessimistic Manichaeanism – with 'sufficient reason' as the darkness, and 'efficient cause' (now conflated with Peirce's pragmatic maxim) as the light. Since there was no necessary connection between the pragmatic maxim and 'objective, impersonal, materialistic' law, he was increasingly driven to have recourse to a very idiosyncratic version of a theory of 'instincts', especially 'the instinct of workmanship' – a non-physiological entity whose 'functional content is serviceability for the ends of life, whatever these ends may be' (Veblen 1914, p. 31). The pragmatic maxim, which started out as a solution to a difficult problem in metaphysics, ended up as a reified 'instinctive' entity.

Early in his career, Veblen's antinomies resonated with the pragmatist philosophy and produced some of his most profound work. For instance, *The Theory of the Leisure Class* may be read as a skilful deployal of the pragmatic maxim, showing that the consequences of an action are an important part of its interpretation, wryly pointing out that 'serviceability' might actually be consistent with waste. 'The Economic Theory of Woman's Dress' (1934, pp. 65–77) is a *tour de force* of Peircian semiotics. By *The Theory of Business Enterprise* another antinomy was posited, pitting 'the machine process' against pecuniary enterprise. This antinomy also resulted in fruitful economic theory (Mirowski 1985), but the tendency to conflate 'science', efficient causal reasoning, and the working or engineering class made its first appearance. Progressively, Veblen came to see the conflicts of science vs. religion, efficiency vs. waste, capitalist vs. worker, and knowledge vs. ignorance as all prototypes of one large dichotomy (Veblen 1914). Everything seemed to conspire to drag down the march of scientific progress as Veblen got older, and this Manichaeanism blunted his earlier sensitivity to the subtle interplay of science and culture – what we have dubbed Peircian hermeneutics – so that by the time he reached *Absentee Ownership*, he could write:

> The technology of physics and chemistry is not derived from established law and custom, and it goes on its way with as nearly a complete disregard of the spiritual truths of law and custom as the circumstances will permit. The reality with which technicians are occupied is of another order of actuality, lying altogether within the three dimensions of the material universe, and running altogether on the logic of material fact.
>
> (Veblen 1923, p. 263)

Perhaps Veblen believed that he could break out of the 'logical circle' (see Veblen 1969, p. 32) by resort to this lofty and other-worldly conception of science, and then use it to claim that he was merely applying 'matter-of-fact' attitudes to the economic sphere. Instead of Peirce's community of inquirers, scientists became for Veblen almost automatons, closer to Dewey's Thought Thinking Itself. In striking similarity to Marx, Veblen also wished to argue that there was a certain inevitability to the whole process: the matter-of-fact efficiency characteristic of the technician would necessarily clash with the anachronistic appeal to inefficiency propped up by the legitimation of natural law by 'captains of industry'; and Veblen intimated that the technicians would defeat the business interests in the long haul (Layton 1962).

Although Veblen's writings are a fertile source of insights into economic theory, the Achilles heel of his later system was his naïve conception of science and the exalted place of the engineer. This epistemological weakness led to two further flaws. First, Veblen did not understand that the neoclassical theory which he so adamantly opposed had a more powerful claim to his brand of scientific legitimacy than he realized, because it later turned out that those self-same engineers would be attracted to the neoclassical brand of social physics. Second, certain particular evolutionary or Peircian aspects of Veblen's thought stood in direct conflict with his later image of science.

The first flaw can go quite some distance in explaining the neglect of Veblen's profound critiques of neoclassical theory, particularly the theory of capital and the theory of production. Veblen clearly believed that natural-law explanations were on the wane in physics, and that economics would eventually follow suit. Obviously, things have not turned out as anticipated. Veblen's neglect of the hermeneutical aspects of science prevented him from understanding how deeply rooted natural-law explanations are in the western cultural matrix, and how significant they were in the nineteenth-century science which he admired: in mechanics; in chemistry; and in energetics. In other words, Veblen had an inadequate comprehension of the DMD thesis.[8] Because of this, he could not comprehend the primal attraction of neoclassical theory, or the extent to which it was a model appropriated lock, stock and barrel from nineteenth-century physics (Mirowski 1984a and 1989). Veblen's assertions that he was a partisan of modern scientific methods appeared weak and unavailing in comparison with the shiny surfaces of neoclassical economic theory. The engineers, with whom Veblen was so enamoured, flooded into economics after his death, and opted to work for the theoretical tradition which they recognized as closest to their previous training (i.e., neoclassicism).

The second flaw in Veblen's epistemology was that he did not realize that some of the more intriguing aspects of his economic theory were in open conflict with his conception of science. In his early essay on Kant, he claimed that 'the play of the faculties of the intellect is free, or but little hampered by the empirical elements in its knowledge' (Veblen 1934, p. 181), but did not maintain this insight in his later work using anthropological sources. He was also very scathing when it came to others' adherence to a naïve sense-data empiricism, as in his critique of the German historical school (Veblen 1969, p. 58), but oblivious to instances of it in some of his descriptions of science.

In his profound series of essays on the preconceptions of economic science, he observed:

> since a strict uniformity is nowhere to be observed in the phenomena with which the investigator is occupied, it has to be found by a laborious interpretation of the phenomena and a diligent abstraction and allowance for

disturbing circumstances, whatever may be the meaning of a disturbing circumstance where causal continuity is denied. In this work of interpretation and expurgation the investigator proceeds on a conviction of the orderliness of natural sequence . . . The endeavor to avoid all metaphysical premises fails here as elsewhere.

(Veblen 1969, p. 162)

This heightened awareness of the presumption of natural sequence was put to good use in Veblen's critique of the 'obvious' neoclassical proposition that the value of outputs must necessarily be equal to the value of inputs, for example.

There are other Peircian themes in Veblen which languish in an under-developed state because of his epistemological position on science. His earliest work on the theory of the leisure class could be read as a prolegomena to a semiotics of economic transactions (Mirowski 1990). The phenomenon of conspicuous consumption indicates that desires and wants can not simply be read from economic behaviour (as has often been claimed under the rubric of 'revealed preference'), but that the interpretative and intentional problems of the actors must also enter into the picture, under-mining any unique reference for the concept of self-interest. In essays such as 'The economic theory of woman's dress', he shows the hermeneutic practice of approaching familiar behaviour as if one were producing an ethnographical report of the behaviour of an alien tribe. His conception of capital as an evolving linchpin of our economic system has interesting parallels with Peirce's idea that natural laws themselves evolve, and thus our interpretations are forced to evolve as well.

These possibilities did not receive the attention they may have deserved; and instead, Veblen became associated in the public mind with the politics of the 'technocratic movement' and a 'soviet of engineers', as the extrapolation of his faith in a self-assured materialist science (Layton 1962).

JOHN R. COMMONS

The Peircian legacy in the work of Commons was more self-conscious and more direct (Ramstaad 1986). In his *magnum opus*, *Institutional Economics* (Commons 1934), he surveyed the philosophical traditions which he saw as nurturing the primary schools of economic thought, and argued that it was time for recent advances in philosophy to prompt a new economic theory.

In the stage of Pragmatism, a return is made to the world of uncertain change, without fore-ordination or metaphysics, whether benevolent or non-benevolent, where we ourselves and the world around us are continually in a changing conflict of interests. . . . Not till we reach John Dewey do we find Peirce expanded to ethics, and not until we reach institutionalist economics do we find it expanded to transactions, going concerns, and Reasonable Value.

(Commons 1934, pp. 107, 155)

Commons followed Peirce in many respects. He, too, was hostile to the Cartesian duality of mind and body (Commons 1934, pp. 16 and 105), and suspected that the said doctrine had served to obscure the problem of conflicts of interest in earlier economic thought. For Commons, both truth and value were defined as the consensus of the relevant investigative community. Contrary to neoclassical biases, mind was not assumed to be a passive receptacle of sense impressions, but rather was seen as an active inventor of meanings, which displayed 'an inseparable aspect of valuing, choosing and acting' (Commons 1934, p. 18). Commons brought these philosophical convictions to bear in his economics, by isolating value as the central epistemological term in economics, and postulating that the definition of value is tentative and evolutionary, constructed by courts in the course of their adjudication of conflicts of interest.

Commons perceptively grasped the importance of the dichotomy between sufficient reason and efficient cause in Veblen's research programme, and yet he rejected Veblen's reification of the dichotomy as an unbridgeable gap:

Veblen's concept of a science was the traditional concept of the physical sciences which rejected all *purpose* in the investigation of the facts. The court's concept of a science was an institutional concept wherein the investigation must start with a public purpose as a primary principle of the science itself. Veblen's elimination of purpose from the scope of science was based on his interpretation of Pragmatism as set forth by James and Dewey. He does not seem to have known the Pragmatism of Peirce, which dealt only with the physical sciences, nor the Pragmatism of the courts, which more nearly followed Dewey.

(Commons 1934, p. 654).

This hermeneutical character of science is an important presupposition of Commons' economics. He insisted that, 'False analogies have arisen in the history of economic thought by transferring to economics the meanings derived from the physical sciences' (Commons 1934, p. 96). If economists had not been so spellbound with the slavish imitation of the outward trappings of physics, they might have admitted that the structures and meanings they had constructed frequently conflicted with the interpretations of the actors so described, and that there had to be some rational means for reconciliation of such divergent constructions. All economic life is interpretative, and there is no more certain recourse than the interpretative practices of the community. This explains why Commons dubbed his theory 'Institutional economics'. As he put it: 'we may define an institution as Collective Action in Control of Individual Action' (Commons 1934, p. 69).

Commons' theory of transactions follows directly from his embrace of what we have called Peircian hermeneutics, as it attempts to supply a theory of semiotics to explain the actors' interpretations of the meanings of legitimate transactions (Ramstaad 1986, pp. 1083–6). To portray a transaction as simple physical transport between two spheres of relative need assumes away all problems of rational cognition (Mirowski, 1989, 1990).

> It is significant that the formula of a transaction may be stated in terms of psychology. . . . All that is needed to shift it to institutional economics is to introduce rights of property; legal units of measurement; the creation, negotiability and release of debt; the enforcement of the two duties of delivery and payment by the collective action of the state.
>
> (Commons 1934, pp. 438–9)

In effect, Commons was invoking Peirce's dictum that every semiotic act must be analysed in terms of the sign itself, the signifier and the interpreter. In his taxonomy of transactions, the signifiers were the actual traders, the interpreters were to be the virtual buyers and sellers and the state apparatus, and the signs were to be the contracts, the debt instruments and all the rest.

Once one sees the transaction for the complex social phenomenon which it is, it should become apparent that conflicts of interest and interpretation would be endemic. Hence, problems of co-ordination within a market system will be rife, and there will be an imperative for some notion of 'reasonable value' to be negotiated. This concept of value can only be historical, and contingent upon the evolution of the interpretative community.

Commons' legacy as an economist was surprisingly consonant with his stated philosophical premises. As is well known, both he and his students were very active in legal and governmental circles, attempting to get courts and legislatures to recognize their role as experimenters as well as mediators. Commons' stance was that he was openly advocating the gradual improvement of capitalism through governmental intervention. Many of the economic functions of American government which we today take for granted were the handiwork of Commons and his students in the first half of the twentieth century.

However, his greatest triumphs in the arena of practice were viewed as liabilities in the arena of economic theory in the next generation. His refrain that there were no 'natural' grounds for economic institutions was read as implying that Commons left no systematic economic theory. The conjuncture of the decline of pragmatism in the US in the 1930s with the rise of a particularly narrow form of positivism sealed the fate of the Commons wing of the Pragmatist institutionalist programme.

POST-1930s INSTITUTIONALISM

The pragmatist view of science had fewer and fewer partisans in the US from the 1920s to the 1960s. The causes of this decline are too baroque to discuss here, but it is obvious that a Cartesian-style positivism rose to predominance and became the premier cultural image of natural knowledge.[9] The Institutionalist school of economics found itself very vulnerable in this harsh new climate. The rival tradition of neoclassical economics was patently more attuned to the trends in philosophy and science, and even went on the offensive, branding its rivals as 'unscientific'. In reaction to this threat, the 'second generation' of institutionalists tended to distance themselves from their heritage of Peircian pragmatism. Two prominent representatives of this reaction were Wesley Clair Mitchell and Clarence Ayres.

Mitchell was a student of Veblen, and received from him an extreme scepticism about the analytic claims of neoclassicism, a scepticism he maintained throughout his career. His early work on monetary history and business cycles were extrapolations of some major Veblenian themes, such as the divergence of financial from material expansion as a cause of macroeconomic instability. However, as Mitchell rose in professional standing, he became the advocate of a very unsophisticated notion of scientific endeavour, in the sense that he became an advocate of the economic scientist as a neutral and impartial gatherer of facts. One of his crowning achievements was to be the prime mover behind the founding of the National Bureau of Economic Research, an organization originally dedicated to the non-partisan support of the collection and analysis of quantitative economic data such as the fledgling national-income accounts.[10]

From some of his comments – such as those in Mitchell (1937, p. 35) – it seems he thought that statistical analyses were somehow separate from and immune to the mechanical analogies imported by neoclassical theory. None the less, it is also clear that his formidable success in capturing funding and support for his Bureau hinged crucially upon his willingness to make use of prevalent impressions of the trappings of scientific rigour. As a result, it was largely due to Mitchell that by mid-century the Institutionalist school was perceived as promoting a form of naïve empiricism without any theory. Protests to the contrary were met with the challenge 'where is your scientific theory?' – which really meant, 'why aren't you using the conventional techniques of physics (such as constrained maximization) as we do?'. Mitchell and his school had no coherent response, since he had already acquiesced to so much of the positivist programme.

Clarence Ayres was another well-known institutionalist who stressed the later, more Manichaean side of Veblen's legacy. Ayres explicitly traced his influence from Dewey: 'It was from John Dewey that I first learned what that way of knowing is. It is what Dewey called the "instrumental" process. This, as Dewey realized, is identical with what Veblen was calling the "technological" process' (Ayres 1961, p. 29; see also McFarland 1986, p. 622). The reification of technology as the sole category of legitimate knowledge, begun by Veblen, was carried to its extreme conclusions by Ayres. In the process, the Peircian pragmatic maxim was stripped of everything but a crude instrumentalism which sought 'to identify the intellectual procedures of science with the use of instruments and at the same time to identify the instruments of scientists with the tools which are still in wider use by artisans and craftsmen' (Ayres 1961, p. 277). While Dewey could hardly be accused of possessing an architectonic, this was certainly a misrepresentation of his position (Rutherford 1981). Where Dewey wanted to portray scientific inquiry as a continuous questioning procedure, Ayres tried to portray it as the accumulation of certain and final knowledge by means of the accumulation of tools and artefacts. While this position had little to do with pragmatism, it did resonate with certain doctrines in the philosophy of science in the 1930s through the 1960s – such as Bridgeman's 'operationalism' and various attempts to define a neutral object language – and therefore it did attract adherents.

The central theme in Ayres' work is the tension and dichotomy between 'ceremonial' and 'technological' or 'instrumental' processes (Waller 1982; Bush 1983). The distinction seems to reduce all social life into an exhaustive partition of non-scientific and scientific endeavour, for Ayres insists that: 'tribal beliefs, and the institutional and ceremonial practices in which they are objectified, are simulacra of scientific knowledge and technical skills' (Ayres 1961, pp. 30–1). Technology is by far the larger category, since it is defined:

> in the broadest possible sense to refer to that whole aspect of human experience and activity which some logicians call operational, and the entire complement of artefacts with which mankind operates. So defined, technology includes mathematical journals and symphonic scores.
>
> (Ayres 1961, p. 278)

This work was more reminiscent of Comte's division of all human knowledge into three stages – the Theological or fictitious, the Metaphysical or abstract, and the Scientific or positive – than it was of any of the writings of Peirce or Dewey. Somewhat incongruously for an Institutionalist, 'ceremonial' practices and habits are equated with institutions, which are then invidiously contrasted with science. Religion, myth, folkways and the *status quo* are at various times tarred with the brush of 'ceremonial' status; but the most concise definition of the concept is provided by Mayhew (1981 pp. 515–6): 'Ceremonialism is a failure to evaluate by testing consequences.' At the end of this road, the pale shadow of pragmatism has become – irony of ironies – a Popperian version of science.

Hence the subtle hermeneutics of Peirce, by way of Dewey, was reduced in Ayres' hands and those of his followers to a very prosaic materialism. 'The "we" who know are not the entire community, or even a majority of all the people . . . such knowledge exists, is a community possession, so to speak accessible to anyone who seeks access to it' (Ayres 1961, p. 34). Knowledge was effectively a physical stock, and the role of community was diminished to the vanishing point. Science was treated as if it were the embodiment of a single method true for all time, although he was negligent when it came to describing precisely what the method consisted of (Ayres 1961, p. 51). Ayres was prone to such *obiter dicta* as 'nothing but science is true or meaningful', or 'Any proposition which is incapable of statement in scientific terms, any phenomenon which is incapable of investigation by scientific methods, is meaningless and worthless as meaning and value are conceived in that universe of discourse' (in Lepley 1949, p. 59). Ayres did temper the harshness of this pronouncement by his reference to the relevant universe of discourse, but he had obviously come a long distance from Peirce's hermeneutics. This increasing stridency in the evocation of science became painfully incongruous to a positivist audience, and pushed institutional economics further and further out on a limb: how could they praise scientific discourse as the only relevant truth criteria, and simultaneous eschew scientific practice as it was understood in mid-twentieth-century America? Where was the mathematical formalism and axiomatization, the systematic hypothesis-testing according to the canons of classical statistical inference, the mathematical models, and the style of studied anonymity of the physics report?

REVOLUTIONS IN SCIENCE AND PHILOSOPHY

A funny thing happened on the way to the Temple of Science. Just as neo-classicism and institutionalism were vying to be the sole legitimate claimant of the mantle of science, science itself changed dramatically. First in the theory of relativity, and then more dramatically in quantum mechanics and cosmology, physics was severely warping the complacent vision of natural law. The particularly Laplacean notion of rigid determinism came unstuck, and the prosaic conception of percepts or sense-data got lost in a whole sequence of counter-intuitive and perverse accounts of space, time, discontinuity, and the interaction of the observer with the natural phenomenon. Eternal verities, such as the conservation of energy and the suprahistorical character of physical law were progressively undermined (Mirowski 1989). Things got so bad that physicists started going around telling people that there could be such a thing as a free lunch.[11] The amazing thing is that much of this drift had been anticipated by Peirce as part of his hypothesis that natural law was itself the product of an evolutionary process.

Philosophers of science felt the tremors under their feet in the 1960s. Analytical philosophy of science had not only been subject to devastating internal criticism, but historians of science such as Thomas Kuhn, Paul Forman, Richard Westfall and others were demonstrating that respected scientists of the past did not conform to the strict positivist code of correct scientific behaviour. Perhaps because they were historians, they grew more curious about the hermeneutic aspects of scientific behaviour. As Kuhn wrote, about scientists:

> When reading the works of an important thinker, look first for the apparent absurdities in the text and ask yourself how a sensible person could have written them. When you find an answer, I continue, when those passages make sense, then you may find that more central passages, ones you previously thought you understood, have changed their meaning.
>
> (Kuhn 1977, p. xii)

Now, if we have difficulties in understanding the paradigm scientists sanctioned by our culture, it is but a short step to assert that the contemporaries of pivotal scientists also had problems of interpretation and understanding their peers. Explicit rules of deduction and induction could not be expected to resolve this problem in all situations, and as a result the entire Cartesian portrayal of science came unravelled for philosophers (Suppe 1977; Laudan 1984; Rorty 1979, 1986).

By the 1980s, it was common to find historians, philosophers, and sociologists of science employing hermeneutic techniques (Latour and Woolgar 1979; Knorr-Cetina and Mulkay 1983; Radnitzky 1973; Ackermann 1985). This development in turn encouraged philosophers to rediscover Peirce and resuscitate the pragmatist tradition in America. Writers such as Richard Rorty, Richard Bernstein, and Karl Apel have put pragmatism back on the philosophical map, proposing to reunite a theory of language and social interaction with a theory of scientific inquiry. As Rorty has written of the new pragmatism:

> [it] is the same as the method of utopian politics or revolutionary science (as opposed to parliamentary politics or normal science). The method is to redescribe lots and lots of things in new ways, until you have created a pattern of linguistic behavior which will tempt the rising generation to adopt it, thereby causing them to look for appropriate new forms of non-linguistic behavior – e.g., the adoption of new scientific equipment or new social institutions. Philosophy, on this model, does not work piece by piece, analyzing concept after concept, or testing thesis after thesis. Rather, it works holistically and pragmatically. . . . It does not pretend to have a better candidate for doing the same old things which we did when we spoke the old way. Rather, it suggests that we might want to stop doing those things and do something else.
>
> (Rorty 1986, p. 4)

The irony of this revival was that the legitimate heirs of the tradition of Peirce in economics were basically unaware of it, remaining wedded to the Cartesian conception of science, which bartered away their legitimacy to neoclassical economics. Although many institutionalist economists maintained a lively interest in philosophical issues, they tended to get sidetracked into such controversies as the meaning of Milton Friedman's essay on 'The methodology of positive economics' (an article so incoherent that it could support any reading), or else into behaviouralism of a mechanistic cast, which neutralized all hermeneutic problems of interpretation.

Worst of all, the lavish praise of science which had been a hallmark of institutionalism from the 1930s to the 1960s grew more and more an embarrassment, both because of the overt scientism of neoclassical theory, and because of the increasing scepticism about the competence and benevolence of the technocrat in a society where the very institution of science seemed an instrument of subjugation and a juggernaut careering out of control. The tragedy was that Institutionalism had lost sight of its bearings, making the mistake of pretending to be a better candidate for doing the same old things which were done when speaking the same old language. In consequence, the research agenda had been set by the neoclassical economists. It was a no-win situation.

THE MODERN REVIVAL OF A PRAGMATIST INSTITUTIONALIST ECONOMICS

There is one more nod to be made in the direction of the DMD thesis, and that is to discuss certain nascent hopeful trends in institutional economics. As the vortex model suggests, one might expect that profound transmutations of our 'natural' concepts would be felt (perhaps with a lag) in the construction of social theory. I should like to argue that this is indeed the case in some recent institutionalist economic research, and that one might extrapolate from present trends to anticipate a full-scale repudiation of Cartesian philosophy of science and an increased reliance on hermeneutic conceptions of the economic actor as well as the role of the economic researcher.

Twentieth-century innovations in physical science have come quite a distance in denying a mechanically determinate world, reinterpreting our ideas of limitation and scarcity, and filling us with disquiet at the boundlessness of chance, chaos, and emergent novelty. Science is making us rudely aware of our role in constructing the world, or as Rorty puts it, 'making truth'. If the DMD thesis is any guide, then we should expect that this progressive awakening should eventually show up in economics. Because neoclassical economics is irreparably committed to the imitation of nineteenth-century physics, the DMD thesis predicts that it will find itself progressively isolated from cultural conceptions, defending an increasingly reactionary conception of 'natural order' as mechanically deterministic and static. Institutional economics, on the other hand, with its Peircian pedigree, should be well-positioned to participate in the reconstruction of economic theory from a hermeneutic perspective. This reconstruction is not merely wishful thinking; there are signs that it is already well under way.

The revitalized Institutionalist tradition cannot consist of a return to Peirce: too much has happened in the interim, in science, philosophy, and economics for that to be a practical course of action. None the less, Peirce and his work might serve as a symbol of the central concept of institutional economics, the idea of collective rationality. The primary lesson of Peirce's philosophy of science is that the validity of science is not encapsulated in a 'method' for all time, and that our criteria of knowledge will always be bound up with the constitution of the community of inquiry. Further, this will not just be true for 'science' writ small, but for all human endeavour. Consequently, the philosophical definition of an 'institution' (with a bow towards Commons) should be 'collective rationality in pursuit of individual rationality'. This does not imply a reversion to a Hegelian *Geist* or Bergsonian *élan vital*; it is not an idealism. Institutions can be understood as socially constructed invariants which provide the actors who participate in them with the means and resources to cope with change and diversity; this is the non-mechanistic definition of individual rationality (Mirowski 1988, 1990).

A prodigious body of institutionalist economic theory can be systematized around this philosophical conception of an institution. We have already mentioned Commons' discussions of transactions as a semiotics of economic trades, as well as his portrayal of value as the outcome of a long history of negotiation in the legal system. There is also Mitchell's gem of an essay on money in economic history, which suggests that money itself is a socially constructed invariant which is intended to stabilize the concept of price, but which inadvertently transforms the very idea of freedom.

Yet it is in more modern writings that one can observe the impact of a hermeneutic philosophy upon economic theory. Wilbur and Harrison (1978) have proposed the vocabulary of 'pattern models' in order to highlight the evolutionary and holistic themes in recent applied work in institutional economics. Samuels (1978) has surveyed the alternative portrayal of information and preferences in many articles in the *Journal of Economic Issues*. The role of mathematics in obscuring the hermeneutic problem of interpretation has been explored with great insight by Dennis (1982).

But more importantly, hermeneutic considerations are beginning to show up in the actual theoretical portrayal of the social actors and their problems. The idea of rule creation as the outcome of a constrained maximization problem has been critiqued with great subtlety by Field (1979, 1984). The proliferation of solution concepts in game theory has been interpreted by Mirowski (1986a) as the breakdown of the mechanistic notion of individual rationality, which had been already anticipated in the philosophy of Peirce and Wittgenstein. Randall Bausor (1986) has demonstrated how complicated it is to model the passage of time from the transactor's point of view. David Levine (1986) has suggested that the problem of firms' interpretations of one another's activities has a direct bearing upon the rate of growth of the macroeconomy. Philip Mirowski (1981) has argued that institutions cannot be explained within the ambit of neoclassical models, because the only legitimate explanation in that sphere is one which reduces the institution to antecedent natural givens, which renders their function incoherent and superfluous. Furthermore, Mirowski (1986b, 1990) attempts to outline the mathematical foundations of institutionalist economics, arguing that the quantitative character of prices and commodities is socially constructed, and suggesting that the institution of money imposes an algebraic group structure which permits the mathematical manipulation of economic categories, and hence reifies the notion of value.

ACKNOWLEDGEMENTS

I would like to thank Anne Mayhew, Marc Tool, Ken Dennis and especially Paul Dale Bush for their comments on an earlier draft of this essay. I am sure that none of them agree with my overall thesis, so they should not be held accountable for the foregoing.

NOTES

1 Evidence for this assertion is presented in detail in Mirowski 1989, Chapters 4–6.
2 See, however, Mirowski (1987a and 1988); Mini (1974).
3 I must stress that what follows is specifically my own reading of Peirce, although it shares many points with Apel (1981). We shall ignore in this essay questions of the wellsprings of Peirce's influences, or the tangled question of his metaphysics. We should caution, however, that some authors in the institutionalist literature (such as Liebhafsky 1986, p. 13) have tried to absolve Peirce of any Hegelian or Continental influence, a thesis I obviously find unpersuasive. On this issue, see Peirce (1958b, p. 283); Thayer (1981) and Apel (1981, p. 201 fn.).
4 This assertion of the self-correcting nature of specifically quantitative induction is perhaps one of the weakest parts of the Peircian corpus, because it does not give any cogent reasons for the privileged character of quantitative evidence. On this issue, see Kuhn (1977). Further, it is easy to devise numerous situations where repeated measurement does not converge upon any particular value. This would especially be true of non-ergodic situations, such as those envisioned in Peirce's own 'evolutionary' laws.
5 Peirce made a number of observations on the role of conservation principles in the construction of the static mechanical world picture, such as Peirce (1935, pp. 15, 20, and 100). It is interesting to compare these statements with the definition (given on p. 108 of this present chapter) of an institution as 'a socially constructed invariant'. See also (Mirowski 1984b).
6 As Peirce saw it:

> But the higher places in science in the coming years are for those who succeed in adapting the methods of one science to the investigation of another. That is where the greatest progress of the passing generation has consisted in. Darwin adapted biology to the methods of Malthus and the economists. Maxwell adapted to the theory of gases the methods of the doctrine of chances, and to electricity the methods of thermodynamics. . . . Cournot adapted to political economy the calculus of variations.

(Peirce 1985a, p. 46)

On this issue, see also Mirowski (1987a and 1989).

7 The reasons for the decline of pragmatism in the 1940s is beyond our mandate in this paper, but see Thayer (1981, pp. 560–3), where it is suggested that pragmatism's alliance with liberal social engineering, its misconstrual as a methodological semantic principle, and Dewey's alliance with the logical positivists (particularly in Dewey 1939b) all served to cripple the programme.

8 Veblen wrote:

> addiction to magical superstition or religious conceptions will necessarily have its effect on the conceptions and logic employed in technological theory and practice, and will impair its efficiency by that much.
>
> (Veblen 1914, p. 41)

Here Veblen clearly understands that science may be influenced by culture as well as vice versa, but notice the derogatory language in reference to non-science, as well as the unfounded assertion that cultural or teleological influences impair the efficiency of scientific logic. Where the DMD thesis posits a vortex, Veblen has two poles of a dichotomy, where one can only pollute the other.

9 See note 7 above.

10 Conventional histories of economic thought have not given sufficient attention to the importance of the institutionalist school for the rise of twenteith century macroeconomics. (Here, see Mirowski 1985.) The position of NBER as a nonpartisan purveyor of data and research was repudiated in the 1970s when Martin Feldstein was installed as director, at which point institutionalist themes disappeared from its agenda.

11 'I have heard it said that there is no such thing as a free lunch. It now appears possible that the universe is a free lunch' (Guth 1983, p. 215).

REFERENCES

Ackermann, Robert (1985) *Data, Instruments and Theory*, Princeton: Princeton University Press.

Apel, Karl (1981) *Charles S. Peirce: From Pragmatism to Pragmaticism*, Amherst: University of Massachusetts Press.

Ayres, Clarence (1961) *Towards a Reasonable Society*, Austin: University of Texas.

——— (1962) *The Theory of Economic Progress*, 2nd edn, New York: Schocken.

——— (1963) 'The legacy of Thorstein Veblen', in *Institutional Economics*, Berkeley: University of California Press.

Barnes, B. and Shapin, S. (eds) (1979) *Natural Order*, Beverly Hills: Sage.

Bausor, Randall (1986) in Mirowski, P. (ed.) *Reconstruction of Economic Theory*, Boston: Kluwer.

Bernstein, Richard (1966) *John Dewey*, New York: Washington Square.

——— (1983) *Beyond Objectivism and Relativism*, Philadelphia: University of Pennsylvania Press.

Bloor, David (1976) *Knowledge and Social Imagery*, London: Routledge & Kegan Paul.

——— (1982) 'Durkheim and Mauss Revisited', *Studies in the History and Philosophy of Science* 13 (Winter): 267–97.

Bush, Paul Dale (1983) 'An exploration of the structural characteristics of a Veblen-Ayres-Foster defined institutional domain', *Journal of Economic Issues* 17 (March): 35–66.

Cahn, S. (ed.) (1977) *New Studies on the Philosophy of John Dewey*, Hanover: University Press of New England.

Commons, John R. (1934) *Institutional Economics*, New York: Macmillan.

Dennis, Ken. (1982) 'Economic theory and the problem of translation', *Journal of Economic Issues* 16 (September): 691–712.

Dewey, John (1931) *Philosophy and Civilization*, New York: Minton Balch.
—— (1938) *Logic: The Theory of Inquiry*, New York: Holt.
—— (1939a) *John Dewey's Philosophy*, New York: Modern Library.
—— (1939b) *Theory of Valuation, vol. 2 of International Encyclopaedia of Unified Science, no. 4*, Chicago: University of Chicago Press.
Douglas, Mary (1970) *Natural Symbols*, London: Barrie & Jenkins.
—— (1975) *Implicit Meanings*, London: Routledge & Kegan Paul.
—— (1986) *How Institutions Think*, Syracuse: Syracuse University Press.
Durkheim, E., and Mauss, M. (1903) *Primitive Classification*, London: Cohen & West.
Dyer, Alan (1986) 'Veblen on scientific creativity', *Journal of Economic Issues* 20 March: 21–41.
Eisele, Carolyn (1957) 'The Peirce-Newcomb correspondence', *Proceedings of the American Philosophical Society*, 101: 409–25.
Field, Alex (1979) 'On the explanation of rules using rational choice models', *Journal of Economic Issues* 13 (March): 49–72.
—— (1984) 'Microeconomics, norms and rationality', *Economic Development and Cultural Change* 32 (July): 683–711.
Guth, Alan (1983) 'Speculations on the origin of the matter, energy and entropy of the universe', in Alan Guth *et al.* (eds) *Asymptotic Realms of Physics*, Cambridge, Mass.: MIT Press.
Hands, D. (1985) 'Karl Popper and economic method', *Economics and Philosophy* 1 (April): 83–99.
Harding, Sandra (ed.) (1976) *Can Theories De Refuted?* Booton: Reidel.
James, William (1975) *The Works of William James: Pragmatism*, eds Fredson Bowers and Ignas K. Skrupskelis, Cambridge, Mass.: Harvard University Press.
Knorr-Cetina, Karin and Mulkay, Michael (1983) *Science Observed*, London: Sage.
Kuhn, Thomas (1977) *The Essential Tension*, Chicago: University of Chicago Press.
Kuklick, Bruce (1984) 'Seven thinkers and how they grew: Descartes, Spinoza, Leibnitz, Locke, Berkeley, Hume, Kant', in Rorey, R., Schneewind, J. and Skinner, Q. (eds) *Philosophy in History*, Cambridge: Cambridge University Press.
Latour, Bruno and Woolgar, Steven (1979) *Natural Order*, Beverly Hills: Sage.
Laudan, Larry (1984) *Science and Values*, Berkeley: University of California Press.
Layton, Edwin (1962) 'Veblen and the engineers', *American Quarterly* 14 (Spring): 64–72.
Lepley, Ray (ed.) (1949) *Value: A Cooperative Inquiry*, New York: Columbia University Press.
Levine, David (1986) in Mirowski, P. *Reconstruction of Economic Theory*, Boston: Kluwer.
Liebhafsky, H. (1986) 'Peirce on the *summum bonum* and the unlimited community', *Journal of Economic Issues* 20 (March): 5–20.
Mayhew, Anne (1981) 'Ayresian technology, technological reasoning, and doomsday', *Journal of Economic Issues* 15 (June): 513–20.
McFarland, Floyd (1986) 'Clarence Ayres and his gospel of technology', *History of Political Economy* 18 (Winter): 617–37.
Mini, Piero (1974) *Economics and Philosophy*, Gainesville: University of Florida Press.
Mirowski, Philip (1981) 'Is there a mathematical neoinstitutional economics?', *Journal of Economic Issues* 15 (September): 593–613.
—— (1984a) 'Physics and the marginalist revolution', *Cambridge Journal of Economics* 8 (December): 361–79.
—— (1984b) 'The role of conservation principles in 20th century economic theory', *Philosophy of the Social Sciences* 14 (December): 461–73.
—— (1985) *The Birth of the Business Cycle*, New York: Garland.

—— (1986a) 'Institutions as solution concepts in a game theory context', in Larry Samuelson (ed.) *Microeconomic Theory*, Hingham, Mass.: Kluwer-Nijhoff.

—— (1986b) 'Mathematical formalism and economic explanation', in Philip Mirowski (ed.) *The Reconstruction of Economic Theory*, Hingham, Mass.: Kluwer-Nijhoff.

—— (1987a) 'Shall I compare thee to a Minkowski-Ricardo-Leontief matrix of the Hicks-Mosak type?', *Economics and Philosophy* 3 (April).

—— (1987b) 'What do markets do?', *Explorations in Economic History* 24 (April): 107–29.

—— (1988) *Against Mechanism*, Totawa, N.J.: Rowman & Littlefield.

—— (1989) *More Heat Than Light: Economics as Social Physics*, New York: Cambridge University Press.

—— (1990) 'Learning the meaning of a dollar', *Social Research* 57: 689–718.

Mitchell, Wesley (1937) *The Backward Art of Spending Money*, New York: McGraw Hill.

Peirce, Charles S. (1934) *Collected Papers*, vol. 5, Cambridge: Harvard University Press.

—— (1935) *Collected Papers*, vol. 6, Cambridge: Harvard University Press.

—— (1958a) *Collected Papers*, vol. 7, Cambridge: Harvard University Press.

—— (1958b) *Collected Papers*, vol. 8, Cambridge: Harvard University Press.

Polanyi, Karl (1968) *The Great Transformation*, Boston: Beacon.

Radnitzky, G. (1973) *Contemporary Schools of Metascience*, Chicago: Regnery.

Ramstaad, Yngve (1986) 'A pragmatist's quest of holistic knowledge', *Journal of Economic Issues* 20 (December): 1067–1106.

Rescher, Nicholas (1978) *Peirce's Philosophy of Science*, Notre Dame: University of Notre Dame.

Rickman, H.P. (1976) 'Introduction', in W. *Dilthey, Selected Writings*, New York: Cambridge University Press.

Rorty, Richard (1979) *Philosophy and the Mirror of Nature*, Princeton: Princeton University Press.

—— (1986) 'The contingency of language', *London Review of Books* 3 (April): 3–7.

Rorty, R., Schneewind, J., and Skinner, Q. (eds) (1984) *Philosophy in History*, Cambridge: Cambridge University Press.

Rutherford, Malcolm (1981) 'Clarence Ayres and the instrumentalist theory of value', *Journal of Economic Issues* 15 (September): 657–74.

Samuels, Warren (1978) 'Information systems, preferences and the economy in the JEI', *Journal of Economic Issues* 12 (March): 23–42.

Scheffler, Israel (1974) *Four Pragmatists*, New York: Humanities.

Suppe, Frederick (1977) *Structure of Scientific Theories*, Urbana: University of Illinois Press.

Thayer, H.S. (1981) *Meaning and Action*, Indianapolis: Hackett.

Tiles, Mary (1984) *Bachelard: Science and Objectivity*, Cambridge: Cambridge University Press.

Veblen, Thorstein (1914) *The Instinct of Workmanship*, New York: Macmillan.

—— (1923) *Absentee Ownership*, New York: Heubsch.

—— (1933) *The Vested Interests and the Common Man*, New York: Viking.

—— (1934) *Essays in Our Changing Order*, New York: Viking.

—— (1969) *The Place of Science in Modern Civilization*, New York: Capricorn.

Waller, William (1982) 'The evolution of the Veblenian dichotomy', *Journal of Economic Issues* 16 (September): 757–71.

White, Morton (1949) *Social Thought in America*, New York: Viking.

Wilber, C. and Harrison, R. (1978) 'The methodological basis in institutional economics', *Journal of Economic Issues* 12 (March): 61–90.

6   The scope and goals of economic science

A Habermasian perspective

Jon D. Wisman

Jürgen Habermas is the most prominent contemporary descendant of the so-called Frankfurt school. The guiding aim of his intellectual endeavours has been to reconstruct social theory so as to reunite theory and practice in a manner which accounts for the complexities of the late twentieth century. This project has entailed not only drawing upon such intellectual giants of the nineteenth and early twentieth century as Marx, Freud, Weber, Dewey, and Durkheim, but also upon practically every notable contemporary philosopher and social theorist.

Over the past 20 years, Habermas's wide-ranging social and philosophical work has had a substantial impact within practically all domains of the social sciences and humanities.[1] Yet surprisingly, the queen of the social sciences, economics, stands out as a striking exception. Perhaps the failure of Habermas' work to penetrate the discourse of economists has to do with the unmerited high degree of methodological confidence within the profession. Apparently unburdened by the ever-present self-doubt and reflection within other 'soft' disciplines about just what it is that their pursuits should be about, economists by and large are considerably more confident that their discipline is on the right track. They typically believe that they are asking the right questions and using the appropriate research strategies to answer them.

But this confidence is by no means universal. Although the overwhelming majority of the profession's rank and file appears confortable, the discipline has long had heterodox schools of Marxists, Institutionalists, and Austrians who have argued – albeit with often radically different reasoning – that to a substantial degree the inadequacies of mainstream economics stem from its faulty methodology. In recent years a growing number of luminaries within the profession have also come to recognize that all is not well within the house of economic science. Some of the frequently heard allegations include: that the discipline has become bogged down in a sort of formalism – a seemingly endless mathematization of a narrow body of theory – which bears little relevance for contemporary concerns;[2] that it has abandoned the classical duty of knowledge to provide public enlightenment; that a misplaced smugness prevents the profession from limiting the disastrous use of economics as ideology. Indeed, it has frequently been alleged of late that economic science is in a state of crisis.

Crisis times are soul-searching times, and the soul of economics has to do with such things as its social function, its scope and its methodology. Jürgen Habermas has made little more than passing comments on the nature of economic science. However, in so far as his work is focused directly upon the question of what the full potential of social thought might be, it has relevance for a science of economics. Two areas in particular where a greater acquaintance with this work might aid economists in improving their discipline concern the social function of knowledge, and the nature of a critical social science. In terms of the social function of economic knowledge, the question has to do with what it is that society could ideally hope for from a science of economics. In terms of the nature of a critical social science, the issue is how economics might at times serve as ideology and how it might more successfully avoid such a fate.

THE SOCIAL FUNCTION OF ECONOMIC KNOWLEDGE

Why do we seek economic knowledge, or for that matter, any knowledge? A common response is that knowledge or, more honorifically, 'truth', is one of those highest ends which are sought for their own sake. Yet clearly such an answer has little explanatory power. It cannot explain why societies would allocate scarce resources toward the production of specific forms of knowledge. A more satisfactory answer, according to Habermas, is to be found by examining the universal conditions of human existence. Knowledge has a 'practical intent'. It stems from and serves 'social practice' in the reproduction of the human species. Social practice, for Habermas, occurs in two distinct, although interdependent, categories: labour and interaction.[3] It is through labour that humans struggle with nature to overcome material privation. It is through communicative interaction within an inherited institutional framework that humans come to agreement as to how they should live together. These categories, although radically different, were inspired by Marx's definition of a mode of production as composed of forces of production and social relations of production.[4]

For Habermas, it is through the social practices of labour and interaction that humans constitute themselves. Labour is, of course, necessitated by scarcity; it mediates between human material needs and wants and the natural world. And, as Marx had emphasized, in this process of working upon and transforming nature, humans also transform themselves. All of human self-formation is not, however, reducible to labour, the material struggle of the species to survive and reproduce. The self-formation process also occurs in social interaction. Because humans are by nature social, there must be a significant degree of social co-ordination. To achieve this, humans interact symbolically, they use language to communicate their wants and intentions. Further, they must often strive for agreement, and this entails an inherent rationality.[5]

Within the social-practice category of labour or work, knowledge is sought which might enable humans to manipulate and control their environments with greater efficiency. This knowledge, then, has an instrumental character – it is 'purposive-rational'. It is expressed through a means–ends form of rationality, what Weber had termed *Zweckrationalität*. This instrumental or technical form of rationality takes ends or goals as given. It is restricted to the discovery of efficient or strategic means for their attainment. The sciences which develop this form of knowledge Habermas terms 'empirical-analytic'.

Within the social practice of interaction, by contrast, knowledge is sought of just what should constitute appropriate norms or goals. This pursuit is carried out through intersubjective communication. It 'is governed by binding *consensual norms*, which define reciprocal expectations about behavior and which must be understood and recognized by at least two acting subjects' (Habermas 1970a, pp. 91–2). This search for truth in communicative action involves a form of rationality which Habermas terms 'practical' or 'communicative'. Actors involved in social interaction must strive to understand the meanings of others. They must participate in a hermeneutical project. The sciences which study this domain Habermas calls the 'cultural', or the 'historical-hermeneutical'. These sciences:

> gain knowledge in a different methodological framework. Here the meaning or validity of propositions is not constituted in the frame of reference of technical control. . . . [These] theories are not constructed deductively and experience is not organized with regard to the success of operations. Access to the facts is provided by the understanding of meaning, not observation. The verification of lawlike hypotheses in the empirical-analytic sciences has its counterpart here in the interpretation of texts. Thus the rules of hermeneutics determine the possible meaning of the validity of statements of the cultural sciences.[6]
>
> (Habermas 1971, p. 309)

For Habermas, the rise of capitalism and modernity generally has witnessed the delegitimation of the historical-hermeneutical sciences. He argues that this development was a consequence of the expansion of what he terms 'subsystems' – such as markets, contract law, and state administration – in which means–ends or instrumental rationality are exercised. These subsystems have encroached ever more on the 'life-world'[7] where citizens participate in discursive will-formation. The life-world has become progressively 'colonized' by social institutions which mechanically, bureaucratically, or technocratically determine social outcomes, such that 'personal relations, services and phases of life are being transformed into objects of administration, or into commodities' (Habermas in Dews 1986, p. 141). And, as personal and social relations become increasingly technical,

'It is characteristic of the pattern of rationalism in capitalist societies that the complex of cognitive-instrumental rationality establishes itself at the cost of practical rationality; communicative relations are reified' (Habermas 1984, p. 363). As this process continued, the social sciences became increasingly positivistic. They imitated the methodological stances of the empirical-analytic sciences and came to see their goal as prediction and control. But the object, the behaviour of which was to be predicted and controlled, was social interaction. Social sciences came to serve as legitimation for technocratic society. The rise to dominance of an instrumental form of social knowledge led to the 'scientization of politics':

> The social potential of science is reduced to the powers of technical control – its potential for enlightened action is no longer considered. . . . Socially effective theory is no longer directed toward the consciousness of human beings who live together and discuss matters with each other, but to the behavior of human beings who manipulate.
>
> (Habermas 1974, pp. 254–5)

In none of the social sciences has this delegitimation of interaction and a hermeneutical approach been more complete than in economics. Given the subject matter of economics, this is perhaps not entirely surprising. Of the social sciences, economics stands closest to the physical sciences. It is concerned with a physical problem, the problem of material scarcity. Part of its social function is to provide knowledge about how nature might more effectively be manipulated and controlled to improve human welfare. In this manner, it shares an instrumental character with what Habermas terms the empirical-analytic sciences. However, economics is also concerned with social interaction. The human struggle with nature does not dictate a unique set of social institutions.[8] Indeed, it is conceivable that even the most efficient social institutions for drawing the most out of nature would not be those which most benefit human welfare. There may well be trade-offs between efficiency and other goals. Ironically, the discipline which is often called the 'science of trade-offs' essentially ignores this question.

Moreover, from a Habermasian perspective, to the extent that economic science ignores social interaction, it is not fully capable of comprehending the evolution of society's productive capacity. The domains of labour and interaction are interdependent, and Habermas frequently tilts towards granting causal determinacy to the latter:

> Rationality structures are embodied not only in amplifications of purposive-rational action – that is, in technologies, strategies, organizations, and qualifications – but also in mediations of communicative action – in the mechanisms for regulating conflict, in world views, and in identity formations. I would even defend the thesis that the development of these normative structures is the pacemaker of social evolution, for new principles of social organization mean new forms of social integration;

and the latter, in turn, first make it possible to implement available productive forces or to generate new ones, as well as making possible a
heightening of social complexity.

(Habermas 1984, p. 120)

The positivistic character of modern economics is reinforced through
both the pedagogy and the practice of the profession. A positivistic
manifesto is frequently stated in textbooks, and as the profession has turned
ever more toward mathematical formalism and econometrics, the positivism has become the common sense of what science is all about. It generally
goes pretty much as follows: economic science is positive, not normative; it
is concerned with 'what is', not with 'what ought to be'; it is concerned with
facts, not values. These facts are 'empirical'; hence, scientifically acceptable
theories are those which have been confirmed through empirical testing (or
in a Popperian fashion, have not yet been falsified by empirical testing).
Values, on the other hand, must be taken as given, as outside the purview of
science.

The reason for adherence to this methodological manifesto is not hard to
find. It is attractive. It enables practitioners of the science to believe that
they are doing 'hard' science, that they are above ideological quibbling.
Indeed, many become convinced that with positivist criteria they possess a
powerful weapon for ridding the discipline of ideology.

Unfortunately, however, the process of science is far more complex than
this positivistic picture suggests. Theory validation, even in the 'hard'
sciences, requires far more than a mechanical process of subjecting
hypotheses to empirical testing. As post-positivistic philosophers have made
clear, science requires intersubjective communication; it requires a hermeneutical process in which practitioners must persuade others of the
validity of their theories and hypotheses. Even empirical results must be
interpreted and these interpretations must be communicated. Science, then,
is very much a social process in which communicative or hermeneutical
rationality plays a central role.[9]

Although the positivistic character of mainstream economics has been
widely discussed, very little attention has been given to the manner in which
the accompanying instrumentalism restricts and delegitimates the realm of
interaction. An instrumental view of science is not, of course, new. The
view that instrumental power is the principal, if not sole, goal of science has
become progressively more widely held since Francis Bacon. Yet it is only
with the advent of Keynesianism that this instrumentalism has become
dominant within economics. From Smith to Keynes, what might be called a
'natural law cosmology' provided little in the way of legitimation for social
intervention into the workings of the economy. The *laissez-faire* view that
the economy is automatically self-adjusting in an ideal manner meant that
economics was to be a passive science. Economic thought was principally
descriptive. The task was to determine scientifically the laws of motion of a

mechanistic, self-regulating natural economic order so as to ensure that interference stemming from ignorance did not threaten this perfect order. By providing an acceptable explanation of why the machine was imperfect, Keynes transformed the goal of economic thought. It was no longer sufficient to describe the economic world, since that world must be actively controlled and manipulated by public policy. Thus, economic thought must strive for explanation and prediction. Economic thought became overtly active or instrumental.

By the 1950s and 1960s this instrumentalism had become the general understanding of the social function of the discipline.[10] But in terms of how economists would come methodologically to understand instrumentalism, it is ironic that Milton Friedman would play an important role, given his stature as a foremost spokesperson for non-intervention. Friedman unwittingly did this in his now classic essay, 'The methodology of positive economics'. He argued that the ultimate goal of a positive science 'is the development of a "theory" or "hypothesis" that yields valid and meaningful (i.e., not truistic) predictions about phenomena' (Friedman 1953, p. 7).[11] This, coupled with his denial of the need for realism of assumptions (Friedman 1953, p. 14), suggests that science is merely an instrument for generating predictions, not explanations.[12] Although Friedman's 'methodological instrumentalism' does not explicitly suggest control and manipulation as the end of science, it has served as a methodological foundation for this view.

It is doubtful, especially in a social science like economics, whether prediction, or even empirical testing more generally, could bear the weight which Friedman would place upon it. But even if it could, the question remains as to whether prediction should be the sole, or even principal goal of economic science. Habermas's social category of interaction suggests that it should not. Economic science is capable of more than merely serving as an engineering tool. It is capable of participating in social enlightenment as to how we might best live economically. It can help society better understand which socio-economic goals might best be pursued. This, of course, means that values would openly enter into the discourse of economists.

Positivistic economics insists that values are beyond the purview of science, if not reason. As Friedman so poignantly put it, value questions involve 'differences about which men ultimately can only fight' (Friedman 1953, p. 5). Habermas does not agree. All knowledge claims, whether of facts or of appropriate norms or values, must be supported by reason. Only through communicative interaction can knowledge claims be redeemed or agreed upon. Along with modern post-positivist philosophers, Habermas rejects the traditional 'foundationalist' hope of finding a secure, solid criterion for judging all knowledge claims. Instead, it is only through communication, intersubjective interaction, that knowledge claims can be supported: 'Post-empiricist philosophy of science has provided good reasons for holding that the unsettled ground of rationally motivated agreement among participants in argumentation is our only foundation – in questions of physics no less than in those of morality' (Habermas 1982, p. 238). What is required is that the discussants be equal partners in open and uncoerced discourse.

Positivistic economics restricts itself to an instrumental or means–ends form of rationality. It restricts itself to discovering efficient means to given goals or ends. But this restrictive stance suggests several disturbing questions: Just what goals are given? Who determines these goals? How are they determined? How do economic scientists become aware of the appropriate goals? And to what extent does economics participate in determining the very goals which it then pretends to take as externally given?

A Habermasian perspective, then, suggests that economic science must address the social practice of interaction. Economists would not dictate appropriate ends or goals: 'in a process of enlightenment there can only be participants' (Habermas 1974, p. 40). Instead, they would participate in the process of public enlightenment as to exactly what ends or goals might constitute the good and just economic order. They would participate in the 'public sphere' where 'public opinion' is formed. This public sphere for Habermas is where citizens openly discuss issues of general social interest as equals. They come together, not as subjects of the state or individuals pursuing their own economic interests, but as citizens.[13] Within a Habermasian perspective, economists would recognize, as did Adam Smith, that economics is a subset of politics. Providing 'advice to the statesman' in a democracy means providing enlightenment for the people, empowering the people to better determine their own destinies.

MAINSTREAM ECONOMICS AND MODERN CAPITALIST SOCIETY

For Habermas, modern social thought has been largely moulded by its formation within the evolution of capitalist society. However, the relationship between thought and the socio-economic context in which it has been nurtured is a dialectical one. Just as, on the one hand, thought is continually reproduced by capitalist institutions and reformed as these institutions change; on the other, this thought provides legitimation for these social institutions.

Habermas has written relatively little concerning modern economic science *per se*, beyond noting that political economy has abandoned its broader earlier concern with society as a whole and became a 'specialized science' that 'concerns itself with the economy as a subsystem of society and absolves itself from questions of legitimacy' (Habermas 1984, p. 4). Nevertheless, his attitude towards the discipline might be inferred from a combination of: his views on social theory generally (discussed above), his attitude towards capitalism, and what he sees as the general nature of a more ideal or rational society.

Habermas is no fan of capitalism. With certain reservations, many of the faults he appears to find with capitalism are those shared within the Marxist traditions.[14] But what appears most central to his critical attitude toward capitalism is less traceable to Marx than to Weber, Lukács, and the earlier Frankfurt school. The institutions of capitalism operate by an instrumental form of action which constricts the realms of communicative interaction. '[W]hat happened to many areas of life in the wake of capitalist modernization [is that] money and power – more concretely, markets and administrations – take over the integrative functions which were formerly fufilled by consensual values and norms, or even by processes of reaching understanding' (Habermas in Dews 1986, p. 175). In this manner, capitalist institutions impede the self-determination of humans through open and equal discourse. Yet unlike many critics of capitalism on the left, Habermas is cautious not to opt merely for a state socialist replacement of capitalism. In fact, his resistance to socialism, conventionally understood as state ownership and control of society's means of production, appears to be founded upon much the same problem: social interaction is constricted in this instance because state administrative action becomes bureaucratic.[15]

Keynesian economics and the 'scientization of politics'

Bureaucratic state administration plagues not just socialism, but modern capitalism as well, albeit to a much lesser extent. Since Keynes' delegitimation of natural law cosmology, the state has increasingly replaced markets in the steering of economic activity within capitalist economies. The Keynesian or neo-Keynesian variant of economics has become the science of this administrative steering. To a considerable degree, this form of economics is a perfect example of what Habermas has in mind when he speaks of the 'scientization of politics'. Within the framework of Keynesian economics, the problems of macroeconomic stability, as well as those of economic justice in the forms of the distribution of income, wealth, and opportunity, become technical questions to be solved by economic experts. Because the problems are understood as merely technical ones, they appear to be beyond the political sphere.[16] The full nature of the problems, as well as the full array of options for their solution, is rarely given an open public forum.[17] Instead, politics is reduced to the electorate's casting a choice for one or another candidate with his or her team of economic experts.

A more concrete example of the manner in which Keynesian economics furthers this 'technocratic consciousness' is to be found in the problem of stagflation. Since the addition of the Phillips Curve analysis to the Keynesian framework in the late 1950s, the depiction of a trade-off between unemployment and inflation has become common. Accordingly, attempts to reduce unemployment are seen as exacerbating inflation, whereas attempts to reduce inflation are seen as resulting in higher unemployment. When translated into politics, this trade-off appears as a scientifically understood inevitability – a harsh fate of a cruel world. The political parties which generally represent the interests of labour typically identify unemployment as the evil to be fought; those generally representing the interests of capital identify inflation as the major problem. The public discussion goes no further and the electorate votes for one or the other.[18]

The presumed trade-off between unemployment and inflation is set forth *ceteris paribus* – that is, assuming no institutional change. But why would economic scientists limit their analysis in this manner? A disinterested observer, not schooled in the nature of modern social thought, might conclude that such reluctance to address questions concerning institutional change belies political conservatism on the part of the economics profession. But although conservatism is the social consequence, it is not intended. Instead, it is for methodological reasons that economists shy away from fully investigating the potential for institutional change: social institutions are built upon and sustained by social values, and the discipline's positivistic credo leads practitioners to believe that a rational understanding of values is not possible. The result, in terms of social consciousness, is that the positivistically defined inflation–unemployment trade-off is what science reveals as our options. Thus, rather than disclosing the realm of social potential, Keynesian economics acts (albeit without intent) to restrict social consciousness as to the options for improving human welfare.[19]

Since the 1930s, Keynesian economics has become the most central intellectual component of a technocratic ideology. The reason for this is that the problem of economic stability has taken on a political importance second only to defence. Thus, from a Habermasian perspective, Keynesian economics is an important component of an ideology, the 'singular achievement' of which is:

> to detach society's self-understanding from the frame of reference of communicative action and from the concepts of symbolic interaction and replace it with a scientific model. Accordingly the culturally defined self-understanding of the social life-world is replaced by the self-reification of men under categories of purposive–rational action and adaptive behavior.

> (Habermas 1970a, pp. 105–6)

Keynesian economics has, of course, suffered a considerable decline both politically and theoretically in recent times in favour of a return of confidence in the 'magic of the market', and a renaissance of the ideology of a natural law cosmology. Habermas does not, however, look upon this general shift as a progressive change. Instead, he sees it as merely a:

> policy of shifting the burden of problems back from the state onto the market – a policy which . . . has nothing to do with democratization, which rather effects a further uncoupling of state activity from the pressure for legitimation emanating from the public sphere, and

understands by 'freedom' not the autonomy of the life-world, but a free
hand for private investors.

(Habermas in Dews 1986, p. 181)

Neoclassical economics and distorted communication

Just what Habermas's ideal society would look like in terms of concrete
social institutions is not clear. He argues for legal equality and maximum
individual self-determination: 'That degree of legal equality should be
achieved which will allow at the same time the greatest possible measure of
individualism, and this means space for individuals to shape their own
lives.' Yet he insists that individual freedom must be understood more
broadly than as a mere 'abstract right', since '[t]he individual cannot be free
unless all are free, and all cannot be free unless all are free in community'
(Habermas in Dews 1986, p. 147). He is also a democrat in the widest sense
of the term.[20] He is committed to open political processes in which all
participate in the determination of their collective fate. He is for 'the
enlightenment of political will, [which] can become effective only within the
communication of citizens' (Habermas 1970a, p. 75). His ideal is the same
as Marx's – that humanity make itself with will and consciousness. This
would require social institutions which provide maximum space for free
human interaction, for uncoerced political discourse. Only through such
discourse can a rational consensus on truth be attained.

But what assurance is there that a consensus is in fact rational? Habermas
argues that there is a rationality embedded within communication itself.
Communication in which understanding is sought always raises certain
validity claims; 'anyone acting communicatively must, in performing any
speech action, raise universal validity claims and suppose that they can be
vindicated' (Habermas 1979, p. 2).[21] In other words, the individual claims
to be: (1) saying something comprehensible; (2) saying something true;
(3) qualified to make the claim; and (4) sincere in making the claim. Participants in fully open and uncoerced conversation reach a rational
consensus only 'by the force of the better argument'. This concept of a
rational consensus suggests what Habermas calls an 'ideal speech situation'.
Indeed, for Habermas, this ideal speech situation is implied in the very
possibility of speech:

an ideal speech situation is necessarily implied in the structure of
potential speech, since all speech, even intentional deception, is oriented
toward the idea of truth. This idea can be analyzed with regard to a
consensus achieved in unrestrained and universal discourse.

(Habermas 1970b, p. 372)

It would, of course, be utopian to suppose that ideal speech situations
might exist in all human interaction. But this utopian conception serves as a
counterfactual against which reality can be compared. It serves in this sense

much as a Weberian 'ideal type'. For present purposes, this utopian conception suggests how, from a Habermasian perspective, neoclassical economics might be seen as uncritical at best and ideological at worst. Neoclassical economics focuses principally upon what Marx termed the 'sphere of circulation' or the market nexus. Self-interested individuals are depicted as entering freely into the transactions of such markets. Indeed, in the history of this doctrine, the expansion of markets has typically been equated with an expansion of human freedom. However, from a Habermasian perspective, and a Marxian perspective generally, the almost exclusive focus on the market nexus reveals a preoccupation with mere appearance or surface reality. The charge is that neoclassical economic doctrine fails to penetrate beneath this surface in such a way as to grasp the underlying causal forces of which markets are merely the epiphenomena.

More concretely, neoclassical economics views individual decision-making in an asocial and ahistorical manner. All actors are formally free in the marketplace in that the market contract cannot be concluded without the voluntary accordance of all trading partners. However, if, as Marx pointed out in the extreme instance, the free choice is to work for the capitalist class or starve, then this idea of freedom is wanting. It is no more than the Mafia's 'offer you can't refuse'. Freedom in this sense is a mockery of the Enlightenment ideal,[22] even if the options in modern capitalism are less stark than 'work or starve'.

Because in a market all participants must agree freely to the contract for a transaction to occur, they appear to be equals in free self-determination. But in an important sense this is merely appearance. They may in fact be highly unequal as a consequence of their socialization and this may bear significantly on how well they fare within a competitive market economy. Mainstream economics ignores the social formation or socialization of its market participants. The resultant ideological thrust is that the child of a Rockefeller and one of a prostitute have equal freedom. Each merits what it achieves; each is to blame for what it fails to achieve.

In a market economy decisions are made instrumentally. Mainstream economics depicts these given ends as utility maximization for the worker/consumer and profit maximization for the firm. The market system minimizes the extent to which workers, consumers, and business decision-makers might meet in what Habermas calls 'discursive will formation' to assume democratic control over the nature of work, over what it is that might constitute rational consumption, and over what might be socially ideal business decisions. Even if neoclassical economics were assumed to capture authentically the individual instrumental decision-making within the market system, it does not do so critically. Consequently it presents the market system itself as a given, if not the most crucial, social component of the natural order.

Habermas's ideal is undistorted communication. The ideal is that participants in discourse put aside all motives but the pursuit of agreement according to the best reasoned argument. In the marketplace, by contrast, the process is instrumental or strategic: the goal is to persuade the other to behave in a manner most advantageous to oneself. This persuasion does not celebrate undistorted communication as an ideal. If undistorted communication should be the most profitable strategy, then so be it. But if distorted communication might be yet more profitable, then it would be the ideal. If sophisticated psychological ruses succeed in persuading the other in one's favour, they are the ideal.[23] This 'psychotechnic manipulation of behaviour' perpetuates a social order in which 'men . . . make their history with will, but without consciousness' (Habermas 1970a, p. 118). The persuasion within the marketplace could not be further from Habermas's ideal in which 'no force except that of the better argument is exercised, and . . . as a result, all motives except that of the cooperative search for truth are excluded' (Habermas 1975, p. 108). And because neoclassical economics uncritically accepts this opportunistic instrumentalism, it fails the standards which Habermas wishes to set for critical social theory.

It is important to note at this point that a substantial portion of the differences between Habermas's and neoclassical economics may be traceable to differing conceptions of human nature. Mainstream economics assumes that all behaviour is not only self-interested, but calculatingly self-interested. Habermas, by contrast, appears to hold out for the possibility of human behaviour, which although perhaps still self-interested, is not calculatingly so: 'I speak of *communicative actions* when social interactions are co-ordinated not through the egocentric calculations of success of every individual but through co-operative achievements of understanding among participants' (Habermas 1982, p. 264). To the extent that this passage implies the possibility of altruism, neoclassical economics would rule it invalid on the grounds of the so-called free-rider problem.[24]

EXPANDING THE DOMAIN OF COMMUNICATIVE ACTION

It is a frustrating aspect of Habermas's project that he has not provided more concrete examples of just what more ideal social institutions might look like. His vagueness on this score is captured in the following passage:

I can imagine the attempt to arrange a society democratically only as a self-controlled learning process. It is a question of finding arrangements which can ground the presumption that the basic institutions of the society and the basic political decisions would meet with the unforced agreement of all those involved, if they could participate, as free and equal, in discursive will-formation. Democratization cannot mean an *a priori* preference for a specific type of organization, for example, for so-called direct democracy.

(Habermas 1984, p. 186)

Presumably, undistorted communication will be necessary for the evolution of more rational social institutions. But this would seem to beg the question of what institutional changes might permit an expansion of realms for undistorted communication. And on this score, it would appear that in spite of Habermas's apparent reticence to address concrete institutional change,[25] there is one area in modern democratic societies that calls for transformation more than any other to be in a better conformity with his conception of democracy as a self-learning process. That area is the workplace. It could be argued that the workplace is the most important remaining domain of unfreedom in modern industrial society. Most workers neither own nor control the tools and resources with which they work. They experience little participation in the nature of one of the most, if not the most, central activities of their lives. They are bossed about, often within highly bureaucratic and authoritarian organizational structures. Because they must frequently take and execute orders uncritically from above, the workplace does not socialize them in democratic self-determination. Indeed, they are socialized in its opposite – in unquestioning obedience to authority. Given the central importance of the workplace, it would be surprising if these authoritarian attitudes did not spill over into other domains of the social world.

A move toward worker ownership and control of the firms in which they work could constitute an important step in the 'decolonization of the life-world'. It would not only directly expand the area of communicative action, it would also be important in socializing citizens to recognizing the rationality of open discursive will-formation in other social spheres. In fact, it seems to fit Habermas's ideal rather closely in so far as that ideal is:

> to arrest the destruction of solidaristic forms of life and to generate new forms of solidaristic collective life – in other words, life-forms with possibilities for expression, with space for moral-practical orientations, life-forms which offer a context within which one's own identity and that of the others can be unfolded less problematically, and in a less damaged way.

> (Habermas in Dews 1986, p. 144)

As an aside, it is interesting to note that workplace democracy is politically attractive from the vantage points of both the right and left. Yet it is neither capitalism nor socialism. The *differentia specifica* of capitalism is that workers are separated from ownership and control of the tools and resources with which they work. The *differentia specifica* of socialism is state ownership of these means of production. Workplace democracy can be conceived to vest ownership, control, and responsibility with those most intimately connected to the means of production. In accordance with the preferences of the political right, it maintains the sanctity of both private property and free markets. And the elimination of current capital–labour strife might well eliminate the need for much state intervention (e.g., in workplace safety, labour−capital dispute arbitration). In accordance with political preferences on the left, workers would no longer be 'alienated' from the means of production. They would work with democratic rights of self-determination in community settings. No longer would an underclass be needed to hold down wages and bear the greatest costs of the deflation-ary phase of the political business cycle which results from capital−labour strife.

At first glance it appears odd that a body of doctrine such as mainstream economics, which has since its modern beginnings celebrated human freedom, would essentially ignore the unfreedom of the workplace. In fact, although workplace democracy has been an important goal of many noted social reformers for practically 200 years, it is possible to take economics degrees in most US colleges and universities without ever coming into contact with the topic. There are several aspects to modern economics which might help clarify this seeming anomaly: as noted earlier, the freedom celebrated by mainstream economics is confined to the decision-making of asocial and ahistorical individuals. There is no systematic inquiry into their socialization, into how their preference functions are formed. The focus is upon the worker's free choice of an employer. In addition, work is typically depicted as yielding disutility and therefore an activity which only a bribe might bring forth. There is little focus on work as an outlet for self-expression and creativity as well as a source of community and solidarity with others. Of course, the depiction of work as unpleasant mirrors the nature of many, if not most, jobs in industrial society. However, the theory does not attempt to clarify why, given our abundance, such work continues to exist, other than to suggest that there is a trade-off between enjoyable work and income, and that free-willed workers must therefore choose the latter.

A third reason why workplace democracy receives so little attention is traceable to the positivist limitation of scope. The question of workplace democracy is one of institutional change; and, as noted earlier, mainstream economics' adherence to positivistic canons of correct scientific procedure results in a reluctance to give theoretical treatment to institutional change. The problem is that institutions are founded on values, and economists fear that to take on such issues is to stray from science. Ironically, the positivist doctrine − which economists believe will protect them from ideology − serves itself as an ideology which blinds them both to the ideological thrust of their own theoretical stance and the need to be ever critical of their own personal preconceptions.

TOWARD A CRITICAL ECONOMIC SCIENCE

To be capable of fully providing public enlightenment, economics would need to abandon its naïve confidence that positivist canons of science can shield the discipline from ideological distortions. It would need to struggle more consciously toward identifying ideology, as well as checking its own vulnerability to serving as ideology. The problem of ideology is, of course, central to Habermas' project. He conceives of his task in much the same manner as did Marx and the earlier Frankfurt school – to set forth the fundaments of critical social theory.[27] Critical social theory would be one capable of self-reflection. It would be capable of the self-examination which promises a more effective rooting out of ideological distortions. By aiding humanity in moving beyond imprisonment in ideology, it would assist humans in assuming mastery of their own destinies.

All social theory serves to legitimate social conditions and action. This social-world legitimation is *per se* neither good nor bad. It is unavoidable. It is the process through which humans give meaning and guidance to their existence.[28] The task of critical social thought is to make this legitimation transparent, to enable us to better understand whether that which is legitimated furthers or impedes human well-being. In pre-modern society, religion served as the predominant over-arching meaning, or legitimation system. In modern times, as Joan Robinson has colourfully put it, economics has essentially replaced religion, and the legitimation task has become that of justifying 'the ways of Mammon to man'.

A critical economic science would strive to demystify or dereify socio-economic institutions to reveal the extent to which, as human products, they are capable of being transformed to improve the human condition. A self-reflective economic science would not only strive to understand itself in terms of its legitimation function, but it would also share this understanding with the public it serves in the struggle for free self-determination. It would aspire, as Richard Bernstein has put it, 'to bring the subjects themselves to full self-consciousness of the contradictions implicit in their material existence, to penetrate the ideological mystifications and forms of false consciousness that distort the meaning of existing social conditions' (Bernstein 1976, p. 182).

Mainstream economics, in its positivistic and instrumental orientation, pretends to be principally concerned with discovering regularities and correlations within the economic order which might permit greater prediction and control of economic phenomena. However, its uncritical stance, combined with its pretence of ethical neutrality, has precluded attempts to differentiate those regularities and correlations representing invariant forms of social life from those which merely 'express ideologically frozen relations of dependence that can in principle be transformed' (Habermas 1971, p. 310). Regularities which represent the ideological imprisonment of humans make predictions of social phenomena more likely. Indeed, the more firmly ideology is entrenched, the greater will be predictive power. Such predictions can become powerful instruments for control and manipulation of society by the state or private centres of concentrated power.

To become a more critical social science in a Habermasian sense, economics would have to embrace a hermeneutical dimension. Others have also argued for the crucial importance of a hermeneutical or interpretive dimension for social theory. But what stands out as unique within Habermas's formulation is his insistence that this interpretive dimension must be supplemented by a critical or self-reflective dimension. The task is not merely to understand meaning and intentionality, but to do so critically. The goal is not merely to understand, but to do so in a manner which enables us to recognize and transcend ideology.[29]

From a Habermasian perspective, a critical economic science would need to be continually aware of both the manner in which it socially evolved and the social functions which it serves. Both dimensions are hermeneutical or interpretive. In seeking an understanding of its own self-formation, economics would probe for the dialectical relationship between the evolution of modern society and modern economic thought. It would need to understand why certain meanings were given to certain economic phenomena as opposed to others. It would need to ask such questions as: By accepting ends or values as externally given, does economics stabilize relations of power by providing them with legitimacy? Why was there such a radical and total shift from what Marx termed a 'sphere of production' perspective to a 'sphere of circulation' perspective in the latter part of the nineteenth century, even though it meant a restriction of scope for the discipline? Why does contemporary economics view individual behaviour in an asocial and ahistorical manner? Why it is that the discipline is preoccupied with a form of formalism which seems to promise so little fruit? Why, in spite of so much evidence to the contrary, does it continue to view the state as a neutral constable of the peace?

In a horizontal dimension, a critical economic science would seek to understand its own social functioning, the manner in which its own categories and conceptual relationships influence the self-understanding of the public it serves. It would recognize the distinction between control and manipulation of the material world and the social world. It would see that whereas providing guidance for the former is part of its liberating potential, to provide either guidance or legitimation for the manipulation and control of the social world is to constrain, if not reduce, human freedom. It would seek to understand economic actors, not merely as mechanical self-interested hedonists, but as social beings who behave with intentions and meanings.[30]

From a Habermasian perspective, then, an ideal economic science would need to embrace two dimensions that currently are accorded no significant role within the mainstream of the discipline. These dimensions are the hermeneutical or interpretative and the critical. Without these two crucial components for social theory, economics is unnecessarily handicapped from aiding humans in their struggle for liberation, not just from material privation, but also from social strife and domination.

NOTES

1 Understandably, this has generated an enormous body of critical books and articles on Habermas's project. For the interested reader, the most comprehensive of these remains McCarthy, 1978.

2 Benjamin Ward has suggested that, since Keynes, economics has undergone a 'formalist revolution' in which 'the proof has replaced the argument' (Ward 1972, p. 41). Piero V. Mini (1974), by contrast, argues that this formalism, what he terms 'the logic of Cartesianism', has plagued economics since its modern beginnings. Robert Kuttner reports that Nobel Laureate Wassily Leontief has become so distressed with the profession's increasing 'preoccupation with imaginary, hypothetical, rather than with observable reality', that he has ceased publishing in economics journals (Kuttner 1985, p. 78).

3 In his earlier work, Habermas conceived of existential human needs as leading to knowledge-constitutive human interests (i.e., general human interests which would serve to guide the search and generation of knowledge). Although Habermas has not fully abandoned this knowledge–interest theory perspective (see Dews 1986, pp. 152, 197), it no longer plays a central role within his more recent work. Instead, the focus has shifted to an examination of the nature of knowledge in the presuppositions of communication.

4 In differentiating his categories from those of Marx, Habermas draws on Max Weber's distinction between purposive-rational action and value-rational action. Weber's distinction, as will be seen below, is evident in Habermas's characterization of different forms of rationality.

5 'If we assume that the human species maintains itself through the socially coordinated activities of its members and that this coordination is established through communication – and in certain spheres of life, through communication aimed at reaching agreement – then the reproduction of the species *also* requires satisfying the conditions of a rationality inherent in communicative action' (Habermas 1984, p. 397).

6 It should be noted that Habermas recognizes the need for a hermeneutical procedure in the natural sciences as well:

> The natural sciences also have to deal with hermeneutic problems on the theoretical, but especially on the metatheoretical level; however, they do not have first to gain access to their object domain through hermeneutic means. The difference between the observer's access to a physically measurable object domain from the third-person perspective, on the one hand, and access to a symbolically prestructured object domain in the performative attitude of a participant in communication, on the other hand, has consequences not only for research *technique*; they reach deeply into the *logic* of investigation in the objectivating and meaning–understanding sciences.
>
> (Habermas 1982, p. 274)

7 For Habermas, the life-world is 'the horizon within which communicative actions are "always already" moving . . . we can think of the lifeworld as represented by a culturally transmitted and linguistically organized stock of interpretative patterns. . . . [It] is given to the experiencing subject as unquestionable' (Habermas 1987, pp. 119, 124, 130).

8 Habermas believes that Marx tended to see labour, or the struggle with nature, as necessitating just such a unique set of social institutions, of determining interaction. That is, according to Habermas's interpretation, Marx often slipped toward reducing interaction to labour alone, to locating the self-formation of the human species as traceable to labour 'in the last instance'.

9 For an extensive treatment of the centrality of this communicative process within economic science, see McCloskey (1985).

10　This instrumentalism, as well as the positivist criteria of theory validation, were most strikingly represented by the explosive rise in the importance of econometrics.

11　This essay is the most frequently cited statement of the appropriate methodology for scientific economics. It often appears in the introductory sections of college course syllabuses and is probably the only methodological essay with which most economists are familiar.

12　For an exposition as well as defence of Friedman's instrumentalism, see Boland (1979).

13　In the sociological language which Habermas employs, economics would complement its 'systems' perspective within which the behaviour of social actors is viewed in a mechanical manner, with a 'life-world' perspective within which importance is given to the meanings and intentions which social actors give to their existence. Habermas insists that these perspectives presuppose each other and that their synthesis is essential if social theory is to realize its full liberating potential.

14　As is the case within the Marxist tradition, Habermas believes internal contradictions threaten capitalism with crises which portend post-capitalist society. However, whereas Marxists have typically located the source of crises within the socio-economic domain, Habermas finds it within the socio-cultural. The contradictions have less to do with labour than with legitimation. For example, since the advent of Keynesian economics, the state has become more overtly involved in ensuring the profitability of private production. Yet this socialization of the conditions of production runs counter to the market logic of just desserts, or of the legitimacy of the private appropriation of surplus value. See, especially, Habermas 1975.

15　'Marx, to be sure, viewed the problem of making history with will and consciousness as one of the *practical* mastery of previously ungoverned processes of social development. Others, however, have understood it as a *technical* problem. They want to bring society under control in the same way as nature by reconstructing it according to the pattern of self-regulated systems of purposive-rational action and adaptive behavior. This intention is to be found not only among technocrats of capitalist planning but also among those of bureaucratic socialism' (Habermas 1970a, pp. 116–17). Although Habermas considers himself a Marxist, he shows no preference for state socialism over capitalism: 'I am unable to persuade myself that, from the standpoint of social evolution, state socialism is any more "mature" or "progressive" than state capitalism' (Habermas in Dews, p. 41).

16　Habermas believes that this has been carried to the point where '[t]he dependence of the professional on the politician appears to have reversed itself' (Habermas 1970a, p. 63).

17　Habermas states the issues more forcefully: 'The solution of technical problems is not dependent on public discussion. Rather, public discussions could render problematic the framework within which the tasks of government action present themselves as technical ones. Therefore the new politics of state interventionism requires a depoliticization of the mass of the population. To the extent that practical questions are eliminated, the public realm also loses its political function' (Habermas 1970a, pp. 103–4).

18　A number of economists on both the right and the left have come to see the modern business cycle as more a political phenomenon than the consequence of more traditional economic forces as elaborated by Marx or Keynes. See, for instance: Nordhaus (1975); Paldam (1981); Heilbroner (1985); Boddy and Crotty (1974).

19　The Keynesian attempt to define a specific minimum of unemployment which can be expected even at 'full employment' provides another example. This minimum is derived analytically *ceteris paribus*, again assuming no institutional change. Because the general thrust of Keynesian economics is to ignore the potential for those institutional changes which might enable a further reduction in the so-called minimum unemployment rate, the public is inclined to believe that such reductions are not scientifically possible.

20 'We shall understand "democracy" to mean the institutionally secured forms of general and public communication that deal with the practical question of how men can and want to live under the objective conditions of their ever-expanding power of control' (Habermas 1970a, p. 57).

21 Habermas calls 'the research program aimed at reconstructing the universal validity basis of speech' *universal pragmatics* (Habermas 1979, p. 5). The sciences within this research programme address competencies which are universal within the human species, such as the ability to understand and speak languages. The most widely known examples of work within this domain are those of Noam Chomsky and Jean Piaget.

22 Even Adam Smith recognized that where the employers and employees are at odds, the freedom of the latter is severely constricted: 'A landlord, a farmer, a master workman, could generally live a year or two upon the stocks which they have already acquired. Many workmen could not subsist a week, few could subsist a month, and scarce any a year without employment' (Smith 1937, p. 66).

23 Those who defend the market order against this Veblenian or Galbraithian charge typically do so by arguing that competition for contracts, even where communication is intentionally distorted, not only educates the individual to new possibilities, but inculcates a more critical potential for discounting false claims. Whatever the merits of this defence it remains largely a phenomenon between individual private actors pursuing their own narrow self-interest. It does not appear to fit Habermas's ideal of individuals deliberating their own public well-being through free and open discourse.

24 Surprisingly, Habermas has not set forth a well-developed theory of human behaviour. Perhaps yet more surprising is that his critics have not taken much note of this. One exception, Agnes Heller, notes that 'Habermasian man has . . . no body, no feelings; the "structure of personality" is identified with cognition, language and interaction.' Consequently, '[t]he question of whether, and, if so, how, distortion of communication is motivated cannot be answered by Habermas; nor can he answer the question of what would motivate us to get rid of the distortion. The assumption that consensus can be achieved in a process of enlightenment is in fact no answer: the *will* to achieve consensus is the problem in question' (Heller 1982, pp. 22, 25).

25 On this score Habermas has stated that 'social theory would be overstepping its competence . . . if it undertook to project desirable forms of life into the future, instead of criticizing existing forms of life' (Habermas in Dews 1986, p. 171). However, it could be argued that Habermas misses an important dimension in just how it is that social thought might abet society in enlightenment as to the nature of the good and just social order. By setting forth 'desirable forms of life' which are argued to be realizable, social theorists provide the public with alternative models which can be discussed within the public forum. Indeed, it is part of the legacy of positivism that social theorists feel constrained from discussing such models at all.

26 Yet Habermas does not apparently view a movement toward workplace democracy as an effective and attractive response to the 'crumbling of the welfare state compromise': 'I wonder . . . if we should not preserve part of today's complexity within the economic system, limiting the discursive formation of the collective will precisely to the decisive and central structures of political power: that is, apart from the labour process as such, to the few but continuously made fundamental decisions which will determine the overall structure of social production

and, naturally, of distribution' (Habermas in Dews 1986, pp. 67, 107). Given the superior efficiency of many worker owned and controlled firms, Habermas's presumption that workplace democracy would necessitate a sacrifice of efficiency is certainly questionable. It could also be argued that in distancing himself from Marx, Habermas has overtly discounted Marx's understanding of the self-creation of humans through labour. However, Habermas at times appears victim to the illusion – which has been presented as horrid by some, and utopian by others – that work is disappearing, or will do so. See, for instance, Habermas in Dews 1986, pp. 140–1.

27 As Habermas's critics have made clear, this is no mean task. The problem is how to move beyond relativism without falling into a discredited objectivism; that is, how can a non-foundationalist grounding for critical theory be established? Habermas's earlier theory of knowledge-guiding human interests and his later theory of communicative action have been attempts to deal with just this problem.

28 Peter L. Berger and Thomas Luckmann have explained the necessity of legitimation in terms of our 'instinct poverty'. Unlike other species, humans possess relatively little in the way of a fixed relationship to their environment. Although humans possess genetically inherited drives, 'these drives are highly unspecialized and undirected'. There is, then, an intrinsic 'world-openness', and it is through cultural institutions and legitimation that a relative 'world-closedness' is achieved. In other words cultural institutions and legitimation complement inherited drives to provide behavioural guidance for humans (Berger and Luckmann 1967, p. 148).

29 This insistence that interpretation must be fused with ideology-critique led to one of the most famous of Habermas's interchanges with another philosopher, Hans-Georg Gadamer. According to Gadamer, Habermas traps himself into the sort of foundationalism which he believes himself to be beyond. For superb treatments of this debate, see McCarthy (1978) pp. 187–93, and McCarthy (1982).

30 The argument that economists must supplement the third-person stance of the detached observer with the first-person stance of the participant observer is seldom heard within the discipline. For an insightful essay on this topic – tellingly not published in an economics journal, see Sivakumar 1986.

REFERENCES

Berger, Peter L. and Luckmann, Thomas (1967) *The Social Construction of Reality* Garden City, N.Y.: Anchor Books.

Berger, Peter L. (1969) *The Sacred Canopy*, New York: Doubleday.

Bernstein, Richard J. (1976) *The Restructuring of Social and Political Theory*, New York: Harcourt Brace Jovanovich.

—— (ed.) (1985) *Habermas and Modernity*, Cambridge: MIT Press.

Boddy, Radford and Crotty, James (1974) 'Class conflict, Keynesian policies, and the business cycle', *Monthly Review* 26 (5), October 1974, pp. 1–7.

Boland, Lawrence (1979) 'A critique of Friedman's critics', *Journal of Economic Literature* 17 (June), pp. 503–22.

Dews, Peter (ed.) (1986) *Habermas, Autonomy and Solidarity: Interviews with Jürgen Habermas*, London: Verso.

Friedman, Milton (1953) 'The methodology of positive economics', *Essays in Positive Economics*, Chicago: University of Chicago Press.

Habermas, Jürgen (1970a) *Toward a Rational Society*, trans. Jeremy J. Shapiro, Boston: Beacon Press.

—— (1970b) 'Toward a theory of communicative competence', Boston: Beacon Press.

—— (1971) *Knowledge and Human Interests*, trans. Jeremy J. Shapiro, Boston: Beacon Press.

—— (1974) *Theory and Practice*, trans. John Viertel, Boston: Beacon Press.

—— (1975) *Legitimation Crisis*, trans. Thomas McCarthy, Boston: Beacon Press.

—— (1979) *Communication and The Evolution of Society*, trans. Thomas McCarthy, Boston: Beacon Press.

—— (1982) 'A reply to my critics', in John B. Thompson and David Held (eds) *Habermas: Critical Debates*, Cambridge, Massachussetts: MIT Press, pp. 219–83.

—— (1984) *The Theory of Communicative Action*, vol. 1, trans. Thomas McCarthy, Boston: Beacon Press.

—— (1987) *The Theory of Communicative Action*, vol. 2, trans. Thomas McCarthy, Boston: Beacon Press.

Heilbroner, Robert L. (1985) *The Nature and Logic of Capitalism*, New York: W.W. Norton.

Heller, Agnes (1982) 'Habermas and Marxism', in John B. Thompson and David Held (eds) *Habermas: Critical Debates*, Cambridge, Massachusetts: MIT Press, pp. 21–41.

Kuttner, Robert (1985) 'The poverty of economics', *The Atlantic Monthly*, Feb., pp. 74–84.

McCarthy, Thomas (1978) *The Critical Theory of Jürgen Habermas*, Cambridge, Massachusetts: MIT Press.

—— (1982) 'Rationality and relativism: Habermas's "overcoming" of hermeneutics', in John B. Thompson and David Held (eds) *Habermas: Critical Debates*, Cambridge, Massachusetts: MIT Press, pp. 57–78.

McCloskey, Donald (1985) *The Rhetoric of Economics*, Madison, Wisconsin: University of Wisconsin Press.

Mini, Piero (1974) *Philosophy and Economics*, Gainseville: University of Florida Press.

Nordhaus, William (1975) 'The political business cycle', *Review of Economic Studies* 42, April, pp. 169–90.

Paldam, Martin (1981) 'An essay on the rationality of economic policy: the test case of the election cycle', *Public Choice* 37, November, pp. 287–305.

Sivakumar, S.S. (1986) 'Is method all madness? Comments from a participant-observer economist', *Social Research* 53 (4), Winter, pp. 615–46.

Smith, Adam (1937 [1776]) *The Wealth of Nations*, New York: Modern Library.

Ynger, Roberto Mangabeira (1975) *Knowledge and Politics*, New York: Free Press.

Ward, Benjamin (1972) *What's Wrong with Economics*, New York: Basic Books.

UNIVERSITY OF BRISTOL
Department of Philosophy

9 Woodland Road
Bristol
BS8 1TB

7 Austrian economics

A hermeneutic approach

Ludwig M. Lachmann

INTRODUCTION

In recent years, hermeneutics as a style of thought has captured the imagination of bold minds and made its impact on a number of disciplines for which it seems to hold a promise of exciting departures. Economics has thus far not been among them. This is the more remarkable since in Germany, at least before the First World War – in the years when the *Methodenstreit* was petering out – the merits of the method of *Verstehen*, backed by the authority of Max Weber, were widely discussed.

During the 1920s, when there was no single dominant school of economic theory in the world, and streams of thought flowing from diverse sources (such as Austrian, Marshallian and Paretian) each had their own sphere of influence, 'interpretive' voices (mostly of Weberian origin) were still audible on occasions. After 1930, however, economists all over the world followed Pareto in embracing the method of classical mechanics as the only truly 'scientific' method. In the decades that followed this became the dominant style of thought in almost all countries. In 1931 the Econometric Society was founded amid much naïve enthusiasm. An arid formalism began to pervade most areas of economics and to sap the vigour of analytical thought. In this milieu, rational action came to be regarded as meaning nothing but the maximization of given functions!

In subsequent decades, economists began to live as if they were in a citadel of their own. Opening new vistas to them will not be an easy task. To those who grew up in isolation, nourished by the products of the textbook industry under the aegis of its scribes and typesetters, these vistas may well become a traumatic experience. So we have reason to go about our task with some care.

As regards the scope and breadth of this chapter, let it be said at once that any attempt on my part to deal with the subject of hermeneutics as a 'style of thought' on as broad a canvas as its present significance and promise to the social sciences (let alone other disciplines) call for, would far surpass my competence and knowledge. In what follows I shall therefore have to confine myself to the significance of hermeneutics for economics – in particular, for the renewal of economic thought. I also propose to restrict this chapter's scope even further by limiting it to Austrian economics, except in the last section.

Twenty years ago, in the Festschrift for Alexander Mahr, Professor of Economics in Vienna, I attempted to show that we have to see the main contribution the Austrians made to the 'subjective revolution' of the 1870s in the 'interpretive turn' (although I did not use these words) which they managed to impart to the evolution of economic thought at that critical period (Lachmann 1977, pp. 45–64). My present purpose is to pursue this line of thought further and explore the possible consequences if a similar 'turn' were to be given to the evolution of contemporary thought by means of ideas grounded in Austrian economics. If modern Austrians were to succeed in replacing the present neoclassical paradigm – an embodiment of desiccated formalism – by a body of thought more congenial to the spirit of hermeneutics, what exactly might they hope to accomplish? Although mainly interested in what Austrian economics might have to say on these matters, we shall find, later on in this chapter, that in this context the work of certain non-Austrian economists as a contribution to hermeneutical thought, even though they were probably unaware of it, is not to be neglected.

WHY HERMENEUTICS?

There are of course many reasons why, and respects in which, the neo-classical textbook paradigm is inadequate. Its level of abstraction is too high and, what is worse, there appears to be no way in which it could be lowered so as to enable us to approach reality gradually. Complaints about the 'scaffolding' that is never removed have been numerous. The paradigm casts no light on everyday life in an industrial world. The 'life-world' in which all our empirical knowledge of social matters is embedded does not exist for it.

But what to Austrians is most objectionable is the neoclassical style of thought, borrowed from classical mechanics, which makes us treat the human mind as a mechanism and its utterances as determined by external circumstances. Action is here confused with mere reaction. There is no choice of ends. Given a 'comprehensive preference field' for each agent, what is there to choose? The outcome of all acts of choice is here pre-determined. In response to changing market prices men perform meaning-less acts of mental gymnastics by sliding up and down their indifference curves. All this is far removed from meaningful action in our 'life-world'.

In reality men make plans to achieve their purposes and later on attempt to carry them out. These plans are based on, and oriented to, means available and ends freely chosen. They may collide with those of others or may turn out to be unachievable for other reasons (e.g., that in the course of action actors become aware that means counted upon are no longer available or show themselves less efficient than they were expected to be). Plans may therefore have to be revised or even abandoned. But whatever happens, observable economic phenomena – such as prices or quantities produced or exchanged – are the outcomes of the interaction of our plans. Action guided by plans causes economic phenomena. We might say that economic phenomena are the outward manifestations of action guided by plans.

Austrian economics is perhaps regarded as lending theoretical expression to the features of everyday life in the type of market economy just described. In its essence Austrian economics may be said to provide a voluntaristic theory of action, not a mechanistic one. Austrians cannot but reject a conceptual scheme, such as the neoclassical, for which man is not a bearer of active thought but a mere bundle of 'dispositions' in the form of a 'comprehensive preference field'. Austrians are thus compelled to look for conceptual schemes informed by a style of thought that is altogether different. Perhaps hermeneutics can provide us with an answer. In this context the following points call for our attention.

Action consists of a sequence of acts to which our mind assigns *meaning*. The elements of action are thus utterances of our minds and have to be treated as such. In studying action and interaction on a social scale our task is therefore an interpretative one; we are concerned with the actors' content of consciousness.

These facts have no counterpart in nature. In our observation of natural phenomena no meaning is accessible to us. All we can do is to put our observations in a certain order, an arbitrary order. In all those cases in which our observations serve a practical purpose, the order we impose on them will depend on this latter. In the absence of a practical purpose, the order will probably conform to the direction of our research interest. Phenomena of human action, by contrast, display an *intrinsic* order we dare not ignore: that which the human actors assigned to them in the making and carrying out of their plans. As social scientists we have no right to substitute our own arbitrary designs for those which are implicit in action shaped by the human will – 'designs' here lending expression to its *intrinsic* meaning.

Plans, of course, often fail. They may fail for a large number of reasons, but one of them, already mentioned above, is of particular interest to us: the collision of one actor's plan with that of others. Such conflict of plans, so far from invalidating the importance of plans for our understanding of forms of interaction, actually shows how important a help they are for our insight into problems here arising. Who would deny that our understanding of the fact that changes in incomes and employment may be due to a failure of savings and investment plans to match, has increased our insight into macroeconomic problems?

A similar conclusion applies to the problem of tracing the unintended consequences of action. This is no doubt one of the tasks of economic theory, but how could we hope to accomplish it unless we have first mastered the theory of intended action? We have to realize that only once we are able to handle the tools of the logic of means and ends – the basis of the voluntaristic theory of action – with some adroitness, can we proceed with confidence to tackle the unintended consequences of action. No mechanistic scheme bound to confuse action with reaction is likely to be of help to us here. The fact that plans guide action and provide it with meaning enables us to find the causes of conflicts of action in the incompatibility of plans constituted by acts of diverse minds. The consequences of action, whether intended or unintended, remain the economist's concern.

Finally, we have to remember that our mind is never 'at rest'. Our thoughts are, for many purposes at least, best regarded as particles of an unending stream, the stream of consciousness. Our knowledge consists of thoughts, and can therefore hardly be regarded as a stock, except at a point of time. Time cannot elapse without the state of knowledge changing. 'Economics, concerned with thoughts and only secondarily with things, the objects of those thoughts, must be as protean as thought itself' (Shackle 1972, p. 246). It is the task of the social sciences to make happenings in this protean realm intelligible to us.

The answer to the question 'why hermeneutics?' is, then, to be found in our need for conceptual schemes more congenial to the freedom of our wills and the requirements of a voluntaristic theory of action than anything we have at present. Is hermeneutics likely to assist us in this endeavour?

WHAT IS HERMENEUTICS?

Hermeneutics connotes the style of thought of classical scholarship. It was at first in the scholarly exegesis of texts that those problems arose which led to the evolution of various methods of interpretation whose relative merits have to be assessed by the criteria of access to intrinsic meaning.

Whenever we read a text, we want to grasp its meaning, and an effort of interpretation is called for. Where our text is of a narrative nature, we must understand how the various parts of the story we are told are related to one another, in order to grasp its full meaning. Where it is of exhortatory character, we need to be sure we understand what we are exhorted to do or to omit. Where it contains a religious or legal prescript, we have to ascertain that we understand precisely to what kind of cases it applies. In all such cases we have to interpret the text to pervade to its meaning.

For centuries past, long before the rise of modern science, scholars have applied these methods, whether they studied the Bible or the Pandects, read Polybius or Tacitus, or translated Averroes or Avicenna from the Arabic. Theirs was a hermeneutical activity.

As we are reading a text, page by page, we do not merely grasp the meaning of sentences and passages, but while doing so we gradually form a notion in our mind of what the author wants to tell us in his work. The meaning of the text as a whole gradually emerges before our eyes from the network of meanings constituted by single passages. When we come across a passage hard to understand we must attempt to interpret it in the light of the 'major meaning' we derive from our reading of the text as a whole.

In all this we are applying a *principle of limited coherence*, the coherence of all the utterances of the same mind. From our general knowledge of life and letters, we feel we have a right to assume that an author will not want to contradict himself. A 'difficult passage' has to be interpreted so as to cohere with what we take to be 'the spirit of the whole'. In awkward cases, where this proves impossible, we may have to revise our interpretation of the 'major meaning' of the text. Or we may conclude that the author 'changed his mind' before writing the passage under examination – that our text is not the manifestation of 'one mind at one time', but that it reflects, almost as a mirror would, the change of the author's mind over time. Since a voluminous text may be the work of many years, the existence of such a possibility is not surprising.

In all these cases our interpretation is an application of critical reason. Hermeneutics is in conformity with the maxims of critical rationalism. Our interpretation of a text is in principle always 'falsifiable'.

How do we pass from letters to life, from ancient texts to modern business transactions? What texts and phenomena of action have in common is that they both are utterances of human minds, that they have to exist as thoughts before they become manifest as observable phenomena. A text needs to be thought out before it is written down, a business transaction before it is entered upon.

A great step forward was taken, and the range of application of hermeneutical method considerably enhanced, when it gradually emerged from the work of historians (already of Greek and Roman historians) that these writers did not merely provide a chronicle of events but attempted to explain these events as human action in terms of ends and means, that they thus attempted to interpret action. This was an important insight of classical scholarship.

It is but a short step from historiography to the theoretical social sciences which produce ideal types of recurrent events, and thus provide historians with the analytical tools they need. And here we reach the point at which we are able to catch a glimpse of what the role of economics as a hermeneutic discipline might be like, and of the kind of 'interpretive turn' we might hope to impart to it.

Most economic phenomena are observable, but our observations need an interpretation of their context if they are to make sense and to add to our knowledge. Only meaningful utterances of a mind lend themselves to interpretation. Furthermore, all human action takes place within a context of 'intersubjectivity'; our common everyday world (the Schutzian 'life-world') in which the meanings we ascribe to our own acts and to those of others are typically not in doubt and taken for granted.

Our empirical knowledge of economic phenomena obtained by observation must in any case be interpreted as embedded within this context. Elucidation of their meaning cannot here mean that the economist as outside observer is entitled to assign to them whatever meaning suits his cognitive purpose. It must mean elucidation of the meaning assigned to them by various actors on the scene of observation within this context of intersubjective meanings.

Hermeneutic interpretation of economic phenomena therefore has to take place within a horizon of established meanings, with one such horizon for each society. Our phenomena observed have to be placed within an order constrained by this framework.

INSTITUTIONS AND THE AUSTRIAN SCHOOL

> Everyone agrees that the modelling of institutions by neoclassical economics is too sparse.
>
> (Hahn 1975, p. 363)

After what has been said in the preceding sections of this chapter, it is not hard to see that a more satisfactory treatment of institutions in economics, or at least one that could satisfy the demands of Austrian economists, will call for the infusion of a sizeable dose of the hermeneutic spirit. Institutions prescribe certain forms of conduct and discourage others. It is clear that those persons who conduct themselves in conformity with them must attribute some *meaning* to them. Such meaning must be elucidated to outside observers.

Or we might say that an institution is a network of constantly renewable meaningful relations between persons and groups of persons who may not all ascribe the same meaning to the same set of relations. The task of the student of institutions is to distil such meanings from his observations and to interpret them to his audience.

It is hardly possible to accuse today's orthodox economics of the neglect of institutions – in the sense that the latter are never mentioned, or at least implied, in their writings. Markets and firms, after all, are institutions. On however high a level of abstraction 'agents' may engage in exchange transactions, the enforceability of contracts and the protection of property are implied. And where would monetary economics be without financial institutions?

What strikes the student of hermeneutics when he approaches our subject is not the fact that institutions are ignored in modern orthodox economics, but the fact that, like natural phenomena, they are treated as externally given conditions of human action – whose origin may not be investigated and whose continued existence is taken for granted. *And nobody asks questions about their meaning.* In fact, few economists today possess a vocabulary that would permit them to ask such questions.

We thus confront a situation in which, while institutions are by no means ignored, most economists do not know what to do with them. They play with them like children playing with ancient coins about whose value and history they know nothing. Institutions belong to the realm of culture, not that of nature. They are immersed in history. Although we can observe their operations, our observations cannot disclose to us what meaning their objects have to those enmeshed in them, a meaning that varies from group to group and over time. It is impossible to elucidate such meaning until we realize that the mode of existence of institutions corresponds to, and varies with, the mode of orientation of those who participate in them. Such a mode of orientation is an element of culture, a web of thought – open to interpretation but not measurable. Most of our contemporaries have to ignore this fact. Plainly, owing to their lack of acquaintance with matters of culture, most of them are hermeneutically disabled. This is the real problem to which Professor Hahn's little euphemism, quoted above, gives rather inadequate expression. How are we to overcome it?

Economic institutions are situated in an area in which the realms of economics and sociology overlap. Terms of co-operation are therefore called for. Needless to say, these will be the easier to find the closer the levels of abstraction on which institutions are discussed in the two disciplines. Perhaps it will be helpful to look at some of the problems arising here from a historical perspective.

The Austrians made their contribution to this field early on, when in most of Europe sociology as an academic discipline did not yet exist. In 1883, in the *Untersuchungen*, Menger introduced the distinction between 'organic' and 'pragmatic' institutions – between those that are the products of spontaneous social processes and those that are products 'of the social will'. Money is an example of the former, legal norms are of the latter variety.

It took more than half a century before Alfred Schutz gained fame as (almost) the first sociologist of the Austrian school and a hermeneutic thinker of the first rank. Ludwig von Mises, for all his avowed apriorism, belonged to the same tradition. Professor Don Lavoie, in his contribution to the Lachmann-Festschrift ('Euclideanism versus hermeneutics: a reinterpretation of Misesian apriorism'), has convincingly argued that we should regard him as an 'interpretive' thinker. Whether von Mises, who was inclined to assign 'interpretation' to historiography only, would have liked the appellation is quite another question.

It is today almost forgotten, but we have reason to remember, that Max Weber, the great protagonist of the hermeneutic method in the social sciences, came across our problem in the early years of the century – the years when the *Methodenstreit* was gradually petering out. He concluded that in order to deal with institutions what was needed was a new discipline – 'economic sociology' – which would supplement, rather than supplant, economic theory as it then existed. In planning (as editor after 1908) what was to be a German encyclopaedia of the social sciences, the *Grundriss der*

Sozialökonomik, Weber decided that he himself would write a volume, *Economy and Society*, devoted to the new discipline, while prominent economists – such as Wieser, Schumpeter and others – would write the volumes on the various parts of economics proper.

It goes without saying that the situation we encounter today in regard to economic institutions is altogether different from that which Weber faced in his time. To him, economic theory meant Austrian economics – which was then enjoying its 'golden decade', the decade before 1914. This was the economic theory to be supplemented by his own work. It seemed reasonable to hope for co-operation between economists and sociologists on an approximately common level of discourse.

Where is such a common level to be found today? As long as economic theory is conducted at a level of abstraction on which meaningful utterances are made to lose their meaning, action appears to flow from (innate?) dispositions, and cultural phenomena are made up to look as though they were phenomena of nature, there can be little hope for bringing institutions into economics. What we need is the descent to a lower level of abstraction on which hermeneutical effort is possible and worthwhile. Economic sociology as a mere supplement to neoclassical theory will not do today.

Institutions reduce uncertainty by circumscribing the range of action of different groups of actors, buyers and sellers, creditors and debtors, employers and employees. We understand how they work by grasping the meaning of the orientation of these groups towards them. For us, orientation is a fundamental hermeneutic concept. Orientation, of course, changes in time, but it cannot be regarded as a 'function' of anything else. It does not fit into a world of 'function-maximizing' agents.

Some crucial problems arise here which concern the relationship between the individual institution and the institutional order as a whole. In a world of change, it seems, each institution has to be flexible but their order must be permanent. 'Law and Order' must be maintained if the market economy is to function. How is this possible? How can the whole persist if none of its parts is permanent?

We might look upon the institutional order as a merchant looks upon his inventory – that is, as consisting entirely of exchangeable parts. In the inventory, however, every part, by virtue of its being of value, is a substitute for every other part. But are all institutions substitutes for one another? Is there no complementarity among them? To the extent to which there is, there are limits to complete flexibility.

Or do we have to conceive of such complementarity in terms of a distinction between fundamental and immutable institutions, and other mutable and flexible ones? If so, might this distinction be a matter of degree rather than category?

In facing these intriguing questions we had better understand what kind of problems they are: problems pertaining to meaning and orientation. At some time it may become desirable, as Weber originally intended, to entrust the task of dealing with these and similar problems to a task force of economic sociologists. It goes without saying, perhaps, that their effort will be more likely to flourish if they are able to count upon a wide and sympathetic audience of other social scientists – among them many, we hope, from the sister discipline of economics.

HERMENEUTICAL ALLIES OF THE AUSTRIANS

Ultimate unifying simplicity is the aim or the dream of natural science in a sense which is not permissible for the study of human affairs. For the disciplines which envisage human conduct, policy, history and institutions, or art in all its forms, are directly and essentially concerned with the manifestations themselves, the manifoldness, the richness and the detailed particular variants and individual facts of these facets of humanity, rather than with dismissing them as the contingent outcomes of some original, general and essential principle which it is the real purpose of science to identify. The science of Nature and the science of Man stand in some sense back to back, the one looking inward at the Origin and the other outward at the Manifestation.

(Shackle 1972, p. 29)

At this juncture it must be one of the aims of economists of the Austrian school to give their discipline an 'interpretive turn' and to bring about the infusion of a considerable dose of the spirit of hermeneutics into the, at present somewhat enfeebled, body of economic thought. No doubt it will be an arduous task. Austrians, fortunately, do not have to shoulder it entirely on their own, but are able to call on some allies for help.

Hermeneutic thought has flowed in the past, and is still flowing today, from a variety of sources. Even within the narrow orbit of economic theory, as currently practised, traces of its influence can still be found today. In earlier decades of this century, as described above, it often had a noticeable influence. What matters more to our present purpose is that there have been, in this century (outside the Austrian ranks), three prominent economic thinkers whose work we may legitimately claim to have been at least strongly affected by hermeneutic influence, even though not all of them may have been aware of it: Knight, Keynes, and Shackle.

Knight at least was well aware of it. He knew Weber's work well, and the influence of the latter is clearly discernible in most of his methodological writings. In his famous (1940) paper, 'What is truth in economics?' originally a review of T.W. Hutchison's first book (published in 1938), Knight had this to say:

The whole subject matter of conduct – interests and motivation – constitutes a different realm of reality from the external world, and this fact gives to its problems a different order of subtlety and complexity than those of the sciences of (unconscious) nature.

The first fact to be recorded is that this realm of reality exists or 'is there'. This fact cannot be proved or argued or 'tested'. If anyone denies that men have interest or that 'we' have a considerable amount of valid knowledge about them, economics and all its works will simply be to such a person what the world of color is to the blind man. But there would still be one difference: a man who is physically, ocularly blind may still be rated of normal intelligence and in his right mind.

Second, as to the manner of our knowing or the source of knowledge; it is obvious that while our knowledge ('correct' observation) of physical human behavior and of correlated changes in the physical objects of non-human nature plays a necessary part in our knowledge of men's interests, the main source, far more important than in our knowledge of physical reality, is the same general process of intercommunication in social inter-course – and especially in that 'causal' intercourse, which has no important direct relation to any 'problem', either of knowledge or of action – which has been found to play a major role in our knowing of the physical world.

(Knight 1940, pp. 27–8)

In the case of Keynes, the hermeneutic quality of his thought is not as easy to document as that of Knight. Keynes was a thinker of an altogether different style, a pragmatist who mostly took very little interest in the methodology of the social sciences. The two passages we quote to attest the hermeneutic quality of his thought are both taken from letters addressed to disciples.

In the summer of 1935, before the publication of Keynes' book, *General Theory*, Robert Bryce, a Canadian student of Keynes, addressed Professor Hayek's seminar at the London School of Economics on the fundamental ideas of the forthcoming book. He appears to have reported to Keynes that at this seminar session most of the discussion turned on the definition of income to be used in the book. Evidently exasperated at this report, Keynes said in his reply to Bryce:

It is, I think, a further illustration of the appalling Scholasticism into which the minds of so many economists have got which allows them to take leave of their intuitions altogether. Yet in writing economics one is not writing a mathematical proof or a legal document. One is trying to arouse and appeal to the reader's intuitions; and if he has worked himself into a state where he has none, one is helpless.

(Keynes 1979, pp. 150–1)

We note that what Keynes here calls 'the reader's intuitions' is precisely what, in the language of phenomenology, would be described as our 'aware-ness of the life-world', and that what he means is just what Knight expressed in the excerpt quoted. The lack of a common vocabulary is one of the obstacles to the diffusion of hermeneutic thought among economists.

In July 1938, in a letter to Harrod, Keynes wrote:

I also want to emphasize strongly the point about economics being a moral science. I mentioned before that it deals with introspection and with values. I might have added that it deals with motives, expectations, psychological uncertainties. One has to be constantly on guard against treating the material as constant and homogeneous.

It is as though the fall of the apple to the ground depended on the apple's motives, on whether it was worthwhile falling to the ground, on whether the ground wanted the apple to fall, and on mistaken calculations on the part of the apple as to how far it was from the center of the earth.

(Keynes 1973, p. 300)

This passage marks Keynes as a subjectivist and an exponent of the hermeneutical style of thought.

Few can doubt that, in the second half of the twentieth century, Shackle as a hermeneutical thinker has been the great torch-bearer of enlightenment in the shadowy realm of economics. The passage quoted at the beginning of this section offers an example of the calibre of his thought. Hard as it is to sum up his achievement, the following reflection provides at least a hint of what we owe to him.

The fundamental flaw of neoclassical methodology lies in the confusion of action with reaction. Man in action is seen as a bundle of dispositions and not a bearer of thought. What difference does it make if we observe rather than ignore these distinctions? In action we reflect on means and ends, trying to fit the former to the latter, make plans and carry them out. As our ends lie in the unknowable (albeit not unimaginable) future, we have to exercise our imagination in reflecting upon them, and such exercise is incompatible with mere 'response to stimulus' or even the 'decoding of signals'.

We always knew, of course, that our plans might fail and our ends prove unattainable. To Shackle we owe the more pervasive insight that any action we start now may have any one of a large number of possible sequels which, if they did occur, might affect the conditions of our own future action, our own future means, leaving thus but little room for the constancy of parameters.

To the names of these three prominent non-Austrian thinkers we must, in justice, add that of Sir John Hicks who, for the last two decades, has often reminded us that economic events take place 'in time' and that men in action do not know the future.

It is not to be denied that 50 years ago the young John Richard Hicks showed himself inspired by the style of thought of classical mechanics, and with remarkable success, espoused the Paretian paradigm from which we are still suffering today. In 1936, at the Econometric Society conference in Oxford, he presided at the opening of that exhibition of Islamic art which brought him instant fame.

But all this happened a long time ago. The mature Sir John Hicks, our contemporary, has long since renounced his early beliefs and disavowed his affiliation to the Paretian paradigm. He now defends the methodological autonomy of economics. 'Economics, accordingly, if it is on the edge of the sciences (as we saw) is also on the edge of history; facing both ways, it is in a key position' (Hicks 1979, p. 4). He also now comes close to Mises in reminding econometricians that:

It is just that economics is in time, in a way that the natural sciences are not. All economic data are dated, so that inductive evidence can never do more than establish a relation which appears to hold within the period to which the data refer.

(Hicks 1979, p. 38)

What is to be done? While some conclusions to be drawn from the argument presented seem obvious, others are less readily discernible at present.

Austrians must join with non-Austrians in an effort to co-ordinate the hermeneutically relevant parts of their respective traditions, a task calling for historical perspicacity in selecting appropriate parts of these traditions as well as some dexterity in handling ideas. In short, the situation demands the typical skills of a 'broker of ideas' who has a flair for fitting together cognate ideas of various origins. Austrians and their hermeneutical allies must also attempt to establish some rapport with other social scientists and philosophers interested in exploring similar themes. The need for an 'economic sociology' in the study of institutions is an obvious example. Another is the need for reaching a new accord between economics and history in the light of what we recently learnt from Hicks (economics is 'facing both ways, it is in a key position') and of what is in any case a corollary of Shackle's teaching (see the quotation on p. 142).

Beyond the horizon constituted by these immediate tasks there loom other, more formidable, problems that will have to be tackled in the future.

The 'market process' is an item high on the agenda of the Austrian research programme. The market, needless to say, offers a particularly fascinating example of an area of intersubjectivity in which vast numbers of men interact with one another in the pursuit of their multifarious needs and interests. It calls for treatment by a method inspired by the hermeneutical style, a method which defies the spirit of orthodox formalism. As regards price formation (for example, a prominent feature of the market process), the different meanings assigned to it by different groups of participants (in particular, price setters and price takers) call for our attention.

At some time in the future the concept of 'plan' − a fundamental hermeneutic notion, as we saw − will have to be introduced into the theory of consumption. If firms make and carry out plans, why not households?

The realm of economics cannot forever remain closed to the rays of hermeneutical enlightenment.

REFERENCES

Hahn, F.H. (1975) 'Revival of political economy: the wrong issues and the wrong argument', *Economic Record*, Sept., p. 363.

Hicks, J.R. (1979) *Causality in Economics*, Oxford: Blackwell.

Hutchison, T.W. (1938) *The Significance and Basic Postulates of Economic Theory*, London: Macmillan.

Keynes, J.M. (1973, 1979) *Collected Writings*, vols XIV (1973) and XXIX (1979).

Knight, F.H. (1940) 'What is truth in economics?', *Journal of Political Economy* 48 (February): 27−8

Lachmann, L.M. (1977) *Capital, Expectations and the Market Process*, Kansas City: Sheed Andrews.

Lavoie, D. (1986) 'Euclideanism versus hermeneutics: a reinterpretation of Misesian apriorism', in Israel M. Kirzner (ed.) *Subjectivism, Intelligibility, and Economic Understanding: Essays in Honor of Ludwig M. Lachmann on his Eightieth Birthday*, New York: New York University Press.

Shackle, G.L.S. (1972) *Epistemics and Economics*, Cambridge: Cambridge University Press.

Weber, M. (1968) *Economy and Society: An Outline of Interpretive Sociology* (ed. by Guenther Roth and Claus Wittich), New York: Bedminster Press.

Part III

Alternative views of hermeneutics from a particular economic standpoint: the controversy in the Austrian school

8 Practical syllogism, entrepreneurship and the invisible hand

A critique of the analytic hermeneutics of G.H. von Wright

Uskali Mäki

SYNOPSIS OF THE ARGUMENT

Question. Are economics and hermeneutics mutually compatible?

Specification 1. Hermeneutics is treated here as providing a method or methods potentially used by economists for understanding economic phenomena.

Specification 2. The method of understanding is considered in its acausal purposive mode, specified as the practical syllogism as formulated by G.H. von Wright.

Specification 3. Economics as the study of the economy is represented by some aspects of Austrian economics, especially Israel Kirzner's theory of entrepreneurship and Carl Menger's theory of the genesis of money.

Specified question. Do Austrian accounts of what is going on in the economy conform to the practical syllogism as a method of acausal understanding?

Answer. No.

Reason 1. Kirzner's theory of entrepreneurial action is dependent on the notion of causal powers, hence not analysable in terms of the acausal version of the practical syllogism.

Reason 2. Austrian invisible hand explanations, Menger's theory of money included, are accounts of irreducibly unintended consequences of individual action, hence not analysable in terms of sequences of practical syllogisms.

THE CHALLENGE OF *VERSTEHEN*

In his much discussed book, *Explanation and Understanding* (1971, Ch. I), Georg Henrik von Wright makes a distinction between two traditions in the philosophy of science, the Galilean and the Aristotelean. While the former is occupied with causal explanation, the latter is concerned with understanding and teleological explanation. Causal explanations, according to the first tradition, conform more or less to the positivistic covering law model, causalistically conceived: they cite general law-like regularities and 'mechanical' causes. Understanding, in turn, uses a technique which, in the context of human action, can be explicated in terms of the Aristotelean practical syllogism which refers not to causes but to reasons – i.e., intentions and beliefs of actors.

It is von Wright's conviction that, while the covering law model is well suited to the natural sciences, it is not appropriate for the social sciences, contrary to what is implied by the methodological monism of positivism. Natural events do have (Humean) causes, unlike human actions with which social sciences are concerned. This is why human action (and anything manifesting it) should not be causally explained but understood in terms of the reasons of the actors. Whereas general (Humean) laws can be found in the natural world, they do not obtain in the human world. Understanding is not dependent on reference to causes and general laws.

Von Wright's view is, of course, a radical restatement of the old methodological dualism according to which sciences are divided between two categories according to the methods they employ to gain a cognitive grasp of the world. Sometimes this methodological division is prefaced by ontic characterizations of two different realms of reality, the natural and the human. A typical combination of these two presumptions gives the view that natural events which are not meaningful in themselves can and should be causally explained, whereas phenomena involving human action do have a meaning, and this makes them – exclusively or together with causal explanation – amenable to understanding or interpretation. (In what follows I usually treat 'interpretation', 'understanding', and '*Verstehen*' as synonymous.)

The tradition of the interpretive approach is far from uniform; rather, its advocates constitute a large, heterogeneous and often quarrelsome family. There are too many doctrines of *Verstehen* to be dealt with in a short essay like this. I will concentrate my comments on what has been called 'analytic hermeneutics' for which one source of inspiration was Wittgenstein's later philosophy.[1] This essay is a critical discussion of one version of analytic hermeneutics as applied to economics.[2]

Once a branch of modern hermeneutics has been selected for consideration, a number of further specifications are needed – such as the possible subjects and objects of *Verstehen* or interpretation. Various subjects can act as interpreters, and various objects can be interpreted. For our purposes, it seems sufficient to recognize two kinds of subject and object – those related to economics and to the economy. The following rough classification is produced:

(A) Interpretation by economists of economic theories and the behaviour of their fellow economists. This is *interpretation within the realm of economics*.

(B) Interpretation of economic agents of themselves and of their surroundings, including the behaviour of other economic agents. This is *interpretation within the realm of the economy*.

(C) Interpretation by economists of economic phenomena, incuding the behaviour of economic agents, institutions and statistics. This is *interpretation across the two realms*.

(A) covers, among other things, what has become known as the rhetoric of economics; (B) may be characterized as part of an ontology of economic life; (C) is an object of the traditional issue of a *Verstehende* method. To confuse these three cases without a systematic reflection of the relations between them is inexcusable, although I admit that the division should not be understood as a strict classification into separately existing worlds of interpretation. It is rather a conceptual division which permits all kinds of overlap and interaction in reality. Indeed, in the final analysis, (C) is not completely independent of (A) and (B), and vice versa. But (C) has some relative independence which makes it a suitable starting point.

I propose to focus my attention on (C). Thus, I will discuss questions of interpreting phenomena related to economic agents and institutions by means of the tools provided by economics. This means that hermeneutics will be dealt with as a potential methodology for studying the economy, that is, *Verstehen* is questioned as a method with applicability in economics. It is in analytic hermeneutics, especially in von Wright's work, that we can find a refined definition of a method of understanding.

Although my remarks on the insistence on studying social – including economic – phenomena on the basis of exclusively interpretive methods will be critical, I am ready to admit that interpretation cannot be avoided in economics, or anywhere else where human action is involved. Indeed, I am willing to subscribe to what may be called *the thesis of the ubiquity of interpretation*: interpretive activity is an aspect of all human life – scientific as well as non-scientific, social scientific as well as natural scientific. We are engaged in interpretive activity as readers of poems or speculators on the stock market; as social scientists recognizing physical movements of human beings as certain kinds of meaningful action, and reading national income statistics; or as natural scientists observing the pointings of a measurement device, and listening to a lecture given by a colleague.

Interpretation appears in many forms, but its ubiquity cannot be denied. However, nothing follows from this in regard to the relative role and power of the methods of causal explanation and interpretive understanding in economics. The question still is this: Is *Verstehen*, in context (C) above, exclusively sufficient and superior to causal explanation?

The above question arises and is specified in the context of the recent revival of hermeneutic ideas among some Austrian economists (see Lachmann 1986, Lavoie 1986, and Ebling 1986). We may now ask: Is *Verstehen* the method of Austrian economics? This question is no doubt ambiguous in many ways. The notion of *Verstehen* will be further specified shortly. 'S is the method of T', in turn, should be understood so as to encompass, 'the actual procedures of T can be reconstructed in terms of S'.

Another specification is this: by 'Austrian economics' I mean economic theories *actually presented* in texts written by people recognized as Austrian economists. Only a very small selection of these theories will be dealt with: namely, Israel Kirzner's theory of entrepreneurship and Carl Menger's theory of the genesis of money.

It seems to me that the hermeneutic revival in Austrian economics has so far remained largely unsettled as to the precise contents of its message. I hope that this paper will help specify the aims and limits of the revivalist efforts.

Underlying von Wright's methodological dualism is the view that positivist explanation in terms of Humean causes is the method of natural sciences, whereas hermeneutic understanding in terms of reasons is the method of social sciences. Replacing positivism by an interpretive approach in social sciences has some undeniable merits. Emphasis on subjectivity and human agency as essential aspects of social reality belongs to these. If this is contrasted to behaviourism in psychology, functionalism in sociology, and 'hydraulic Keynesianism' in macroeconomics (see Coddington 1976), it should be clear that there is a vast difference between focusing on empirical regularities or structural dependencies without the mediation of human consciousness on the one hand, and studying social phenomena as meaningful imprints of the human will on the other.

My complaints begin with the observation that von Wright shares with some other hermeneutic dualists some suspicious premises underlying the picture given about the situation in the philosophy of science. First, it is often assumed that positivism and hermeneutics together exhaust the set of philosophical options in methodology, the problem then being the division of sciences between the purviews of the two approaches. One important consequence of this assumption is the choice given to any student of society and social science: if you do not want to be a positivist, all there is left is hermeneutics. Secondly, it is assumed by some hermeneuticists that positivism – with its Humean conception of law and causation – is the correct theory of natural sciences.[3]

I find it obvious that both of these assumptions are false. Not positivism but some other philosophy – such as some version of scientific realism – may be the correct (or the most plausible, or the most progressive) theory of the natural sciences. I will not argue for this hypothesis here; it is sufficient merely to introduce a plausible non-hermeneutic rival to positivism in order to establish the rejection of the first assumption. Positivism and hermeneutics do not exhaust our methodological options.

Rejection of the two assumptions does not, of course, imply anything about the role and power of the method of *Verstehen* in social sciences – about whether hermeneutics is correct as *the* social scientific methodology. However, it is clear that their rejection makes it a legitimate project to challenge, on a non-positivistic basis, the exclusive status ascribed by some to the doctrine of acausal understanding.

The third methodological option I have in mind rejects Humean notions of law and causation, and is careful about the limits of the covering law model of explanation, while at the same time insisting on causal notions and explanatory ambitions. I will argue that this kind of scientific realism can be flexibly applied to the methodology of the social sciences without bringing in some of the most serious positivist vices. I will argue that causal explanation of social (and economic) phenomena on a non-Humean basis is possible without destroying human subjectivity and that Austrian economics exemplifies this approach. On the negative side, I will argue that the method of *Verstehen*, compared with this approach, may turn out to be shallow in results and restricted in scope. At the same time, it has to be emphasized that the version of scientific realism I am employing as my background incorporates many hermeneutic insights – it is hermeneutically enlightened scientific realism.[4]

PRACTICAL SYLLOGISM AND ENTREPRENEURIAL ACTION

Selection of the analytic branch of the doctrine of understanding as our focus of attention does not yet unambiguously determine the characteristics of the operation of understanding. At least three kinds of such an operation can be distinguished (see Collin 1985). They differ from each other in regard to the presumed 'ontological basis' of interpretation and to the ways this basis is supposed to convey understanding. They have the common feature that interpretation is concerned with human action; and they all conceive of action as somehow meaningful. Meaningfulness is an ambiguous notion which becomes specified by each approach in its own way. The three modes of interpretation are based, respectively, on goals, rules, and semantic meanings. The focus of this essay will be on the goals-approach, formulated loosely as follows.

(G) Phenomena of human action can be interpreted in terms of the *goals or purposes* of that action. Purposefulness of action amounts to its directedness towards some goal which is valued by the actor as an end. Action is understood by referring to the intention of the actor to achieve the goal, and to the beliefs of the actor concerning the required means. Pursuit of a goal is one of the senses in which action may be said to be meaningful.[5]

The three modes of *Verstehen* are often unreflectively confused with each other (though it is possible to combine any two – or perhaps all – of them to provide more encompassing approaches). In the tradition of Austrian economics it is possible to find emphases on each of the senses of meaningfulness of human action – some but not all of them accompanied by a commitment to a hermeneutic approach. Goal-directedness is a primary theme in Mises (1949), Lachmann (1986), and Kirzner (1976); rule-following has an important role in Hayek (1973); and meaning-conveying has been dealt with by Ebeling (1986). The bulk of the discussion which follows will focus upon the goal-directedness or purposefulness of human action in the context of Austrian economics.

The question is now as follows: Are those Austrian economic theories that have a special concern with the purposefulness of human action instances of (G)? The search for an answer to this question has to begin with a suggested specification of the purposive mode. For this purpose I will now turn to von Wright's formulation of the practical syllogism (PS).[6]

Let us begin with the following simple version of the practical syllogism (von Wright 1971, p. 96):

(PS1)   Agent *A* intends to bring about *p*.
        A considers that he cannot bring about *p* unless he does *a*.
        _____

        Therefore, *A* sets himself to do *a*.

This scheme can be used in answering the question 'Why does *A* proceed to do *a*?', or 'Why does *A* do *a*?'. The information given in the premises about the intentions and beliefs of the agent is then mentioned in the answer, beginning with 'Because . . .'. It is this answer that provides us with an *understanding* of *A*'s action, or its teleological explanation, as von Wright wants to put it. Let us call this PS-understanding or PS-interpretation.

The first (major) premise of the practical syllogism concerns the intentions, aims, goals, purposes, etc. of the agent under consideration. The second (minor) premise is about the epistemic attitudes of the agent, his or her means-ends beliefs. An important point to be noted here is that it is sufficient for the operation of understanding an action that the agent has some beliefs about the appropriate means; it is not required of those beliefs that they are true.

The action is believed by the agent to be causally related to the end in view. In this way, causation does have a role in practical inference. But when used for understanding human action, the practical syllogism does not, in von Wright's view, provide causal explanation of action. This is so because he subscribes to the so-called *logical connection argument*: the facts described by the premises and the conclusion of the syllogism are logically or conceptually connected. This, von Wright and others claim, precludes any causal connection between them; (Humean) causation would require logical independence of cause and effect. But since intention plus belief and the respective action are conceptually or logically dependent, the former cannot cause the latter. Thus, human action cannot be causally explained by referring to intentions and beliefs as its causes (see von Wright 1971, pp. 93–4, 107–17).

As it stands, (PS1) is too simple as a scheme for understanding human action in excluding, for instance, the time factor. The final qualified formulation of the syllogism provided by von Wright (1971, p. 107) is as follows:

(PS2)   From now on *A* intends to bring about *p* at time *t*.
        From now on *A* considers that, unless he does *a* no later than at
        time *t'*, he cannot bring about *p* at time *t*.

Therefore, no later than when he thinks time *t'* has arrived, *A* sets
himself to do *a*, unless he forgets about the time or is prevented.

There are three moments of time here, *t* (the time of the goal realization), *t'*
(the time of acting), and now. 'From now on' refers to the time interval
between the present moment and *t'*. In addition, two more qualifications
are introduced in (PS2): the agent is not to forget the time and the intended
action is not to be prevented by any external circumstance. (Note that
change in intentions or beliefs or both is not excluded; as a consequence of
such a change the original practical inference would 'dissolve' and be
replaced by another one with new premises.) The purpose of all these qualifications is to make the practical syllogism logically binding; given the facts
represented by the premises, and given the action represented by the
conclusion, there is a relation of logical necessity connecting the premises
and the conclusion. Note, however, that this is 'a necessity conceived *ex
post actu*': the action must already be there in order to have been necessitated by the syllogistic reasoning (von Wright 1971, p. 117).

Economists typically seem to make statements about individual action.
More precisely, those statements often concern action by groups or
organizations such as households and business firms. It is one of the
simplifications of standard economic theory that households and firms are
treated as if they were individuals. This is an interesting problem in its own
right, but I will refrain from dealing with it here and take, in a more neutral
mode, 'agents' − such as 'consumers' and 'producers' and especially
'entrepreneurs' − as the values of the variable *A*, and their actions as the
values of the variable *a* in (PS1) or (PS2).

Various properties, aims and beliefs, are attributed to consumers and
producers by economists. Consumers are said rationally to maximize their
utility, and to have beliefs about the relevant conditions of their action,
such as the types of goods available in the market, and their prices.
Producers are postulated to have maximum profits as the aim of their
action, and to have beliefs about the conditions in the factor and product
markets. Beliefs of both consumers and producers may be assumed to exist
in various degrees of completeness and certainty.

As an illustration, we may apply the simple scheme (PS1) to the case of
producer behaviour in standard neoclassical theory with timeless equilibrating mechanisms. An introductory textbook case of a price taker choosing
the amount of his output might look roughly like this:

(PS3)   Producer *B* intends to maximize his profits, $\pi = TR - TC$.
        B believes that unless he produces the amount of q* of his output so
        as to establish $MC = MR$, π will not be maximized.

Therefore, *B* sets himself to produce q* of his output.

But we are not now interested in the structure of standard neoclassical reasoning. The question we have to tackle is this: Does (PS2) capture the nature of human action as depicted by Austrian economic theory? As a potential Austrian *analysandum* for an inquiry in terms of (PS2) I will consider the theory of entrepreneurship developed recently by Israel Kirzner (1973, 1979, 1985). The question is now this: Does (PS2) capture the nature of entrepreneurial action as depicted in Kirzner's theory?

Let us begin with the major premise of (PS2). It clearly implies the acknowledgement of the essential purposefulness of human action. This is something that has been vigorously emphasized by Austrian economists, and it is no doubt also built into Kirzner's theory. There is the postulate of the general and overriding purpose of human agents to improve their own position, and this is implied in each of the more specific objectives of action, entrepreneurial profit-seeking included.

In general, the time factor is given special emphasis in the Austrian theory, and the treatment of profit-seeking is no exception. A simple point is that, like all action, profit-seeking action takes time. Furthermore, maximum profit as the objective of entrepreneurial action is dealt with by Kirzner in its *ex ante* role. It is *anticipated* profit that serves as an incentive to entrepreneurial action. Pure entrepreneurial profit is based on perceived price differentials in the market – hence, it depends on the violation of Jevons' Law of Indifference. It is the surplus of sales revenues over total relevant purchase outlays, provided this surplus has been discovered by the entrepreneur. It is conceived by the agent as the future result of his action.

To conclude, it seems perfectly sensible to provide the following reconstruction of this aspect of the notion of purposeful profit-seeking in terms of the formulation of the major premise of (PS2): From t on, an entrepreneur, E_i, pursues maximum pure profit as an end to be realized at time t''. Note that I have relaxed the restriction on the scheme imposed by the formulation in terms of 'now'. Note also that while the formulation captures some aspects of the time-dimension of profit-seeking, it also contains the less than perfectly plausible idealization that the agent already has in mind at t the time (t'') of the fulfilment of his intention. Let us assume, however, that this idealization does not affect the likelihood that (PS2) will adequately characterize the nature of entrepreneurial action.

The minor premise of the practical syllogism is a reflection of the kind of concern that has been given an extremely important status in the Austrian tradition of economics. Reference to what has usually been called agents' 'knowledge', 'information', and 'expectations' of market conditions and available means of profit-seeking action have been of central importance to Austrian theorizing. The minor premise of either (PS1) or (PS2) implies a kind of subjectivism about beliefs due to its indifference with respect to truth. It is obvious that this subjectivism is shared by Kirzner's theory of entrepreneurial action. He writes that he is not 'concerned with the truth or correctness of the knowledge people possess' (Kirzner 1979, p. 139). He is interested in beliefs and other epistemic attitudes only 'to the extent that people's actions can be recognized as the consistent expression of these beliefs, expectations, and speculation' (Kirzner 1979, p. 140). This is in accord with the view implied in the practical syllogism.[7]

To show that intentions and beliefs have a prominent role in the Austrian theory is not yet proof of its hermeneutic and non-causalist character. I will now present an analysis suggesting that it does not have such a character. Commentators have pointed to several problems in the practical syllogism as a device of understanding (see, e.g., Tuomela 1977, pp. 170–205). Here it is sufficient to concentrate on two problems, because these two reveal divergences between the doctrine of PS-understanding and the Austrian theory of entrepreneurship. The first problem is that there is nothing in the syllogism to tell us what enables and activates people to act in accordance with their intentions and epistemic attitudes. The second problem is that revision of intentions and beliefs – no doubt a permanent feature of human life – remains unaccountable given the conceptual resources provided by the syllogism. It is my suggestion that these problems do not arise in the Austrian theory thanks to the notion of entrepreneurial alertness which is given a central role by Kirzner. I further suggest that alertness can be understood as a causal power, which has critical consequences with respect to the syllogism. I will now deal with each of the two problems in turn.

Consider von Wright's (1971, p. 116) example of a man 'resolved to shoot the tyrant. He stands in front of the beast, aiming at him with his loaded revolver. But nothing happens'. We find that the man was not 'physically prevented from carrying his intention into effect', did not forget about the time, did not give up his intention, nor did he revise his beliefs about the situation. He just did not act as intended. It is notable that no explanation of this kind of event can be given in the framework of the practical syllogism. The only consequence that is permitted to follow from the possibility of the above sort of inaction is the restriction of the necessity of practical inference to necessity *ex post actu*: an action has to take place in order to have been necessitated by the relevant intentions and beliefs (von Wright 1971, p. 117). This implies a kind of asymmetry in our accounts of action and inaction where the relevant intentions and epistemic attitudes are present: action allegedly can be accounted for while inaction cannot. The latter remains a mystery.

To step in front of a tyrant aiming a loaded gun at him is an achievement in itself. Most of us never get so far: we stay at home and deliberate about the premises of a practical syllogism in the first person (e.g., 'I intend to liberate my country from tyranny', and 'to make my country free I have to shoot the tyrant'). But that is it. The intentions and epistemic attitudes do not turn into action. This seems to be a common phenomenon. Introspectively, most of my intentions never get translated into action – that is, most of my intentions are not efficacious. It would thus seem that the practical syllogism is helpless with respect to an important category of phenomena related to intentions, beliefs, and human action: failures to act. Something is missing in the syllogism.

What we need to add to the accounts of human action and inaction alike to make them symmetrical is a set of notions of factors that help turn intentions into actions. In the case of action all of these factors are present, while in the case of inaction at least some of them are absent. Without these notions the practical syllogism remains restricted in scope (because it does not encompass inactions) and shallow within its scope (because it does not mention all the factors that have a role in generating actual actions).

One suggestion of how to specify the notion of a central factor in the set is to say that it has the general character of a *causal power* that is being exercised when suitable conditions obtain (see, e.g., Harré and Secord 1972, Chs. 12–13; Harré and Madden 1975, Chs. 5–6; Harré 1983, Ch. 7; Chisholm 1976, Ch. 2). Having the power to act in a certain way is to be capable of acting that way; it is to be in a state of readiness to act that way; it is to act that way if the appropriate conditions obtain; and it is to act that way by virtue of an intrinsic nature. Powers in this sense are akin to tendencies, drives, excited capabilities, grounded dispositions or propensities and the like. Loaded guns and runners at the starting line are paradigmatic cases of entities with causal powers. Human powers, when embedded in intentions and beliefs, make these causally efficacious. They are part of the definition of ourselves as *agents*.[8]

To refer back to von Wright's example above, a possible explanation of the failure to act on the part of the potential assassin is that he did not have the required power to implement his intention; we can say this because it was assumed that the appropriate conditions did obtain. The rest of us even lack the power to step in front of the tyrant.

I am now ready to make a crucial point about the Austrian theory of entrepreneurial action. It is in the form of the following suggestion: a central ingredient in entrepreneurship according to Kirzner's theory, namely *entrepreneurial alertness, is best understood as a causal power*. Kirzner's work does not provide a strict definition of entrepreneurial alertness that would immediately justify my interpretation. But I hope to show that his several characterizations of alertness give support to the suggestion.

While Mises (1949, p. 336) talks about the superior 'mental power and energy' of entrepreneurs, I have not found the term 'power' used by Kirzner in this context. But Kirzner uses several other terms that are akin to causal powers. 'Ability' is one of them: 'Entrepreneurial alertness consists, after all, in the *ability* to notice without search opportunities that have been hitherto overlooked' (Kirzner 1979, p. 148; my italics). So is 'propensity': 'Human alertness at all times furnishes agents with the *propensity* to discover information that will be useful for them' (Kirzner 1985, p. 12; my italics). 'Tendency' is still another: alertness is 'a *tendency* for man to notice those [facts] that constitute possible opportunities for gainful action on his part' (Kirzner 1979, p. 29; my italics).

That alertness has a role in prompting entrepreneurs to act, becomes clear from the following: 'If one has become sufficiently alerted to the existence of an opportunity . . . it becomes virtually impossible to imagine not taking advantage of the opportunity so discovered' (Kirzner 1985, p. 22). And more explicitly: 'Purposive human action involves a posture of alertness toward the discovery of as yet unperceived opportunities and their exploitation' (Kirzner 1979, p. 109).

Some further characteristics, typical of causal powers in general, are attributed to alertness by Kirzner (1985), which gives support to my interpretation. Entrepreneurial alertness is said to be something that can be *'inspired'* by 'the lure of market profits' (p. 61), or by 'freedom of entrepreneurial entry' (p. 91); it can be *'tapped'* (p. 25) or *'switched on'* by the incentive of 'the pure gain' (pp. 58–9). But alertness can also remain *'latent and untapped'* and *'inert'* (p. 25). The italicized (the italics are mine) expressions give further reason to think of entrepreneurial alertness as a causal power inherent in human agents that has to be stimulated in order for it to manifest or actualize itself. *Entrepreneurial action, then, is the exercise of the causal power of entrepreneurial alertness.*

This also means that, for Kirzner, alertness is no mere behavioural regularity or disposition. It is rather a human power that has a grounding in the nature of the persons who have that power. As such, alertness is a property that mediates between a person's behavioural dispositions and nature. What, then, is the grounding or nature that gives rise to entrepreneurial alertness? Kirzner only gives hints at an answer and says that we do not know much about the psychological basis of alertness, though it would be good to know more about it (Kirzner 1979, p. 26). That he thinks there *is* such a basis becomes evident, however, when he talks about 'the qualities that make for entrepreneurial alertness' and refers to 'restive temperament, thirst for adventure, ambition, and imagination' (Kirzner 1985, pp. 26 and 89), as well as 'vision, boldness, determination, and creativity' (p. 64).[9]

Let us now turn to the second problem of the practical syllogism. Actors are allowed to revise their intentions and epistemic attitudes in von Wright's account of human action. Each pair of intentions and beliefs is accompanied by a corresponding practical syllogism; so that when intentions and/or beliefs change, a particular syllogism has to be replaced by another one. However, the resources of the practical syllogism turn out to be incomplete in that they do not enable us to explain why it is that actors revise their purposes and beliefs. This inability is a characteristic feature of the practical syllogism: changes in the premises have to be taken as exogenously given. This implies another restriction in the scope of the syllogism.

I will now try to show that the notion of entrepreneurial alertness, understood as a causal power, saves the Austrian theory from such shortcoming. If this claim is true, then it provides another reason for objecting to the idea that the Austrian theory of entrepreneurial action conforms to the hermeneutic practical syllogism. After all, it seems to me that the syllogism may be better equipped to clarify some aspects of what Kirzner calls 'Robbinsian' maximizing behaviour.

Robbinsian economizing as constrained optimization is action within a given means–end framework. The actor has a hierarchy (in terms of importance) of a multiplicity of given ends and a set of given means that are scarce in the sense that they do not enable the realization of all the ends at the same time. The actor solves this 'economic problem' by choosing a course of action which maximizes his/her utility. He or she does this by employing available means to promote achieving various ends in varying degrees so as to achieve the grand goal, maximum utility (see Robbins 1935, pp. 12–16). Alertness, and with it entrepreneurship, are lacking in any Robbinsian theory: any such theory 'only applies after a person is confronted with opportunities; for it does not explain how that person learns about opportunities in the first place' (Kirzner 1979, p. 7). It follows that '[t]here is nothing in the formulation of the economizing view of the decision that tells us how, in the absence of unexplained exogenous changes, one pattern of relevant ends–means comes to be replaced by another' (Kirzner 1973, p. 36; italics deleted). Robbinsian action, in short, does not encompass the change in means–ends frameworks.

In contrast, entrepreneurial action is not restricted to given frameworks of scarce means and multiple ends: it is based on 'alertness toward new valuations with respect to ends, new availability of means' (Kirzner 1979, p. 109). Without giving up pure profit as their grand goal, indeed in order to promote its attainment, entrepreneurs are apt to revise their means–ends frameworks by virtue of their alertness. Successive frameworks do not remain unconnected as they do in the case of Robbinsian economizing, because 'recognizing this entrepreneurial element may make it possible to view a succession of different decisions by the same individual as a logically unified *sequence*, with each decision comprehensible as the logical outcome of the prior decision' (Kirzner 1973, p. 36). In sum, by postulating the power of alertness to entrepreneurs, the Austrian theory gains the ability to give an account of how and why agents change their intentions and beliefs. The practical syllogism as formulated by von Wright does not have this ability.

I have argued that entrepreneurial alertness, as characterized by Kirzner, is a causal power. As such it makes it both possible and likely for entrepreneurs to hold, revise, and exercise certain sorts of intentions and beliefs. A few remarks will clarify some of the implications of this interpretation.

First, while I have proposed to analyse entrepreneurial action partly in causal terms, I do not mean to do this in terms of (Humean) causal sequences of events but in terms of causal powers. That is, what seems relevant here is not event causation but rather what has recently come to be called agent causation.[10] Second, characterizing action in causal terms does not undermine the fundamentally intentional or purposeful character of human action, so much emphasized in the Austrian tradition of economics. Purposefulness and causality are both built into the notion of entrepreneurial action; action is determined both causally and intentionally without contradiction. Third, causation of human action is compatible with the idea of free will, another topic dear to Austrian economists. It may be argued more strongly that the notion of free will presupposes analysing agency in terms of causal powers. Fourth, and most importantly from the point of view of my overall argument, it follows from my suggestion that the hermeneutical practical syllogism does not succeed in analysing the Austrian account of entrepreneurial action. The structure and content of the Austrian account is not that of von Wrightian PS-understanding but of a version of causal explanation. This is not to say that it is the primary purpose of Austrian theory to explain entrepreneurial action, but that, in its attempts to explain something else, it builds upon an account of action that is partly causal.

It is to the primary *explananda* of Austrian theory that I now turn. I will argue that the prospects of hermeneutic PS-interpretation thus become even more problematic.

UNINTENDED CONSEQUENCES AND THE INVISIBLE HAND

Although human action is typically intentional, it usually has consequences that were not intended by the actor. To clarify the idea of unintended consequences I would like to introduce the concept of *the sphere of intendedness*: every intended result of an action belongs to the sphere of intendedness of this action by the actor. It is also possible to think of the sphere of intendedness as part of the action itself, together with the underlying intentions, beliefs, powers, plans, etc.

The same type of behaviour may be accompanied by various spheres of intendedness. Take the example of A's turning the handle of a window. It may be that it is only this event which belongs to A's sphere of intendedness: A intended to bring about nothing more than the turning of the handle. But it may also be that A intended to open the window; the sphere would accordingly be larger. It would grow even larger than that if A, say, intended to find out what made the strange noise she had heard from the street, or to get some fresh air into the room. Suppose, however, that this is the limit of A's sphere of intendedness in the case of turning the handle. But A's action may have other consequences as well. The heating costs of the building may become slightly higher than they would have been if she had not opened the window (suppose it was winter). The temperature of the room may drop so as to make D (who also was in the room and had incipient influenza) sneeze just as A was passing; as a consequence, after a couple of days A will have influenza. Worst of all, A will not recover soon enough to be able to give her presidential address at the Annual Meeting of the Society for Interpretive Economics. None of these consequences was intended by A; they are not within the sphere of intendedness of her original innocent act. What is most important, these consequences cannot be accounted for by referring to A's intentions and beliefs. The practical syllogism becomes restricted in scope.

Economics is often concerned with invisible-hand processes, and these are not quite like the one described above. There are, however, important similarities. In both cases the actions of agents have consequences which go beyond their spheres of intendedness. In both cases, what happens beyond the limits of the sphere is, I would like to argue, causally determined. In the above example, the causal process is partly natural: decline in temperature, sneeze, propagation through the air of the virus carriers, etc. In an invisible-hand process, whereby economic institutions and phenomena emerge, causation is primarily a social process.

My point may become clearer if von Wright's terminology is used. A typical action may be said to have 'inner' and 'outer' aspects. The inner aspect consists of the mental states and processes which manifest themselves in bodily behaviour, in the outer aspect of an action. Von Wright (1971, pp. 86–7) further distinguishes between 'immediate' and 'remote' outer aspects of an action: 'The immediate outer aspect is muscular activity – e.g. a turning of the hand. The remote outer aspect is some event for which this muscular activity is causally responsible – e.g. the turning of a handle or the opening of a window.'

In addition, von Wright (1971, pp. 87–8) defines *'performance'* as an action which has a phase in its outer aspect – which he calls the *'result'* – that has to materialize in order for the action to have been completed. It is von Wright's view that results of an action – such as the window opening – are conceptually connected with the action itself, which implies that results are intended by the actor. In my terminology, results belong to the sphere of intendedness of an action.

Let us familiarize ourselves with these concepts in an economic context. A typical – maybe the most important – action discussed by economists is that of a transaction or an act of exchange in the market. The inner aspect of an exchange, though much simplified by an economist, seems to be within the purview of the discipline; talk about utility, maximization, knowledge, expectations, etc. is an expression of this. The economist seems to be much less interested in the immediate outer aspect of an exchange; it is usually taken for granted that the bodily movements of passing items of the generally accepted media of exchange, and receiving items of usable goods in return, succeed as required. It is the remote outer aspect of an act of exchange that interests the economist – namely, the fact that certain amounts of goods and money change owners. This is, for an economist, also the result of a transaction: it is intended by the market agents, and its accomplishment completes an act of exchange. An isolated act of exchange, then, is a performance for an economic theorist.[11]

However, there are typically several agents in the market, and a number of exchanges take place. The exchanges by different agents are independent of each other in that they are not connected by a common plan of the agents. They are, however, interdependent – in that their relations are established by the market mechanism. As a consequence of these independent–interdependent exchanges, a co-ordinative system of relative prices emerges. This system is a social fact which is not a 'result' of any individual or collective action; it does not lie within the sphere of intendedness of any actor, individual, or collective. Agents do jointly bring it about; but bringing it about is not anybody's or any group's performance. Note that this way of talking presupposes the notion of collective or group intention – or 'we-intention' as it is sometimes called[12] – in addition to that of individual intention (or 'I-intention'), with the notions of result and performance defined in terms of these two notions of intention. The point can now be formulated as the statement that the system of relative prices is a social fact that is neither I-intended nor we-intended.

The concept of the sphere of intendedness is also related to Anscombe's (1957, paragraphs 26–29) notion of *'intentional under a description'*. To show this we may sharpen our previous concepts and follow von Wright (1971, p. 88) by distinguishing between the *result* of an action and its causal *antecedents* and *consequences* – the latter two being causes and effects of the former. While the result is, in von Wright's opinion, intrinsically (conceptually) connected with the action, this is not the case with the antecedents and consequences of the action. For instance, certain bodily movements of a person are causal antecedents of his act of opening a window. A decrease in the temperature in a room may be a causal consequence of the result of the act. Where the dividing lines between the results, antecedents, and consequences of an action are drawn depends on what the intention behind the action focuses on. Whereas results are intended, antecedents and consequences are not. The dividing lines can be moved by changing the description which deems an action intentional. For example, when describing a given action, we may move from (i) 'she turned the handle' to (ii) 'she opened the window' to (iii) 'she cooled the room' (von Wright 1971, p. 89).

This may be taken to mean that by moving from one description to another we turn consequences into results and results into causal antecendents. For instance, when moving from (i) to (ii) we conceptualize the turning of the handle (which was a result) as a causal antecedent; and the opening of the window (which was a causal consequence) as a result. It is clear that several such descriptions may be true of an action – the sphere of intendedness may be stretched quite far. Which one of the possible descriptions is true depends on the focus of the intention of the acting agent. However, there are certainly actions for which there is a limit beyond which the sphere cannot be stretched. If an action is described as intentional beyond this limit, it will be a false description. There are consequences of individual action that cannot be truthfully described as its results. It may be true that

A intentionally cooled the room, but it is probably not true that it was an intended result of her act of cooling the room that she could not deliver the presidential address.

Not all unintended consequences of individual action are mediated by an invisible-hand process. For this reason, and because many economic explanations make reference to that process, we have to specify what is characteristic of those unintended consequences that are being generated or mediated by the invisible hand (let us call them '*invisible-hand consequences*'). At least the following special features have to be mentioned:

(i) An invisible-hand consequence is a consequence of actions by several actors. An individual actor is not sufficient to generate such a consequence; a collective – in fact, a 'large' collective – of actors is needed. On this basis, the failure of *A* to give her presidential address, in the example above, is to be excluded.

(ii) The members of the collective or group have to be unconnected by a we-intention to bring about the consequence. The consequence is unintended by the collective as well as by any of its individual members. In other words, the actions of the individuals in the group are 'dispersed' – that is, unco-ordinated by a common plan (although they are co-ordinated by their social consequences).

(iii) The class of invisible-hand consequences comprises social institutions, such as money, as well as large-scale social events, such as changes in many relative prices. One individual becoming unable to deliver a presidential address thus will not do so on this account either.

(iv) Invisible-hand consequences, though unintended, are by and large beneficial to members of the collective. Thus, various kinds of undesired *and* undesirable consequences or 'perverse effects' in the narrow sense (see Boudon 1982) are not invisible-hand consequences in the traditional sense of economics, Austrian theory included (though it is evident that perverse effects in the wide sense are also relevant to standard economic theory; just think of the problem of externalities). This is one more reason why the fate of our poor hermeneuticist who caught a cold is to be excluded.

Of course, this list does not exhaust the characteristic features of invisible-hand consequences, but it will do for our purposes.

An *invisible-hand process*, in turn, is a process whereby invisible-hand consequences are generated. Thus, the above characteristics of invisible-hand consequences serve to define aspects of the process, too. A couple of additional points have to be mentioned. First, the set of invisible-hand processes comprises both processes of origin or emergence, and processes of maintenance or preservation. Second, as I will argue in the next section, an invisible-hand process is essentially a causal process.

Finally, an *invisible-hand explanation* is an explanation which has an invisible-hand consequence as the *explanandum* and an invisible-hand process as the *explanans*. The next section will be devoted to further scrutiny of invisible-hand explanations, but let it be noted here that the point I am making there is that there is no contradiction between these explanations being causal explanations and their *explanantia*, having intentional individual actions as their components.[13]

Menger's theory of the origin of money is a paradigmatic case of invisible-hand explanation in Austrian economics (see Menger 1892, 1950, 1963; O'Driscoll 1986; Koppl 1984). A rough outline of some of its more important ingredients will neatly illustrate the essentials of invisible-hand explanation.

That Menger thinks there are institutions which satisfy at least the above conditions (ii), (iii), and (iv) for identifying something as an invisible-hand consequence is implied in his explanation-oriented question: 'How can it be that the institutions which serve the common welfare and are extremely significant for its development come into being without a *common will* directed toward establishing them?' (Menger 1963, p. 146). That condition (i) is satisfied and that condition (iii) is satisfied in cases other than institutions proper becomes evident when we quote from the words of Menger (1963, p. 158): 'a large number of the phenomena of economy . . . e.g., market prices, wages, interest rates, etc., have come into existence in exactly the same way as those social institutions. . . . For they, too, as a rule are not the result of socially teleological causes, but the unintended result of innumerable efforts of economic subjects pursuing *individual* interests'. That Menger focused his attention primarily on the invisible-hand processes of origination and emergence is evidenced in the above quotations by the expressions 'coming into being' and 'coming into existence'.

Menger's 'evolutionary account' of the genesis of money begins with a description of the situation of pure barter. In this state market agents suffer from poor liquidity and high transaction costs. An essential condition for the invisible-hand process to get started is the perception by market-agents of differences between commodities as to their *Absatzfähigkeit*, their saleability or marketability – that is, the facility with which commodities can be disposed of in a market at going prices. This facility consists of such factors as the time required for selling a commodity and the quantity of the commodity that can be sold at one time, and it is dependent – among other things – on the value, transportability, and preservability of commodities (see Menger 1892, pp. 243–7). Basing their actions on this perception, individual market agents in entrepreneurial pursuit of their self-interest in an immediate satisfaction of their own needs, begin one after another to exchange their commodities for those that are more saleable in order to secure the provision of those that they require for satisfying their consumption needs. Menger put it this way:

> As *each* economizing individual becomes increasingly more aware of his economic interest, he is led by this *interest, without any agreement, without legislative compulsion and even without regard to the public*

interest, to give his commodities in exchange for other, more saleable, commodities, even if he does not need them for any immediate consumption purposes.

(Menger 1950, p. 260)

This leads to an improvement in the liquidity of market agents, which helps to decrease their future transaction costs. The process, once started, continues in a cumulative, self-enforcing fashion. In the end, the commodity which enjoys the best saleability properties becomes selected as the universally accepted medium of exchange. Money is born.

I would like to discuss the above process metaphorically. Let us say that by making a choice between available media of exchange the agent of each transaction in the process 'votes' for one particular medium and by doing so raises its 'popularity'. The more popular a medium is, the more likely it is that future transactors will vote for it; hence the self-enforcing character of the process. The voting process goes on and is not finished until one medium of exchange becomes 'elected': it becomes so popular that it is established as *the* generally accepted medium of exchange (of course, this medium is continuously being 're-elected'; thus, the voting process in fact never gets finished). I will use this 'voting' metaphor shortly.

That the general conditions of invisible-hand consequences and processes are also fulfilled by Menger's account of the origin of money can easily be shown. He says that 'money is not the product of an agreement on the part of economizing men nor the product of legislative acts. No one invented it'. (Menger 1950, p. 262). Thus, money is not a result of an I-intention or a we-intention. It is rather 'the spontaneous outcome, the unpremeditated resultant, of particular, individual efforts of the members of a society' (Menger 1892, p. 250). Moreover, just as is required of an invisible-hand consequence in the present sense, the institution of money is also beneficial to the members of society, in that the money commodity is 'in the interest of every one to accept in exchange for his own less saleable goods' (Menger 1892, p. 248).

EXPLANATION, UNDERSTANDING, AND THE INVISIBLE HAND

What is the general nature of an adequate account of the unintended consequences of individual action when those consequences have been shaped by an invisible-hand process? Does interpretive understanding have a role in this account? Is the practical syllogism, as a representative of the interpretive mode (G), of any help? Are its limits co-extensive with the limits of spheres of intendedness? Does causation, after all, have a role?

I have argued that understanding based merely on an acausalistically conceived practical syllogism (PS) is shallow and restricted in scope in the case of individual action. I will now argue that there are also other restrictions to its scope: it does not suffice to account for those economic phenomena and institutions which have emerged as consequences of invisible-hand processes.

Let us now test the potential of PS-interpretation in the case of accounting for invisible-hand consequences. I would like to suggest a possible reconstruction of an invisible-hand explanation which is a variation of von Wright's (1971, pp. 139–143) characterization of what he calls a 'quasi-causal' explanation of an historical event. This kind of explanation points out a sequence of actions (each of them accounted for by means of a practical syllogism) in which the result of each action constitutes part of the situation in which the next action takes place. The structure of the sequence can be represented as in Figure 8.1.

Figure 8.1 Quasi-causal explanation

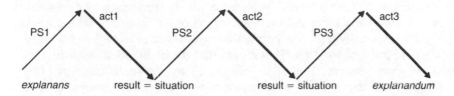

Von Wright's example takes the generation of World War I as the *explanandum*. He says that the explanation is quasi-*causal*, because it looks as if the murder in Sarajevo, the *explanans*, causally brought about the war. However, it is only *quasi*-causal since the connection was mediated by a number of actions plus practical reasonings supporting those actions with no nomic relation involved. Of course, the *explanans* itself was intentionally generated by the reasons of the murderer and his supporting group.

Now one might want to suggest that, for instance, the Mengerian explanation of money should be reconstructed in the same way, in terms of a sequence of practical syllogisms. To each individual transactor would be attributed the intention to improve his or her position and the relevant beliefs about the situation in regard to the available media of exchange and their saleability. The situation changes (the media of exchange change as to their 'popularity'; in every transaction one or the other medium has been 'voted for') as a result of each transaction, thereafter constituting a new starting point for the next transactor. In general terms, the spheres of intendedness of the actors would, so to speak, be connected at the edges. *The notion of global unintendedness would become reduced to the notion of a sequence of local intendedness.* The institution of money would, in this way, be intentionally understood, not causally explained. The same kind of reconstruction might be applicable in the case of the explanation of a system of relative prices.

There are several problems with the above suggestion. First, the causalist arguments against the intentionalist version of the practical syllogism provided earlier will also retain their force in the case of a sequence of practical syllogisms. A conjunction of non-explanatory or superficially explanatory reasonings is no less non-explanatory or superficial than each individual reasoning. However, this is a point of shallowness rather than scope, because inaction does not have a constructive role in the generation of money or relative prices.

Second, it seems to me that, after all, each of the practical syllogisms inevitably leaves room for unintended consequences in the sequence; the net consisting of the local spheres of intendedness is not completely tight. This is because, to take the example of money, one important consequence of each action in the sequence is a change in the popularity of the available media of exchange, and these changes typically do not belong to the agents' spheres of intendedness. Only in rare cases could we think of a change in popularity as a result intended by a transactor. In these cases, the epistemic competence of the actor and the reach of his or her sphere of intendedness would be especially high. I presume that typical actors in typical situations were (and are) not like that. This means that the unintended element in the invisible-hand process cannot be eliminated by the reconstruction of an invisible-hand explanation as a sequence of practical syllogisms. In conclusion, practical syllogism is restricted in scope: it cannot encompass an important set of *explananda* of economics.

Third, the sequencing of the account is problematic in itself. This is especially clear in the case of an account of a system of relative prices. Market agents may act more or less co-temporally, responding to and creating situations which do not follow each other in a neat sequential order, one action not regularly being dependent on the result of the previous one. In response to this, some people may suggest that sequencing can be justified as a harmless simplification. My reply would be that this kind of simplification would be no less harmful than the simplification in neo-classical general-equilibrium theory, vehemently opposed by the Austrians, that all transactions take place simultaneously.

Fourth, and least important, there is the practical problem related to the length of the sequence in invisible-hand processes. It may be possible to mention the stages leading from Sarajevo to the war, but not those leading to the emergence of money. The obvious way of escaping this difficulty is to omit most of the 'stages' and concentrate on only a few crucial ones, on those at which important transformations occurred in the development of the media of exchange. The practical syllogisms included in such an abridged account would then be simplified accounts of some crucial, representative actions. It seems that Menger's evolutionary account can be read as having this character. Thus, it would seem that simplifications involved in this strategy are more or less harmless.

It follows from the above critical points (especially the second and third points) that we should accept something like the representation shown in

Figure 8.2 as a closer approximation of an invisible-hand process than Figure 8.1. Two modifications to Figure 8.1 are suggested. First, Figure 8.2 rejects the idea of a neat sequential order. Second, Figure 8.2 incorporates the claim that it is not the intended results of earlier actions (depicted as R) that, as such, constitute the situations (S) perceived by agents of later actions. The relevant situations are not results but rather unintended consequences of preceding actions. There is a gap between results and situations represented by the squared circle.

Figure 8.2 Invisible-hand explanation

R S   Result ≠ Situation = Consequence

In order to suggest one interpretation of an important aspect of invisible-hand explanation we have to penetrate the secret of the squared circle. Menger's story will serve as an illustration. I submit that the squared circle symbolizes *the three-fold relation of a redescription*. This relation connects three items to one another. First, there is the *real element* in the economic process. Second, there is the *description* of the real event as a result of an individual action – that is, as something that intendedly promotes satisfying the self-interest of the acting agent. Third, there is the *redescription* of the element as an event of 'voting for' a particular medium of exchange. The redescription tells us what, from the point of view of the invisible-hand process, the event is – namely, an increase in popularity of the medium selected.

The description tells us what happens within the sphere of intendedness of a transactor. The agent intends to bring about a result that promotes his self-interest and acts in accordance with this intention, with his beliefs about the situation and with whatever powers he may possess. By the same act of transaction, however, he brings about something that he did not intend, though this, too, is ultimately in accord with his self-interest. The action is intentional under the description (A) 'He increased his liquidity', but not under the redescription (B) 'He increased the popularity of this medium of exchange', or, 'He voted for this medium of exchange'. (A) describes a performance, whereas (B) does not. Voting is typically intentional action, but in this case, typically, it is not. By using the term metaphorically, we can avoid conceiving of voting as intentional under the redescription.

To clarify the point further I submit that we make a distinction between describing an action in terms of the related intentions and describing it in terms of its outcomes, let us call them 'intention-descriptions' and 'outcome-descriptions'. In the case of (A) and (B) this implies making a distinction between the pair of description and redescription,

(A′) 'a pursuing of one's self interest by choosing the medium of exchange *x*'

and

(B′) 'a voting for the medium of exchange *x*',

on the one hand, and the pair,

(A″) 'an increase in one's individual liquidity'
and
(B″) 'an increase in *x*'s public popularity',

on the other.

It should now be obvious that *an action redescribed in terms of (B′) and (B″) cannot be accounted for in terms of (PS2)*, even if complemented with the notion of human causal powers. If formulated as stating that an agent had the intention of bringing about an increase in the public popularity of *x*, the major premise of (PS2) would most likely be false and hence would not serve to make the action understandable. This is a crucial point, because it is the conjunction of (B′) and (B″) that tells us something about how situations for further actions are generated as consequences of previous actions.

We can use the ambiguous notion of 'by' to clarify some of the relations that prevail between various elements under consideration. Note that (A′) is already formulated in terms of a 'by'. Here it denotes a means–ends relation: an end is pursued *by* some means. The same sense of 'by' is employed if we say that an agent did what (A″) describes *by* doing what (A′) describes. Even the pair (B′) and (B″) can perhaps be connected by a 'by' in this sense, providing it is kept in mind that language here is deliberately metaphorical. The important point is that the meaning of 'by' is different when we say that an agent did what (B′) describes *by* doing what (A′) describes, or that he did what (B″) describes *by* doing what (A″) describes, or, by virtue of transitivity, that he did what (B″) describes *by* doing what (A′) describes. In spite of their differences, these two senses of 'by' seem to be similar in one respect: they denote a causal relation. It would seem obvious enough that 'by' (in its 'means–ends' sense) designates a causal notion. However, it will have to be argued that the second sense is causal, although the reason is relatively simple.

There is a non-causal sense of 'by' that is related to the mode (R) of hermeneutic understanding (see note 5). When we say, for example, that 'Matti voted for Teppo by writing "Teppo" on a piece of paper which he dropped in a box', we do not presume that Matti's voting was caused by his writing, etc. Instead, what we say presupposes the existence of a rule or social convention which prescribes that Matti's writing 'Teppo', etc. (or Matti's raising his hand or Matti's shouting) means Matti's voting for Teppo. The rule is a constitutive rule (see Searle 1969, pp. 33–5) which prescribes that Matti's writing constitutes Matti's voting. Whether or not this view is correct, it should be clear that there is a difference in regard to the meaning of 'by' between:

(1) '*A* voted for *x* by writing "*x*" on a piece of paper etc.'

and

(2) '*A* voted for *x* by using *x* as his medium of exchange in pursuing his self-interest.'

There is a thread of social convention and usually one of intention that connect the two sides of 'by' in (1), but these threads are missing in (2). We can say that, by virtue of a convention, *A*'s writing etc. is regarded as *A*'s voting, and usually also that *A* intended to vote by writing, etc. These sorts of things cannot be said in the case of (2). Statement (2), I argue, relates the two sides of 'by' by a causal connection.

The two sides of 'by' in (2), I suggest, are connected by the causal relation of *bringing about*. A reformulation in these terms is as follows:

(2') '*A* brought about the voting for *x* by using *x* as his medium of exchange in pursuing his self-interest.'

That what we have here is the relation of 'bringing about' should be uncontroversial. That this relation is a causal relation should also be evident. Consequently, we may formulate:

(2″) '*A* caused the voting for *x* by using *x* as his medium of exchange in pursuing his self-interest.'

Loaded with human powers, economic agents also bring about intended results. In a case like (2'), agents bring about unintended consequences. The transformation of intended results into unintended invisible-hand consequences is contingent upon appropriate social conditions such as, in this case, the dispersion of decision-making and the co-ordination of decisions in the market. These factors may be regarded as necessary causal conditions for the causal bringing about of invisible-hand consequences by individual agents. These consequences would not emerge in the absence of those social conditions, but these conditions do not bring about the consequences. Individual agents do. We may say that, in the presence of the market system, the individual agents acquire the causal power to bring about invisible-hand consequences such as 'votings for' mediums of exchange and, ultimately, the emergence of money. The invisible-hand process in question is a socially conditioned causal process with intentional agents as the initiators and mediators.

It is important to understand that the above rough draft of a causal account of economic institutions and the phenomena related to them does not eliminate genuine human agency. It is still true that human actors, by their intentional actions, bring about the institutions and their behaviour; that is, that social phenomena 'are generated by deliberate, purposeful human action' (Kirzner 1979, p. 151). However, it is not true that the actors purposefully generate all of those phenomena. The generation is a causal process whereby results of action are transformed into consequences of action. For this reason it is not true that explanations of these consequences of actions are reduced only to intentional accounts of those actions. Thus, it makes no sense to ask the question: 'Why did the actors bring about these particular institutions and phenomena?' It makes no sense, because it is typically presupposed in such a question that the answer lies in the actors' reasons (one possible answer could be, 'Because they wanted to have a society like this.'). But it makes sense to ask, 'How did the actors bring about these things?' And a simplified Austrian answer would be, 'By pursuing improvement in their own position under market conditions.' That is, they did one thing by doing another thing. It also makes sense to ask, 'Why do these institutions exist and these phenomena take place?' And the answer would be a more comprehensive answer to the above 'how' question. In this way, causal explanation, not being reducible to hermeneutic PS-understanding, is dependent on theoretical description.

CONCLUSION

I have argued that invisible-hand consequences are causally generated. More precisely, I have argued that they are doubly caused. Invisible-hand consequences are caused by a social mechanism in which individual action has a central role, and individual action is generated in part by the causal power of entrepreneurial alertness. Note that at no point is Humean causation presupposed. Thus, Austrian invisible-hand explanation would seem to represent a third way between positivistic explanation and hermeneutic PS-understanding. If my arguments are acceptable, two conclusions can be drawn from them. First, important parts of existing Austrian economic theory do not conform to that version of analytic hermeneutics which builds upon the acausalistically understood practical syllogism. Second, von Wright and other hermeneuticists who hold an acausalist view of legitimate social scientific understanding have been given a case that subscribes both to the spirit of subjectivism that it shares with hermeneutics and to the idea of causal explanation.

Of course, both analytic hermeneuticists and those Austrian economists who commit themselves to hermeneutic ideas can respond to these statements by denying the Austrian theories of entrepreneurship and the invisible hand their legitimacy as adequate theories of society. This would, indeed, seem to be the only option open to somebody like von Wright in his 1971 book.[14] However, Austrian hermeneuticists have another alternative. This is to opt for some other version of hermeneutical understanding as the *analysans* of Austrian economic theory. This also brings out one important restriction of this essay. Namely, it follows from focusing on one tributary of a wider stream that the implications of my critical remarks cannot always, at least without modification, be applied to other tributaries as well. I hope, however, that my tentative remarks will have some relevance in assessing other versions from the angle of economic methodology. I also hope that, to promote genuine argument, these other versions will be formulated with the same rigour that characterizes the analytical hermeneutics of von Wright.

ACNOWLEDGEMENTS

I wish to thank Israel Kirzner, Martin Kusch, Don Lavoie, Raimo Tuomela, and Georg Henrik von Wright for comments on an earlier draft. Financial support from the Yrjö Jahnsson Foundation is gratefully acknowledged.

NOTES

1 This post-Wittgensteinian branch of the philosophy of interpretive social sciences is closely related to the analytic philosophy of language, and it has been cultivated mainly in Britain and Scandinavia. For general accounts, see Apel 1967 and Howard 1982, Ch. 1. Some important though far from unified representatives are Winch 1958, Louch 1966, Taylor 1971, von Wright 1971. For a collection of essays on and inspired by von Wright's approach, see Manninen and Tuomela 1976.
2 To my knowledge, analytic hermeneutics has not been utilized or adopted by economists or methodologists of economics, unlike, say, Alfred Schütz's phenomenological variety of the interpretive approach.
3 Conceptual ambiguities abound here. First, von Wright (1971, p. 93) defines *Humean causation* in terms of the logical or conceptual independence of cause and effect, whereas this notion is often understood as primarily involving the constant conjunction view of causation. Of course, no inconsistency prevails between these two meanings of the term. Second, von Wright's (ibid., p. 4) characterization of *positivism* is extremely broad and vague. In his view, positivism is a doctrine which subscribes to methodological monism, to the conception that mathematical physics provides an ideal for all science, and to the tenet that scientific explanation should be causal and nomological. These characteristics may be misleading, since only by combining (one or more of) them with certain ontological, semantical, and epistemological views based on the notion of observability can we hope to distinguish positivism proper from other doctrines that may accept one or more of the three characteristics. Of course, often the best thing might be to avoid using such highly ambiguous terms as 'positivism' altogether.
4 I do not intend to discuss explicitly questions of scientific realism in this paper. For a reconstructive analysis of explanatory theorizing in Austrian economics in terms of some explicitly scientific-realist presuppositions, see Mäki (1990a and 1990b).
5 The other two modes of interpretation can be characterized in the following way:

(R) Phenomena of human action can be interpreted in terms of the *rules* to which action conforms. Action is rule-following if e.g., it is performed out of a feeling of obligation to act in compliance with a rule and not based on calculations of the preferred outcome. Action is understood by referring to recognition of a rule and compliance with it by the actor. Rule-following is one of the senses in which action may be said to be meaningful.

(M) Phenomena of human action can be interpreted in terms of the *semantic meaning* that the actor wishes to convey by her or his act. Meaning-conveying action is communication of messages, i.e. beliefs in something being the case, from actors to audiences by means of symbols; speech acts, for instance, use spoken language. Action is understood by referring to the communicative intentions of the actor and to the semantic meaning of the communicative vehicles used. Meaning-conveying is one of the senses in which action may be said to be meaningful.

6 It is a common difficulty with methods of hermeneutic understanding that they have seldom been given rigorous articulations. The practical syllogism, as formulated by von Wright, is an exception in this respect.

7 It may sometimes be misleading that Austrian economists often use the word 'knowledge' when they talk about beliefs in the strict philosophical sense. Knowledge, in the sense of traditional epistemology, implies both belief and truth, while belief implies neither truth nor knowledge. Continuity between disciplines in terminological matters and benefits of greater conceptual clarity might be forthcoming if Austrians consistently adopted the philosophical terminology about belief and knowledge.

8 It is interesting to note that in his manipulation theory of causation, von Wright (1971, pp. 48–54; see also von Wright 1974, pp. 64–74) maintains that agency is conceptually prior to causation (because, he thinks, it is human agents who give rise to causal sequences by manipulating the world). According to the view suggested here, however, it is the other way round: causality (in the sense of causal powers, not in that of causal sequences as in von Wright) is conceptually prior to agency.

9 In private correspondence, Kirzner has told me that it seems to him that my interpretation of his work 'is accurate' and that I am 'correct in describing entrepreneurial alertness as representing . . . "causal power" '. His only concern is that by using the term 'power' we may give rise to a misunderstanding to the effect that alertness is something that can be deliberately deployed by agents. This misinterpretation should, indeed, be avoided by abstracting from such possible unnecessary connotations of 'power'. That these connotations are unnecessary is evidenced by the fact that we can speak also about natural agents (such as helium atoms, DNA molecules, pieces of coal, birch trees, elephants) as having causal powers that are exercised with no one deliberately deploying them.

10 Note that von Wright (1974, p. 49) explicitly rejects the notion of agent causation; event causation is the only variety of causation he accepts.

11 The degree to which ordinary action theory simplifies social scientifically relevant human action is revealed nicely here. Think of a typical act of exchange across national borders in a modern setting. The good being sold and bought is shipped from one country to another, which often takes a long time. The process is mediated by complicated technical devices and by a large number of bodily movements by several persons – most of whom are not the agents of this particular transaction. The corresponding payment for the good is transmitted by electronic means, again mediated by bodily movements of several persons, and possibly taking place in many stages. Thus, what amounts to a simple case of an exchange for economics, turns out to be extremely complicated for action theory. But, as I said, the outer aspect of an action is not of great interest for general economic theory and the simplification of the actual situation implied in action theory may thus be justified. It is another matter whether the simplification in economic theory concerning the inner aspect is justified or not.

12 For a discussion of we-intentions, see Tuomela (1984, pp. 31–54).
13 For discussions of invisible-hand explanation, see Ullmann-Margalit (1978), Elster (1979, pp. 28–35), Tuomela (1984, pp. 448–54), Koppl (1984), Vanberg (1986), Langlois (1986).
14 In his 1971 book, von Wright conceives of the scope of the practical syllogism widely enough to cover all social science: 'Broadly speaking, what the subsumption-theoretic [covering-law] model is to causal explanation and explanation in the natural sciences, the practical syllogism is to teleological explanation and explanation in history and the social sciences' (p. 27). In private correspondence, von Wright now says that he no longer regards the scope of the PS-scheme as encompassing as he used to.

REFERENCES

Anscombe, G.E.M. (1957) *Intention*, Oxford: Basil Blackwell.
Apel, Karl-Otto (1967) *Analytical Philosophy of Language and the Geisteswissenschaften*, Dordrecht: Reidel.
Boudon, Raymond (1982) *The Unintended Consequences of Social Action*, New York: St Martin's Press.
Chisholm, Roderick (1976) *Person and Object*, London: Allen & Unwin.
Coddington, Alan (1976) 'Keynesian economics: the search for first principles', *Journal of Economic Literature* 14 (Dec.): 1258–73.
Collin, Finn (1985) *Theory and Understanding*, Oxford: Basil Blackwell.
Ebeling, Richard (1986) 'Toward a hermeneutical economics: expectations, prices, and the role of interpretation in a theory of the market process', in Israel Kirzner (ed.) *Subjectivism, Intelligibility, and Economic Understanding*, New York: New York University Press.
Elster, Jon (1979) *The Ulysses and the Sirens*, Cambridge: Cambridge University Press.
Harré, Rom (1983) *Personal Being*, Oxford: Basil Blackwell.
—— and Madden, Edward (1975) *Causal Powers*, Oxford: Basil Blackwell.
—— and Secord, Paul (1972) *The Explanation of Social Behaviour*, Oxford: Basil Blackwell.
Hayek, F.A. von (1973) *Law, Legislation and Liberty*, vol. 1, London: Routledge & Kegan Paul.
Howard, Roy J. (1982) *Three Faces of Hermeneutics*, Berkeley: University of California Press.
Kirzner, Israel (1973) *Competition and Entrepreneurship*, Chicago: Chicago University Press.
—— (1976) *The Economic Point of View*, Kansas City: Sheed & Ward 1976.
—— (1979) *Perception, Opportunity, and Profit*, Chicago: Chicago University Press.
—— (1985) *Discovery and the Capitalist Process*, Chicago: Chicago University Press.
Koppl, Roger (1984) 'Marginal explanations or do economists use invisible hand explanations?' mimeo.
Lachmann, Ludwig (1986) *Market as an Economic Process*, Oxford: Basil Blackwell.
Langlois, Richard (1986) 'Rationality, institutions, and explanation', in R. Langlois (ed.) *Economics as a Process: Essays in the New Institutional Economics*, Cambridge: Cambridge University Press.
Lavoie, Don (1986) 'Euclideanism versus hermeneutics: a reinterpretation of Misesian apriorism', in Israel Kirzner (ed.) *Subjectivism, Intelligibility, and Economic Understanding*, New York: New York University Press.

Louch, A.R. (1966) *Explanation and Human Action*, Oxford: Basil Blackwell.

Manninen, Juha and Tuomela, Raimo (eds) (1976) *Essays on Explanation and Understanding*, Dordrecht: Reidel.

Menger, Carl (1892) 'On the origin of money', *Economic Journal* 2 (June): 239–55.

—— (1950) *Principles of Economics*, New York: New York University Press.

—— (1963) *Problems of Economics and Sociology*, Urbana: University of Illinois Press.

Mises, Ludwig von (1949) *Human Action: A Treatise on Economics*, New Haven: Yale University Press.

Mäki, Uskali (1990a) 'Scientific realism and Austrian explanation', *Review of Political Economy* 2, pp. 310–44.

—— (1990b) 'Mengerian economics in realist perspective', *History of Political Economy* 22 (forthcoming).

O'Driscoll, Gerald (1986) 'Money: Menger's evolutionary theory', *History of Political Economy*,

Robbins, Lionel (1935) *An Essay on the Nature and Significance of Economic Science*, London: Macmillan.

Searle, John (1969) *Speech Acts*, Cambridge: Cambridge University Press.

Taylor, Charles (1971) 'Interpretation and the sciences of man', *Review of Metaphysics* 25, pp. 3–51.

Tuomela, Raimo (1977) *Human Action and its Explanation*, Dordrecht: Reidel.

—— (1984) *A Theory of Social Action*, Dordrecht: Reidel.

Ullmann-Margalit, Edna (1978) 'Invisible-hand explanations', *Synthese* 39 (Oct): 263–91.

Vanberg, Viktor (1986) 'Spontaneous market order and social rules: a critical examination of F.A. Hayek's theory of cultural evolution', *Economics and Philosophy* 2 (April): 75–100.

Winch, Peter (1958) *The Idea of a Social Science and Its Relation to Philosophy*, London: Routledge & Kegan Paul.

Wright, Georg Henrik von (1971) *Explanation and Understanding*, London: Routledge & Kegan Paul.

—— (1974) *Causality and Determinism*, New York: Columbia University Press.

9 What is a price? Explanation and understanding

(With apologies to Paul Ricoeur)

Richard M. Ebeling

INTRODUCTION

One of the central concepts of economic analysis is that of price. Indeed, it is probably little exaggeration to say that it was the discernment of the significance of prices in the network of market exchanges that enabled economics to emerge as an autonomous field for investigation. It came to be seen that it was the structure of market prices, and the responses to changes in those market prices by participants in the social division of labour, that made possible the emergence and maintenance of a spontaneous order of economic relationships.

The existence of such a spontaneous market order and the place of prices in it has been appreciated for thousands of years.[1] Yet it has only been in the last 250 years that truly systematic analyses of market orders and the role of prices have been undertaken. Particularly following the publication of David Hume's essay, 'Of the balance of trade', in the middle of the eighteenth century, the self-regulatory qualities of a market-pricing system has been a central theme of economic analysis. Hume argued that discrepancies in the prices at which goods were sold at different locations would set in motion shifts in market supplies and demands until prices had adjusted sufficiently to bring both domestic and international trade into balance (see Hume 1985, pp. 308–26; also Hume 1970, pp. 60–77).

Through most of the nineteenth century, the classical economists had focused on the processes of change and adjustment when agents in the market discovered such discrepancies between cost and selling prices (see McNulty 1967, p. 75–90; McNulty 1968, pp. 639–56; cf. also Robbins 1952, p. 16). But for the past 100 years the central concern of neoclassical economics has been to *explain the logic of what prices do* (i.e. what role and function they perform, in a hypothetical state of general equilibrium). What neoclassical economics has failed to do to any significant degree is to provide an analysis of the process of how prices are formed in markets (cf. Mayer 1932, pp. 147–239b and von Mises 1966 [1949] pp. 350–7 and 710–15). Nor has it offered any *understanding* of how market participants *interpret* changing market conditions as expressed in prices, and which enables the maintenance of a spontaneous order of interdependent social actors through appropriate responses in individual actions.

Now such a claim will strike most economists as either confusing or as proof that the person making the charge does not know what economics has been about for the past 100 years. But I think it is a more damning statement about the state of contemporary economics that most economists would not comprehend what was meant in contrasting an *explanation of prices* with an *understanding of prices*.

It is for this reason that Paul Ricoeur's essay, 'What is a text? Explanation and understanding', has been chosen as the inspiration and guiding framework for this paper. The question, 'What is a text?' as I shall attempt to show, has its counterpart in the question, 'What is a price?' Both a text and a price reflect human intentionality: in the case of a text the desire by an individual to convey knowledge about some aspect of the natural or social worlds, or of his thoughts and beliefs, to anonymous others separated from him by time and space; in the case of a price, the desires of individuals to obtain goods and services from anonymous others also separated from them by time and space. And both texts and prices must be interpreted by those others to discern the meanings they contain. Furthermore, as Ricoeur has argued, once written, a text takes on an existence of its own now that it is 'objectified' and separated from its author. Market prices have a similar characteristic, since they represent the composite outcome of many interacting supplier and demander choices, and since the unintended result of a multitude of actions are separate from the individual 'authors' whose decisions have generated those composite results.

WHAT IS A TEXT? EXPLANATION AND UNDERSTANDING

It seems possible to situate explanation and interpretation along a unique *hermeneutical arc* and to integrate the opposed attitudes of explanation and understanding within an overall conception of reading as the recovery of meaning.

(Ricoeur 1981, p. 161)

One of the consistent characteristics of Paul Ricoeur's writings is his ability in demonstrating compatibility and even complementarity between concepts and theories traditionally considered to be in diametric opposition. His analysis of the relationship between 'explanation' and 'understanding' in the human sciences is an example of one of his most successful reconciliations. And as in many of his other intellectual excursions, he returns to the genesis of things in the history of ideas. He reminds the reader that it is in Wilhelm Dilthey's writings that the supposed dichotomy between explanation and understanding was most clearly articulated:

The human sciences are distinguished from the natural sciences in that the latter take as their object features which appear to consciousness as coming from outside, as phenomena . . . for the former, in contrast, the object appears as coming from within, as a reality. . . . It follows therefore that for the natural sciences an ordering of nature is achieved only through a succession of conclusions by means of linking of hypotheses. For the human sciences, on the contrary, it follows that the connectedness of psychic life is given as an original and general foundation. Nature we explain, we understand mental life.

(quoted in Howard 1982, pp. 15–16)

But he also reminds the reader that Dilthey pointed out that the process of interpersonal understanding is not undertaken directly (i.e. not on the basis of any direct insight into the intentionalities of men but rather through the external *manifestations* of human actions). In Dilthey's own words, the human spirit 'speaks to us from stone, marble, musical compositions, gestures, words and writings, from actions, economic arrangements and constitutions, and has to be interpreted' (Dilthey 1982, p. 247). Interpretation, therefore, is the art of understanding the meanings of human intentions as they have left their trace in the form of sediments of past human conduct (Ricoeur 1981, pp. 150–1).

It is at this point that a tension arises concerning the presumed dichotomy between explanation and understanding. While understanding for Dilthey rests on the idea of an empathetic psychologizing, this psychologizing is undertaken through the mediations of those sediments left by previous human acts. What, then, are the criteria for evaluating the validity of any interpretations made of these 'objectifications' of human intentions? As Ricoeur expresses it:

Although this distinction between explanation and understanding seems clear at first, it becomes increasingly obscure as soon as we ask ourselves about the *conditions of scientificity* of interpretation. Explanation has been expelled from the field of the human sciences; but the conflict reappears at the very heart of the concept of interpretation between, on the one hand, the intuitive and unverifiable character of the psychologizing concept of understanding to which interpretation is subordinated, and on the other hand the demand for objectivity which belongs to the very notion of human science. The splitting of hermeneutics between its psychologizing tendency and its search for a logic of interpretation ultimately calls into question the relation between understanding and interpretation.

(Ricoeur 1981, p. 151)

A solution of the dilemma can be found, Ricoeur believes, through a reflection on the nature of a text, a reflection that suggests a new relationship between explanation and understanding.

What *is* a text? A text, Ricoeur says, 'is any discourse fixed by writing . . . fixation by writing is constitutive of the text itself' (Ricoeur 1981, p. 145). While writing appears to be merely a linear script of what has been spoken, writing radically transforms the discursive process. In spoken discourse, there are certain unique qualities that are abridged through the recourse to writing. The act of speech, and its tacit assumption of speaker and listener, implies that the parties to the exchange share at that moment in time a common world. Participants share a common environment; they can exchange questions and answers through direct dialogue; and the referents of speech can more easily be grasped or 'pointed to' through interaction of the minds present simultaneously at a specific time and place.

All of this is thrown into upheaval with the transformation of communication from the intimacy of the spoken word to the anonymity of the written word:

> the reader takes the place of the interlocutor, just as writing takes the place of speaking and the speaker. . . . Dialogue is an exchange of questions and answers; there is no exchange of this sort between the writer and the reader. The writer does not respond to the reader. Rather, the book divides the act of writing and the act of reading into two sides, between which there is no communication. The reader is absent from the act of writing; the writer is absent from the act of reading. The text thus produces a double eclipse of the reader and the writer. It thereby replaces the relation of dialogue, which directly connects the voice of one to the hearing of the other.
>
> (Ricoeur 1981, pp. 146–7)

Writing, therefore, intercepts the discursive exchanges. Writing is now one side of the communicative act and becomes as a consequence an 'intention-to-say'. 'The emancipation of the text from the oral situation,' Ricoeur argues, 'entails a veritable upheaval in the relations between language and the world, as well as in the relation between language and the various subjectivities concerned (that of the author and that of the reader)' (Ricoeur 1981, p. 147). The anchoring of language to that commonly shared world of speaker and listener is broken. 'The movement of reference toward the act of showing is intercepted, at the same time as dialogue is interrupted by the text' (Ricoeur 1981, p. 148). The text now takes on an autonomy, an existence of its own. It is freed to be placed into relationships with other texts, and in other settings of time and place. 'Words cease to efface themselves in front of things; written words become words for themselves' (Ricoeur 1981, p. 149).

If the written word creates a distanciation, a separation of the writer from what he has written and the reader from the author, how does one approach the text? What now, is the meaning of the text? How shall the intentionalities objectified in the text be interpreted? Ricoeur considers two possible ways. One way is to treat the text 'as a wordless and authorless object' in which 'we explain the text in terms of its internal relations, its structure'. The other way is to restore the text as a 'living communication' in which 'we interpret the text' and rediscover the meanings that were captured in it as a telling (Ricoeur 1981, p. 152).

What does it mean to explain the text in terms of its internal relations and structures? Robert Scholes, a proponent of the 'structuralist approach', helps us with this question:

> Under semiotic inspection neither the author nor the reader is free to make meaning. Regardless, as author and reader they are traversed by codes that enable their communicative adventures at the cost of setting limits to the messages they can exchange. A literary text, then, is not simply a set of words, but . . . a network of codes that enables the marks on the page to be read as a text of a particular sort.
>
> (Scholes 1982, p. 110)

Within this perspective, explaining the text becomes an explanation of the language of that text as a game of rules, or 'codes', the logic of which specifies and permits the use of words and language units (e.g. the sentence) in certain ways and not in others. Explanation in this sense means the *logic of language* separate from and regardless of the particular message that any concrete text written by a certain author at a moment in time and place was meant to convey. When analysed in terms of the logic of language, the text is lifted out of the context of its historicity – its making and meaning – and transformed into an entity lacking both temporality and speciality. It is reduced to and examined in terms of its purely formal properties. The text in a fundamental sense is dehumanized. In other words, the intentionality of the text's creator as it is to be found in the communication now only has meaning as an example of the general linguistic rules to which any specific text may be reduced, and which may be discerned to reside in any text of a particular type.

But what is the purpose of such an explanation of the text? It was seen earlier that human intentionalities left their traces in 'objectified' tracks of signs, symbols, monuments, and manuscripts. An understanding of them and their meaning was only possible through the mediation of interpretation. Yet the validity of interpretation required a basis of evaluation. The logic of language is, therefore, a set of explanatory tools – a 'textual way of thinking' with which to approach the written word and give it order and internally consistent relationships for general intelligibility (Ricoeur 1978, pp. 153–4).

In Ricoeur's eyes, the development of a logic of language is a means not an end. It is a way to reapproach the text and undertake the art of interpretation. If it were not, if the means become the end of the analysis, it would be reduced to a sterile game. Only by returning to the meaning of the text, by refocusing upon a world of subjects, subjectivities, and intentionalities, can explanation fulfil its task – to facilitate understanding through the mediation of interpretation. And by returning to the text as communication it now not only has internal structure but meaning as a narrative entered into and followed by the reading subject.

By itself, structural analysis – the logic of language – is a static analysis, a logic of timeless, interdependent relationships among word codes and rules.[2] The task is completed only by moving on to the dynamics of the narrative of the text – in which specificity, temporality, and a unique succession of meaningfully structured events and ideas represent the context of understanding. *The focus of attention is shifted to the text within the structure, rather than the structure within the text.* The determinateness of the structural analysis is replaced by the patterned path of the tale of the text. In Ricoeur's words:

> Following a story, correlatively, is understanding the successive actions, thoughts and feelings in question insofar as they present a certain directedness. By this I mean that we are pushed ahead by this development and that we reply to its impetus with expectations concerning the outcome and the completion of the entire process. In this sense, the story's conclusion is the pole of attraction of the entire development. But a narrative conclusion can be neither deduced nor predicted. There is no story if our attention is not moved along by a thousand contingencies. This is why a story has to be followed to its conclusion. So rather than being predictable, a conclusion must be acceptable.
>
> (Ricoeur 1980, p. 170)

Thus, the hermeneutical arc is completed. 'Naïve' interpretation is replaced with structures of formal explanation, which then guide the reader back to the actual texts for critical interpretations of the meanings and intentionalities within them.

EXPLANATION WITHOUT UNDERSTANDING: THE MEANING OF PRICE IN FORMAL ECONOMIC ANALYSIS

> what we have in mind . . . is not to pose and solve the problem in question as if it were a real problem in a given concrete situation, but solely to formulate scientifically the nature of the problem which actually arises in the market where it is solved empirically. . . . What must we do in order to prove that the theoretical solution is identically the solution worked out by the market? Our task is very simple: we need only show that the upward and downward movements of prices solve the system of equations of offer and demand by a process of groping.
>
> (Walras 1954, pp. 157 and 170)

Neoclassical economists in general begin their analysis with the individual human decision-maker. After all, only individuals evaluate, prefer, choose, and exchange. The *explanatory schema, the analytical grid*, that they use for coherence and universal applicability is the *logic of choice*. The formal structure of choice is demonstrated to be a matter of a certain invariant relationship between diverse, competing ends and limited means which have alternative uses, under a particular set of general assumptions: that a chooser can rank alternatives in order of importance; will experience a diminishing marginal utility or usefulness from each additional unit of a means applied to any specific end; can decide whether the application of an additional unit of a means will have a higher marginal utility in one use rather than another; and can co-ordinate, or bring into equilibrium, his own actions in such a manner that no reallocation of the means available to him can bring about a net improvement in his particular circumstance.

From the perspective of the logic of choice, all of the concepts and categories usually specified as 'economic' can be seen as being present in every conscious human decision in which the means are found to be insufficient in relation to the ends: cost and benefit, profit and loss, exchange and price. This has been succinctly expressed in relation to the concept of exchange by R.G. Collingwood in his essay 'Economics as a philosphical science':

> there is no such thing as an exchange between persons. What one person gives, the other does not take. I may give a piece of bread for a cup of milk; but what I give is not the bread, but my eating of the bread, and this is not what the other party gets; he gets *his* eating of the bread, which is an utterly different thing. The real exchange is my giving up the eating of bread and getting the drinking of milk; and there is another exchange, that of his drinking against his eating, on the part of the person with whom I am said to exchange commodities. All exchange, in the only sense in which there can be a real exchange, is an exchange between one person and himself; and since exchange, understood as the relation between means and ends, is the essence of economic action, all the essentials of economic theory can be worked out with reference to a single person. Indeed, it is only *so* that they can be intelligibly worked out.
>
> (Collingwood 1925, pp. 169–70)

What, then, is a price? In this context it is, as Philip Wicksteed clearly stated, the alternative foregone:

> the price paid stands for the alternatives foregone; so that ultimately the price we pay for getting this consists in going without that (which we want) or putting up with the other (which we dislike).
>
> (Wicksteed 1933, p. 93)

The price is the cost of the choice. Using Collingwood's example, for one individual it is the foregone eating of a piece of bread for the drinking of a cup of milk; for the other, it is the foregone drinking of a cup of milk for the eating of a piece of bread. The external manifestation of their decisions, the transfer of bread and milk, is ultimately only the consummation of respective exchanges in the minds of the two, after they individually conclude that the price to be paid is worth it in terms of what was to be acquired. It is the pricing and exchanging in the minds of the individuals that can be seen as the ultimate foundation of the economic process.

By focusing attention purely upon the decision-making process in the mind of each individual, neoclassical economic theory shoves into an obscure corner of the analytical background an essential element inherent in the very nature of the market process: that the fulfilment of the exchanges made in the mind of each requires a *meeting of the minds* of the two. Neither can consummate their intention and pay the price they are willing to incur without the consent and assistance of the other. Their *intentionalities are interdependent*. But the assistance of each through exchange requires an understanding of the intention of the other. And an understanding of the other's intention requires an interpretation of his plans and actions.

In the logic of choice, where the focus of the analysis is on one mind, an understanding of price is acquired through an explanation of price as the cost of a decision. Choice is explained as selection among alternatives and the terms at which alternatives may be obtained are their prices for the individual. But in an arena of multiple minds, *prices are not merely generalized constraints*, but a means for communication with others concerning one's own intentions and the reciprocal actions desired from those others in the nexus of exchange. Prices now enter as a potentially co-ordinating element in the arena of interpersonal relationships. In order to fulfil this role, however, the actors in the market must understand the meanings of others as externalized in the form of ratios of exchange between commodities traded.

Rather than understanding the process of interpersonal interpretation of prices, neo-classical economics has predominantly directed its attention to a formal explanation of the logic of prices, conceived as generalized constraints. In the logic of market prices, actors are conceived as *re*actors; they become the evaluators of goods, but neither the doers nor interpreters of acts. They neither offer nor interpret prices, for in the formalized schema the market participants neither communicate nor respond to each other. Rather, they simply, and *individually*, register the alternative quantities of goods they would be willing to buy or sell along a hypothetical spectrum of higher or lower prices that are both 'given' and given to them.

In this analytical schema of things, prices are not used by actors to interpretively co-ordinate; rather, their role is to equilibrate logically. The 'individual experiment' (in which n number of anonymous choosers are confronted with a family of buy and sell prices) is followed by a 'market experiment' (from which equilibrium values of demand and supply are determined by simultaneously varying the prices of the n goods in question until all prices have moved in the respective directions *logically necessary* for a general clearing of all markets).

Human action is removed from the scene and replaced with quantitative relationships. The heterogeneity of conduct is replaced with the homogeneity of amounts. And an arid explanation of the relationships among magnitudes at alternative ratios and rates becomes the end of economics.

EXPLANATION WITH UNDERSTANDING: THE MEANING OF PRICE IN INTERPRETIVE ECONOMIC ANALYSIS

We may regard the price system as a vast network of communications through which knowledge is at once transmitted from each market to the remotest corners of the economy. . . . But . . . in a world of continuous change . . . knowledge derived from price messages becomes problematical . . . [price] information therefore requires interpretation (the messages have to be 'decoded') in order to be transformed into knowledge, and all such knowledge is bound to be imperfect knowledge.

(Lachmann 1978 [1956], pp. 21–2)

Neoclassical economic analysis detaches the logic of choice and price from its natural moorings in the context of human action. The logic of choice, as we saw, concerns the appropriate allocation of given means among alternative and given ends that have been ranked in order of importance. The concept of *action*, on the other hand, as developed for example by Ludwig von Mises, focuses on the *mental doings* of men by which the 'givens' of the logic of choice are created and given contextual or *subjective meaning* by the actor, without which the content of choice would have no intelligibility for human understanding. As Mises (1966) put it concisely: 'Economics is not about things and tangible material objects; it is about men, their meanings and actions.' The mental doings behind all human action involve the creation of pictures of imagined alternative courses of action and the arrangement of their various elements in men's minds. For example, what are the 'costs' of alternative actions and what are the relevant dimensions of 'sooner' or 'later' in a particular mode of conduct? These mental pictures in the minds of men, in turn, guide their actions. These imagined possibilities are maps that men draw in their minds and from which they select some possibilities and set aside others and for which they initiate actions for their materialization in a journey into an uncertain future (see Mises 1966, pp. 13–14 and 92–118; see also Cranach and Harré 1983, pp. 1–73; and Brenner 1981, pp. 1–27).

When looked at from the context of 'action', men also *create their own prices*. What they imagine as possible alternative circumstances, what they 'see' as means to their attainment, and how they estimate the trade-offs between them, establish the constraints inhibiting the achievement of their desired ends. Whether their beliefs and expectations turn out to be 'objectively' correct or not they still serve as the points of orientation for all they say or do. Experience may override and modify men's mental creations, but it can never replace them.

I have argued that while price and exchange were ultimately acts of the individual mind, their consumption requires a meeting of the minds in a setting of interdependent intentionalities. The assistance of each through exchange requires an understanding of the other. And an understanding of the other's intentions requires an interpretation of his actions.

Neoclassical economics, with its arid formalism, has closed itself off from a serious posing of such questions. Much can be gained, on the other hand, by taking a look at some of the contributions in neighbouring social disciplines. And it is particularly in the sociological writings of Max Weber and Alfred Schutz that some useful conceptual tools for an interpretive economics may be found.

The hallmark of Max Weber's approach is his emphasis on the subject-ively meaningful act. Human behaviour takes on the characteristic of 'action' when that behaviour has a meaning expressible by the actor in terms of the goal towards the achievement of which the action is directed. Human action incorporates a 'social' aspect when it contains awareness of the behaviour of some other human actor. Human actions take on the character of a 'mutual orientation' when the actors incorporate into their respective actions an appreciation of the actions of the others (Weber 1978, pp. 4–31). The words most frequently employed by the economist represent notions of such mutual orientation. 'Market', 'buyer', 'seller', 'com-petition', 'fidelity to contracts', all imply behavioural expectations concern-ing attitudes, conduct and response in the context of particular circum-stances that actors would intend for themselves and expect from others (Weber 1978, p. 27). As Weber clearly expresses it, 'exchange' would be meaningless without the presence of a mutual orientation in which the transactors assign a particular type of meaning to their specific doings:

> Let us suppose that two men who otherwise engage in no 'social relation'
> . . . meet and 'exchange' two objects. We are inclined to think that a mere
> description of what can be observed during this exchange – muscular
> movements and, if some words were 'spoken', the sounds which, so to
> say, constitute the 'matter' or 'material' of the behavior – would in no
> sense comprehend the 'essence' of what happens. This is quite correct.
> The 'essence' of what happens is constituted by the 'meaning' which the
> two parties ascribe to their observable behaviour, a 'meaning' which
> 'regulates' the course of their future conduct. Without this 'meaning', we
> are inclined to say, an 'exchange' is neither empirically possible nor
> conceptually imaginable.
>
> (Weber 1977 [1907], p. 109)

The actors possess a mutual understanding of each other when they have interpretively grasped the meaning to be discovered in the action of the other (Weber 1978, pp. 8–9).

But how are interpretive judgements to be made as to the meanings to be discerned in the actions of others? Here Alfred Schutz comes to our assist-ance. And he aids us through his developments and improvements on

Wilhelm Dilthey's idea of 'structures of intersubjective meaning' and Max Weber's conception of the 'ideal type'. We all are born into an ongoing social world already containing commonly shared structures of inter-subjective meaning. They define objects and situations, relationships and feelings (Shutz 1973, pp. 7–11). Through a process of inculcation beginning in childhood, we are introduced to that world, and come to 'see' in various actions, things and situations the same potential meanings that others do (e.g. this individual is a 'bank teller', this object is a 'door stop', this experience is 'professional recognition', this situation is a 'riot' or 'trading on the stock exchange'). This commonly shared world enables individuals to understand both themselves and others as manifested in various words and deeds.

Within the commonly shared world of intersubjective meaning, indi-viduals experience each other in varying degrees of intimacy and anonymity, what Schutz characterizes as 'ideal types'. At one extreme all other members of the social world are experienced merely as the anonymous 'others', typified in terms of those general characteristics discernible in all men (i.e. choosers of ends, appliers of means, doers of acts). At the other extreme is the face-to-face relationship in which individuals construct composite images in their minds of the particular person in question (i.e. an 'ideal type' of that individual's characteristics and personality traits that make him what he seems to be in our eyes). And in the middle are 'ideal types' that represent concrete generalizations concerning behavioural motivations and patterns of action that have come to be expected from any individual in the particular social or economic role or situation referred to.

The 'ideal types', as developed by Schutz, serve the role of explanatory schemata for the purpose of interpretive understanding in the concrete social world of everyday life: for example, any individual motivated by this goal or endeavour will 'typically' act in the following manner . . . ; or any individual performing this particular task will 'typically' fulfil the require-ments of that task in the following manner. . . . In turn, similar 'ideal typical' explanatory schemata tacitly exist in the minds of social actors and serve as the basis upon which individuals are able to form expectational judgements as to the meanings of others with whom they interact. They enable each individual to both understand and anticipate to varying degrees the likely conduct of others in alternative circumstances (see Schutz 1976, pp. 20–63; see also Ebeling 1987, pp. 50–61).

An understanding of prices in the market requires a situating of prices in the context of the intentionalities they reflect. By themselves, prices are nothing more than quantitative ratios – magnitudes of things. They become more than this when viewed from within the setting in which they arise, and they arise from the actions of men. The intentionalities of men *as reflected* in prices are what require interpretation, and not the prices themselves. *The prices of the market are indicators and not signals* – that is, they register changes, but by themselves they do not specify what is to be done.

How then are prices used and how are markets co-ordinated? Since Friedrich A. von Hayek's essays on 'Economics and knowledge' and 'The use of knowledge in society', it has generally come to be recognized that what is of crucial importance with the emergence of a division of labour is the accompanying division of knowledge. Once an economic order goes beyond a certain threshold level of increasing complexity, it transcends the ability of any mind or group of minds to collect, integrate, and evaluate the knowledge upon which a complex economy relies (see Hayek 1948, pp. 33–56 and 77–91).

In 'The use of knowledge in society' Hayek emphasized the distinction between scientific knowledge (which is recordable, transferable and permanently available) with the special practical knowledge of time and place (which is specific to changing, local circumstances). Practical knowledge concerns the workplace, resource availabilities, production eccentricities and labour skills that could never be passed on to a central planner and still be effectively used.

More recently, Don Lavoie has reinforced the Hayekian idea of 'special knowledge of time and place' by pointing out the importance of Michael Polanyi's insight into the nature of tacit or inarticulate knowledge. This is the type of knowledge that is crucial for the undertaking of practically all daily and scientific tasks, yet can never be converted into an 'objective' form capable of being transferred to another human being without losing some of its essential properties (see Lavoie 1985, pp. 56–64 and 251–65).

Yet, by themselves, neither Hayekian nor Polanyian knowledge specifies the particular type of knowledge that enables the process of price interpretation to generate a pattern of market co-ordination. If one reads Hayek carefully, it is sometimes unclear whether or not he assumes that the messages conveyed by market prices are unambiguous, and that the only problem is whether those possessing the particular and changing knowledge of the resource and production possibilities in various corners of the division of labour can bring that special knowledge to bear.[3] In the case of Polanyi, most of his examples about the uses of inarticulate knowledge refer to 'skills' and scientific creativity.

The particular knowledge that is the basis upon which price interpretation is undertaken is that of the 'structures of intersubjective meaning' and 'ideal types'. But it, too, is a knowledge that is divided among time and place and almost always in an inarticulate, non-quantitative form. While most people in a community or society would share a vast multitude of 'ideal types' in common, the process of division of labour would result in a differentiation in both the types and degrees of specificity of various 'ideal types' possessed in the minds of the market participants. There results a particular kind of social distribution of knowledge (Schutz 1976, pp. 120–34).

The 'ideal types' that different individuals will construct in their minds, and which serve them in interpreting the market, will be products of experience with the specific markets within which they operate, the particular set of customers with whom they normally do business, and the tangles they have had with competitors selling the same or substitute goods. Particular changes in market conditions or movements of prices will result in the individual being confronted with the dilemma of interpreting market indicators (prices). In other words, when he is juxtapositioning, integrating and structuring the 'ideal types' he has to draw upon, he has to do it in ways that seem relevant *to him*. The question about which of the 'ideal types' and what relationships between them will be relevant in a particular circumstance, will only be known to him, and involves an intellectual exercise that will often be a classic instance of Polanyi's conception of tacit knowledge.

Yet, regardless of the 'tacit' or 'inarticulate' nature of the 'ideal typifications' and their use in the minds of the market actors, they nevertheless remain the social background to the market foreground upon which decisions will have to be made by the participants in the nexus of exchange. Without such a stock of social knowledge, the actors could neither evaluate a change observed in the market prices relevant to their own lines of production, nor estimate consumers' response to a self-initiated change in the price of their own product, or a change in its qualities or characteristics. A furniture manufacturer, for example, must interpret the state of the market for furniture concerning the styles, quantities and various prices for the furniture he could construct. To make his pricing and product decisions, he must draw upon his accumulated experience, knowledge, and 'feeling' for the market.

One of the consequences of the development of the market economy during the past 200 years has been that a diminishing portion of output is 'made-to-order', (i.e. with specification of what product or characteristics are desired before production begins, through prior face-to-face discourse between seller and buyer). Production is usually undertaken in advance for anonymous 'others' on the basis of judgement and speculation on the producer's part. This has meant that 'price' is not merely the consummation of a literal meeting of two minds who conclude terms of trade on the basis of bargaining through conversation. Prices, as historical artefacts (the terms of trade of past acts of exchange), must serve as indicators of future possibilities towards which present actions are to be oriented.

Generalizations must be made about the participants in the market who may be potential customers of the good in question, or competitive rivals in a line of production. The producer's informal and tacit generalizations of his accumulated experiences, knowledge and feelings about his corner of the market and those in it *are* his 'ideal typifications'. *They* are what enable him to use the prices of the market for purposes of interpretation.[4]

As long as formal, neoclassical price theory is separated from an understanding of the social context within which the laws of price manifest and work themselves out, the task of price theory remains incomplete. Neoclassical economics constructs a rarified, rigorous, timeless logic of the formal function of prices in the market; but the interpretative arc – by which Ricoeur means an integration of theory with the world it is meant to comprehend for the purposes of understanding – is left incomplete.

It is true that in elementary textbooks and in informal conversations among themselves, economists tell 'stories' about how the laws of economics and price work in the 'real world'. And in these informal 'tales' they introduce actions, plans, discoveries and temporal–sequential adjustments. This is analogous to the linguist who, in trying to show how the 'rules' of a language work in practice, makes up concrete sentences for purposes of example. Both exercises are indispensable for grasping the logic behind either language or market relationships; but in neither case is this a return to the text or a return to the actual setting of the market requiring interpretation.

Economists have either remained at the rarified level of abstract formalism and model-building or claimed to have returned to the 'real world' through applications of formal, mathematical theory via statistical constructions. In the former case, they abstract from the interpretive dimension represented by the 'social structures of intersubjective meaning' and the 'ideal typification' process of which it is composed. In the latter case, they decompose the structure of market and price relationships and reconstitute them in the form of various frequency distributions, mean averages and stochastic processes. This method of analysis has its counterpart in those textual interpreters who attempt to understand the *meaning* of a text by reducing the text to various word classes and then test their interpretive hypothesis concerning its 'meaning' in terms of word frequencies. Such exercises may very well have certain linguistic functions, but they would not help in the necessary task of what is normally meant by 'understanding' the meaning of the text.

The consequence of reducing economic phenomena to statistical aggregates is to submerge sequential–temporal relationships between both the actions of the individual market participants and the *pricing process and patterns* that emerge out of the intersecting of a multitude of individual plans in the social market arena. By transforming the actual and existing structures and price relationships of the market into a statistical image, economists following this method do not succeed in understanding the market; instead, they create a *different* pattern of relationships that may appear to possess 'interesting' properties, but which usually have little to do with the 'real world'.[5]

CONCLUSION: COMPLETING THE INTERPRETIVE ARC

In the movement from an explanation of the logical function of prices for market equilibrium to an understanding of the social process of the formation and interpersonal interpretation of prices for market co-ordination there appears to be a loss in both rigour and determination. The formal and axiomatic structure dissolves away into something more ambiguous, tentative and open to different meanings and 'interpretations'. The solid foundation of what is traditionally considered the method of scientific reasoning and evidence seems to slide from beneath our feet. We enter an arena in which scholarly discourse appears to become mere 'opinion' and 'judgement'.

This sense of ambiguity seems to arise from two sources. The first comes from the analytical isolation that economists have progressively imposed on themselves. The excursions, for example, that economists have made into other social sciences have resulted in the application of the formal structures of economic theory to a variety of new settings and situations. Economists, for the most part, have assumed that possession of the right 'technique' is all one needs, and that the technique for answering one type of question is appropriate for all types of questions. If one views all problems in the social sciences as only involving the working out of solution sets for individual maximization of utility, profit or product (subject to alternative constraints), then all social sciences are reducible to the logic of choice narrowly defined.

If, however, instead of defining 'price' only as a generalized constraint from the individual's point of view, 'price' is also looked upon as a social means for mutual orientation of individual plans in a system of division of labour, then one technique does not fit all problems. The economist must now truly become a *social* scientist. He can achieve this, not by superimposing his established method of analysis on other disciplines, but rather by inquiring into the methods of those other disciplines to see what useful analytical tools have been developed to grapple with problems of understanding *social* action.[6] Social action is by its nature *interpretive* action, and therefore its analysis requires the methods that have been developed in other social disciplines for understanding the processes through which individuals interpret one another's meanings and actions. An illusionary exactitude and determinateness is gained by economists only through their peculiar definition of 'the economic problem'. Ambiguity seems to reign everywhere outside of this definition only because of their methodological pretence that excludes other methods as 'unscientific'.

It is this 'positivist' presence (that is in disarray and in retreat in the philosophy of science) that is the second source of this ambiguity. As Donald McCloskey has eloquently and convincingly shown in his (1985) book, *The Rhetoric of Economics*, the 'positivist' criteria are not, and have not been, the basis for defending alternative propositions and hypotheses in economics. Rather than being an 'objective' standard, 'positivism' has itself been a particular form of argumentation to justify and rationalize the acceptance of one type of scientific approach and one type of theory-formation peculiar to it. A high 'r-square' is not an answer but an argument. It is an evaluational standard within one way of ordering and arranging 'the facts' of the world, and presumes prior justification of that view of things through argumentation and persuasion.

What are acceptable answers depends upon the questions that have been asked. No answer is right or wrong separate from the context of the problem under discussion and what is considered a suitable answer in terms of the subject-matter and its properties (cf. Collingwood 1944, pp. 24–33). The logic of price can provide determinate answers within various ranges, given particular types of questions asked. But once the logic of price is placed within the wider context of the social arena in which actual choices and human interaction have been and are being undertaken, it is no longer the answer but an explanatory tool for an interpretive understanding of men and their meanings and actions. It is a method for rational argument to persuade others about the cogency of various narratives and 'stories' about the 'real world'. There are various ways to order and interpret 'the facts' of the ongoing market process consistent with the logic of price. The art is to demonstrate through rhetoric and discourse the superiority of one interpretative schema over another to the others participating in the scholarly conversation. And in the process of doing so one moves from explanation to understanding and thereby completes the interpretive arc in economics.

NOTES

1 As the Chinese historian, Ssu-ma Ch'ien, observed:

> Society obviously must have farmers before it can eat; foresters, fishermen, miners, etc., before it can make use of natural resources; craftsmen before it can have manufactured goods; and merchants before they can be distributed. But once they exist, what need is there for government directives, mobilizations of labor, or periodic assemblies? Each man has only to be left to utilize his own abilities and exert his strength to obtain what he wishes. Thus, when a commodity is very cheap, it invites a rise in price; when it is very expensive, it invites a reduction. When each person works away at his own occupation and delights in his own business then, like water flowing downward, goods will naturally flow forth ceaselessly day and night without having been summoned and the people will produce commodities without having been asked. Does this not tally with reason? Is it not a natural result?
>
> (Ssu-ma Ch'ien, trans. Watson 1969, p. 334)

Ssu-ma Ch'ien was born in 145 BC and died around 90 BC.

2 It is noteworthy that Ferdinand de Saussure, a founder of structural analysis, appears to have been inspired in developing his approach from classical economics and the notion of an interdependent equilibrium within a system (see Strickland 1981, p. 19).

3 I have discussed Hayek's argument on this point at greater length in other essays (see Ebeling 1985 and 1986a).

4 cf. Ebeling (1988), in which I explain the way in which Mises believed that 'ideal types' could and did serve as the tool for interpersonal forecasting in the market arena. See also Machlup (1978, part IV, pp. 207–301), in which the 'ideal type' is defended both as a tool of analysis for the economist and as a method for interpersonal interpretation by social and market participants.

5 I have attempted to deal more fully with the wrong turn that I see in the reduction of economic relationships to statistical classes of events in my (1985) essay on 'Hermeneutics and the interpretive element in the analysis of the market process';

also in my (1986) review essay 'Looking backwards: the message is in the method', which discusses *Which Road to the Past?* by Robert Fogel and R.G. Elton.

6 cf. Ronald H. Coase's (1978) paper on 'Economics and contiguous disciplines', in which from a different perspective the argument is made that economics' imperialism towards other social sciences is likely to be short-lived.

In the end, economics will be enriched by seeing what it can learn and incorporate from other social sciences for understanding the workings of the market.

REFERENCES

Brenner, Michael (ed.) (1981) *The Structure of Action*, London: Basil Blackwell.

Coase, Ronald H. (1978) 'Economics and contiguous disciplines', *Journal of Legal Studies* 7 (June), pp. 201–11.

Collingwood, R.G. (1925) 'Economics as a philosophical science', *International Journal of Ethics* xxxv pp. 169–70.

—— (1944) 'Question and answer', in R.G. Collingwood, *An Autobiography*, Harmondsworth, Middx.: Penguin Books.

Cranach, Mario von and Harré, Rom (eds) (1983) *The Analysis of Action*, Cambridge: Cambridge University Press, pp. 1–73.

Dilthey, Wilhelm (1982) *Selected Writings*, Cambridge: Cambridge University Press.

Ebeling, Richard M. (1986a) 'Toward a hermeneutical economics', in Israel M. Kirzner (ed.) *Subjectivity, Intelligibility and Understanding, Essays in Honor of Ludwig M. Lachmann*, New York: New York University Press.

—— (1986b) 'Looking backwards: the message is in the method', *Market Process Newsletter* (Fall).

—— (1985) 'Hermeneutics and the interpretive element in the analysis of the market process', *Center for the Study of Market Processes, Working Paper* no. 16, Fairfax, Virginia: George Mason University.

—— (1987) 'Cooperation in anonymity', *Critical Review* (Fall), pp. 50–61.

—— (1988) 'Expectations and expectations-formation in Ludwig von Mises' theory of the market process', in *Market Process*, vol. 6, no. 1, Fairfax, Virginia: George Mason University, pp. 12–18.

Hayek, Friedrich A. von (1948) *Individualism and Economic Order*, Chicago: University of Chicago Press, pp. 33–56 and 77–91.

Howard, Roy J. (1982) *Three Faces of Hermeneutics*, Berkeley: University of California Press, pp. 15–16.

Hume, David (1970) *Writings in Economics*, ed. by Eugene Rotwein, Madison: University of Wisconsin Press, pp. 60–77.

—— (1985) *Essays: Moral, Political and Literary*, Indianapolis: Liberty Classics, pp. 308–26.

Lachmann, Ludwig M. (1978 [1956]) *Capital and its Structure*, Kansas City: Sheed Andrews & McMeel, Inc., pp. 21–2.

Lavoie, Don (1985) *National Economic Planning: What is Left?*, Cambridge, Mass.: Ballinger Publishing Co., pp. 56–64 and 251–65.

Machlup, Fritz (1978) 'On ideal types and the interpretation of rationality', *Methodology of Economics and Other Social Sciences*, New York: Academic Press, Part iv, pp. 207–301.

Mayer, Hans (1932) 'Der Erkenntniswert der Funktionellen preistheorien', in Hans Mayer, Frank A. Fetter and Richard Reich (eds) *Die Wirtshaftstheorie der Geganwert*, vol. 2, Vienna: Springer-Verlag, pp. 147–239b.

McCloskey, Donald N. (1985) *The Rhetoric of Economics*, Madison: University of Wisconsin Press.

McNulty, Paul J. (1967) 'A note on the history of perfect competition', *Journal of Political Economy* 1 (Aug.), pp. 75–90.
—— (1968) 'The meaning of competition', *Quarterly Journal of Economics* (Nov.), pp. 639–56.
Mises, Ludwig von (1966 [1949]) *Human Action, A Treatise on Economics*, 3rd revised edition, Chicago: Henry Regnary Co., pp. 350–7 and 710–15.
Ricoeur, Paul (1978) 'Explanation and understanding: on some remarkable connections among the theory of the text, theory of action, and theory of history', in Charles E. Reagan and David Stewart (eds) *The Philosophy of Paul Ricoeur*, Boston: Beacon Press, pp. 153–4.
—— (1980) 'Narrative time', in W.J.T. Mitchell, *On Narrative*, Chicago: University of Chicago Press, p. 170.
—— (1981) 'What is a text? Explanation and understanding', in P. Ricoeur *Hermeneutics and the Human Sciences*, Cambridge: Cambridge University Press.
Robbins, Lionel (1952) *The Theory of Economic Policy in English Classical Political Economy*, London: Macmillan & Co. Ltd.
Scholes, Robert (1982) *Semiotics and Interpretation*, New Haven, Conn.: Yale University Press.
Schutz, Alfred (1973) 'Common-sense and scientific interpretation of human action', in Maurice Nathanson (ed.) *Collected Works*, vol. I, The Hague: Martinus Nijhoff, pp. 7–11.
—— (1976) 'The dimension of the social world' and 'The well-informed citizen: an essay on the social distribution of knowledge', in Arvid Broderson (ed.) *Collected Works*, vol. II, The Hague: Martinus Nijhoff, pp. 20–63 and 120–34.
Ssu-ma Ch'ien (1969) *Records of the Historian*, chapters from the *SCHI CHI*, translated by Burton Watson, New York: Columbia University Press.
Strickland, Geoffrey (1981) *Structuralism or Criticism? Thoughts on How to Read*, Cambridge: Cambridge University Press.
Walras, Leon (1954) *Elements of a Pure Economics*, New York: Augustus M. Kelley.
Weber, Max (1977 [1907]) *Critique of Stammler*, New York: The Free Press.
—— (1978) *Economy and Society: An Outline of Interpretive Sociology*, Berkeley: University of California Press.
Wicksteed, Philip H. (1933) [1910]) *Common Sense of Political Economy*, vol. 1, London: Routledge & Kegan Paul.

10 The economics of rationality and the rationality of economics

Ralph A. Rector

INTRODUCTION

In this essay I question whether or not a frequently employed standard of economic rationality can be defended. Numerous economists now use models based on a 'rational expectations' hypothesis by which decision-makers are assumed to make rational economic projections. Economists typically define rational expectations (RE) as predictions that are based on all relevant information. The rational expectations hypothesis has been criticized for not realistically describing the way decisions are actually made. This lack of realism is usually substantiated by *psychological* studies of 'real' people in experimental situations. The first section of this paper introduces an alternative critique which, rather than challenging the empirical realism of RE directly, tentatively adopts the RE view to determine whether it produces expectations that are *epistemically* justified.

Imagine that we were suddenly able to communicate with 'agents' in an RE model. Among other things, they could tell us what they expect the future to look like. It is usually taken for granted that agents in RE models are rational by definition; but suppose we questioned the rationality of some of their projections. These agents would tell us that their beliefs are justified by the assumption of economic rationality used in RE models. Economic rationality would, in this case, be virtually synonymous with epistemic justification. We could then analyse the claim that agents in RE models are rational, by investigating the epistemic dimension of their beliefs. In the second part of this paper I develop an epistemological framework for analysing rational expectations.

An important similarity between epistemic justification and economic rationality is the element of definitiveness they provide. Theories of epistemic justification are designed to eliminate the relativist problem of having several contradictory beliefs which seem to be true. Such conflicts cause practical difficulties. More important, relativism has been characterized as a serious theoretical problem because it seems to lead to the sceptical conclusion that we lack knowledge altogether. The economic assumption of rationality is designed to prevent a similar problem in formal models. It helps ensure that there will be a single, determinate mathematical solution to equations in these models. The RE hypothesis does not guarantee that expectations will always be precisely correct. However, it does ensure that agents in the same model would not disagree about how expectations should be formed.

Agents in an RE model that lacked some standard of justification would be left with beliefs that were relativistic; they would have no reason to favour one expectation over another. From the economists' perspective, this would result in mathematical models that could not be solved. If all predictions about the future were relative, then each would carry equal weight; one belief would be no better than another, so there would be no justification for relying on any one belief. Viewed theoretically, agents would not possess any *knowledge* of the economy because their beliefs could not be justified. This is clearly at odds with the intent of RE theorists, who assume that subjects in their models know a great deal about the economy.

In their attempts to avoid the problems of relativism and scepticism, philosophers have proposed two basic types of justificatory theories: foundationalism and coherence. These theories are described and evaluated in the third and fourth sections of this chapter. I intend to show how the economic assumption of rationality could be viewed in the context of foundational and coherence theories, and to indicate why both theories lead to relativistic beliefs for agents in RE models. If I am right in this claim, then, according to the prominent theories of knowledge and the standard definition of rationality, agents in RE models are not rational after all.

In light of the objections raised against foundationalist and coherence theories I also examine an alternative account of rationality and justification. The fifth section of the chapter briefly describes how Hans-Georg Gadamer's work in philosophical hermeneutics can be used to analyse epistemic justification and address the problem of relativism. Finally, I indicate in the sixth section some of the changes that would be required in our understanding of the economy and economic theory if we were to adopt a hermeneutical view of rationality. The analysis offered in this concluding section can be viewed as a *prima facie* defence of the newly emerging practice of economic analysis known as 'the interpretive approach'.

Description of RE theory

John Muth is generally credited as the first to employ the rational-expectations hypothesis in an economic model (Muth 1961).[1] According to Muth, expectations are formed rationally when they forecast outcomes that do not contain any systematic errors. For Muth, rational expectations are not 'perfect' in the sense that they are error-free. Instead, expectations are rational when all the relevant data have been taken into account. By examining the relevant data, all consistent statistical patterns can be identified and incorporated in the formation of expectations. Only random factors, which by definition are inherently unpredictable, prevent these rational expectations from being perfect.[2]

Muth devised an ingenious method for incorporating the hypothesis of rational expectations into economic models. He recommended that the theories used to model rational economic events also be used to model predictions concerning future economic situations. According to Muth:

> expectations, since they are informed predictions of future events, are essentially the same as the predictions of the relevant economic theory. At the risk of confusing this purely descriptive hypothesis with a pronounce-ment as to what firms ought to do, we call such expectations 'rational'.
>
> (Muth 1961, p. 316)

Incorporating the rational expectations hypothesis into economic models involves three conceptual steps. Economists first develop techniques for describing economic data and expectations in terms of probability density functions. These functions express numerical 'facts' about the economy (e.g. unemployment rate, inflation rate) as the result of underlying or 'structural' relationships in the economy. Second, they model the processes of expectations-formation as a series of solutions to probability density functions. Finally, they define the expectations-formation functions to be the same as the structural functions which produce data observed in the actual economy. Economists commonly believe that the expectations made by subjects in their models are rational because the functions used to generate expectations are equivalent to those used to model the underlying structure of the economy.

Psychological versus philosophical critiques of RE

Since the early 1970s, something of an academic 'growth industry' has emerged, with an increasing number of economists using RE models to analyse public-policy questions. Despite their widespread application, RE models have been sharply criticized by some economists and by scholars in other disciplines. Among the many criticisms that have been made, the one most frequently raised is the implausibility of assuming that economic agents always, or even frequently, form expectations that meet the RE standard of rationality. In its general form, this complaint is similar to the critique developed in this essay. The difference is that the standard objection is commonly based on psychological studies of decision-making,[3] whereas the approach taken here is based on a philosophical analysis of the rationality hypothesis. More specifically, the focus of this study is on the epistemic authority that agents in rational expectations models may be said to possess. It is important to distinguish between the psychological and epistemic critiques, because RE theorists have already developed more or less persuasive responses to challenges offered by psychologists. If the philosophical and psychological critiques are the same, then economists may already have answers to the questions raised in this essay.

The psychological and philosophical critiques of economic rationality differ in two respects. First, different types of agents are studied. Psychological critiques often rely on experiments which demonstrate that when individuals are faced with certain kinds of choices they frequently violate the laws of probability and are therefore not rational. Economists typically reject the relevance of these results because they concern the rationality of real decision-makers. For the positivist, the decision to include the RE hypothesis is based on tests regarding the accuracy of predictions made by these models. From this perspective, economic models need only assume that it is 'as if' real agents were rational. The criterion of predictive success and the use of 'as if' assumptions may answer the challenge posed by the psychologist; it does not answer the epistemic question regarding the *meaning* of rationality, and it does not address the problem of defending the claim that RE *models* are populated by rational agents.

A second difference is that psychological studies test for the truthfulness of beliefs while philosophical studies include tests for the justification of these beliefs. Behavioural psychology deals primarily with the efficacy of beliefs. From this point of view there is little to distinguish the choices made by humans and those of other animals: both are information-processing organisms that make decisions which are, to a greater or lesser degree, correct. In psychological studies involving humans, the 'subjects' predict which event is most likely to occur, or they choose which wager has the greatest expected pay-off. In a related set of experiments, economists have observed the behaviour of rats to determine if their choices are consistent with economic assumptions of rationality (Kagel 1981). Behavioural studies such as these focus on the decision-makers' abilities to make accurate choices. Both psychologists and philosophers study the context in which truthful beliefs are formed. Philosophers extend this analysis to include beliefs that are true and *justified*. Richard Rorty notes that:

> Awareness in the first sense is manifested by rats and amoebas and computers; it is simply reliable signaling. Awareness in the second sense is manifested only by beings whose behavior we can construe as the utterance of sentences with the intention of justifying the utterance of other sentences. In this latter sense awareness is justified true belief – knowledge – but in the former sense it is ability to respond to stimuli.
>
> (Rorty 1979, pp. 182–3)

If the distinction between truth and justification is ignored, then rationality can be defined as correctly employing the laws of probability. According to this definition, agents in RE models may indeed be rational. The philosophical view of *knowledge* is different from the psychological account of rationality because knowledge involves more than arriving at a correct conclusion.[4] Lehrer notes that knowledge 'is not merely the acquisition of information but the certification of that information as trust-worthy' (Lehrer 1986, p. 5). There is a normative aspect in the epistemic account of justification which is missing from the psychological.[5] If we take the purpose of a belief to be that of making a true affirmation, then epistemic justification addresses the question of whether, given the available information, a subject *should* hold a belief.[6] Sellars explains that:

> in characterizing an episode or state as that of *knowing*, we are not giving an empirical description of that episode or state; we are placing it in the logical space of reasons, of justifying and being able to justify what one says.
>
> (Sellars 1963, p. 169)

It is not enough that agents' expectations accurately correspond to predictions derived from the economist's probability functions. For subjects in RE models to *know* something, their expectations must be in a 'logical space of reasons'.

EPISTEMIC ANALYSIS OF RE

According to the traditional definition of knowledge, a proposition must be true, it must be believed, and the belief must be justifiable.[7] This definition of knowledge can also be applied to agents in RE models, but the specification of belief, truth, and justification depends on the type of model being analysed. The first type, hypothetical models, are purely theoretical and are not intended to represent an actual economy. Empirical models are the second type, and are designed to represent aspects of a real economy.

In an RE model of a purely hypothetical economy, agents' *beliefs* would consist of the numeric values they expect the model to generate. These beliefs or expectations are *true* if the expected values correspond to the results of equations that represent their economy's structure. If challenged, the agents in these models could *justify* their beliefs by arguing that their expectations-formation processes were designed by the model-building economist to be rational. The equations which generate predicted values correspond to the equations that describe the way their economy works. It is assumed that the economist has not omitted anything from the agents' decision-making functions which would make their expectations more accurate. This is a plausible assumption because we expect the economist to have complete knowledge of all the relevant data for a hypothetical world.

Now consider an RE model designed to represent an actual economy. Because of the differences between non-empirical and empirical models, changes in the specification of belief, truth, and justification are required. Unlike the case involving an imaginary economy, *beliefs* or expectations in an empirical model would refer to events in an economy external to the model. *Truth* would be defined as a correspondence between empirical values that are produced by the model's expectation-formation equations and the quantified measures of actual economic phenomena.[8] Beliefs would be *justified* by agents in the empirical model if they could demonstrate that the beliefs were produced by processes that made use of all relevant data. In the case of hypothetical models, this meant that all the pertinent data regarding the model had to be taken into account. For empirical models the situation is somewhat different.

The economist constructing an empirical model is not at liberty to specify an arbitrary set of probability density functions and he cannot directly observe these functions in the economy. Of course, this is not a requirement unique to RE theorists. Economists are generally expected to provide reasons for accepting empirical models as accurate representations of the economy.. The question this chapter addresses is whether economists can do this in such a way as to claim that agents in empirical RE models have *rational* expectations.

If challenged to defend the rationality of their expectations, RE agents in empirical models could offer a two-part argument. First, their expectations are generated exclusively by the mathematical functions supplied by the economist and, second, the formulas they use are the product of a rational study of the economy. If the *economist* has been rational in specifying the mathematical functions, and if he has designed the model correctly, then *agents* in these models have a basis for justifying their rational expectations.[9] As Brian Loasby observes: 'Modern theories of "rational expectations" require agents to believe what the analyst knows to be true' (Loasby 1982, p. 113). RE agents could argue that their expectations are justified because the economist has knowledge of the economy, and their expectation-formation functions fully incorporate this knowledge.

The problem of epistemic regress

The preceding examination of belief, truth, and justification provides an account of what it means for RE agents to have knowledge of the economy. Despite the fact that this analysis makes the description of knowledge clearer in some respects, it also introduces significant ambiguities. An important issue to be resolved is the definition of the concept 'rational economist'. If the standard of rationality applied to agents is applied to economists, then economists are rational when they make the best use of all relevant data. Such data could be divided into two categories. First, the rational economist must be aware of all information available about the economy. This would include empirical data that are regularly used in economic models as well as any other data that might be relevant. A second category of information concerns the techniques used to specify probability functions and construct analytic models. Given the RE definition of rationality, the rational economist should know about all the relevant econometric techniques for identifying systematic patterns in the economy, and should be aware of all the possible mathematical and statistical procedures for incorporating these patterns into an economic model. It is obvious that these are impossibly strict demands. No economist could ever meet the requirements of rationality that agents in RE models are assumed to satisfy.

The practical problems of satisfying the RE standard of rationality are enough to warrant scepticism with regard to the knowledge possessed by economists and agents in RE models, but these difficulties are similar to those raised by the previously described psychological studies. If this were the only conclusion from an epistemic analysis of RE models, then nothing new would be added to the standard critique. Epistemic analysis discloses another problem. The new complication is an infinite regress of the arguments used to justify beliefs. The following sections of this paper focus on the implications of this logical problem.

Assume for a moment that there exists an economist who is rational in the sense that he is aware of all relevant data. Such an economist must still use his judgement: he must decide how to use this information. In evaluating the economic data he must decide such things as: which measures of economic phenomena to include in his model; which time periods to include in the statistical tests; what level of aggregation to employ, etc. In addition, there is a vast array of mathematical and statistical methods for identifying systematic patterns in the data. These options introduce a new level of complexity into the definition of rationality for the economist.

At one level, economists can refer to empirical observations and formal techniques to defend their beliefs about the economy, but at another level this justification must itself be defended. Philosopher James Jason notes that: 'in any epistemology one needs *some* principle governing the use of justification techniques. . . . Otherwise, any proof technique, any logic would be acceptable' (Jason 1986, p. 51). A rational economist must therefore be more than psychologically aware of economic data and techniques of model-building. He or she must also be rational in choosing the data and techniques that best identify systematic patterns in the economy. For this normative judgement to be rational, it too must be based on all relevant data. For example, there are numerous types of interest rates and these are measured in a number of ways. Economists constructing macroeconomic models must decide which measure of the interest rate best identifies systematic processes. Rational economists will not only be *aware* of the data and analytical tools available, they will also be able to *justify* their choice of economic variables and estimating techniques.

In his book on rational expectations, Steven Sheffrin provides an example of the problems encountered in correctly identifying which techniques and data to use. He compares the work of Robert Barro and David Small, and notes that a 'key difficulty of any work of this nature is the identification of forecast equations for money growth with agents' actual expectations'. Sheffrin observes that the debate between these two economists over the best way to eliminate systematic error 'illustrates the difficulty of ascertaining exactly what a "rational" agent should know'

(Sheffrin 1983, p. 61). The decision that all 'systematic error' has been eliminated presents a logical difficulty, since arguments justifying this decision must be made, and these arguments rest on other judgements which themselves require justification. Because the justification for this new set of beliefs depends on the justification of antecedent beliefs, and the justification for these antecedent beliefs requires yet another set of beliefs, and so on, the process of justification becomes an infinite regress.[10]

The issue of justification has become so important to philosophers that at least one scholar has suggested that epistemology be described as the theory of justification rather than the theory of knowledge (Kekes 1977). Though few philosophers take such an extreme view, most would probably agree with John Pollock that: 'The central problem of epistemology is to give an account of when beliefs are justified' (Pollock 1984, p. 103). Despite the many differences between recent theories of knowledge, all include attempts to address the problem of an infinite regress of justifications.[11] The problem is considered serious because it precludes the use of a truthful basis on which knowledge claims can be supported. Philosophers have thought that without such a foundation the regress of justifications leads to relativism or scepticism.[12]

THE METHOD OF FOUNDATIONALISM

Many renowned philosophers have considered the theory of foundationalism to be the most promising strategy for solving the regress problem.[13] The goal of foundationalism is to identify a set of privileged 'basic' beliefs which are 'immediately' justified, and then demonstrate that these beliefs provide a basis for epistemically justifying all other beliefs. The foundationalist approach to justifying beliefs has been common among philosophers since the emergence of western philosophy. In the words of Nicholas Rescher, foundationalism 'represents the predominant and most strikingly prominent approach to Western epistemology, deep-rooted throughout the Western tradition from Aristotle through Descartes to the present day' (Rescher 1979, p. 54). Most forms of foundationalism contain two criteria that may be identified as the 'privileged justification rule' and the 'dependency rule':

1 *Privileged Justification Rule*: There exists a set of immediately justified observations or beliefs such that epistemic justification for each member of the set does not depend exclusively on the prior justification of other observations or beliefs.
2 *Dependency Rule*: Epistemic justification for all true non-basic beliefs must ultimately be derived from the set of basic beliefs: that is, from beliefs that satisfy the Privileged Justification Rule.

Foundationalism claims that the only way to halt the regress of epistemic justifications is to anchor non-basic beliefs to a foundation of basic beliefs. At one time foundationalists argued that basic beliefs must be objective, certain and absolute.[14] The philosopher C.I. Lewis, for example, warned that unless such a bedrock is correctly identified:

> any citation of evidence for a statement about objective reality, and any mentionable corroboration of it, will become involved in an indefinite regress of the merely probable – or else it will go round in a circle – and here probability will fail to be genuine. If anything is to be probable, then something must be certain. . . . We do have such absolute certainties, in the sense data initiating belief and in those passages of experience which later may confirm it.
>
> (Lewis 1946, p. 186)

Because of problems encountered in identifying incorrigible beliefs, recent versions of foundationalism have abandoned references to axiomatic, incorrigible, intuitive, immediate, primitive, and self-evident beliefs in favour of those that are self-justifying, self-presenting or self-warranted.[15] Regardless of the subtle differences between these descriptions, it has been assumed that foundational beliefs are in some sense basic or simply 'given'.

Foundationalism has often been compared to Euclidean geometry because of the geometric-like structure that links the justification of non-basic to basic beliefs. The structure connects the claims of justification to a set of axioms by way of a linear claim of inferences. Rescher notes the 'Euclidean approach' is 'the paradigm model of cognitive systemization throughout the mainstream of Western philosophy' (Rescher 1979, p. 53). This geometric analogy can be expanded somewhat if we visualize foundationalism as an epistemic structure with basic beliefs on the lower level supporting beliefs at all higher levels. The levels are connected in such a way that whatever happens to change beliefs in the 'superstructure' will not affect the foundational beliefs. Rescher suggests that the structure can be viewed as a 'vast inverted pyramid that represents the total body of knowledge' with the foundational beliefs representing the pyramid's apex (Rescher 1979, p. 41).

Empirical observations, such as perceptions, are sometimes offered as an example of a source for basic beliefs. Williams, for example, cites a foundational-type theory as '*the* empiricist theory of perceptual knowledge' (Williams 1977, p. 25). Rorty suggests that one reason why empirical beliefs seem to qualify as immediate beliefs is that we can be certain about them 'because of their causes rather than because of the arguments given for them'. (Rorty 1979, p. 157). Beliefs based on perceptions have been considered foundational because of the 'grip' a perceived object is thought to have on us. According to this view, an object is known objectively because, as philosopher Laurence BonJour notes, it is 'simply given to or thrust upon the mind' (BonJour 1985, p. 60).

If an indubitable epistemic foundation for justification can be discovered then there exists an objective and universal basis for choosing between competing knowledge claims. It has often been assumed that the task of philosophy is to derive a universal epistemic standard of this type (Rorty 1979). An economist could defend the claim that he was rational by appealing to a foundationalist standard that solved the infinite regress puzzle. If it exists, the foundationalist standard could be used to justify a rational economist's claim that he had taken all relevant information into account. However, faced with sophisticated challenges to their theories, foundationalists repeatedly have been unable to defend systems of knowledge that rely on basic beliefs. To a growing number of philosophers it appears unlikely that such a defence is possible.

Problems with foundationalism

Critics of foundationalism usually begin by questioning whether the foundationalist has identified beliefs which are actually self-justifying. They then question whether the set of basic beliefs is sufficient to justify all non-basic beliefs. It is far beyond the scope of this paper to review all the objections raised against the various forms of foundationalism.[16] Instead, the justification of beliefs based on perceptions will be analysed to illustrate two difficulties with foundationalist-type theories. Beliefs based on perceptions are commonly accepted as given by most people and have been treated as foundational by numerous philosophers.[17] Perceptual awareness is usually assumed to produce 'hard' or 'brute' facts because it is immediate, but this evidence is at least conceivably subject to revision. We learn, for example, that under fluorescent lighting objects of a certain colour will appear differently than they do when they are exposed to sunlight. There is also evidence that the human eye and mind must learn to integrate the 'raw data' of sense perception to form images of objects. Unless this learning process is guided exclusively by the nature of the object (and not 'constructed' in part by the perceiver), the resulting image will be influenced by perceptual interpretations and judgements that are independent of the external world. Perceptual judgements formed in this manner would appear to violate foundationalism's privileged justification rule. For Rescher, as for many other modern philosophers, 'The consideration that we have no *direct* access to the truth regarding the *modus operandi* of the world we inhabit is perhaps the most fundamental fact of epistemology' (Rescher 1979, p. 35).

A slightly modified view of foundationalism claims that the conditions under which the perceptual object is observed must be taken into account. Unfortunately, we cannot step outside the sensory-perceptual process to judge whether there are conditions that distort our current perceptions. We can only appeal to other perceptions or other beliefs. To evaluate the reliability of the perceptual process, some additional standard must be applied; however, appealing to beliefs outside the set of givens runs counter to the strategy on which foundationalism is based. Relying on an additional standard puts in motion the regress of justifications which foundationalism was designed to prevent.

A second challenge facing foundationalism concerns its ability to construct the inferential linkage that connects basic beliefs to all other beliefs. The foundationalist must demonstrate that the context of basic beliefs is sufficiently rich to confer justification independently on to other beliefs. Within the philosophy of science, most scholars have rejected the view that unidirectional linkage connects basic observations with the more complex elements of explanatory theory. Instead, observations themselves are considered to be 'theory-laden'. Rorty notes:

> We cannot determine relevance by focusing on subject matter and saying, for example, 'Don't bother with what Scripture said God did, just look at the planets and see what *they* do'. *Mere* looking at the planets will be of no help in choosing our model of the heavens, any more than *mere* reading of Scripture.
>
> (Rorty 1979, p. 332)

Similar statements could be made for the social sciences. There is little reason to believe that concepts such as the state, economy, or society can ultimately be inferred from basic beliefs.

Foundationalist theories have played a pivotal role in philosophy, and philosophers do not take lightly the fact that these theories are unable to solve the regress problem. The apparent failure of foundationalism has led some to advocate abandoning epistemic investigations and even philosophy itself. Even for scholars who are reluctant to abandon epistemology, the relativist position may seem to be an increasingly attractive alternative.

Foundationalism and economic methodology

Even though philosophers have identified many weaknesses in foundationalism, the foundationalist approach is still relied on by many economists who advocate methodological positivism.[18] In economics, the classic statement regarding positivist methodology is Milton Friedman's essay 'The methodology of positive economics' (Friedman 1953). In this article Friedman draws on positivist and instrumentalist theories to form a foundationalist-type standard. He employs this methodological standard to show why assumptions made in economic models are often unrealistic. Friedman claims that assumptions in economic theories are similar to the assumption of a perfect vacuum in theories regarding gravity: 'Truly important and significant hypotheses will be found to have "assumptions" that are wildly inaccurate descriptive representations of reality, and, in general, the more significant the theory, the more unrealistic the assumptions (in this sense)' (Friedman 1953, p. 14).

For example, few economists believe that economic agents are sophisticated enough to calculate the expected value of economic variables by solving probability density functions. Theorists would have serious problems if the validity of formal RE models depended on a realistic representation of agents and the decision-making procedures actually used by producers and consumers. Friedman states that in most cases such realism is not necessary because economists can employ the hypothesis that agents:

> behave *as if* they were seeking rationally to maximize their expected returns . . . and had full knowledge of the data needed to succeed in this attempt; *as if*, that is, they knew the relevant cost and demand functions, calculated marginal cost and marginal revenue from all actions open to them, and pushed each line of action to the point at which the relevant marginal cost and marginal revenue were equal.[19]
>
> (Friedman 1953, pp. 21−2)

For the positivist, the test of an economic model is not how closely the assumptions correspond to the world but how accurately the model predicts future conditions. The decisive test is a pragmatic decision about how well the hypothesis 'works' for the phenomena it seeks to explain.

Friedman's approach can be interpreted as a foundationalist methodology that consists of two types of basic beliefs: first, beliefs that support an instrumentalist procedure for verifying and falsifying theories; second, beliefs that justify a positivist method for specifying data.[20] The initial set of basic beliefs justifies the use of a general rule for testing economic theories. This is the rule that predictions generated from a formal mathematical model should be compared to empirical observations. The second set of basic beliefs provides an epistemic justification for the objective, measurable observations that are incorporated into economic models and used to identify the numerical targets that predictive models are designed to hit.

Many economists implicitly attempt to solve the problem of epistemic regress when they adopt a methodology similar to Friedman's. Consider, for example, two common beliefs that economists have about economic models. Each rests directly on the foundationalist qualities of methodological positivism. The first belief is that the method of testing models allows the use of unrealistic assumptions. The justification for this practice is not based on a comparison of assumptions with empirical observations. Instead, the positivist justification for making unrealistic assumptions stems directly from a rule for model-testing which is treated as a given. The second belief is that predictions made by the model can be treated as 'self-evident' givens that do not have to be interpreted by making reference to any beliefs other than those regarding the empirical data used in the model and the formal characteristics of the model itself.

Problems with positivism

As recent debates show, economists are beginning to question the mainstream view of what qualifies as economic data and how theories should be evaluated.[21] These debates take on added significance when we consider whether positivism offers a viable solution to the problem of epistemic regress.

Because positivist methodology is based largely on foundationalism, many of the critiques against foundationalism in philosophy apply to the economic methodology used by most RE theorists. For example, it is doubtful whether the positivist standard for testing hypotheses actually satisfies the requirements of basic beliefs. To employ the predictive mechanism suggested by Friedman, we must compare a model's predictions with observations concerning the world. The problem with this method is that there are no known procedures for making 'direct' observations of economic phenomena. Friedman himself points out that the evidence used to test formal models is never conclusive. Comparison of observations with predictions is never free from what Friedman calls 'the background of the scientists', and thus 'the weight of evidence for or against a hypothesis can never be assessed completely "objectively" ' (Friedman 1953, p. 30). Since the process of classifying, aggregating, and measuring economic data necessarily involves the use of background judgements, beliefs based on empirical observations cannot be justified directly. The background context used to interpret observations must also be justified, and this generates the regress that foundationalism seeks to avoid.

There are also difficulties with the positivist criteria for making empirical observations. The positivist standard justifies an absence of qualitative analysis because this type of data cannot be incorporated into predictive models. Formal predictive models are often assumed to be the only method appropriate for studying economic phenomena and addressing economic questions. The difficulty with this view is that it cannot be defended purely on positivist grounds, since the positivist standard for deciding which phenomena are important and which questions are relevant must be justified. Despite the positivist claim to the contrary, a theory's validity is never completely dependent on the pragmatic criteria of whether it 'works', because the criteria used to measure success must be examined.

When the positivists' standard of success is questioned, economists often interpret the challenge as an argument against using models which include unrealistic assumptions. Realistic assumptions are not important to positivists, therefore challenges to the appropriateness of positivism are sometimes dismissed as irrelevant. The positivists' position is that the *only* appropriate test is of the model's predictive ability. This response overlooks the fact that it is not only the *model's* assumptions that are being questioned, the assumptions of *positivism* are being challenged as well. The question, then, is whether the standards for success dictated by positivism are appropriate for studying all or even any economic issues. Positivism does not address this question and thus cannot solve the regress problem.

THE COHERENCE STRATEGY

As indicated earlier, the foundationalism method of relying on basic beliefs has not produced a solution to the regress problem. Given the objections raised against the use of basic beliefs, a promising alternative would appear to be a theory based on the overall coherence of beliefs which does not depend on basic beliefs. Two of the most comprehensive theories of this type are those developed by Nicholas Rescher and Lawrence BonJour. The following discussion of coherence theories is based primarily on their work.[22]

Since coherence theories lack basic beliefs, the structure of justification in these theories is different from that of foundationalism. The foundationalist structure resembles a tree in which all the branches lead to a foundation of basic beliefs. In contrast to this linear formation, coherence theories rely on models from network or systems theory. The epistemological standard of coherence is applied to the entire system of beliefs rather than to specific beliefs. In his text on epistemology Jonathan Dancy notes that, for coherence theories: 'The *set* is coherent to the extent that the members are mutually explanatory and consistent' (Dancy 1985, p. 112, my italics). Justification in coherence theories depends on the ability of a belief to increase the coherence of this interconnected system of beliefs.[23]

Coherence theorists view system circularity as the primary method of solving the regress problem. At the same time they want to avoid the type of circular argumentation in which a belief justifies itself because this would open the door to relativism and scepticism. In place of this vicious circularity, coherence theories adopt a holistic strategy in which 'beliefs are justified by being inferentially related to other beliefs in the overall context of a coherent system' (BonJour 1985, p. 90).

Rather than linking one belief to another, justification by coherence involves a process of examining specific beliefs in the context of the entire system. Rescher describes the coherence approach as:

> iterative and cyclical; one is constantly looking back to old points from new perspectives, using a process of feedback to bring new elucidations to bear retrospectively on proceeding analysis. What determines correctness here is the matter of over-all fit, through which every element of the whole interlocks with some others.
>
> (Rescher 1979, p. 107)

According to coherence theorists, adoption of a system-standard avoids the problem of a belief justifying itself.

Coherence theory and rational economics

While foundationalism is perhaps the most obvious method for demonstrating the rationality of expectations, the coherence strategy represents another alternative for defending the claim that RE agents and economists are rational. Indeed, there is a remarkable consistency between the RE hypothesis and the coherence approach as Timo Airaksinen's fairly typical definition of the coherence theory demonstrates:

First S must collect a set of data which includes all relevant 'information' concerning his target-propositions. Then S applies some special reasoning methods to his data: S takes a consistent or inconsistent D [set of data], forms its maximal consistent subsets and derives the logical consequences from one or more suitably selected subsets.

(Airaksinen 1978, pp. 265–6)

Robert Lucas, a leading RE theorist, explains how a coherence-type approach could be applied. He suggests that we think of rational expectations as one stage of an ongoing process of adaptive behaviour that constitutes a 'trial-and-error process through which our modes of behavior are determined' (Lucas 1987, p. 217). According to Lucas, adaptive and RE theories are different but not mutually exclusive.

Lucas notes that no currently available economic theory, including RE, provides a useful basis for modelling adaptive processes. Instead, economic models start with 'decision rules that are steady states of some adaptive process, decision rules that are found to work over a range of situations and hence are no longer revised appreciably as more experience accumulates' (Lucas 1987, p. 218). Economists and agents in RE models could view the coherence standard as an adaptive context within which rational expectations are made. Lucas' reference to this context as a 'steady state' condition seems to come directly from the type of systems theories that coherentists such as Rescher refer to. The standard of a 'steady state' together with the related criterion of 'ordered wholeness' are often used to describe systems which have reached a high degree of coherence.[24]

In addition to his implicit references to a coherence-type standard Lucas also notes that adaptive processes produce pragmatic rules which 'work over a range of situations'. He views adaptive expectations as the context within which expectations are judged to be rational. As I indicate below, Rescher and other advocates of the coherence theory adopt a similar approach.

Problems with coherence theories

The coherence method for terminating the regress of justifications is in many ways an improvement over foundationalism, but numerous criticisms have been raised against it. These objections include: (1) the lack of empirical inputs; (2) inter-system indeterminacy; (3) ambiguous coherence criteria; (4) vicious circularity; and (5) a problematic view of truth. If substantiated, these objections would undermine the coherence defence of rationality. The following sections contain a brief review of these problems.

The lack of empirical inputs

The 'lack of empirical inputs' objection is based on the claim that the coherence standard is detached from reality. A standard of justification based exclusively on coherence seems to ignore the fact that at least some empirical beliefs must be justified – not because of their relation to other beliefs but because of their source, an 'outside world'. For example, without empirical inputs it may be possible for agents in an RE model to form a highly coherent set of fictional beliefs that is totally unrelated to the real economy. Several philosophers consider this type of objection to be the primary attack on coherence theories (Dancy 1985, p. 120; BonJour 1985, p. 111).[25] As Rorty has observed: 'Holistic theories seem to license everyone to construct his own little whole – his own little paradigm, his own little practice, his own litte language-game – and then crawl into it' (Rorty 1979, p. 317).

In answer to this objection several advocates of coherence theories have agreed that coherence theories must include some empirical inputs.[26] This requirement appears similar to the foundationalist rule of privileged justification, but it is also consistent with the coherence approach. 'It is important to stress that the need for inputs is inevitable in the realm of factual knowledge; but this unavoidable recourse is not a concession to foundationalism. The coherentist's inputs are raw materials and not themselves finished products' (Rescher 1979, p. 69). Like Rescher, BonJour admits that empirical inputs are required: 'it is possible to identify certain beliefs as cognitively spontaneous; and also to determine that certain classes of such spontaneous beliefs are, *as judged from within the system*, reliable, that is, likely to be true' (BonJour 1985, p. 138). He notes that coherence theories, in fact, require such inputs (BonJour 1985, p. 141).

Although beliefs based on empirical inputs are thus 'privileged' – in the sense that they cannot be completely ignored – coherentists point out that the process of justifying them is no different from that used to justify other beliefs. These inputs, which BonJour calls cognitively spontaneous, are not afforded the special role of foundationalist basic beliefs, but are instead tested like other beliefs. The general test is whether they increase system coherence. Instead of being 'immediately justified' they are assumed to be plausible candidates for justified beliefs, where the degree of plausibility is determined in part by considering whether beliefs of a similar 'type' have historically added to the system's coherence. Ultimately, empirical beliefs as a class are required because cognitive systems exist largely to help us to interact successfully with an empirical world. The important point is that, even though in principle the cognitive system must include some empirical inputs, individual empirical beliefs are not justified because of their source but because they enhance the system's coherence.

Inter-system indeterminacy

A second objection to the coherence theory is that it does not provide an adequate standard for choosing between competing coherence systems.[27] Critics claim that the coherence standard does not guarantee that a single system will be optimally coherent (Sosa 1980, p. 557). The coherence theory must therefore not only provide a standard for deciding which beliefs should be included in cognitive systems, it must also address the possibility of having to choose between a variety of equally coherent but mutually inconsistent systems.

The justification of individual beliefs is ambiguous when the choice of cognitive systems is indeterminate. If economists and RE agents cannot rationally choose between different sets of expectation-formation approaches that contain equally coherent sets of equations, then they cannot justify their expectations. Stating this argument somewhat differently, since it is conceivable that any belief could be a member of *some* coherent system, the inability to decide between competing systems appears to make all beliefs equally justified and thereby forces the coherentist to accept relativism and scepticism.

In addition to the more obvious problems of system indeterminacy, the challenge also contains an implicit presupposition which, when questioned, exposes further difficulties. The indeterminacy objection assumes that the choice between competing holistic systems occurs outside the context of the competing systems. This assumption is subject to the same arguments made against the foundationalist 'privileged justification rule'. Foundationalist theories have been unable to justify basic beliefs without relying on other beliefs that must be defended. This problem creates a dilemma for coherentists who must choose between two or more competing systems.

On the one hand, if the context for choosing between competing theories is assumed to be the correct foundation for making such choices, then it is subject to the criticisms that have already been raised against basic beliefs. On the other hand, if the choice of evaluative contexts is justified by appealing to another coherence standard, then the infinite regress problem cannot be solved. Any 'meta-system' used to justify the choice between cognitive systems would face the problem of indeterminacy. The attempt to justify a meta-system by appealing to yet another context-based standard would initiate a regress of justifications.

Because foundational and coherence theories face a similar difficulty, the problem of system indeterminacy cannot be used as an argument favouring the foundationalist view over the coherence approach. This is a weak defence, leaving both theories open to the charge of relativism and scepticism.

Ambiguous coherence criteria

The coherence standard is generally recognized as a measure of how well a system 'hangs together' but there is no consensus on the exact meaning of the term 'coherence'. In addition to the obvious standard of logical consistency, coherence theories typically include criteria such as comprehensiveness, cohesiveness, uniformity, simplicity, and regularity.[28] Rather than specifying a single coherence rule, coherence theories usually include a combination of rules that act as the standard of system coherence.[29] This can lead to difficulties when the importance of two or more measures of coherence must be compared. Rescher, for example, notes that individual measures or 'desiderata' may conflict with each other in concrete cases. Rather than rejecting one of these rules he suggests a pluralistic approach. 'The pluralism of desiderata – the fact that each must be taken in context of others within the overall picture of systematicity – means that in the pursuit of these factors we must moderate them to one another' (Rescher 1979, pp. 16–17). For example, in the tension generated between coherence rules, some degree of simplicity may have to be sacrificed for a gain in uniformity. RE agents might have to weigh the loss of completeness associated with one set of equations against the greater accuracy of another set that is less comprehensive. Rescher even admits that, while no one wants an inconsistent belief system for its own sake, it may be advisable to accept some measure of inconsistency in exchange for an increase in the degree of completeness (Rescher 1979, pp. 176–7).[30]

The solution to this problem requires the introduction of coherence 'meta-criteria' which regulate the use of individual rules. The meta-criteria can be thought of as a special class of beliefs – namely 'epistemic beliefs' – which define what constitutes a properly constructed cognitive system.[31] Epistemic beliefs could determine the weights assigned to various coherence criteria – such as completeness, consistency, etc. The correct assignment of weights is important because a change in the relative significance of one of the criteria could affect the system's coherence. As with other beliefs, these must pass the coherence test of epistemic justification.

Rescher argues that epistemic beliefs can 'break the regress of justifying theses by theses' because they are 'justified by reference to certain *practical* criteria (preeminently, success in prediction and efficacy in control)' (Rescher 1979, p. 93). He suggests that the coherence standard could be justified by using a pragmatic cost–benefit analysis to determine the 'trade-off' between employing various measures of coherence (Rescher 1979, pp. 11–12).[32] This approach does not solve the regress problem. Rescher's cost–benefit standard cannot be justified on the basis of its ability to increase system coherence because it also used to determine the meaning of coherence.[33] In his article on the economic theory of cost–benefit analysis Israel Kirzner notes: 'No matter how calculative a man's behavior may be, it seems impossible to avoid having accepted, without calculation, some framework within which to self-consciously engage in cost–benefit comparisons' (Kirzner 1982a, pp. 144–5).[34]

By relying on a methodology such as the cost–benefit analysis, coherentists are forced to adopt an approach that is at odds with the coherence strategy. As Cornman has noted, some form of foundationalist theory is necessary to show that probabilities or something else should be used to establish the maximally consistent set of beliefs (Cornman 1977, p. 295).[35]

Since in the absence of a foundationalist solution to the regress problem, Rescher's method for identifying 'practical criteria' cannot break the process of epistemic regress.[36]

Vicious circularity

Coherentists could answer the charge that the coherence standard is ambiguous by claiming that epistemic beliefs, like all other beliefs, are justified within the coherence system. This gives rise to the fourth objection, that the coherence theory must adopt a circular argument.[37] Coherentists would be guilty of circular reasoning if, on the one hand, the justification of epistemic beliefs depends on whether these beliefs increase the system's coherence while, on the other hand, the same beliefs are used to define and measure coherence.

In coherence theories *individual* beliefs are justified if they increase the degree of *system* coherence. The charge of circularity applies only if this relationship is reversed – that is, if the coherence of the system is determined by the status of a belief's justification. Coherence theories appear to avoid this reversal by separating the judgement of justification from the judgement of what constitutes coherence. The difficulty in the case of epistemic beliefs is that this separation is not possible. The beliefs that are being justified are beliefs about the standard of coherence. In this more complex case it appears that a thoroughly consistent coherence approach must ultimately include circular arguments.

A problematic view of truth

As an epistemological theory, the coherence strategy is useful only if it justifies beliefs that are true. The final objection to the coherence theory is that there are no necessary reasons why internal coherence produces true beliefs about an external world.

It is often assumed that beliefs are true when they correspond to reality. Philosophers refer to this approach as a correspondence theory of truth. In addition to its common-sense appeal, Rorty characterizes this view as '*the* philosophical urge'. It is the feeling that true assertions and actions must ' "correspond" to something apart from what people are saying and doing' (Rorty 1979, p. 179). Coherentists such as Rescher and BonJour have suggested that the coherence theory of justification be combined with a correspondence view of truth because coherence theories cannot by themselves provide an adequate definition of truth (Rescher 1973, p. 23; 1979, p. 66; BonJour 1985, p. 88).[38]

In correspondence theories, beliefs are true when a specific relation exists between an object and a subject's belief about the object. This relationship is one of 'agreement' between either a subject and an object or between a belief and something else which does not depend on the belief for its existence.

Because of this agreement, the correspondence theory is often called a 'picture theory' of truth. Beliefs which correspond to objects are beliefs which faithfully reproduce the objects in such a way that a successful comparison can be made between the belief's original object and the reproduction.

Correspondence can also be thought of as a confrontation. If I act on the false belief that the door before me is open, I am (perhaps painfully) confronted with the fact that it is not. I directly confront reality with my belief by comparing 'the facts' with my belief. If I then claim that the door is closed, the correspondence theorist would explain that this belief is true because it corresponds to the fact that the door *is* closed.

Coherentists who claim that beliefs are true because they correspond to reality must demonstrate why an *internal* relationship between beliefs is reason enough to believe there is an *external* relation between the belief and the world. For Rescher and BonJour, this relationship exists because the coherence theory requires observahional or empirical inputs (Rescher 1979, p. 102). BonJour, for example, states that:

> the basic metaheory requires observational or empirical inputs (Rescher 1979, p. 102). BonJour, for example, states that:
> the basic metajustificatory argument for such a coherence theory is that the best *explanation* for this sort of *prima facie* improbable agreement between large numbers of cognitively spontaneous beliefs is that they are so caused as to truly reflect external reality.   (BonJour 1985, p. 138)

The problem with this approach is that it forces empirical inputs to perform a role which the coherence theory cannot justify.

Since all inputs are, at best, only candidates for inclusion in the cognitive system, they cannot act as independent sources to test whether the system is 'getting it right'. As Rescher points out, we not only reject theories because they do not fit the data, we also, '(and not infrequently) [proceed] conversely as well, rejecting data because they do not fit our accepted theories' (Rescher 1979, p. 83). Even though the source of cognitively spontaneous beliefs may be an independent world, inputs are always subject to a test that is based on the coherence of all beliefs, empirical and non-empirical. The inclusion of empirical inputs does not guarantee that the belief system will 'correspond' with an external world.

The inability to appeal directly to the 'facts of reality' leads Rescher to suggest that: 'Room must be made for the operation of the *theory-external* controls of a factor that is essentially disjoint from the purely cognitive realm – to wit, pragmatic efficacy' (Rescher 1979, p. 100). However, standards of pragmatic efficacy cannot solve the regress problem because they presuppose an understanding of what it means for a belief to 'work'. Pragmatic considerations are clearly one aspect of coherence but they are not external controls that allow us to get outside the cognitive system.[39]

A HERMENEUTICAL APPROACH TO RATIONALITY AND JUSTIFICATION

Despite the advantages of the coherence approach, economists and RE agents cannot rely on it to avoid the problem of relativism, because coherence theories have not solved the problem of epistemic regress. Of the five objections raised against the coherence theory only the first has been answered in any satisfactory way. The concept of spontaneous inputs suggested by BonJour and others allows empirical inputs to enter the cognitive system and assists in determining the coherence of the system. However, these inputs cannot correct the remaining defects. They do not, for example, provide a means for choosing between competing systems or of identifying the proper coherence standards. It appears that the only way to address these problems is by introducing coherence meta-criteria that create further difficulties. There is no way for the coherentist to avoid circular reasoning and at the same time use the coherence standard to justify the meta-criteria. This difficulty has led some to suggest that foundationalist-like approaches be used to defend the coherence theory. Unfortunately, coherentists have been no more successful in justifying coherence meta-criteria than foundationalists have been in justifying basic beliefs.

An alternative epistemological approach is Gadamer's philosophical hermeneutics, which does not rely on 'external' standards to justify beliefs. For Gadamer, it would be impossible to apply such criteria because there is no vantage point from which the totality of a cognitive structure can be evaluated. The reason why this internal position cannot be overcome is that cognitive systems are not restricted to the beliefs of autonomous individuals. Rather, cognitive systems are part of the culture that individuals participate in. From this perspective, epistemic justifications must be from 'within' an inter-subjective shared cognitive process. The shared contexts of languages and traditions provide a social network in which beliefs are formed and evaluated. Gadamer notes that 'we always stand within tradition, and this is no objectifying process, i.e., we do not conceive of what tradition says as something other, something alien. It is always part of us' (Gadamer 1975, p. 250).

As participants in a cultural tradition we often implicitly rely on beliefs which might be termed 'spontaneous conceptual inputs'.[40] Just as coherence theorists have shown that *empirical* inputs are essential, Gadamer's analysis has expanded the class of cognitively spontaneous inputs to include *epistemic* beliefs. (By epistemic beliefs I mean to include beliefs such as those that make a coherence standard of justification meaningful, or beliefs that could be identified as coherence meta-criteria.)

Gadamer often describes these and other cognitive inputs as 'prejudices' or prejudgements. It should be emphasized that these beliefs are inputs and not the product of a purely subjective process. By prejudices he does not mean subjective judgements that are produced by autonomous individuals isolated from tradition, or beliefs that are arbitrarily related to reality. The generation of inputs is not controlled according to 'a "procedure" or a method, which the interpreter must of himself bring to bear', instead they are given to the individual (Gadamer 1975, p. 263). The beliefs which Gadamer refers to as given are not the same as the foundationalist's set of basic beliefs, but are instead similar to empirical beliefs in coherence theories.[41] They are spontaneous in the sense that they happen *to* us through our use of language. As a group they cannot be ignored, but individual inputs can be challenged and rejected.

Spontaneous epistemic beliefs provide the common base or ground rules for what participants in a linguistic community will accept as common sense and persuasive argumentation. These beliefs are the presuppositions or pre-judgements that make understanding possible. From the perspective of coherence theory they provide a context in which all beliefs, including coherence criteria, are interpreted, evaluated, and justified. Rather than representing obstacles to justification, prejudgements are essential inputs to the process of forming true beliefs. They include the tacit assumptions that lie behind the way we frame problems and ask questions. Even the most formalistic of scientific investigations must rely on prejudices such as these. Gadamer observes that:

> Whoever wants to understand something already brings along something that anticipatorily joins him with what he wants to understand – a sustaining agreement. . . . This includes as well the practice of any truly vital science. It, too, is never a simple application of knowledge and methods to an arbitrary object. Only one who stands within a given science has questions posed for him. How much the problems, thought experiences, needs, and hopes proper to an age also mirror the direction of interest of science and research is common knowledge for any historian of science.
>
> (Gadamer 1981, p. 136)

The regress of justification stops when epistemic inputs are used to justify a belief. Because they are inputs in the conceptual system there is no way to get beyond or 'behind' them. We inevitably reach a point in defending our beliefs when we say our belief is justified because of what it *means* to justify a belief. Rather than relying on the coherentist method of employing an explicit meta-criterion, epistemic inputs provide a linguistic context in which concepts such as justification are understood. It is within this context that the regress of justifications terminates. The solution to the problem of what justifies a belief is much the same as that provided by coherentists. The answer is that the belief adds to the coherence of the entire system of beliefs. If we then question the standard used to measure coherence we can report that it is a standard that has 'worked' for us in the past. Of course, this pragmatic defence must itself be justified within the context provided by prejudgements, because the meaning of success must be considered.[42]

Many philosophers and economists have thought of the pragmatic standard of 'success' as a standard that eliminates the need for presuppositions. Gadamer examines the nature of presuppositions not to deny the validity of pragmatic tests but rather to defend them. In this respect, the crucial function that prejudices perform in Gadamer's analysis of understanding is closely related to Michael Polanyi's use of tacit knowledge (Polanyi 1962). Tacit or background beliefs provide the basis for the judgements made in using the trial-and-error procedure of pragmatism. They provide the context within which new experiments are devised and new results are interpreted. When we advance reasons for accepting one interpretation over another, we appeal in part to this tacit dimension. Pre-reflective beliefs play an important role in the application of pragmatic standards. For Gadamer, the justification for why we measure success in a particular way is ultimately given by the tradition in which we participate, and, more specifically, through language (Gadamer 1975, p. 430).

Language as a mediator

Gadamer's appeal to tradition and language provides a means of ending the regress of justifications, but critics have identified other difficulties with philosophical hermeneutics. For example, Gadamer's view of language has been criticized because it seems to eliminate the need to discuss the truth or falsity of beliefs about objects in the world. Objects are not usually thought of as existing in a linguistic sense. In the previous discussion of the correspondence theory, I have discussed the common belief that objects exist in themselves, independent from conceptual systems and languages. An often heard claim is that hermeneutics ignores the existence of real objects and is only concerned with how objects are represented in language. These critics conclude that if this is all there is to hermeneutics then it is merely 'talk about talk'. Another way of expressing this objection is that the hermeneutical account of justification applies only to the use of words and not to our knowledge of real things that exist apart from language.

This critique is often made by those who associate traditional theories of truth with Gadamer's view of justification. This type of criticism misses the point, because Gadamer rejects the correspondence approach of separating objects from knowing subjects. For Gadamer, knowable objects do not exist in a 'pure' state separate from a cognitive process. Objects which could be said to exist independent of a subject's projections are not a part of the world which presents itself to us. Gadamer does not deny that there is a world-in-itself (Gadamer 1975, p. 406). He notes, for example, that in understanding a text: 'even if it must always be understood in different ways, it is still the same text presenting itself to us in these different ways' (Gadamer 1975, p. 359). Nevertheless, Gadamer does challenge the fundamental distinction between objects and subjects that the correspondence theory rests on, and he bases his view of hermeneutics on an alternative understanding of truth.

In brief, Gadamer rejects the view that words are substitutes for independent 'objects' and that language is a tool that can be manipulated by an autonomous 'subject'. Instead, he regards language as a context within which both objects and subjects are given meaning.[43] The understanding we have of objects from within the context of language is not something that can be compared with objects viewed from an Archimedean point that lies outside language.[44] Gadamer notes that:

> to live in a linguistic world, as one does as a member of a linguistic community, does not mean that one is placed within an environment as animals are in theirs. We cannot see a linguistic world from above in this way, for there is no point of view outside the experience of the world in language from which it could itself become an object.
>
> (Gadamer 1975, p. 410)

For Gadamer, words are not the 'copies' of objects but instead are elements in the process by which objects come into language (Gadamer 1975, p. 377).[45] It is important to recognize that this process does not result in the 'world' becoming an object that stands apart from language: 'Rather the object of knowledge and of statements is already enclosed within the world horizon of language' (Gadamer 1975, p. 408). Objects are not first experienced apart from language and then categorized within a linguistic context. Instead, it is language that makes the original experience of the world possible:

> The experience is not wordless to begin with and then an object of reflection by being named, by being subsumed under the universality of the word. Rather, it is part of experience itself that it seeks and finds words that express it.
>
> (Gadamer 1975, p. 377)

Within any language there is an important sense in which certain words are appropriate for the object being described. Gadamer's point is that neither the object nor the subject can be the dominant 'controlling' influence in determining the appropriateness of words.[46] Just as words are not 'copies' of autonomous objects, words are not used by autonomous subjects who somehow exercise 'external' control. Instead of either the object or the subject controlling language, both are understood 'within' a linguistic framework. Language is the context which allows people to converse about an object and ultimately to arrive at true beliefs. It is the 'middle ground in which understanding and agreement concerning the object takes place between two people' (Gadamer 1975, pp. 345–6). Gadamer tells us in the concluding pages of *Truth and Method* that his 'enquiry has been guided by the basic idea that language is a central point where "I" and world meet or, rather, manifest their original unity' (Gadamer 1975, p. 431).

By rejecting the standard account of the relationship between object and subject, Gadamer refuses to accept the view that truth refers to the relationship between objects-in-themselves on the one hand and ideas which are somehow independent of language on the other. For Gadamer, both the object and the subject are linguistically constituted, there is no 'possible position outside the human, linguistic world' from which words could be compared to beings-in-themselves. Even those forms of awareness which are not explicitly linguistic presuppose language (Gadamer 1975, p. 360).[47]

Critics who claim that Gadamer's linguistic approach makes truth unrelated to reality often miss the point of Gadamer's analysis. Truths are absolute only in the context of language because there is nothing other than language that beliefs can be compared with. Understanding is essentially a linguistic event that:

> transcends all the relativities of the positing of being, because it embraces all being-in-itself, in whatever relationships (relativities) it appears. The linguistic quality of our experience of the world is prior, as contrasted with everything that is recognized and addressed as being.
>
> (Gadamer 1975, p. 408)

Truth for Gadamer could be viewed as a form of coherence in which objects are part of the coherence context. Given the difference between this approach to ontology and that of the correspondence theory, it would perhaps be better to identify Gadamer's views as representing a 'coordination' theory of knowledge.[48] Rather than corresponding one to the other, there is a co-ordination of objects and ideas in language. The fact that meanings are formed within this context does not imply that Gadamer's theory is merely 'talk about talk' rather than being 'talk about reality'. There is no talk of reality which is not also 'about talk'.

Addressing the problem of relativism

As with foundationalism, pragmatism, and coherentism, Gadamer's hermeneutical views have been criticized for being relativistic. Many philosophers have assumed that true beliefs must be justified according to standards that are unequivocal, universal, and unchanging. Even if philosophical hermeneutics stops the regress of justifications and overcomes the objection that it is unrelated to reality, it still appears to these critics to be relativistic. Perhaps the most troubling aspect of Gadamer's philosophy is his view that the process of reaching true beliefs presupposes the existence of unexamined prejudices which may vary from one tradition to another. Since there is no context other than tradition within which epistemic justification can be decided, differences between traditions that result in diverse truth claims appear to produce relativistic beliefs. By arguing that subjects cannot 'look' at objects in a way that is independent from their tradition, Gadamer seems by his own analysis to support relativism. In response to this charge, Gadamer admits that all perspectives are relative to some context but he argues that this does not prevent beliefs from being true.

> [T]here is no possible consciousness, however infinite, in which the 'object' that is handed down would appear in the light of eternity. Every assimilation of tradition is historically different: which does not mean that every one represents only an imperfect understanding of it. Rather, every one is the experience of a 'view' of the object itself.
>
> (Gadamer 1975, p. 430)

The concept of a 'hermeneutical circle' is sometimes used to indicate how truth and justification occur within an on-going process. Gadamer makes use of the concept of a hermeneutical circle to explain that 'the movement of understanding is constantly from the whole to the part and back to the whole. . . . The harmony of all the details with the whole is the criterion of correct understanding' (Gadamer 1975, p. 236). In Gadamer's view, it is the circular movement between parts and wholes, combined with the anticipation of how ideas will fit together, which provides a 'process' view of justification.

> A person who is trying to understand a text is always performing an act of projecting. He projects before himself a meaning for the text as a whole as soon as some initial meaning emerges in the text. Again, the latter emerges only because he is reading the text with particular expectations in regard to a certain meaning. The working out of this fore-project, which is constantly revised in terms of what emerges as he penetrates into the meaning, is understanding what is there.
>
> (Gadamer 1975, p. 236)

For Gadamer, all beliefs incorporate *anticipations* regarding the best way to organize conceptual systems into a coherent whole. Because we cannot 'close' our conceptual system we cannot escape the necessity of adopting some prejudgements. This does not mean that we are forced to accept our presuppositions passively. Just as empirical inputs allow us to investigate empirical objects, our tradition provides us with questions that allow us to examine closely the prejudices that underlie our claim of understanding. Hermeneutical philosophers, such as Gadamer, emphasizes the need to be open to perspectives that reveal objects in new ways, and to consider different ways of interpreting objects. This openness, in turn, causes tacit beliefs to be revealed and evaluated because it forces us to test their ability to co-ordinate internal relationships within the cognitive system.

Gadamer's view of beliefs as being guided by projections or anticipations is remarkably similar to certain aspects of Karl Popper's evolutionary epistemology. Popper defends the view that expectations must precede observations and that both are revised through a trial-and-error process (Popper 1979, p. 344).

> Knowledge never begins from nothing, but always from some background knowledge – knowledge which at the moment is taken for granted – together with some difficulties, some problems. These as a rule arise from the clash between, on the one side, expectations inherent in our background knowledge and, on the other side, some new findings, such as our observations or some hypotheses suggested by them.
>
> (Popper 1979, p. 71)

Popper sees this projection as an essential component of all understanding, including sensory awareness. Sense organs, prejudices, scientific theories, and language are alike in that they are blind to phenomena which they do not anticipate. Popper rejects the view that direct observations are possible, arguing instead that data are 'interpretations which incorporate theories and prejudices and which, like theories, are impregnated with conjectural expectations' (Popper 1979, p. 145).[49]

Prejudices, like Popper's scientific conjectures, do not form a harmonious set but often emerge as conceptual competitors that are continually being put at risk and questioned in light of what other prejudices and conjectures indicate. When we ask questions about objects, we place them in particular perspectives by defining the legitimate bounds for meaningful answers (Gadamer 1975, p. 326; 1981, p. 164). In the process of answering one question other questions arise, including some that challenge our presuppositions. As out prejudices are revealed through this competitive process, we disclose truths about ourselves and the object (Gadamer 1975, p. 266).

Unlike coherentists, who attempt to find external epistemic beliefs that are unchanging, Gadamer recognizes that the justification of beliefs is an ongoing process. Establishing the system's coherence is a constant process in which individuals both receive inputs from, and contribute to, their tradition. Joel Weinsheimer notes that the 'finitude of interpretation', which lacks both a beginning and an end, 'has profound consequences for our conception of truth, for it suggests that if there is any truth at all, it occurs not at the beginning or the end but in the process of interpretation' (Weinsheimer 1985, p. 254). Because we are always within a tradition that includes an epistemic process of justification, we cannot refer to a static relation of fixed correspondence or a set of absolute coherence standards.

Gadamer's work demonstrates that when we question the legitimacy of our beliefs we rely on more than a formal methodology that can be made fully explicit. We must also employ extra-methodological standards. Gadamer identifies the source of these standards as prejudices that are available to us through our participation in a tradition. Susan Hekman observes that : 'True prejudices are always self-reflexive, that is, they reveal us to ourselves; they are prejudices that constitute our way of life and our self-understanding' (Hekman 1986, pp. 114–5).

PHILOSOPHICAL HERMENEUTICS AND THE INTERPRETIVE APPROACH

Gadamer's understanding of rationality and justification challenges the positivist approach in several respects. As previously stated, agents in RE models are judged to be rational when their expectation-formation process makes the best use of all relevant information. Because economists have no theory that explains how agents create their own models of the economy, it is assumed that agents are rational when they adopt the model constructed by the economist. In other words, agents in RE models must rely on the economist to identify all the systematic trends in the relevant data. The question of epistemic justification arises when economists must defend the claim that they themselves could be 'rational' agents. The RE standard of rationality is consistent with both foundationalist and coherentist theories of justification. The problem is that RE agents and economists cannot use these theories to defend their rationality because neither theory solves the infinite regress problem.

Although Gadamer's philosophical analysis is largely consistent with a coherence approach, his concept of prejudgements provides a means for overcoming objections raised against traditional coherence theories. Gadamer in effect identifies prejudgements as conceptual inputs which help determine the meaning and justification of standards such as coherence and rationality. Philosophic hermeneutics provides economists with an effective solution to the regress problem and offers a justification for the claim that they are rational.

Whether they realize it or not, economists must rely on tacit presuppositions. Without numerous unstated assumptions they could not decide which economic phenomena to study, which research techniques to use and which interpretations of the results to accept. According to hermeneutical philosophers, such evaluations could never be based on a set of basic beliefs or universal standards of coherence. Unlike the economists and philosophers who attempt to take explicit account of all the relevant data, Gadamer's analysis indicates that presuppositions or prejudices play an important role in justifying the rationality of economists.

In contrast to economists' claims of rationality, Gadamer's analysis does not apply to agents in RE models. Economists who are participants in a scientific community share a language, tradition, and history. From the perspective of RE theory, no purpose would be served by introducing these interpretive contexts into RE models. RE agents do not have to interpret the formal decision-making algorithms that are explicitly given to them. From the agents' perspective, the economist has already determined what their expectations mean. Decision algorithms used in RE models can be viewed as basic beliefs or coherent systems which may be consistent with either the foundationalist or coherentist approaches to justification. However, they are fundamentally different from the given beliefs which economists rely on and those identified by hermeneutical philosophers.

RE economists who use philosophical hermeneutics to defend the claim that they are rational cannot use the same standard to justify the rationality of RE agents. This discrepancy presents obvious problems for those economists who believe that there is a universal standard of rationality. Other economists may not be troubled by this inconsistency because they do not see how the problem affects the day-to-day practice of economic analysis. They may decide to ignore the inconsistency or perhaps argue that the dichotomy can be defended. Another strategy for coping with the problem of contradictory rationality standards is to consider how economic analysis would differ if the beliefs of RE agents were judged by the same standard of rationality that economists apply to themselves.

One key difference would be a new understanding of the meaning of 'expectations'. From a hermeneutical perspective, expectations are projections made by agents about economic and other social phenomena. These projections are distinguished from a positivist view because they are not 'copies' of patterns or trends that exist independently of the agents' expectation-formation process. The difference centres on the relation between the subject that forms the expectation and the object about which the expectation is formed. The process of forming expectations contains an ontological character that is ignored by the positivist separation of subject and object. Friedrich von Hayek's work on the relationship between economics and knowledge leads him to a similar observation. '[O]ur senses recognize (or better: "project", or "read into" the world) patterns which we are in fact not able discursively to describe and perhaps may never be able to specify' (Hayek 1967, p. 53). The objects about which economic agents form expectations are not immediately observable as foundationalist 'givens' or even coherentist 'wholes'. This is because the very existence of these objects is in part dependent on the interpretive context within which agents understand the opportunities and obstacles they face.[50]

This emphasis on the agents' perspective will be familiar to economists who have studied the history of the 'subjectivist' tradition in economics. Subjectivism became an accepted part of neoclassical theory when economists recognized that economic value is not an 'objective' object. With the success of the marginalist revolution, most economists now concede the importance of subjective *value* in price theory. However, mainstream economic theory has not yet accounted for the 'subjectivity' of agents' *interpretations*. From an interpretive perspective, it is impossible to look at objective data directly to determine what economic agents are forming judgements or expectations about. Instead, as Gerald O'Driscoll and Mario Rizzo put it:

[the] 'level of reality' that is important is the 'realm of *subjective meaning*'. The objects of economic activity are thus not even definable except in terms of what actors perceive them to be. A price is not merely a number placed on a label but, more fundamentally, the conditions of exchange on which A and B purposefully interact.

(O'Driscoll and Rizzo 1985, p. 18)

From an interpretive point of view, rational agents cannot respond automatically to 'objective' events, such as price changes, because there are no events that could elicit such responses. Consider the information that a price 'conveys' to the manager of a store. Richard Ebeling notes that a price can convey many different 'signals': the need to relocate the store; increase advertising; change product line; or alter the quality of goods for sale. In fact there are no unambiguous or objective signals that could be sent to the store owner (Ebeling 1986, p. 45). As Mark Addleson observes:

Market prices do not serve as 'points of orientation' in any deterministic sense. Whatever information is *judged* to be relevant has to be *interpreted*. Its significance has to be evaluated and weighed in the process of forming expectations and making decisions.

(Addleson 1986, pp. 12–13)

A hermeneutical view of economic theory differs from positivism because it does not ignore agents' interpretive contexts. Interpretive economics bases its understanding of economic events in part on the meanings and interpretations that economic actors give to these events. A closely related 'unit of analysis' is Ludwig Lachmann's concept of the agent's plan (Lachmann 1971). The concept of the plan brings together the forward-looking aspect of expectations and the interpretive context in which these expectations are understood. It provides a basis for theories that explain how individuals interact to produce both micro- and macro-economic phenomena.

The interpretive view of agents' expectations is consistent with the approach economists take when forming theories about the economy. Even economists who claim that their work is based on the methodology of positivism rely on presuppositions that supplement positivist tenets. By failing to recognize the importance of the interpretive dimension in the development of their own understanding of the economy, positivists have overlooked the limitations of not having interpretive-type agents in their models. Instead of taking account of the interpretive schemes that real economic decision-makers use to interpret the relevant data of the market, positivists believe they can objectively decide which data are relevant and how they should be interpreted. These decisions are then codified in formal RE models to provide the standard of rationality that is appropriate for agents in these models. Given the ontological nature of expectations described above, such economists should consider whether they are even studying the same 'objects' that actors in the real economy are forming expectations about.

For example, the development and implementation of corporate strategies depends in part on the interpretations which senior managers make regarding a wide variety of data. The information available to these decision-makers often includes consumer marketing surveys, internal efficiency reports, evaluations of competitive threats, etc. In addition to assessing the environment outside the firm, the company must also consider whether internal factors such as organizational structures and financial plans are consistent with their strategic goals. Choices made on the basis of this information depend on the interpretive framework that decision-makers find themselves in. Seen in this context, the economists' understanding of data regarding factors used in the production of economic goods should be based in part on the agents' interpretations. This approach is especially important if an adequate understanding of market processes such as technological innovation are to be developed. From a positivist perspective, interpretive-type data appear irrelevant because they cannot be formalized as testable for quantitative predictions. In contrast to this view, interpretive economists believe that our understanding of important social phenomena has been hindered by the positivist standard of relevancy.

Critics might charge that there is no point in developing theories of the economy if these theories contain nothing other than the opinions of agents. It might appear that the role of the economist is reduced to that of an historian who collects vague impressions about what consumers and producers think of the economy. This view misrepresents the interpretive approach in two ways. First, although it is important to consider the understanding that agents attach to their plans, the economist is not bound by these interpretations. The interpretive economist is not attempting to effect a kind of 'psychic transposition' or 'empathetic understanding' concerning the meaning which economic subjects give to the plans they author. Gadamer notes that: 'The horizon of understanding cannot be limited either by what the writer had originally in mind, or by the horizon of the person to whom the text was originally addressed' (Gadamer 1975, p. 356). The economist, in fact, often performs an important service by showing that the effects of agents' plans were different from those which were intended by the agents. Interpretive economics is interested precisely in the process by which unintended consequences emerge and affect future plans and outcomes. The requirement that an understanding of agents' plans be included in economic analysis means that the economists' explanation of unintended consequences must be related to the agents' perspective.

Another critique of interpretive theory is that it focuses on data which are purely 'subjective'. It is ironic that an approach based on philosophical hermeneutics has been challenged in this way. Interpretive analysis employing Gadamer's understanding of presuppositions does not view expectations as being formed in isolation of social, historical, and linguistic contexts. The interpretive framework in which economic plans emerge are not subjective in the sense that they are the result of an autonomous process that agents engage in. Instead, as previously stated, these expectations are formed in an intersubjective context. Ebeling explains that: 'The social standardizations of role and function in the form of typical modes of conduct serve as the foundations for the construction of expectations by agents in the social and economic arenas' (Ebeling 1986, p. 48). This suggests that instead of collecting isolated impressions about economic events, the interpretive economist investigates *social* patterns that define the conceptual frameworks within which agents make their plans.

The inclusion of the agents' intersubjective context in economic theorizing clearly distinguishes the hermeneutical-based, interpretive approach from positivist methodology. In addition, the interpretive view of rationality sheds new light on the criticism that RE theory is based on an unrealistic assumption of rationality. The argument that 'real' decision-makers are not rational is based on the unwarranted assumption that the RE view of rationality is justifiable. This view of rationality cannot be consistently defended when the process of justifying the agents' beliefs includes an examination of positivist methodology. As the preceding analysis of foundational and coherence epistemology indicates, these theories can at best provide only a partial defence for the claim that agents in RE models are rational. In addition, philosophical hermeneutics solves many of the problems of justification and truth that economists face, but it cannot be applied to agents in RE models.

From an interpretive perspective, agents in economic models could be considered rational if they were more like 'real' economic agents. Thus, the epistemological and ontological analysis presented in this chapter complements the alternatives suggested by psychologists and others who find RE theory to be unrealistic. It is not 'real' agents that are irrational but, instead, the agents in RE models. Rather than indicating why real agents are not rational, the analysis of actual economic decision-making should be seen as an alternative which promises a view of rationality and of economic theory that is more justifiable than that of rational expectations.

ACKNOWLEDGEMENTS

I wish gratefully to acknowledge the valuable advice of Don Lavoie and Lynn Newbill, although I assume responsibility for any errors.

NOTES

1 For a general introduction to RE models, see Attfield, Demery and Duck (1985), Havrilesky (1985), Klamer (1984), and Sheffrin (1983).
2 RE theorists do not argue that their statistical approach is an attempt to

compensate for imperfections such as 'lapses in closure and completeness'. Their definition of 'imperfect' knowledge would therefore be somewhat different from the description given by Brodbeck (1962).

3 For example, see Hogarth and Reder (1987).

4 While most philosophers seem to agree that both truth and justification are required for knowledge, there are differences of opinion regarding the exact relation between these two requirements. For example, see Chisholm (1986), Cohen (1983), and Gill (1985).

5 But, as Firth points out, the normative aspect is not in the sense of an ethical question to which someone would reply: ' "Because you will be happier (or more loyal to your friends) if you believe these statements rather than those" ' (Firth 1964, p. 549).

6 For a more detailed discussion on epistemic justifications see Alston (1985).

7 While the justified true belief (JTB) account enjoys widespread popularity among philosophers, it has, for the last two decades, been roundly criticized for failing to account adequately for knowledge. Beginning with Gettier's article (Gettier 1963), philosophers have constructed hypothetical examples showing that a person may hold a justified true belief, and yet it would be false to say that this person knows what they justifiably believe. Despite this weakness, I will use the JTB definition of knowledge for two reasons: first, no consensus has developed among philosophers that a superior alternative exists; and second, I do not think the Gettier-type problems affect the critique of justification offered in this essay.

8 This description of truth is based on the well-known 'correspondence theory of truth' described later in this chapter.

9 It may appear that agents could offer a different defence that would eliminate the requirement that the economist be rational. We could imagine, for example, that agents have justified their beliefs by conducting their own tests to see if any systematic errors result from following the model's decision-rules. However, independent tests such as these do not eliminate the need for the economist to be a rational agent. Only if the economist has taken into account all relevant information about both the economy and possible testing procedures can we be sure that an enterprising agent will not find some remaining systematic error. If the economist has not eliminated the error from the model's equations then the agents in the model are not rational. In other words, for agents in the model to be rational the economist must himself be a rational agent.

10 The regress would terminate if the economist could claim that it was only important that he *be* justified in his belief rather than actually *providing* a justification. This view reflects the difference between justifying and being justified: a person's belief could be justified even though they could not defend it themselves. However, this approach merely shifts the burden of justification. It must in principle be possible to justify the belief. The epistemic question of justification occurs precisely because we want to know that we are justified.

11 For an overview to issues related to this problem see Alston (1985), Moser (1985), and Simson (1986). Although I refer to this as the problem of infinite regress, I agree with Alston that, in practice, justifications often become circular rather than regressing in a linear sequence. However, I think that referring to the justifications as circular obscures the root problem – which is avoiding the infinite regress. Circularity is but one of several unsuccessful solutions to that problem.

12 It should be noted, however, that philosophers such as Annis reject the regress argument on the grounds that it 'involves confusing the epistemological question of when a belief is justified with the meta-epistemological question of how we know or can justify a theory of justification' (Annis 1982, p. 54). I do not find

this view convincing. If the only restraint on what justifies beliefs is the existence of *some* theory of justification, arbitrary theories could be concocted to justify almost any belief. Such a result is clearly at odds with the purpose of deriving epistemological theories of justification.

13 Recent advocates include Firth (1964), Chisholm (1980), Pollock (1974), Alston (1976c), and Van Cleve (1979). Also see Stiffler (1984) and references for additional approaches to foundationalism.

With few exceptions philosophers have rejected scepticism and instead have tried to address the regress problem directly. There are three generally acknowledged responses to the regress problem. First, it might be possible to accept the infinite regress of justifications but deny the charge that it precludes epistemic justification. Second, there may exist 'foundational' or 'basic' beliefs which do not receive epistemic justification from other beliefs but are nevertheless justifiable and are the basis on which all other beliefs derive their justification. Finally, the regress might not be a linear progression but instead a circular structure of beliefs or systems of beliefs that are used to justify themselves.

14 The requirement that the foundation of knowledge must be certain has been associated with a 'strong version' of foundationalism by some philosophers. For examples of weak or 'relativized' foundationalism, see Annis (1977), Alston (1976a, 1976c), and Van Cleve (1979). Others who argue that basic beliefs in foundationalism can be fallible include Alston (1976a, 1976c) and Pastin (1975).

15 See, for example, Chisholm (1980) and Pastin (1978).

16 See, for example, Goodman (1978), Lehrer (1974), Putnam (1981), Rorty (1979), and Will (1977).

17 For an overview to problems related to foundationalism and perception, see Alston (1986).

18 This similarity is not surprising because, as Hornstein (1982) has observed, positivist epistemic theories are often sophisticated versions of foundationalism.

19 Muth also relies on the 'as if' argument (Muth 1961).

20 It is perhaps worth noting that the assumptions identified by Friedman are not basic beliefs because they do not confer justification onto other beliefs. Rather, their justification depends on beliefs about the model's predictive ability which, in turn, is dependent on the givens of empirical observation and the methods of model-testing.

21 See, for example, McCloskey (1985).

22 In addition, Quine (1953), Aune (1967), Harman (1973), Lehrer (1974), Sellars (1963, 1973, 1979), and Blanshard (1939) have developed different versions of the coherence theory. Other related proposals include systems epistemology and contextualism. On systems theory see Seidler (1979) and references. On contextualism see Annis (1978) and Simson (1986).

23 It is important to note that the coherence standard involves more than a logical consistency between beliefs. Even foundationalist theories are 'coherent' in this sense. The difference between the two theories depends less on the absence or presence of a 'coherence' criterion and more on whether or not the standard is based on the coherence of the entire set of beliefs.

24 The roles of steady states and ordered wholeness are described in Laszlo (1972). In his systems theory of cognition Laszlo refers to the concept of ordered wholeness and to an adaptive process that is similar to the one described by Lucas (Laszlo 1972, p. 120).

25 Other philosophers consider this a straw-man argument because all the leading advocates of coherence agree that some input from the world is necessary. See Brandt (1985).

26 In defence of his coherence theory Lehrer also allows for inputs which are 'immediate and noninferential' but he states that these beliefs must be justified

because of their coherence with 'acceptance systems'. Leherer's theory of justification seems to include some beliefs that can be 'immediately justified' (Lehrer 1986, p. 21). However, his statements about the relationship between immediately justified beliefs and the system of beliefs appear to be inconsistent. While Lehrer explains that the coherence theory is compatible with the claim 'that there are some beliefs that are justified in themselves without argument', he also states that 'even immediate knowledge depends on coherence' (Lehrer 1986, pp. 21 and 22).

27 The indeterminacy problem is independent of the first objection that the coherence standard does not allow for empirical inputs. Since the standard refers to internal coherence with *all* beliefs, allowing inputs would not prevent some *systems* from being equally coherent while remaining inconsistent with each other.

28 Another alternative suggested by Moser is to replace 'positive' criteria such as those listed in the text with 'negative' criteria which determine whether a belief will *reduce* a system's coherence (Moser 1984).

29 However, at least one advocate of the coherence approach claims that coherence is universally recognizable as being the standard of 'rationality'. Larmore states:

> Coherence, then, underlies what I described as the contextualist justification of epistemological and theoretical standards. . . . [R]ationality enjoins that we strive for overall and mutual coherence, and thus any new standard must cohere with our more significant and steadfast beliefs . . . This *norm of coherence* constitutes a sense of rationality that, I again wish to insist, has been universally shared.
>
> (Larmore 1986, p. 158, my italics)

Unfortunately, Larmore does not explicitly define this norm nor does he provide convincing evidence that such a norm is universal.

30 On the need to allow for inconsistent beliefs in coherence theories see Foley (1979).

31 Rescher identifies these epistemic beliefs as '*principles* that are no less crucial to the make-up of the system than the theses it accommodates' (Rescher 1979, p. 5). BonJour refers to them as 'laws and principles which underlie the various subsystems of beliefs and provide a significant degree of inferential connection between [beliefs]' (BonJour 1985, p. 97).

32 In contrast to Rescher's attempt to justify the coherence standard, BonJour claims that even if the coherence standard is ambiguous this cannot be counted as an argument in favour of foundationalism. If the meaning of coherence is vague, then this creates a problem for 'any theory which makes any substantial use of the concept of coherence, and this arguably includes all theories of knowledge which are even minimally adequate' (BonJour 1985, p. 154). This admission weakens the ability of foundationalists to use the ambiguity objections against the coherence theory but it does not address the question of epistemic regress. A sceptic could easily interpret BonJour's admission to be an argument for rejecting all theories of knowledge.

33 Justification of coherence criteria is further complicated by the claim that coherence must involve not only a judgement about the current state of the system, it must also reflect a degree of long-run coherence. BonJour claims that:

> the force of a coherentist justification depends ultimately on the fact that the system of beliefs in question is not only coherent at a moment (as a result which could be achieved by arbitrary fiat), but remains coherent in the long

run. It is only such long-run coherence which provides any compelling reason for thinking that the beliefs of the system are likely to be true.

(BonJour 1985, p. 135)

While BonJour's point is well-taken it appears to raise difficulties because the meaning of 'the long run' must be specified. Is it too much to expect that our cognitive system remain stable for 10 years, 10 months, or 10 days? However these questions are resolved, the standard for judging whether there is an 'adequate' degree of temporal stability in the cognitive system would itself have to be justified, and this would lead to another regress of justifications.

34 Even if the coherence standard could be justified by appealing to a 'supra-coherence' standard that remained within the frame of a cognitive system, this would not solve the regress problem because the supra-coherence standard must also be justified. See Airaksinen (1982) for a more detailed discussion of the regress problem in coherence theories.

35 Lemos is equally critical of BonJour's definition of coherentism because it leads to an infinite regress. Lemos notes that 'BonJour's argument, if directed towards the coherence theory, would require a reason, or in his view a justified belief, that any belief cohering with certain other beliefs is likely to be true; and this belief would itself require a justified belief as its source of justification and so on and so on' (Lemos 1982, p. 308). An example of this sequence is provided by BonJour in his defence of an 'observational requirement'. After identifying this requirement as an epistemic belief, he states that the justification for it is that it contributes 'to the overall interconnectedness and thus coherence of the system' (BonJour 1985, p. 243). The observational requirement is an epistemic belief that is justified by another epistemic belief, namely that of overall interconnectedness. As Lemos notes, this does not solve the regress problem because the new epistemic belief must also be justified. Goldman makes a similar argument against Williams' use of a 'second order' concept (Goldman 1981, p. 208).

36 This criticism also applies to Lehrer's suggestion that inputs to coherent systems be evaluated on the basis of an acceptance system that is 'an integrated system of probabilities' (Lehrer 1986, p. 20).

37 An example of the circularity objection is found in Alston (1986, pp. 25–6).

38 In a departure from his earlier position, Rescher has more recently suggested that 'if one is prepared to consider coherence in an *idealized* perspective – as *optimal* coherence with a *perfected* data base, rather than as a matter of apparent coherence with the imperfect data we actually have in hand – then an essential link between truth and coherence emerges' (Rescher 1985, p. 796). However, this is not a practical alternative to the correspondence theory of truth. The internal coherence standard cannot provide an idealized perspective for deciding whether optimal coherence has been reached. To determine whether such an optimum has been reached we would have to jettison the cognitive system and then, from a position external to the system, compare it to 'the world'.

39 See Lehe (1983) on the internal nature of the pragmatic standard.

40 Numerous philosophers have made similar references to spontaneous inputs that serve as the terminal point for justifications. Bruzina, for example, states that Husserl insisted 'that for rational statement, only the moment of *spontaneous assent in view exclusively of unqualified evidentness*, in accord with intentional orientations, can serve, or else it is not an instance of *knowing*' (Bruzina 1981, p. 365). The concept of groundless beliefs as developed by Wittgenstein and others, such as Malcolm (1977) and Nielsen (1981), also appear to be similar. More recently, Lehrer has noted that 'our judgements of reasonableness are implicitly relative to some assumptions and system that we unreflectively take for granted' (Lehrer 1986, p. 9). A common element in each case is the implicit appeal to beliefs that provide for us the *meaning* of a coherence-type test.

41 Because some of the inputs are epistemic beliefs, it may appear that hermeneutics is a foundationalist theory. There is, however, an important difference between 'foundationalism' and 'foundations'. Krausz observes that foundationalism 'is a theory or theories presuming privileged access' while foundations 'concern the ways in which we settle cognitive claims about the world(s) into which we inquire'. He notes that '[o]pposition to foundationalism does not rule out the consideration of foundations. Indeed, no systematic inquiry can be without foundations' (Krausz 1984, p. 398). Epistemic inputs can be challenged like other beliefs. Based on the distinction made by Krausz, epistemic inputs can provide part of the foundation for justification without requiring that the theory be foundational.

42 Larmore has criticized Gadamer's hermeneutical analysis because it fails to make proper use of a pragmatic account of knowledge similar to Rescher's (Larmore 1986). However, in a passage from *Truth and Method*, Gadamer explicitly adopts the pragmatic view Larmore accuses him of failing to appreciate.

> The fact that experience is valid, so long as it is not contradicted by new experiences (*ubi non reperitur instantia contradictoria*), is clearly character-istic of the general nature of experience, no matter whether we are dealing with its scientific form, in the modern experiment, or with the experience of daily life that men have always had.
>
> (Gadamer 1975, p. 314)

43 However, he is careful to distinguish objects and subjects from language. Gadamer notes that it would be erroneous to think that 'everything' is only language and a language event. See Gadamer (1975, p. xxii) and Hekman (1986, p. 112).

44 Rorty notes: 'We do indeed need to give up the notion of "data and interpretation" with its suggestion that if we could get to the *real* data, unpolluted by our choice of language, we should be "grounding" rational choice' (Rorty 1979, p. 325).

45 Other philosophers have taken a similar position. For example, Wittgenstein rejected a 'correspondence' theory of language in favour of a view that language expressed a 'coherent' world view. He also argued that truth could not be determined outside the context of language (Lilla 1984).

46 In Rescher's view, cognitive systematization 'is intimately intertwined with that of *planning* in its generic sense of the rational organization of materials' (Rescher 1979, p. 14). For Rescher, this planning and 'control over nature leads us to an *interventionist* theory of knowledge' (Rescher 1979, p. 103). In contrast with this view, Gadamer's understanding of the subject/object relationship leads him to reject the view that subjects can stand outside their conceptual system or nature and exercise 'control' over them. For Gadamer, understanding does not mean that we have the ability to control nature but rather that 'we are able to cope with an experience by grasping it in language' (Gadamer 1975, p. 411).

47 A similar ontological point is made by Lehe who notes that:

> The only world that makes any sense to us is that which we understand within the context of our conceptual framework. . . . As soon as we specify anything at all determinate about the world, we are already operating within a con-ceptual framework or theory of some sort and are no longer concerned with a world radically independent of our thought. To be concerned with a world in that sense is to think the unthinkable.
>
> (Lehe 1983, p. 182)

48 Gadamer, for example, notes: 'We are simply following an internal necessity of the thing itself if we go beyond the idea of the object and the objectivity of

understanding, towards the idea of the coordination of subject and object' (Gadamer 1975, p. 418). When describing the 'best fit' criteria, Rescher has also characterized the coherence theory as one of co-ordination (Rescher 1979, p. 155).

49 Gadamer has recognized this similarity. He writes that:

> the theory of trial and error that Popper worked out is not at all confined to the logic of specialized inquiry . . . it makes plain a notion of logical rationality that reaches far beyond the field of scientific research and describes the basic structures of all rationality, even that of practical reason.
>
> (Gadamer 1981, p. 165)

50 See Lavoie (1987) for a more complete discussion of issues regarding the interpretation of economic data by agents.

REFERENCES

Addleson, Mark (1986) 'Radical subjectivism and the language of Austrian economics', in Israel Kirzner (ed.) *Subjectivism, Intelligibility, and Economic Understanding*, New York: New York University Press, pp. 1–15.
Airaksinen, Timo (1978) 'Five types of knowledge', *American Philosophical Quarterly* 15, pp. 263–74.
—— (1981) 'On nonfoundationalist theories of epistemic justification', *The Southern Journal of Philosophy* 19, pp. 403–23.
—— (1982) 'Contextualism, a new theory of epistemic justification?', *Philosophia* 12, pp. 37–50.
Alston, W.P. (1976a) 'Has foundationalism been refuted?', *Philosophical Studies* 29, pp. 287–305.
—— (1976b) 'Self-warrant: a neglected form of privileged access', *American Philosophical Quarterly* 13, pp. 257–72.
—— (1976c) 'Two types of foundationalism', *The Journal of Philosophy* 73, pp. 165–85.
—— (1985) 'Concepts of epistemic justification', *The Monist* 68, pp. 57–89.
—— (1986) 'Epistemic circularity', *Philosophy and Phenomenological Research* 47, pp. 1–30.
Annis, David B. (1977) 'Epistemic foundationalism', *Philosophical Studies* 31, pp. 345–52.
—— (1978) 'A contextualist theory of epistemic justification', *The American Philosophical Quarterly* 15, pp. 213–19.
—— (1982) 'The social and cultural component of epistemic justification', *Philosophia* 12, pp. 51–4.
Attfield, C.L.F., Demery, D., and Duck, N.W. (1985) *Rational Expectations in Macroeconomics*, Oxford: Basil Blackwell.
Aune, B. (1967) *Knowledge, Mind and Nature*, New York: Random House.
Blanshard, Brand (1939) *The Nature of Thought*, London: George Allen & Unwin.
BonJour, Laurence (1976) 'The coherence theory of empirical knowledge', *Philosophical Studies* 30, pp. 281–312.
—— (1985) *The Structure of Empirical Knowledge*, Cambridge, Mass.: Harvard University Press.
Brandt, R.B. (1985) 'The concept of rational belief', *The Monist* 68, pp. 3–23.
Brodbeck, May (1962) 'Explanations, predictions, and "imperfect" knowledge', in Feigl and Maxwell (eds) *Minnesota Studies in the Philosophy of Science*, vol. 3.
Bruzina, Ronald (1981) 'Dependence on language and the autonomy of reason: an Husserlian perspective', *Man and World* 14, pp. 355–68.

Chisholm, Roderick M. (1980) *Theory of Knowledge*, Englewood Cliffs, N.J.: Prentice-Hall.
—— (1982) *The Foundations of Knowing*, Minneapolis: University of Minnesota Press.
—— (1986) 'The place of epistemic justification', *Philosophical Topics* 14, pp. 85–92.
Cohen, Stewart (1983) 'Justification and truth', *Philosophical Studies* 46, pp. 279–95.
Cornman, James W. (1977) 'Foundational versus nonfoundational theories of empirical justification', *American Philosophical Quarterly* 14, pp. 287–97.
Dancy, Jonathan (1985) *An Introduction to Contemporary Epistemology*, Oxford: Basil Blackwell.
Ebeling, Richard (1986) 'Toward a hermeneutical economics: expectations, prices, and the role of interpretation in a theory of the market process', in Kirzner (ed.) *Method, Process and Austrian Economics*, pp. 39–55.
Feigl, H. and Maxwell, G. (eds) (1962) *Minnesota Studies in the Philosophy of Science*, vol. 3, Minneapolis: University of Minnesota Press.
Firth, R. (1964) 'Coherence, certainty, and epistemic priority', *Journal of Philosophy* 61, pp. 545–57.
Foley, Richard (1979) 'Justified inconsistent beliefs', *American Philosophical Quarterly* 16, pp. 247–57.
—— (1980) 'Chisholm and coherence', *Philosophical Studies* 38, pp. 53–63.
Friedman, Milton (1953) 'The methodology of positive economics', in Friedman, *Essays In Positive Economics*, Chicago: University of Chicago Press, pp. 3–43.
Gadamer, Hans-Georg (1975) *Truth and Method*, New York: Crossroad Publishing Company.
—— (1981) *Reason in the Age of Science*, Cambridge, Mass.: MIT Press.
Gettier, Edmund (1963) 'Is justified true belief knowledge?', *Analysis* 23, pp. 121–3.
Gill, Jerry H. (1985) 'Knowledge as justified belief, period', *International Philosophical Quarterly* 25, pp. 381–91.
Goldman, Alan H. (1979) 'Appearing statements and epistemological foundations', *Metaphilosophy* 10, pp. 227–46.
—— (1981) 'The death of epistemology: a premature burial', *Pacific Philosophical Quarterly* 62, pp. 203–10.
Goodman, Nelson (1978) *Ways of Worldmaking*, Indianapolis: Hackett.
Harman, G. (1973) *Thought*, Princeton, N.J.: Princeton University Press.
Havrilesky, Thomas (1985) *Modern Concepts In Macroeconomics*, Arlington Heights, Ill.: Harlan Davidson.
Hayek, F.A. (1967) 'Rules, perception and intelligibility', in Hayek, *Studies in Philosophy, Politics, and Economics*, Chicago: University of Chicago Press, pp. 43–65.
Hekman, Susan J. (1986) *Hermeneutics and the Sociology of Knowledge*, Notre Dame, Indiana: University of Notre Dame Press.
Hogarth, Robin and Reder, Melvin (eds) (1987) *Rational Choice: The Contrast Between Economics and Psychology*, Chicago: University of Chicago Press.
Hornstein, Norbert (1982) 'Foundationalism and Quine's indeterminacy of translation thesis', *Social Research* 49, pp. 32–67.
Jason, G. James (1986) 'Epistemologies and apologies', *Dialectica* 40, pp. 45–58.
Kagel, John H. (1981) 'Demand curves for animal consumers', *Quarterly Journal of Economics* 96, pp. 1–16.
Kekes, John (1977) 'Recent trends and future prospects in epistemology', *Metaphilosophy* 8, pp. 87–107.
Kirzner, Israel (ed.) (1982a) *Method, Process, and Austrian Economics*, Lexington, Mass.: Lexington Books.

—— (1982b) 'Uncertainty, discovery, and human action: a study of the entre-preneurial profile in the Miseian system', in Kirzner (ed.) *Method, Process, and Austrian Economics*, pp. 139–59.

—— (ed.) (1986) *Subjectivism, Intelligibility and Economic Understanding*, New York: New York University Press.

Klamer, Arjo (1984) *Conversations with Economists*, Totowa, N.J.: Rowman & Allanheld.

Krausz, Michael (1984) 'Relativism and foundationalism: some distinctions and strategies', *The Monist* 67, pp. 395–404.

Lachmann, Ludwig M. (1971) *The Legacy of Max Weber*, Berkeley: The Glendessary Press.

Larmore, Charles (1986) 'Tradition, objectivity, and hermeneutics', in Wachter-hauser (ed.) *Hermeneutics and Modern Philosophy*, pp. 147–67.

Laszlo, Ervin (1972) *Introduction To Systems Philosophy*, New York: Harper & Row.

Lavoie, Don (1987) 'The accounting of interpretations and the interpretation of accounts: the communicative function of "The Language of Business"', *Accounting Organizations and Society* 18, pp. 579–604.

Lehe, Robert Tad (1983) 'Coherence – criterion and nature of truth', *Idealistic Studies* 13, pp. 177–89.

Lehrer, Keith (1974) *Knowledge*, Oxford: Oxford University Press.

—— (1986) 'The coherence theory of knowledge', *Philosophical Topics* 14, pp. 5–25.

Lemos, Noah M. (1982) 'Coherence and epistemic priority', *Philosophical Studies* 41, pp. 299–315.

Lewis, C.I. (1946) *An Analysis of Knowledge and Valuation*, La Salle, Ill.: Open Court.

Lilla, Mark (1984) 'On Goodman, Putnam, and Rorty: the return to the "given"', *Partisian Review Two* 51, pp. 220–35.

Loasby, Brian J. (1982) 'Economics of dispersed and incomplete information', in Kirzner (ed.) *Method, Process, and Austrian Economics*, pp. 111–29.

Lucas, Jr., Robert E. (1987) 'Adaptive behavior and economic theory', in Hogarth and Reder (eds) *Rational Choice: The Contrast Between Economics and Psychology*, pp. 217–42.

Malcolm, Norman (1977) *Thought and Knowledge*, Ithaca, N.Y.: Cornell University Press.

McCloskey, Donald (1985) *The Rhetoric of Economics*, Madison: University of Wisconsin Press.

Moser, Paul K. (1984) 'On negative coherentism and subjective justification', *The Southern Journal of Philosophy* 22, pp. 83–90.

—— (1985) 'Whither infinite regress of justification?', *The Southern Journal of Philosophy* 23, pp. 65–74.

Muth, John (1961) 'Rational expectations and the theory of price movements', *Econometrica* 29, pp. 315–35.

Nielsen, Kai (1981) 'On the rationality of groundless believing', *Idealistic Studies* 11, pp. 215–29.

O'Driscoll, Gerald P. and Rizzo, Mario J. (1985) *The Economics of Time and Ignorance*, Oxford: Basil Blackwell.

Pappas, George S. (ed.) (1979) *Justification and Knowledge*, Dordrecht: Reidel.

—— and Swain, Marshall (eds) (1978) *Essays on Knowledge and Justification*, Ithaca: Cornell University Press.

Pastin, Mark (1975) 'C.I. Lewis's radical foundationalism', *Nous* 9, pp. 407–20.

—— (1978) 'Modest foundationalism and self-warrant', in Pappas and Swain, 1978, pp. 279–88.

Polanyi, Michael (1962) *Personal Knowledge: Towards a Post-Critical Philosophy*, Chicago: University of Chicago Press.

Pollock, John, L. (1974) *Knowledge and Justification*, Princeton: Princeton University Press.

—— (1984) 'Reliability and justified belief', *Canadian Journal of Philosophy* 14, pp. 103–14.

Popper, Karl R. (1979) *Objective Knowledge*, Oxford: Clarendon Press.

Putnam, Hilary (1981) *Reason, Truth and History*, Cambridge: Cambridge University Press.

Quine, W.V.O. (1953) 'Two dogmas of empiricism', in Quine *From a Logical Point of View*, Cambridge, Mass.: Harvard University Press, pp. 20–46.

Rescher, N. (1973) *The Coherence Theory of Truth*, London: Oxford University Press.

—— (1979) *Cognitive Systematization: A Systems-Theoretic Approach to a Coherent Theory of Knowledge*. Totowa, N.J.: Rowman & Littlefield.

—— (1985) 'Truth as ideal coherence', *The Review of Metaphysics* 38, pp. 795–806.

Rorty, Richard (1979) *Philosophy and the Mirror of Nature*, Princeton: Princeton University Press.

Seidler, Michael J. (1979) 'Problems of systems epistemology', *International Philosophical Quarterly* 19, pp. 29–60.

Sellars, W.S. (1963) *Science, Perception, and Reality*, London: Routledge & Kegan Paul.

—— (1973) 'Givenness and explanatory coherence', *Journal of Philosophy* 70, pp. 612–24.

—— (1979) 'More on givenness and explanatory coherence', in G.S. Pappas (ed.) *Justification and Knowledge: New Studies in Epistemology*, Dordrecht, Holland: D. Reidel Publishing Co., pp. 169–82.

Sheffrin, Steven (1983) *Rational Expectations*, Cambridge: Cambridge University Press.

Simson, Rosalind S. (1986) 'An internalist view of the epistemic regress problem', *Philosophy and Phenomenological Research* 47, pp. 179–208.

Sosa, Ernest (1980) 'The foundations of foundationalism', *Nous* 14, pp. 547–64.

Stiffler, Eric (1984) 'A definition of foundationalism', *Metaphilosophy* 15, pp. 16–25.

Suppe, Frederick (1977) *The Structure of Scientific Theories*, Cambridge: Cambridge University Press.

Van Cleve, James (1979) 'Foundationalism, epistemic principles, and the Cartesian circle', *The Philosophical Review* 88, pp. 55–91.

Wachterhauser, Brice R. (ed.) (1986) *Hermeneutics and Modern Philosophy*, Albany: State University of New York Press.

Weinsheimer, Joel C. (1985) *Gadamer's Hermeneutics: A Reading of Truth and Method*, New Haven, Conn.: Yale University Press.

Will, Frederick (1977) *Induction and Justification*, Ithaca, N.Y.: Cornell University Press.

Williams, Michael (1977) *Groundless Belief: An Essay on The Possibility of Epistemology*, New Haven: Yale University Press.

—— (1980) 'Coherence, justification, and truth', *Review of Metaphysics* 34, pp. 243–72.

—— (1986) 'Do we (epistemologists) need a theory of truth?', *Philosophical Topics* 14, pp. 223–42.

Part IV

Hermeneutical reason: applications in macro, micro, and public policy

11 On the microfoundations of money
Walrasian and Mengerian approaches reconsidered in the light of Richard Rorty's critique of foundationalism

Randall Kroszner

Many philosophers have endeavoured to find a foundation for knowledge – that is, to outline a well-defined reliable scientific method which provides access to the facts of the matter under study. While operating on a less grand scale, economists have adopted a parallel style of inquiry. When the traditional models were gradually revealed to shed only a dim light on many aspects of macroeconomic and monetary phenomena, the hue and cry went up for foundations. The problem, many economists believe, is that these models are *ad hoc* and at odds with other approaches in the body of economic thought. Economists turned to the elegant and relatively recently 'perfected' Walrasian 'general equilibrium' framework (to be discussed below) as the saviour from the difficulties attributed to the *ad hoc* approach. Grounding our inquiry in this highly regarded model of micro-economic interaction would thus be the way in which to structure our study of macroeconomic and monetary phenomena.

Richard Rorty has boldly attacked the parallel demand for foundations of knowledge in philosophy as nothing more than a strait-jacket on inquiry. By employing themes developed by Rorty in his critique of foundationalism, we will try to illuminate some of the current controversies within economics which revolve around the microfoundations of macroeconomics, focusing on monetary phenomena.

PHILOSOPHIC BACKGROUND

Before embarking upon the analysis of the discussion of foundations in economics, I will attempt in this section to give a flavour of Rorty's argument, highlighting the aspects that are most directly applicable to the problem at hand.[1] Developing a theme from the work of Hans-Georg Gadamer, Rorty takes a radical stand on what constitutes hermeneutics. In contrast to Wilhelm Dilthey and his followers – including Charles Taylor and Hubert Dreyfus – Rorty sees it not as '*the* method of the social sciences' but rather as an 'attitude' or 'intellectual position one arrives at when one puts aside the idea of "method" and the cluster of other Cartesian and Kantian ideas within which it is embedded' (Rorty 1980, p. 39). Rorty comes to this 'radical' Gadamerian perspective by way of a critique of the philosophic enterprise as a foundational discipline. He sees this enterprise inevitably as an attempt to put blinders on discussion rather than open it up. In Rorty's view, an epistemology-based philosophic enterprise has tyrannized systematic inquiry by trying to legislate what can and cannot be done in the so-called scientific acquisition of knowledge. From Plato to Descartes to Kant to the logical positivists, the notion that the mind or our reason has a 'privileged access' to an objective external reality has formed a core of philosophy. The objective has thus been to delineate the method we can follow in order to gain this access to reliable 'scientific' knowledge. Drawing on criticisms by W.v.O. Quine, Wilfred Sellars, and the pragmatists William James and John Dewey, Rorty (1979) disposes of this approach to knowledge and foundationalist philosophy itself, thereby undermining the dictatorship of philosophy or any particular method over enquiry.[2]

The work of the pragmatists and the compelling attacks on necessity and essence by these thinkers, Rorty argues, render the 'privileged access' position − of access to the world independent of human interpretation − untenable: 'We can only make sense of accounting for [the world] in terms useful for this or that human purpose, but we cannot make sense of describing it "in its *own* terms" ' (Rorty 1980, p. 40). We are not able to step outside of the world and observe it from a 'god's-eye' point of view. Our models or ways of speaking should not be construed as representation of some external realm, the essence of which we wish to capture in a model. The goal of a correspondence between our model and 'the world out there' is illusory, for we cannot know what is out there without employing some human filter. Since we are unable to step outside and look in, we can focus instead upon coherence and usefulness, rather than correspondence, in judging our models and theories.

The 'scientific method' has been dethroned as the ruler of the realm of knowledge acquisition, and no new leader need take its place. The usefulness of mechanical and formal ways of speaking in fields such as physics and engineering is no reason to insist that other disciplines adopt a similar vocabulary in order to achieve success. The demarcation of science from non-science has been used as an obstacle to inquiry rather than as an epistemological way by which to separate the wheat from the chaff. As Rorty explains:

> [i]t may be that the only people who still care deeply about the distinctions between science and art, between the cognitive and the non-cognitive, are the bureaucrats who give out grants, the educational administrators, and us professors of philosophy.
>
> (Rorty 1980, p. 45)

The ideas that Rorty develops are in response to the attempts to ground the whole enterprise of knowledge acquisition and not simply to ground the structure of inquiry within a particular discipline. The offending attitudes that Rorty identifies, however, also affect discussion within individual disciplines, as our examination of the general-equilibrium microfoundations of macroeconomics will demonstrate. The application of Rorty's insights to these issues – in particular to the microfoundations of money – helps to illuminate the debates and dissolve some of the controversies.

We begin with a consideration of the Walrasian 'general equilibrium' (GE) model, and the debate among economists over the purposes it may serve. This is the construct in which economists attempt to ground such phenomena as money. Rather than providing a basis for 'representation' of economic phenomena, the GE construct may be more usefully considered as a moneyless comparison point which is used to sharpen other approaches. We then apply the insights arising from this reconsideration of the purposes of the GE model, and its putative foundational role in economics, to some studies of non-Walrasian theories that attempt to integrate disequilibrium processes. The focus will be upon the interpretation of Carl Menger's notion of marketability in his theory of the origin and evolution of money. Our purpose is to illustrate how interplay, rather than 'communion', of theories furthers our understanding of monetary phenomena. The 'confrontation' of the Mengerian and Walrasian approaches helps to illuminate the strengths and weaknesses of each, and to avoid the pitfalls of attempting to render them commensurable. We finally turn to Menger's evolutionary approach itself and examine how certain essentialist biases in the standard interpretation may have unnecessarily limited the range of questions it can usefully address.

THE USES AND PURPOSES OF 'GENERAL EQUILIBRIUM'

The incompatibility of micro and macro theorizing can be salubrious to both ways of thinking without needing to declare one the victor. Through a study of contrasts, practitioners in each sub-discipline may come to understand their own efforts more clearly without feeling that legitimacy is lost if one's theories are not a direct lineal descendant of others' mental handiwork. If one really does desire a unified approach, then attempting to graft one framework on top of another will not be adequate. Focusing on how economic activities, institutions, and plans cohere, instead of narrowly searching for the prime mover, may be a more fruitful way of generating insights in economics.

The search for underpinnings of macroeconomic theorizing stems as much from the disappointments in applying macroeconomics in the policy realm as from failures in theory. Economists have sought comfort, or perhaps refuge, in the GE model. Great strides have been made during the past half century in developing the structure and implications of this model. There is hope that by grounding macroeconomic and monetary theory in this model, the success of the GE approach in the 'micro' realm would rub off. In this way, for many economists, the GE approach fulfils the role of the 'language of unified science' which would provide the key to all economic understanding.[3] It is precisely the reshaping of all inquiry in the form of one successful line which 'blocks the road of inquiry' (Rorty 1979, pp. 349 and 367).

The elegant edifice of GE theory had been erected without reference to money (see Arrow and Hahn 1971, and Weintraub 1979, for detailed discussions). The GE model attempts to provide an account of how the market allocates resources among atomistic individuals through the price mechanism. The economy is characterized in formal mathematical terms, and conditions for existence, optimality, and other properties of equilibrium are derived. Speaking loosely, the allocation is accomplished through a central auctioneer who calls out a set of prices for everything in the economy and then costlessly gathers information from market participants to discover what demand and supply would be for each good at the announced prices. The auctioneer then calculates a new set of prices aimed at eliminating disparities between supply and demand: when the total quantity demanded of a good exceeds the total quantity supplied, the price of that good will rise; conversely, prices fall for those goods in excess supply. These calculations underscore the interdependence of markets for the different commodities. The auctioneer then calls out a new price structure, and the adjustment process continues through successive rounds until equilibrium is achieved where supply and demand are exactly balanced for all commodities. Actual trading occurs only at the final equilibrium-prices stage and not during the *tâtonnement*, or 'groping' process.

Theorists have expended much effort in an attempt to integrate money into this framework, but the theory has stubbornly rejected it. Any good may serve as the *numéraire* accounting unit to express the commodity ratios declared by the auctioneer. Since all trades costlessly take place in the blink of an eye (or the rap of an auctioneer's gavel) at known equilibrium commodity ratios in perfectly organized markets, there is no use for a medium of exchange and money has no role.

What are the conclusions to be drawn from this tension between GE theory and money for monetary theory? The implications depend upon the purpose to which one wishes to put the theory and what one demands from a theory.

If the purpose of GE theory is to illuminate directly the way in which the economy operates, then this approach is a failure – as Janos Kornai (1971), for example, has convincingly argued. Prices are not formed by a central figure dutifully taking account of the preferences and incomes of atomistic individuals in order to ensure simultaneous market clearing for all goods. Furthermore, the technical mathematical requirements for the results of GE theorizing are also inapplicable to most, if not all, functioning markets. Responding to such assaults upon GE, the eminent theorist Frank Hahn questions the standard for theory evaluation in these 'realism' criticisms:

'It is Kornai's besetting sin that he writes as if such a lunatic claim [that GE models describe the economy] had ever been entertained' (Hahn 1973b, p. 329).

There is a quite different and more useful conception of the GE enterprise. If, following Friedrich Hayek (1941, pp. 21 and 23), one believes that GE theory is of a 'purely fictitious character' and so may serve as 'a kind of foil', the absence of money (and many other important features of the economy) need not be a strike against the approach. On the contrary, Hayek (1941, p. 28) argues: 'it seems to be a weakness of the traditional use of the concept of [general] equilibrium that it has been confined to cases where some specious "reality" could be claimed for it'.

The defence of GE theorizing on this basis is consistent with a hermeneutic and pragmatic enterprise. It explicitly rejects the positivist and foundationalist belief that the scientist's job 'is a matter of conforming to, copying, mirroring a supposedly "objective" nature' (Madison 1987, p. 4). This position emphasizes that we may well be able to gain valuable insight into a problem through a model which has no pretensions to correspond in any direct way to the phenomenon under study. In his inaugural lecture at Cambridge, Hahn (1973a, p. 8) is quite explicit on this point: an Arrow–Debreu equilibrium is not representative of and should not be conceived of as a 'termination of actual processes'. 'Indeed,' Hahn (1973a, p. 21) believes, 'one of the reasons why an equilibrium notion is useful is that it serves to make precise the limits of economic analysis'.

As Hahn (1973a and 1973b) develops his argument, however, he abandons a hermeneutic approach and falls prey to foundationalist traps. In his defence of the GE construct, Hahn outlines what he considers to be the three most valuable functions in its role as a foil. We can classify the first two as 'therapeutic' and the third as 'positive'.

The first therapeutic use of GE theory is to clarify policy debate. Hahn argues that GE theory provides a neat framework in which to unearth unstated assumptions upon which policy recommendations may rest, and to identify unintended effects that come about due to the interrelatedness of economic activities. The GE enterprise has unquestionably heightened economists' awareness of many 'indirect' or so-called GE effects of policies, and has underscored the limited validity of theoretical results that ignore these feedback processes.

It is not clear, however, whether these benefits could not have been obtained from systematic economic analysis based upon something other than Walrasian GE theory (see Hausman 1981, pp. 152–3).[4] Even if GE theory were able to identify effects that other perspectives could not, the model rarely gives us any hint of their relative magnitude and importance.[5] In addition, since important policy-relevant aspects of the economy may be absent from the model, the use of GE theory in policy analysis may confound rather than clarify debate. The model's virtues as a foil for economic theory may become its drawbacks for policy analysis. Its often valuable role in sharpening the arguments in certain types of inquiries does not justify making it the touchstone for all economic debate.

Hahn offers a second therapeutic f unction of GE theory. He argues that:

> Arrow and Debreu show what the world would have to look like if the claim [that the 'invisible hand' operates efficiently to coordinate the actions of purely self-interested individuals] is to be true. In doing this they provide the most potent avenue of falsification of the claims.
>
> (Hahn 1973b, p. 324)

The great contrast of the Arrow–Debreu world with our own, Hahn believes, has served to shake the profession of the belief in the applicability of Adam Smith's metaphor. Hahn's claim, however, fails on two levels. In a technical sense, the assertion that the Arrow–Debreu GE model describes the only possible structure in which an invisible hand effectively operates is incorrect. As Daniel Hausman (1981, p. 152) has pointed out: 'If GE models were needed for this purpose, they would not help anyway, since the existence proofs the models present do not show what conditions are necessary, but only what conditions are sufficient for competitive equilibrium.'

Even if the claim were technically valid, it assumes that the processes Adam Smith considered are translatable into the GE model. To limit the conception of the invisible hand to the mathematical formulation of the GE world, as Hahn has done, shows how the emphasis on a restrictive set of techniques can eliminate fruitful paths of inquiry.[6] The notion of invisible-hand processes has proved to be an effective device in the social sciences and philosophical inquiry without reference to Arrow–Debreu techniques or a GE setting (see, for example, Hayek 1973, Nozick 1974, and Ullmann-Margalit 1978). The spontaneous ordering of self-interested individuals cannot be captured fully in terms of the formal equations of the GE model. An attempt to do so robs the notion of its power to illuminate economic and social processes because its purpose is to shed light on the adaptation and co-ordination of individuals under ever-changing circumstances known to no central figure. Since a perfectly informed auctioneer construct is central to GE theory, there is little scope for the operation of an invisible-hand process. An invisible hand interpreted in a non-mechanistic manner is unlikely to be associated with the Arrow–Debreu world, and so not 'falsified'. Hahn's interpretation of the Smithian process reveals a faith in commensurability of all forms of economic theorizing with GE modelling, hence a faith in the GE framework as the language of a unified economic science.

Hahn directly compromises the hermeneutic argument in favour of GE work with his third and 'positive' role for GE. He claims that it provides a 'starting point from which it is possible to advance towards a descriptive theory' (Hahn 1973b, p. 324). The weaknesses of current models should not be used to criticize the merit of the whole enterprise, that is, the theorems of Debreu are only an early stage in the development of GE theory (Hahn 1973b, p. 329). Is there a persuasive argument for refining GE for descriptive theory rather than looking to an alternative? Beyond simple assertion, Hahn does not explain '*how* general equilibrium models help economists advance toward an adequate economic theory' (Hausman 1981, p. 153). The promise that Hahn held out in 1973 for extensions entailing 'sequence economies, stochastic equilibria, and equilbria relative to information structures' has yet to be fulfilled (see Hahn, 1973b, p. 323). Hahn's assessment that when one studies GE theory 'one is not engaged in description at all' (1973b, p. 323) is no less apposite today. Should this be considered a failure of GE theory? Was not the explicit 'unrealism' of GE models held to be a virtue?

If the value of GE theory lay primarily in its role as tool for confronting other theories as a foil, then the 'lack of progress in description' is not a shortcoming at all. To argue that GE is a useful foil and that it simultaneously forms the basis of a description-oriented research programme is problematic (see Cowen and Fink 1985). Why must we demand that this form of theorizing, simply because of its elegance and success in a limited realm, provide *the* springboard for building theories to serve very different purposes? This unwarranted extrapolation of the mechanical and formal approach from one field into another forms the fundamental *non sequitur* of what Hayek (1979) labels 'scientism'. Hahn ignores his own pragmatic dictum that 'the question [of what approach to take] turns on how it can be usefully tamed to serve the analyst and practitioner' (1973b, p. 326).

TOOLS AND METHODS

In much of economics today, tools rule. Economists have developed a high degree of sophistication in various branches of mathematics and brought these methods to bear on the analysis of economic problems, often with fine results. The work of Debreu, Arrow, McKenzie and others erected the elegant structure of the modern GE model.[7] Unfortunately, the success in application of mathematical methods has given a special stature to the use of the methods themselves.[8]

Rigour has typically come to be defined by a limited set of techniques, and so economists have become to some extent prisoners of their tools. In this way, the realm of scholarly discourse has been unnecessarily narrowed. When Hahn speaks of using the equilibrium notion to show the 'limits of economic analysis', he has in mind a rather specific type of analysis, defined more by the use of particular techniques than by economic reasoning broadly construed. Rigour, brillance, and insight may be manifest without use of these techniques. Rather than drawing from an expansive toolbox in order to crack an interesting economic nut, economists often define what is 'interesting' by tractability through the use of a much smaller toolbox. Issues are ignored, or are examined from a restricted perspective, because of the narrow range of techniques considered appropriate.[9]

Rorty (1980, p. 43) has argued that high moral standards and keen insight have often been confused with the adherence to rigorous and restrictive scientific methodological canons.[10] The notion of what it is to be rigorous and scientific is itself 'hammered out' in the process of inquiry (Rorty 1979, p. 330). A healthy rivalry of approaches enriches discourse in a discipline; the belief that the appropriate method of acquiring knowledge of a subject is *a priori* known and immutable can only 'block the road of inquiry'.

The meeting of contrasting approaches to a problem can serve to sharpen the various perspectives without declaring one fit and the others unfit. Quine (1980; see Romanos 1983 for an overview) has been the seminal thinker in developing the notion that different languages, different systems of thought within a language, and even the meaning of a common language among different individuals, are not amenable to a unique and fixed translation scheme. The arguments that show that the 'correct' translation of Balzac is not a meaningful notion also imply that we are lacking a unique translation of the entire French language. More fundamentally, even among speakers of a common tongue, words are not fixed – in that each conjures very different associations and mental images to the various speakers. There is, as Quine has put it, 'no fact of the matter'.

From these insights concerning 'radical translation', neither Quine nor his followers (including Rorty) would then conclude that the whole enterprise of translation or communication should be abandoned. Simply because we know from the start that we cannot 'get it right' implies neither that we should not be engaged in the activity nor that we should stop writing or speaking in one language or the other. In this view, we can argue that GE theory can quite ably fulfil some therapeutic analytic purposes as a foil without denigrating its value by also claiming that it might not be an appropriate basis for the investigation of many economic questions. As a moneyless reference point, GE may provide a coherent model with which other frameworks may be fruitfully compared.

Anthropologist Clifford Geertz (1979 and 1986) has developed an analogous theme in his 'From the native's point of view' and 'The uses of diversity'. We cannot jump out of our skin and understand an alien or aboriginal culture in its own terms. We can confront, observe, and interact with the natives or members of another culture and gain from the encounter without ever doing more than attempting to understand them and their culture by our own lights. The sense of what natives are 'really like' stems not strictly from sympathetically accepting and living their way of life, for this experience simply constitutes part of the investigator's own biography, not theirs (Geertz 1979, p. 241). We further our understanding, Geertz argues (1979, p. 241) not through 'communion' but through an exploration of 'the character of the space' that separates the cultures (Geertz 1986, p. 270).[11]

Through 'the process of playing vocabularies and cultures off against each other' (Rorty 1982, p. xxxvii), we can come to an improved self-understanding and enjoy some cross-fertilization without feeling the need for an integration and reconciliation of the differences. Different theories and alternative approaches can meet on peacable terms, question each other and perhaps thereby raise new questions about themselves, without a victor being declared, and have it be quite useful to both. Applying this perspective, we can see that the attempts to introduce money into the GE framework may be a misguided attempt to enforce a uniformity of approach that does not improve our understanding.[12]

Rather than focus effort on the attempt to force money into this construct, economists might better employ other approaches to monetary theory, using GE theory as a comparison framework rather than the only correct framework. With the foil purpose of GE theory in mind, questions of the compatibility of micro and macro dissolve. There is little reason, then, for GE theory to be a foundation for anything – particularly macro theories that try to capture what we see around us. Since GE theory may be interpreted, most usefully, as a device to show what is not, one should register no surprise nor express anguish that GE theory is at odds with macro models that endeavour to explain observed economy-wide fluctuations. It is precisely the incommensurability of the GE world and ours that makes the study of GE interesting. By grappling with the differences and noting the failures of a one-to-one mapping, we gain a better grasp of economic processes. In the same way that confrontation with alien cultures can lead to a richer understanding of our own without any need to feel we must adopt or adapt to the foreign characteristics, macro and micro theory may benefit from each other without collapsing into a strictly unified approach. Such a hermeneutic attitude (Rorty 1979, Part Three, and 1980) eases the anxieties about micro-foundations and opens alternative approaches to monetary theory, without rejecting the value of GE theorizing within its appropriate sphere.

A confrontation and attempted assimilation can also highlight the limits of an approach. Negishi (1985) and Nagatani (1978) have recently attempted to integrate Carl Menger's insights on money with the tools of GE analysis. The rather uncomfortable and unsuccessful result provides a demonstration of the limitations of the tools, rather than their applicability. But the attempt has also served to emphasize an aspect of Menger's theory that has not received adequate attention – his emphasis on the organization of markets. In order to appreciate the indirect benefits of this attempted 'translation', we will first examine Menger's theory of money and markets and then explore how the direct confrontation has generated the insights mentioned above.

MONEY AND MARKETS

The 'invisible hand' approach to monetary theory pioneered by Menger (1981 [1871], 1892) and developed by Ludwig von Mises (1971 [1912]) holds that money is the outcome of a process of the spontaneous interaction of self-interested individuals. Without centralized co-ordination, our bartering ancestors gradually came to accept certain commodities, not because they wanted them for direct consumption purposes, but because they felt they could trade them with others for what they wanted. These commodities, which emerged to overcome the 'double coincidence of wants' problem through their saleability, came to constitute money. Without conscious design, money arose as the most saleable or liquid of all items that are traded. The purchasing power of money could then be traced back through time to its origin in the value attached to the commodity in its 'pre-monetary' uses; this is the so-called regression theorem (Mises 1971 [1912]). These arguments account for our present monetary institutions by examining the historical process that brought us to the current state.

While Menger's followers in the Austrian school have emphasized the spontaneous and unplanned character of money's emergence, others have focused upon different themes in Menger's theory.[13] Economists concerned with microfoundations issues – such as Negishi (1985), Hahn and Negishi (1962), and Nagatani (1978) – whose perspectives are that of mainstream mathemathatical theorists, have emphasized the theory of markets that underlies Menger's explanation. The key to both Menger's monetary theory and his theory of price formation is the organization of markets. For Menger, the number of traders, the 'thickness' or 'thinness' of markets, the degree to which participants are informed, and the scope and ease of inter-linkage between related markets are crucial. This emphasis on the organization of markets and their 'imperfections' sharply contrasts with the highly organized, complete, and so-called perfect markets of the Walrasian system.

The degree of organization and co-ordination of the market has a significant effect upon the process of price formation and supply-and-demand balancing. The technological, institutional, and legal factors influencing the structure and operation of markets for different wares are typically brushed aside. Menger uttered a lament as applicable today as it was in the late nineteenth century – that in economics the 'investigation into the phenomena of price has been directed almost exclusively to the quantities of the commodities exchanged and not as well to the greater or lesser facility with which wares may also be disposed of at normal prices' (quoted in Negishi 1985, p. 161). Negishi argues that the focus on the organization of market institutions in Menger's theory of markets provides a viable basis around which to build a systematic alternative to the standard institutionless GE framework. 'In other words,' Negishi (1985, p. 161) concludes, 'Menger's theory of the marketability of commodities is a first attempt at non-Walrasian economics'.

The Walrasian 'auctioneer' construct abstracts from institutional considerations. The assumption of a centralized price maker – who takes into account 'notional' supplies and demands at different prices in order to arrive at a price that eliminates actual excess supply and demand – requires complete co-ordination and free information flows among all markets. In addition, the prohibition against 'false trading' (that is, exchanges that occur at prices other than the equilibrium vector) eliminates an important mechanism of price adjustment in imperfect markets (that is, arbitrage). In their history of the marginal revolution in economics, Walsh and Grahm argue that: '[p]erhaps the most important abstraction [from the actual problems of exchange in the neo-classical model springing from the marginal revolution] is the notion of a *single set of prices* applying simultaneously to all transactions' (1980, p. 170). 'Even though [Menger] is regarded as one of the three founders of the modern neo-classical tradition,' they note that he was the only one of the Menger, Jevons, Walras trio 'unwilling to make this assumption' (Walsh and Grahm 1980, p. 170; see also Jaffe 1976, and Streissler 1973).

Menger wished to highlight co-ordination difficulties in order to understand how these could be overcome through actual market institutions and practices; hence, understanding of the purposes and functioning of the market mechanism was of paramount importance. Menger expressed his dismay that:

> the fact that different goods cannot be exchanged for each other with equal facility was given only scant attention until now [i.e. 1871]. Yet the obvious differences in marketability of commodities is a phenomenon of such far-reaching practical importance, the success of the economic activity of producers and merchants depending to a very great extent on a correct understanding of the influences here operative . . . that economics must study it.
>
> (Menger 1981 [1871], p. 242)

Menger did not argue that it was impossible for markets to arrive at an equilibrating price. Rather, he wanted to study those obstacles to that end, since they are ubiquitous and have such great impact upon the price setting process.[14]

The core ideas of Menger's approach are what would be typically translated as frictions or imperfections in today's economic vocabulary, but they take on these trivializing and negative appellations due to the dominance of the GE way of thinking. The Mengerian and Walrasian systems, while sharing many insights such as marginal utility, have very different foci to their theoretical structures.[15] The absence of problems of market organization in the Walrasian system helped thinkers schooled in this tradition to emphasize Menger's insights on this issue, which those trained in the Austrian tradition have not. The attempt to integrate the Mengerian ideas as a modification of the basic GE model (for example, Negishi 1985 and

Nagatani 1978) has not met with much success. Its problems, as we shall see in the next section, illustrates the limits of GE modelling and reiterates the value of GE as a foil by further illuminating Menger's approach.

A NON-WALRASIAN PROCESS AND MENGER'S THEORY OF MARKETABILITY

In a non-Walrasian process, trading takes place during the price-formation process.[16] Instead of depending upon the auctioneer to cry out prices, this model relies upon the agents to come together and strike deals at prevailing prices in order to allocate resources. Given that all trades must be feasible (that is, agents cannot exceed their budget constraint which is calculated by evaluating their endowment at prevailing prices), transactions occur when utility can be increased through trade. Prior to the final iteration, the prices at which trade occurs are not equilibrium prices so markets will not be clearing until equilibrium is achieved.

The modern non-Walrasian economists interpret Menger's marketability theory in the following manner: when the suppliers are on the short side of the market (that is, excess demand at the current price), the good is considered to be highly marketable; conversely, when the buyers are on the short side of the market (that is, excess supply at the current price), the good is considered to be of low marketability. Underlying the approach is a fixprice assumption that prices are stuck over some relevant time period during which transactions occur. Negishi provides the interpretation that each producer/supplier perceives a downward-sloping demand curve:

> not particularly because it is a monopolist, nor because its product is differentiated, but more fundamentally because the market in which the commodity is sold is poorly organized, so that the larger amount of the commodity can be disposed of in the market only with the less favorable price.
>
> (Negishi 1985, p. 163)

This conclusion by Negishi, to which Menger would no doubt assent, is arrived at through a very different analysis than that found in Menger. This non-Walrasian process does not fulfil the purpose of providing an alternative perspective free from the Walrasian 'auctioneer' and 'highly organized' markets. The approach entails curiously limited notions of an imperfect market institution and disequilibrium. Markets are not so imperfect as to allow excess demands and excess supplies for a commodity to occur together.

As Frank Fisher has explained the non-Walrasian process:

> there may be of course either unsatisfied demand or unsatisfied supply . . . [but] *markets are sufficiently well organized that there are not both.* In other words, there may be people who wish to sell apples at the current

prices and cannot or there may be people who wish to buy apples at the current prices and cannot, but there are not simultaneously both unsatisfied sellers and unsatisfied buyers. [italics added]

(Fisher 1976, p. 13)

Markets are so well co-ordinated that if one store sells out of a good all others must also. They all must sell at the same price and cannot change their price over the trading period. The so-called imperfection in the market arises from the exogenously given inability to alter the price. The imperfection gives rise to the disequilibrium in which all unsatisfied agents find themselves on the same side of the market. This state of affairs, then, determines which goods are of high and which are of low marketability.

Much has been lost in the attempted translation of Menger's theory of market and marketability into the vocabulary of GE theory. Economic activity for Menger does not typically take place under such well-regulated conditions. Since there is no completely connected market for most goods, there are typically a number of 'markets' for a good which are not fully integrated. Under these conditions, there may be no single market price for the goods that prevails simultaneously throughout the economy.[17] Because of the single-price market structure, we can then agree with Weintraub, who argues that the non-Walrasian process: 'really is better thought of as being carried out by the auctioneer, although he is no longer constrained to preclude disequilibrium transactions' (Weintraub 1979, p. 118). As in the Walrasian GE model, the auctioneer calls out prices, gathers the supply and demand data, and calculates new prices in successive rounds. Unlike the GE model, the auctioneer permits trades in each round at the just announced prices. The auctioneer uses the post-trade data to determine the prices for the next round, so keeping track of the shifting endowments of the economic agents is the twist introduced.

Although these short side-models do permit some enrichment of the standard Walrasian framework, the approach does not alter the basic limitations of the Walrasian model.[18] The confrontation of Mengerian theory and the GE model, however, has helped both to clarify the limits of GE modelling and to bring out the richness of the theory of market organization underlying Menger's invisible-hand account of the origin of money.

The focus on differential marketability arising from this dialogue also sheds light on the difficulties modern theorists have had in putting money into a GE setting. With imperfectly co-ordinated markets, we can follow Menger's outline of how media of exchange may emerge as the goods that are the most easily marketable. In a Walrasian world of complete and perfect markets co-ordinated under the ever-watchful auctioneer, every good enjoys equal (and perfect) marketability. It then becomes apparent why the Walrasian framework has been so resistant to the inclusion of money. Any good can serve as the *numéraire* accounting unit, and perfect market co-ordination relieves any need for exchange media. A distinct money would be redundant in such an economy. As Nagatani (1978, p. 106) states: 'The Walrasian model may be interpreted as a barter model without the double coincidence of wants condition, i.e., all commodities are equally acceptable in exchange.' The use of the auctioneer concept permits one to bypass all questions concerning the organization of markets. In this way, the importance of the differential marketability of commodities has been ignored. In the next section, we shall see that essentialist biases also have restricted the development of insights concerning differential marketability.

FURTHER DEVELOPMENTS OF MONEY AND MARKETS: THE SEPARATION OF THE UNIT OF ACCOUNT AND MEDIA OF EXCHANGE

The Mengerian theory does not require a perfect market in the monetary commodity and an imperfect one in all the rest: 'All this superior saleableness [of the money commodities] depends only upon the relatively inferior saleableness of every other kind of commodity, by which alone they have been able to become *generally* acceptable means of exchange' (Menger 1892, p. 249; see also Nagatani 1978, p. 116). The crucial notion behind Menger's theory is the *relative* marketability and acceptability of goods, with the hierarchy of saleability due to technological, institutional, legal, and psychological factors. As we shall see, Menger and his followers were led by an 'essentialist' attitude to lose sight of the distinction in degree, and so to portray it as an absolute one. This way of thinking has caused monetary theorizing to be too tightly tied to a particular set of institutions to allow these theorists to fully exploit the theory of marketability and monetary evolution.

A consequence of this overly sharp distinction has been a neglect of the theory's implications concerning the possible separation of the medium of exchange function from the unit of account.[19] There is the possibility that the transactions media would no longer be fixed in terms of an accounting unit. For example, the idea that shares of publicly traded common stock or claims to real assets might circulate is being given serious consideration among leading monetary theorists. Even Milton Friedman (see Friedman 1984, 1986, and Friedman and Schwartz 1986), the doyen of monetarism, is beginning to reconsider his stand in face of the issues raised by the 'new monetary economics' (Hall 1982).[20]

That Menger, Mises, and their followers did not attempt to take the evolution of money a step further, and to consider the separation of functions, stems from their interpretation of the saleability argument. It is here that Rorty's hermeneutic attitude can be applied to help us understand why this evolutionary argument was not developed further. The desire to isolate the essence of money led to an excessive emphasis on cleanly demarcating it from other goods, even though this impulse ran contrary to the role of relative marketability in the theory of the origin of money. Money is then distinguished from other commodities by being not simply the most marketable good but by being 'absolutely' marketable. The special property of 'perfect' saleability comes to define money itself. The initial criterion that identified money's saleability relative to other goods gave way to a strict zero–one distinction that has hindered the investigation of the evolution processes that could result in the separation of the media of exchange from the accounting unit. The achievement of perfect saleability thus becomes the final stage in monetary evolution. Categorizing money in this way obscures the very important observation that even in a monetary economy some items are easier to 'turn over' than others (that is, goods may be placed on a continuum from least to most saleable).

Certainly, this critical view does not imply that we forswear any sort of classification scheme in systematic inquiry. The choice from the multiple and not necessarily commensurable ways in which to organize our thoughts in a particular discipline will have an important impact on the questions we ask and the answers we obtain (see Quine 1980, pp. 20–46; Aumann 1985; and Bernstein 1983, p. 102). To put specific prior demands upon what must be included in a theory, and how phenomena will be represented, can unnecessarily restrict inquiry and blind investigators to other possibly more fruitful organizations of ideas and ways to slice up reality. Roger Garrison (1984), for example, has pointed out limitations in the range of issues that can be examined in a macroeconomic modelling framework without a nontrivial role for money to play. In order to redress this narrowness, Garrison goes beyond developing a framework in which money has a crucial position to assert that money is a 'universal of macroeconomic theorizing'. The same essentialist impulse that lies behind the conceptual transition from money as the most saleable to the perfectly saleable good motivates this demand for a 'language of unified (macro)economic science'. Cutting off consideration of theories that do not conform to some prior mould that claims to capture the essence of reality is unlikely to be a fruitful approach. As Rorty (1982, p. xlvi) argues, we should regard 'all vocabularies [e.g. models] as tools for accomplishing purposes and none as representations of how things really are'.

Money itself is a rather slippery notion; demanding that a theory include 'money' is particularly problematic. Definitional difficulties abound on a variety of levels. At the quantitative level, the US Federal Reserve calculates a variety of numbers that represent the 'money supply', ranging from so-called narrow definitions (including currency and reserves) to much broader measures. As innovations in the financial sector have occurred, changes in the definitions were felt to be necessary. This demonstrates that the institutional dependence of money is taken quite seriously. Some monetarists have urged an instrumentalist position – that we should consider the measure that best fits a regression equation with nominal variables (such as GNP) to constitute the money supply.

At a more abstract level, money is often defined in terms of the purposes it serves – medium of exchange, unit of account, and store of value. Recent work in monetary theory, however, has raised the question of the bundling of these fuctions: Can they be separated and what are the consequences of doing so? The essential functions of money may be, and to differing degrees are, served by other assets or goods in the economy. How well must these functions have to be performed in order for something to be deemed money and something not?

The attempt to provide a strict demarcation of money from non-money is at the root of these problems. The 'moneyness' is not a binary variable – some things have it more than others and the 'moneyness' of a particular good changes over time and circumstance.[21] The well-known example of the use of cigarettes in Second World War POW camps to fulfil monetary functions illustrates the point (Radford 1945). Menger and others wish to describe money as the item with the most 'moneyness', but then go on to talk about the 'perfect' or 'absolute' saleability of money. Some economists earlier in this century explicitly recognized that such talk hindered the development of monetary theory.[22]

Benjamin M. Anderson (1917) was the first to point out that the 'in kind' distinction between money and all other goods led the Austrians to overlook an extremely important implication of the emergence of money. As Anderson put it:

> I think that the distinction [between the saleability of money and other goods] remains a distinction of degree . . . the development of money while it adds to the saleability of the money-commodity, *also adds to the saleability of other goods*.
>
> (Anderson 1917, p. 406)

The advent of the money economy enhances the saleability of commodities through efficiencies that arise from: (1) a generally acceptable medium of exchange; and (2) the existence of a *numéraire* price system itself (that is, the unit of account). With the notable exception of Niehans (1978, pp. 121ff), these characteristics typically are blurred in the monetary-theory literature. It is the former function that is usually stressed, for it is the medium of exchange function that allows the 'double coincidence of wants' problem to be circumvented. Anderson finds that this emphasis has led to some misunderstanding of the relationship between a barter and a money economy. Anderson argues that if we redress this imbalance and give the unit of account function its due, then: '[m]oney . . . facilitates exchange not merely by acting as a medium of exchange'. He says further:

> The money economy has made barter *easier* rather than harder. . . . The feature of the money economy which has thus refined and improved barter is the *standard of value (common measure of value)* function of money. This standard of value function, be it noted, makes no call on

money itself, necessarily. The *medium of exchange* and *'bearer of options'* functions of money are the chief sources of such addition to the value of money as come from money-use. But the fact that goods have money-prices, which can be compared with one another easily, in objective terms, makes barter, and barter equivalents, a highly convenient and very important feature of the most developed commercial system.

(Anderson 1917, p. 201)

The process whereby money's saleability brings about the increased marketability of other goods may be able to bring about the end of money itself as *the* medium of exchange. Active spot and futures markets are organized for a variety of commodities and financial instruments. Organized exchanges, clearing houses and clearing-house networks are set up to help co-ordinate the different markets, and, in so doing, actually reduce the requirements for money as *the* medium of exchange. Transactions are settled without the medium in mutually cancelling balances, really a refined form of barter. Financial instruments besides money are accepted as the final means of payment,[23] and a growing range of transactions take place without money.[24] Anderson explains that, as other goods and instruments gain in saleability, then:

money tends to lose its *differential advantage* in this respect, and so tends to lose that portion of its value which comes from money-use. If all things . . . were equally saleable, there would be no *raison d'être* for money, and gold would have only the value that comes from its commodity functions.

(Anderson 1917, pp. 477–8)

As markets develop in a monetized economy, money loses its special position in the economy. More and more acceptable substitutes arise, and an ever growing number of transactions in the economy occur without money as we know it. Various assets – perhaps interest-paying bearer bonds and equity instruments – are used to settle accounts. Many of the 'exchange media' will thus no longer be fixed in terms of the unit of account. The holding of these assets does not entail the forgoing of interest and earnings as the holding of money does. Without legal restrictions on the media, these instruments will 'portfolio-dominate' money (that is, people will no longer wish to hold any non-interest bearing claims fixed in terms of the unit of account).[25] The monetary functions can become partially or totally separated as acceptable and 'portfolio-dominant' assets displace the money we use today in the settlement of transactions. The value of the accounting unit, which persists as the new media of exchange arise, can be traced back to its origin in the interaction of individuals in the market-place in the same way that the purchasing power of money was traced back to its commodity origin in Mises' (1971 [1912]) 'regression theorem'. Drawing on this analogy with Mises' account, we might characterize this explanation of the further evolution towards separation and refined barter as a 'progression theorem'.[26] Thus, a decentralized decision-making process can explain, first, the emergence of a 'money' combining both the unit of account and medium of exchange to overcome the inconveniences of 'crude' barter, and, second, the separation of functions as 'money' enhances the saleability of other goods.

SUMMARY AND CONCLUDING REMARKS

The application of some of the ideas and arguments developed by Richard Rorty on foundationalism have helped to illuminate a number of foundationalist issues within economic theory. The purposes and limits of the Walrasian general-equilibrium (GE) model were clarified, and the desire to ground monetary theory – or any other aspect of economics – in this construct was brought into question. The moneyless and institutionless GE world may provide a valuable foil as a reference point against which to sharpen other theories, even if those theories are populated by money and institutions and are directed toward achieving different goals.

Economists need not feel uneasy with incompatibilities among the branches of the discipline since much can be learned from studying the differences. Different vocabularies and models fulfil different purposes. Playing them off against each other rather than having them do battle in a winner-takes-all game helps to highlight their strengths and weaknesses. In our application, a relatively neglected but important aspect of Menger's monetary economics – that is, the organization of markets – was emphasized by way of contrast with the GE model in which markets are perfectly organized. In addition, the pitfalls of an essentialist approach to monetary theory were shown through the limits that were placed on the interpretation of Menger's ideas on the marketability of the monetary asset. Rather than demand that a theory explain money in a very narrow sense, or that money is a necessary component of all discussion about macroeconomics, one can consider a broader model that accounts for money's rise and its possible fall. By being willing to entertain alternative classification schemes and ways of organizing our thought, we can raise new questions and extend our understanding into areas that our theories could not and did not attempt to address. After opening the discourse to include such alternatives, we can then explore the merits of the various theories, sharpening our understanding through their interplay.

ACKNOWLEDGEMENTS

My thanks are due to Tyler Cowen, Daniel Klein, Don Lavoie, Mario Rizzo, Jeremy Shearmur, and seminar participants at Duke University for helpful suggestions.

NOTES

1 See Madison (1987) and Bernstein (1983) for a more complete explication of hermeneutics and the 'critique of foundationalism'.

2 Friedrich von Hayek, has also condemned this narrow view of inquiry under the label of 'scientism' which he describes as 'a very prejudiced approach which, before it has considered its subject, claims to know what is the most appropriate way of investigating it' (Hayek 1979, p. 24).

3 When asked by Arjo Klamer to comment on the contrast between new classical economics and monetarism, the eminent monetarist Karl Brunner replied that much of the new classical economics suffers from the Cartesian fallacy:

> This idea has had a strong influence on philosophy but also upon the program of the new classical economics best represented by Neil Wallace [see, e.g., Kareken and Wallace 1980] . . . You are not allowed to talk about money if you have not derived from 'first principles' a specification of all the items which are money . . . Adherence to the Cartesian principle would condemn science to stagnation.
>
> (Klamer 1983, p. 195)

4 Consequences of policies have been effectively analysed and assumptions ferreted out using, for example, process and order analysis (Marget 1966, vol. II, and Hayek 1941) as well as public-choice theory (Buchanan and Tollison 1984).

5 In order to address the empirical relevance issues, 'computable GE' models have been developed which permit 'simulations' to be done measuring the impact of these effects (Shoven and Whalley 1972). The results, however, are highly sensitive to both the calibration of the initial parameters and the specific structure (e.g., number of sectors) of the model.

6 More on how the dominance of tools in economists' thinking narrows discourse in the discipline in the following section.

7 See Weintraub (1983) for a history of the solution of the GE existence problem.

8 Technical flourish can come to replace economic insight. An analogous complaint has become a commonplace among music critics: the technical virtuosity of even second-rank pianists far exceeds that of the greats from the past, but the passion and originality is to a large extent absent – the interpretation lacks imagination and interest. See Hayek (1979) and Rorty (1980) on the general impact of scientism, and Lavoie (1986) for its influence specifically in economics.

9 As Donald McCloskey (1986, p. 162) has expressed, this notion – restricting ourselves to formal techniques – 'is to imitate the drunk who looks for his wallet under the lamp post because the light is better there'.

10 Rorty points to Thomas Kuhn's (1970, 1977) work in the history and sociology of science to support his claim that: 'What we mistook for the ennobling effects of obedience to methodological canons were merely the moral virtues which are encouraged by certain sorts of disciplinary matrices' (Rorty 1980, p. 43). That is, although a mechanistic and formalistic approach and vocabulary has been rather 'useful for purposes of prediction and control' in the natural sciences, there is no reason to then conclude that this type of description is more 'absolute' or less 'subject-related' (i.e. 'objective') than alternative approaches.

11 Geertz elaborates:

> The uses of cultural diversity . . . lie . . . along the lines of defining the terrain reason must cross if its modest rewards are to be reached and realized. This terrain is uneven, full of sudden faults and dangerous passages where accidents can and do happen, and crossing it, or trying to, does little or

nothing to smooth it out to a level, safe, unbroken plain, but simply makes visible its clefts and contours.'

(Geertz 1986, p. 270)

12 Demands that any useful macroeconomic construct must contain 'money' are similarly misguided (e.g. Garrison 1984). The problems of demanding in advance specific structures of theories is precisely the foundationalist legislation of a discipline that Rorty (1979, esp. pp. 155–64) attacks. Also see Hayek (1979). More on the place of 'money' in macroeconomic theory below.

13 A recent exception in the Austrian literature is O'Driscoll (1986a).

14 Note that Keynes (1936) had a similar research agenda in mind, in that he did not argue that a 'full employment equilibrium' price vector could not exist, as some have interpreted him, but rather that he wished to understand the failure of the price mechanism to bring about equilibrium (see Weintraub 1979, pp. 115–8).

15 Quine (1980 [1951], pp. 20–46) thinks of theories as lattices of interrelated propositions and concepts, with some more in the centre and others more on the edge of the web. What is at the heart of the Mengerian web is on the edge of the Walrasian web. In the terms of Lakatos' (1970) development of Quine's imagery, each of these economic 'research programs' has a different theoretical 'hard core'.

16 The non-Walrasian mechanism discussed here is also called the Hahn process, originating with Hahn and Negishi (1962). See Weintraub (1979, pp. 109–26), Negishi (1985), and Arrow and Hahn (1971) for more complete and formal expositions.

17 Erich Streissler (1973, p. 169) has argued that this lack of *the* market price due to difficulties of co-ordinating traders: 'is, I think, perhaps the most important part of Menger's vision of the working of the economy'. See also Walsh and Grahm (1980) cited above.

18 Hahn's (1985, pp. 370, 377) recent evaluation of such models is not sanguine: 'while no doubt something has been learned from the fixed-price model, it is high time to get on. . . . Fix-price theory is a striking example of an attempt to take a short cut. Too much effort has gone into it.'

19 Although this problem was raised earlier (see discussion of Anderson 1917 below), only recently has this possibility and its relation to Austrian monetary theory begun to receive attention again. See Cowen and Kroszner (1987 and 1989b), Greenfield and Yeager (1983), Wallace (1983), and Hall (1982). O'Driscoll (1985 and 1986b) and White (1984) provide critical views.

20 Friedman explains:

> there is a need for either some anchor to provide long-term price predictability, some substitute for convertibility into a commodity, or, alternatively, some device that would make predictability unnecessary. Many anchors and devices have been suggested, from monetary growth rules to tabular standards to the separation of the medium of exchange from the unit of account. As yet, no consensus has been reached among them

(Friedman 1986, p. 646)

21 Cowen and Kroszner (1989a) and references therein provide historical examples of alternative and changing monetary institutions and the impact of the legal background on what takes on 'moneyness'. In a formal setting, Chang *et al.* (1983) have shown that if money market instruments are introduced into the standard 'money-bonds' portfolio model, then a zero cash-balance equilibrium obtains.

22 Keynes (1936, p. 239) was well aware that 'liquidity' must not be regarded as an absolute but did not develop the point further.

23 See Williams (1986) and Telser (1981) on commodities futures markets as substitutes for money markets.

24 Automobile and other durable goods 'trade-ins', real-estate swaps, stock 'conversion' provisions of bonds, and mergers through stock transfer and other 'non-cash' means may also be considered forms of barter, rendering a medium of exchange at least to some extent superfluous. Instruments – from the venerable bill of exchange to modern money-market mutual fund shares – can not only reduce the quantity of the exchange media required to sustain a given level of transactions at a given set of prices, but also act as a substitute for the medium in circulation (see, e.g., Greidanus 1932).

25 See, for example, Wallace (1983). Considerations of risk-bearing and calculational inconveniences which may militate against the disappearance of money as we know it are discussed in Cowen and Kroszner (1989b).

26 See Yeager (1985) and Cowen and Kroszner (1989b) for a discussion of the origin and stability of the accounting unit in a separated system.

REFERENCES

Anderson, Benjamin M. (1917) *The Value of Money*, New York: Macmillan.

Arrow, Kenneth and Hahn, Frank (1971) *General Competitive Analysis*, San Francisco: Holden Day.

Aumann, Robert J. (1985) 'What is game theory trying to accomplish?' in Arrow and Honkapokja, *Frontiers of Economics*, pp. 28–76.

Bernstein, Richard J. (1983) *Beyond Objectivism and Relativism: Science, Hermeneutics, and Praxis*, Philadelphia: University of Pennsylvania Press.

Buchanan, James and Tollison, Robert (eds) (1984) *The Theory of Public Choice – II*, Ann Arbor: University of Michigan Press.

Chang, Winston, Hamberg, Daniel and Hirata, Junichi (1983) 'Liquidity preference as behavior towards risk is a demand for short-term securities – not money', *American Economic Review* 73 (June) pp. 420–7.

Cowen, Tyler and Fink, Richard (1985) 'Inconsistent equilibrium constructs: the evenly rotating economy of Mises and Rothbard', *American Economic Review* 75 (September) pp. 866–9.

—— and Kroszner, Randall (1987) 'The development of the new monetary economics', *Journal of Political Economy* 95 (June) pp. 567–90.

Cowen, Tyler and Kroszner, Randall (1989a) 'Banking in Scotland before 1844: a model for *laissez-faire*?' *Journal of Money, Credit, and Banking* 21 (May) pp. 221–31.

—— (1989b) 'The evolution of an unregulated payments system', unpublished MS, Harvard University, revised.

Fisher, Franklin (1976) 'The stability of general equilibrium: results and problems', in Michael Artis and Robert Nobay (eds), *Essays in Economic Analysis*, Cambridge: Cambridge University Press.

Friedman, Milton (1984) 'Financial futures markets and tabular standards', *Journal of Political Economy* 92 (February) pp. 165–7.

—— (1986) 'Some thoughts on monetary policy', *Contemporary Policy Issues* 4 (January) pp. 1–9.

—— and Schwartz, Anna J. (1986) 'Has government any role in money?' *Journal of Monetary Economics* 17 (January) pp. 37–62.

Garrison, Roger (1984) 'Time and money: the universals of macroeconomic theorizing', *Journal of Macroeconomics* 6 (Spring) pp. 197–213.

Geertz, Clifford (1979) 'From the native's point of view', in Paul Rabinow and

William Sullivan (eds), *Interpretive Social Science: A Reader*, Berkeley: University of California Press.

—— (1986) 'The uses of diversity', in Sterling M. McMurrin (ed.) *Tanner Lectures on Human Values*, vol. VII, Cambridge: Cambridge University Press.

Greenfield, Robert L. and Yeager, Leland B. (1983) 'A *laissez-faire* approach to monetary stability', *Journal of Money, Credit, and Banking* 15 (August) pp. 302–315.

Greidanus, T. (1932) *The Value of Money*, London: P.S. King.

Hahn, Frank (1973a) *On the Notion of Equilibrium in Economics*, Cambridge: Cambridge University Press.

—— (1973b) 'The winter of our discontent', *Economica* 40, pp. 322–30.

—— (1985) 'Comment on "Fix-Price Models"', in Arrow and Honkapokja *Frontiers of Economics*, pp. 368–78.

—— and Negishi, T. (1962) 'A theorem on non-*tâtonnement* stability', *Econometrica* 30 (July) pp. 463–9.

Hall, Robert, E. (1982) 'Monetary trends in the United States and the United Kingdom: a review from the perspective of new developments in monetary economics', *Journal of Economic Literature* 20 (December) pp. 1552–6.

Hausman, Daniel (1981) *Capital, Profits, and Prices*, New York: Columbia University Press.

Hayek, Friedrich A. von (1941) *The Pure Theory of Capital*, Chicago: University of Chicago Press.

—— (1973) *Law, Legislation, and Liberty: Rules and Order*, Chicago: University of Chicago Press.

—— (1979) *The Counter-Revolution of Science*, Indianapolis: Liberty Press.

Jaffe, William (1976) 'Menger, Jevons, and Walras de-homogenized', *Economic Inquiry* 14 (December) pp. 511–24.

Kareken, John H. and Wallace, Neil (1980) *Models of Monetary Economies*, Minneapolis: Federal Reserve Bank of Minneapolis.

Keynes, John Maynard (1936) *The General Theory of Employment, Interest and Money*, New York: Harcourt, Brace & Co.

Klamer, Arjo (1983) *Conversations with Economists*, Totowa, N.J.: Rowman & Allenheld.

Knapp, G.F. (1924) *The State Theory of Money*, London: Macmillan.

Kornai, Janos (1971) *Anti-Equilibrium*, New York: American Elsevier.

Kuhn, Thomas (1970) *The Structure of Scientific Revolutions*, 2nd edn, Chicago: University of Chicago Press.

—— (1977) *The Essential Tension*, Chicago: University of Chicago Press.

Lakatos, Imre (1970) 'Falsification and the methodology of scientific research programmes', in Lakatos and Alan Musgrave (eds) *Criticism and the Growth of Knowledge*, Cambridge: Cambridge University Press.

Lavoie, Don (1986) 'The present status of interpretation in economics', unpublished MS, George Mason University.

Madison, G.B. (1987) 'Hans-Georg Gadamer's contribution to philosophy and its significance for economics', unpublished MS.

Marget, Arthur (1966) *The Theory of Prices*, New York: Augustus M. Kelly.

McCloskey, Donald (1986) *The Rhetoric of Economics*, Madison: University of Wisconsin Press.

Menger, Carl (1981 [1871]) *Principles of Economics*, New York: New York University Press.

—— (1892) 'On the origin of money', *Economic Journal* 2 (June) pp. 239–55.

Mises, Ludwig von (1971 [1912]) *The Theory of Money and Credit*, Irvington-on-Hudson, N.Y.: The Foundation for Economic Education.

Nagatani, Keizo (1978) *Monetary Theory*, New York: North-Holland.

Negishi, T. (1985) *Economic Theories in a Non-Walrasian Tradition*, Cambridge: Cambridge University Press.

Niehans, Jürg (1978) *The Theory of Money*, Baltimore: Johns Hopkins University Press.

Nozick, Robert (1974) *Anarchy, State, and Utopia*, New York: Basic Books.

O'Driscoll, Gerald P., Jr. (1985) 'Money in a deregulated financial system', *Economic Review*, Federal Reserve Bank of Dallas (May) pp. 1–12.

—— (1986a) 'Money: Menger's evolutionary theory', *History of Political Economy* 18 (Winter) pp. 601–16.

—— (1986b) 'Deregulation and monetary reform', *Economic Review*, Federal Reserve Bank of Dallas (July) pp. 19–31.

Quine, Willard van Orman (1980 [1951]) *From a Logical Point of View: Nine Logico-Philosophical Essays*, Cambridge: Harvard University Press.

Radford, R.A. (1945) 'The economic organization of a P.O.W. camp', *Economica* 17, pp. 189–201.

Romanos, George D. (1983) *Quine and Analytic Philosophy*, Cambridge, Mass.: MIT Press.

Rorty, Richard (1979) *Philosophy and the Mirror of Nature*, Princeton, N.J.: Princeton University Press.

—— (1980) 'A reply to Dreyfus and Taylor', *Review of Metaphysics* 34, pp. 39–46.

—— (1982) *Consequences of Pragmatism*, Minneapolis: University of Minnesota Press.

Shoven, John and Whalley, John (1972) 'A general equilibrium calculation of the effects of differential taxation of income from capital in the U.S.', *Journal of Public Economics* 1, pp. 281–321.

Streissler, Erich (1973) 'Menger's theories of money and uncertainty – a modern interpretation', in John Hicks and W. Weber (eds), *Carl Menger and the Austrian School of Economic*, Oxford: Clarendon Press.

Telser, Lester (1981) 'Why are there organized futures markets?' *Journal of Law and Economics* 24 (April): pp. 1–22.

Ullmann-Margalit, Edna (1978) 'Invisible hand explanations', *Synthese* 39 (October) pp. 263–91.

Wallace, Neil (1983) 'A legal restrictions theory of the demand for "money" and the role of monetary policy', *Federal Reserve Bank of Minneapolis Quarterly Review* (Winter) pp. 1–7.

Walsh, V. and Grahm, H. (1980) *Classical and Neoclassical Theories of General Equilibrium*, New York: Oxford University Press.

Weintraub, E. Roy (1979) *Microfoundations: The Compatibility of Microeconomics and Macroeconomics*, Cambridge: Cambridge University Press.

—— (1983) 'On the existence of a competitive equilibrium: 1930–1954', *Journal of Economic Literature* 21 (March) pp. 1–39.

White, Lawrence H. (1984) 'Competitive payments systems and the unit of account', *American Economic Review* 74 (September) pp. 699–712.

Williams Jeffrey (1986) *The Economic Function of Futures Markets*, Cambridge: Cambridge University Press.

Yeager, Leland B. (1985) 'Comment on Cowen and Kroszner', unpublished MS.

12 Self-interpretation, attention, and language
Implications for economics of Charles Taylor's hermeneutics[1]

Lawrence A. Berger

> I can't as yet 'know myself', as the inscription at Delphi enjoins, and so long as that ignorance remains it seems to me ridiculous to inquire into extraneous matters.
>
> (Socrates, in *Phaedrus*, 230A)

Charles Taylor has been a major force in presenting hermeneutical thought to the Anglo-American community. The purpose of this chapter is to review relevant segments of Taylor's (1985) two-volume work, *Philosophical Papers* (hereinafter referred to as *Papers*), and to explore the implications for economics. Two themes which run throughout Taylor's work are: (1) man is a self-interpreting animal; and (2) self-interpretation takes place within a linguistic background of distinctions of worth – a realm of qualitative contrast which is irreducible to the various formulae so popular in today's social sciences. The main thesis presented herein is that the link between economics and hermeneutics lies in the notion of attention. It is argued that attention and language are intimately related, and that attention is to economics as language is to hermeneutics. Thus arises the intimate relationship between economics and hermeneutics.

SELF-INTERPRETING UTILITY FUNCTIONS

In a paper entitled 'Self-interpreting animals' (*Papers* I/2), Taylor lays out the thesis which is central to hermeneutical thought. There is a realm of what are called 'subject-referring emotions' which lies at the heart of human motivation and action. These emotions are partly constituted by our self-understandings, and change as our articulations of them change. We are engaged in a life-long process of interpreting these feelings, and the very articulation shapes them and thus what we are. It is in this sense that we are self-interpreting animals; our interpretations of ourselves play an important role in our very constitution. Taylor argues that any social science which would purport to explain human activity cannot bypass this domain. It is not objectifiable, not amenable to the techniques of the natural sciences, for the articulations refer to emotions which are themselves constituted by articulations. This is the realm of subject-referring, experience-dependent properties which cannot be traced back to physical realities, such as underlying physiological states. We are in the realm of what it is to be human.

In 'The concept of a person' (*Papers* I/4), Taylor contrasts the hermeneutical view of human agency with the atomistic perspective implicit in the mainstream of today's social sciences. In the atomist view, which has its roots in the Enlightenment, people are characterized as conscious individuals who are completely transparent to themselves. They have the power to represent independent objects more or less accurately. This view is quite prominent in economics. The agent has a clear understanding of his preferences, which are represented by his utility function. The process of representing his feelings, his preferences for things and situations has no effect on this independent utility function. On the other hand, for Taylor, the crucial thing about agents is that things matter to them; things have a significance for them. The fact that we feel emotion means that we are moved by the significance of a particular state of affairs. The articulation of an emotion is our understanding of our particular situation and its 'import' for us. This self-understanding can be more or less correct; but the representation is not about an independent object, for the formulation is constitutive of the emotion.

In 'Interpretation and the sciences of man' (*Papers* II/1), Taylor argues that the human sciences cannot avoid the question of interpretation. There are no 'brute data' free from judgement in this realm. When studying human motivation and action, it is impossible to avoid the question of the meanings of situations to the agents involved in them. There is a hermeneutical circle of feelings, emotions, situations and actions, the meaning of which is always relative to other meanings. Any understanding of meaning must ultimately appeal to a field of social practices. These social practices in turn depend upon a language of mutual action and communication which makes the distinctions necessary for the practices. Social practices cannot be brute data, for they are 'partly constituted by certain ways of talking about them'. One must understand the language, the underlying configuration of meanings, in order to understand the practices.

Practices are constituted by self-definitions of social agents, implicit in the underlying language, which involve visions of self and relation to others and society. These are 'intersubjective meanings', which are in the practices themselves, not in the minds of the agents. Practices are modes of mutual action and social relation, not aggregations of individual actions. Intersubjective meanings are the 'common terms of reference' which allow the convergence or divergence of beliefs.

Taylor also discusses what he calls 'common meanings', which are not just intersubjective but are 'common reference points' – objects in the world that everybody shares. They are the basis of community, requiring a powerful net of intersubjective meanings. Reciprocally, powerful common meanings result in the formation of a greater web of intersubjective meanings as people live in community; and a strong ser... of community means 'spontaneous cohesion' between its members and less necessity to use force.

SOCIAL THEORY AS PRACTICE

A recent review (Hands 1987) of the implications of Taylor's thought for economics saw Taylor as arguing in 'Social theory as practice' (*Papers* II/3) that economics can be successful by following the method of natural science. This was an unfortunate reading, for Taylor gives the example of inflation as a problem which has shaken economists' faith in this regard, and which drags them unwillingly into the realm of self-understanding which he claims is unavoidable in social theorizing. Taylor does believe that there can be certain regularities of economic life which may be relatively resistant to changes in self-understanding. Winter (1986) has argued in a similar fashion that neoclassical techniques would appear to be appropriate in a very limited realm – in which agents are repeatedly exposed to a situation which varies little over time. Taylor does not say that economics as a whole is an exception, but rather that some economic theories would appear to be refutable if the promised results of their application were not forthcoming. He then writes:

> And even these seemingly clear cases of verifiable theory may turn out to be muddy. Suppose the defenders of monetarism try to save it from the discredit of its failure as a policy by arguing that extraneous cultural or political factors – managerial practices, trade union rigidities – prevented its beneficent effects from ensuing. Won't we have to follow the argument back into the domain where theories as self-definitions shape our practice?
>
> (Taylor, *Papers*, II, p. 114)

As it is currently constituted, economic theory depends on a limited view of human motivation and action. Taylor argues that the apparent success of economics rest largely on the currently predominant cultural conditions which allow us to 'be confident that in some department of their lives people will behave according to rather tightly calculable considerations of instrumental rationality' (*Papers*, II, p. 103). Today's societies do not form a timeless cultural matrix which would allow economics as currently constituted to aspire to the status of a universal, objective science. 'Rather than being theories about how things always operate, they actually end up strengthening one way of acting over others' (*Papers*, II, p. 103). A change in the self-understanding of society could result in a change in the culture, which in turn would mean that we could no longer depend so much on people behaving according to the regularities of instrumental reason.

In 'Social theory as practice', Taylor is concerned with how it is possible to validate theories in the social sciences. He begins by examining the relationship between theory and practice. In the natural sciences, we learn about underlying processes and adjust our practices accordingly. This has no apparent influence on the underlying mechanisms themselves. In the social sciences, however, the objects of study are themselves partly constituted by knowledge, and as such may change when theories are applied to them. For the practices are themselves the objects of study in social science, and cannot be separated from the everyday understandings – the self-descriptions which constitute them.

In this paper, Taylor introduces a subject of profound importance for economic thought. He discusses the notion of 'shared goods' as an example of a theory which challenges our everyday (atomist) understanding. Falling under the category of the 'common meanings' discussed above, a shared good is by definition something that is sought after and cherished in common. This is to be differentiated from a 'convergent good', which may be an object of common interest, but could exist without such interest. Taylor gives the example of the law of the citizen republic as a shared good. Action takes its significance in relation to the laws. Since the key characteristic of the hermeneutical agent is that things matter, that she is moved by what is significant and meaningful, the fact that the significance is shared means that our way of acting together is qualitatively different. We can 'become capable of acting together in a spontaneously self-disciplining way, the secret of the strength of the republics' (*Papers*, II p. 96).

Taylor contrasts the theory of shared goods with the atomist approach underlying economic theory. Atomist theories predominate in the everyday understanding of western society, and thus the practices of interest to economic theory are informed by such theories. He gives the example of the common understanding of the political process, in which society is understood as the interaction of individual agents. There is no room here for a theory in which action also takes place in a context of shared goods. From the perspective of shared goods, atomist theories represent a degenerate case. A society informed by an atomist theory 'would be a society so fragmented that it was capable of very little common action, and was constantly on the point of stasis or stalemate' (*Papers*, II, p. 99). It is vital that social choice proceed under the right intentional description – policies must 'be adopted as the right form of a common purpose, and not as the point of convergence of individual aims' (*Papers*, II, p. 100).

It may be argued (Hands 1987) that economics is indeed cognizant of the interpretive dimension of human action, since it employs intentional explanations in its model building. But the question is whether the discipline employs the right kind of intentional explanation. Atomist theories go hand in hand with the objectivist assumptions of complete self-transparency in which desires, preferences and goals are clear and unproblematic. The only problem is achieving such aims in the face of 'technological' constraints. This is very different from the view of the agent implicit in the theory of shared goods. How is it possible to adjudicate between competing social theories such as atomism and shared goods?

For Taylor, the key lies in the quality of practice each informs. Social theories must be tested in practice in order to be able to judge their worth. Since the social practices – the objects of study of social science – are partly constituted by the self-understandings of the agents involved, social theories can influence the self-definitions and, thus, the objects of study themselves. A simple correspondence model will not suffice here. The best theory will 'bring practices out in the clear'; it will make possible a more effective practice. It provides the constitutive understanding necessary for 'continuing, purified, reformed practice'. Practices have a point; and social theories offer a clear account of the goods, the norms involved. If the theory is wrong, the goods involved will not be realized; the practices will be self-defeating. The more perspicuous view will allow more effective action, which overcomes 'previously muddled, self-defeating activity'. The proof of validity lies in a changed quality of practice, one which is 'less stumbling' in producing the desired goods. To be put to the test, the theory must be generally accepted by the practising community, and its impact (through a changed self-understanding) assessed. Up to that point, we have only the test of the persuasiveness of the arguments in the theory's behalf, which must consider how the theory would affect practice.

WHAT IS A GOOD?

Hermeneutical thought suggests that economics should ask its self-definition. What is economics about? Its self-understanding must be as clear as possible in order for its practice to be of the highest quality. Economics is said to be about resources, or goods. But what is a resource? Is there anything in this world which could not be put to some use? If we are only interested in resources which are 'scarce', what does this say to the status of humans as resources? No; economics is about human action and interaction in the world. It is about human energy and motivation. Under this definition, it is clear that the success of economics depends on its depth of understanding of what it is to be human.

Taylor (*Papers* I/4) is offering another view of the agent of economic theory. She is one to whom things matter, who is moved to action by matters of significance. The hermeneutical agent may have a more or less finely articulated understanding of the emotions which reflect the significance of the situations in which she is embedded. There are matters of pride, shame, moral goodness, evil, dignity, sense of worth, and love which make up a realm which clearly differentiates the human. In particular, being a moral agent means being sensitive to certain standards; it means being a self-evaluating being (Hirschman 1984). It means recognizing that we are subject to *higher demands* – that we can wish to achieve *higher goods*. These are peculiarly human concerns, matters of the deepest significance for us as humans.

For Taylor, to be human is to exist in a space defined by distinctions of worth – in which we may evaluate ourselves. Self-interpreting animals can only be understood against this linguistic background, which is formed by the 'continuing conversation of humanity'. These interpretations can be more or less correct; one cannot just think anything about oneself and have it be self-fulfilling. We can be deluded about ourselves, and the result is not just the absence of correspondence, an incorrect representation, but rather 'in some form inauthenticity, bad faith, self-delusion, repression of one's human feelings, or something of the kind' (*Papers*, II, p. 26). For Taylor, the depth of self-understanding determines the quality of human motivation and action.

When considered from this perspective, the notion of human ends which are absolutely describable becomes quite problematic. Beyond the physiological regularities of the needs for food, shelter, etc., human ends reside in the self-interpretive realm. Here the question is not how to achieve absolutely defined ends, but rather how to achieve the finest articulation, the most profound understanding of ourselves. It is a question of 'practical deliberation' on the true form of human emotions.

In 'The diversity of goods' (*Papers* II/9), Taylor (in a fashion reminiscent of Knight 1935, Ch. 1) discusses the limitations of utilitarianism. Utility theory assumes that what counts for human happiness can be clearly ascertained as fact; it ignores distinctions between qualities of action, or modes of life. There is an evaluation of action, of being a certain way, which does not depend on the consequences of action. The necessity to recognize these qualitative distinctions, which differentiate between the noble and the base, the higher and lower, cannot be eliminated by a calculus of utils. Just as Hirschman (1984, p. 91) discusses 'striving', Taylor notes that personal integrity, for example, can be a central goal which has an overriding influence on action. Moral demands and other standards of action are higher goods which are worthy of pursuit in a special way. We recognize the higher value of integrity, charity, and rationality; we aspire to be motivated in certain ways. Here Taylor, along with Hirschman, cites Frankfurt's (1971) distinction between first- and second-order desires. We are considered deficient if we do not have higher goals, whereas it does not matter if we have ordinary goals or not.

Taylor claims that much of human behaviour is only explicable in terms of qualitative contrast. There are goods which are of ultimate importance, which make the most important demands. There is a plurality, a diversity of such goods. Decisions here cannot be made on the basis of a single consideration procedure, for this cannot do justice to the diversity of goods. Counting utils is a 'bogus exactness', which leaves out all that cannot be calculated.

What sort of 'goods' are the concern of economic theory? Where is the line drawn? Are shared goods and the associated questions of unity and strength of community in its domain? Taylor is calling for a transformation of much of economic theory at its very roots. The test of such a theory would come in the quality of life in a world whose self-definition was informed by the theory. But what would such a theory look like? What is the link between economics and hermeneutics?

ATTENTION AND LANGUAGE

I would like to suggest that attention is the link. Attention is a most commonly used word . . . just the stuff of which economic theories are made. In the terms of modern cognitive psychology, attention is a limited capacity resource for mental operations. The extent to which attentional capacity is exhausted is a function of intensity of effort and/or the demands of the task at hand. Attention is also considered to be a selection mechanism, and the object of attention consists of those stimuli selected out of all possible perceptions impinging on the senses.

Attention and language are intimately related. Attention is a selection mechanism, and interpretation is a process of selective attention to those aspects of a matter which are more salient than others. Clarity results as attention is brought to bear on our worldly engagements. As these affairs come to light, what was previously unclear becomes more finely articulated. More clarity with respect to the import of these situations means that the associated practices are more effective in producing the desired goods. The movement of attention in articulation and interpretation shapes our language and the social environment in which we find ourselves situated.

The intimate relationship between attention and language is evident in Taylor's 'Theories of meaning' (*Papers* I/10). In contrast to the designative view of language, Taylor cites Humboldt's notion of the primacy of the activity of speaking, in which language is constantly being made and modified. Language formulates what was only implicit, and allows a proper focus on the matter in question. Articulation brings matters into focus, as a feature is identified; and an articulated view grasps how the different features or aspects of a matter are related. Language draws boundaries in which certain features become salient. Through language we 'delimit what we are attending to in the matter at hand' (*Papers*, I, p. 258).

Language places matters out in the open between interlocutors, in 'public space'. This is the realm of common meanings and shared goods. Public space is a 'common vantage point from which we survey the world together'. It is not a coincidence of individual states, but a 'common act of focusing'. Taylor claims that it is not possible to understand how society works without some notion of public space. Public space is where we jointly attend to the matters which lie at the heart of human action, matters which have been selected for concern (Douglas and Wildavsky 1982).

The relations between language and human emotion and social practices are most important in Taylor's work. Language 'provides the medium through which . . . the characteristically human concerns, can impinge on us at all' (*Papers*, I, p. 260). It provides the background upon which distinctions of worth are made. A language of qualitative contrasts is necessary in order for us to focus on the standards by which we judge our actions and self-worth. A discussion of the relation between attention and economics will now argue that attention plays a role similar to that of language in hermeneutics.

ATTENTION AND ECONOMICS

Economics is about human effort; and the essence of effort is attention (Kahneman 1973; Eysenck 1982). McCloskey (1985, p. 79) has defined labour as 'conscientious attentiveness'. Attention is how we apply ourselves in the course of daily life. My assertion is that attention is a central element in knowledge, communication, and therefore in all economic phenomena. The manner in which attention is paid influences both what comes to be known and the extent of communication which takes place in any situation. A study which would aspire to explain human activity must take cognizance of the attentional deployment of the agents under investigation.

In his 1967 study of the behaviour of sub-human primates, M.R.A. Chance of the University of Birmingham came to a most important conception: the structure of attention, which he defined as the joint movement of attention of the members of a social unit. Chance and Larsen (1976) viewed attention structure as central to the co-ordination of all behaviour. The structure of attention forms the network of communication between individuals, and lies at the heart of the system of resource deployment. Our world is constituted by encounters with others through resources which are animated by practical attentiveness. Resources in the system of deployment are far from lifeless; they reflect the marks left by those individuals standing behind them. The quality of life is directly dependent on the quality of practical attentiveness in day-to-day activities.

The importance of attention as an economic resource has already been noted by the theorists of bounded rationality. In a section entitled 'Attention as the scarce resource', Herbert Simon (1978, p. 13) writes: 'I am not aware that there has been any systematic development of a theory of information and communication that treats attention rather than information as the scarce resource'. James March (1982, p. 30) declares: 'The key scarce resource is attention; and theories of limited rationality are, for the most part, theories of the allocation of attention'. Communication takes place when there is a common object of attention – the centre of attention – which is the focal point that allows co-ordinated action. In rational-expectations models it is implicitly assumed that the random variables comprising the 'underlying situation' are the centre of attention – the common focus for all agents allowing the convergence of understanding. The attentional deployment of economic agents is the great unspoken assumption of economic theory.

Attention should not be thought of as an ordinary resource. It is not something that one can 'economize'; it is rather a dynamic of the 'one', of the economic agent, itself. As March (1988, pp. 3–4) has remarked: 'the organization of attention [is] a central process out of which decisions arise . . . choice [is] driven by attention allocation'. The study of attentional deployment means to get at our 'being in the world', the fact that we are always situated, always 'already engaged in coping with our world, dealing with the things in it, at grips with them' (Taylor 1987, p. 476). This is the prior process which economics must fathom instead of positing priors over states of the world. It is the partly pre-theoretical orientation which determines our stance in the world and resultant deployment of resources.

A hermeneutic approach to economics would make attention a centre-piece. Current economic theory assumes detached, rational agents who perceive their situations from a transcendent position. They calculate optimal actions on the basis of disinterested observations which have no effect on the objects making up the economic environment. The hermeneutic agent, on the other hand, is historically situated. She is interested, concerned, and embedded in her situations prior to any calculations of trade-offs. The attention of the hermeneutic agent is deployed in worldly engagements which shape the very environment in which she is situated. Thus the hermeneutic environment is profoundly historical in nature.

The historical movement of attention is not to be explained by recourse to calculations of trade-offs with respect to given objects in the economic environment. Consider, for example, the following familiar situation. A scholar submits the fruits of her labour to a respected journal, and receives a review focused on certain aspects of the paper. After she invests considerable effort in responding to the criticisms, a second review (by the same reader) finds difficulties with other aspects which were virtually unchanged and unaffected by the other revisions. How is this inefficient disposition of human resources to be explained? Perhaps the referee had nagging doubts which he was unable to articulate during the first review. Or perhaps the revision facilitated a clearer focus on the paper as a whole. In any case, the simple fact is that circumstances led him to attend more seriously to those aspects which were neglected during the first evaluation.

Did the referee initially take a calculated risk by overlooking some items of crucial importance? The problem would be viewed in standard theory as a trade-off between the disutility of attending and the embarrassment of a poor report. The resulting stochastic process would assume objectively perceived disutilities and an optimal expenditure of effort. But what led to the particular choice of focus during the first review? Is this again to be explained by a utility calculus over all possible aspects of the paper?

In order to address the question, it is necessary to inquire into the actual process of attending to the text. The reader begins with a set of initial interests which orient him toward certain aspects of the manuscript. These initial interests can be more or less influenced by activities in which he has recently been engaged. As the reading progresses, these 'pre-understandings'

(Gadamer 1975) change as the text is encountered. The particular aspects selected for concern shift as the engagement with the text develops. One does not know in advance what one will discover. Since the situation is changing over time, the decision with respect to the optimal amount of effort to expend on each possible aspect must be continually re-evaluated. But in order to focus on the text, one must set such calculations aside and immerse oneself in the historical situation. One must be embedded in the act of reading itself. Thus the act of attending cannot be explained by assuming that the reader calculates trade-offs, for the reading cannot proceed if attention must continually be diverted to the utility calculus.

In inquiring into the particular path taken during the review of the manuscript, it is also necessary to consider all concomitant demands on the attention of the reader. Was he pressed with other matters? Upset with affairs at home or on the job? The details of one's entire life situation at the time will influence how one attends to the task at hand. The lapse of attention during the first review can hardly be explained as the outcome of a random process, with objective mean and variance which depends on the calculation of an isolated ego. The very actualization of such a calculation would itself be contingent on a particular attentional deployment in that it must be embedded in an historical situation. Rather than positing detached observers viewing affairs from afar, the total shifting complex of demands on attention (which themselves depend on previous deployments) must be considered in understanding human activity.[2]

It has been argued that attentional deployment cannot be explained by recourse to calculations with respect to underlying objects constituting the economic environment. In addition, these objects are themselves shaped by the worldly engagements of economic agents. In current theory, utility and cost functions are considered to be the given objects forming the economic environment. Rational, disinterested agents observe these objects and make their choices. Hermeneutic theory, on the other hand, recognizes that utility and technology are constituted by knowledge, and as such are subject to change as attention is paid to them by interested individuals. Thus attention shapes the very environment in which the agents find themselves situated.

The supporting argument with respect to utility has already been made. Utility is a proxy for human emotionality. Economists talk about maximizing happiness, about 'pleasure machines'. Utility functions should be called emotion functions; and, when considered from this perspective, the specification of such functions becomes quite problematic. For emotion does not exist by itself, completely irrational as it were. There is always an accompanying cognition (Clarke and Fiske 1982; Izard 1977), an articulation of oneself. One's feelings change as they are articulated; thus, attending to one's utility function can change it.

Attention also shapes technology, or more generally the historical situation/institutional environment in which we find ourselves embedded. I will consider cost functions, human skills, household production functions, organizational decision processes, and financial markets as part of the historical situation.

Radner and Rothschild (1975) studied the allocation of effort in the firm. Managers have many possible activities to which they may attend. They can learn about operations, communicate with suppliers, customers, and employees, etc. Radner and Rothschild hypothesized that attended activities will tend to improve, while unattended activities will tend to deteriorate. The firm's cost function is determined by which rule of thumb is used in the selection process. This determines how economy is practised in the organization.

The key idea is that attending to the cost function changes it. Cost functions are not objects, like mountains, waiting to be climbed; they are not separate from the learning process. Of course, humans are very important components of 'cost functions'. Simon (1965) claimed that the bulk of the productive wealth in an economy resides in our minds, and pointed to the rapid post-war reconstruction of Europe as evidence in behalf of the assertion. Attention is central to the development of human skills; psychology recognizes how cognitive structures develop as the result of the investment of attentional energy (see, for example, Eysenck 1982).

The general law noted by Radner and Rothschild with respect to attended and unattended activities also applies to household-production functions. For example, how long will a given pair of shoes last? If one is heedful of the process of consumption of the resource (that is, if one pays careful attention while walking) one may practise economy. Another example is whether an individual will decide to eat one more unnecessary serving. This depends on whether attention is captured by the thought of food, or if the individual directly attends to the physical reality of the overextended stomach. (The notion of not wasting, or needlessly using, things is noticeably absent from explicit consideration in economic theory.)

March and Olsen (1976) have highlighted attention as a scarce resource in their study of organizational decision-making. Who is attending to what and when is a critical determinant of organizational dynamics. Rather than an abstract maximization subject to constraints, March and Olsen find decision-making to be highly contextual, in concert with hermeneutical thought (see, for example, Rommetveit 1987). At any given point in time, there is a complex mix of choices, problems, solutions looking for problems, and outside claims on the attention of decision makers. Thus the attention given to a particular decision will depend on the total nexus of situations which demand attention. Short spans of volatile attention underlying decisions and communication in general make for the turbulent environment presented by March and Olsen. This is the antithesis of the simple 'underlying situation' facilitating common understanding in the rational-expectations models.

The chaotic picture of organizational life provided by March and Olsen may be extended to the system as a whole. Attention brings affairs to light.

A change in the deployment of attention brings new affairs to light, resulting in a change in system performance. Scarcity of attention means that a great many situations go unattended, resulting in systemic instability. This phenomenon is particularly apparent in financial markets. Participants focus on good news in bull markets, for instance, as euphoria captures the bulk of attention. Scarcity of attention is evident in the short memories exhibited by market participants (Minsky 1975; Guttentag and Herring 1984). As the peak is reached, the focus shifts to previously overlooked negative factors – resulting in a dramatic change in system performance. The perspective of the aggregate is determined by the micro-level deployment of attention.

The focus of attention is important in financial markets. The markets used to focus on the money supply; today it is world financial markets and the trade and budget deficits. Market participants always watch the Dow-Jones Index and the various support levels – there are Federal Reserve watchers and dollar watchers. There are fads (see, for example, Shiller 1984) in which investors become interested in particular companies or sectors of the economy, just as in the academic world some research areas are 'hotter' than others. Agents pay attention to these at the expense of others. It may be said that a market is efficient when all factors get paid the 'appropriate amount' of attention, though this can be a more or less problematic notion depending on how much the attention itself affects the outcome. In any case, there can be bias in the perspective of the aggregate when, for example, a fad captures all the attention.[3]

I have argued that utility and technology are constituted by knowledge, and that attending to utility and cost functions can change them. What can it mean for such functions to be the objects of 'common knowledge', as is frequently assumed by economists? Common knowledge requires a joint focus of attention, which means that communication has taken place. Common knowledge cannot be assumed without explicitly detailing the actual communicative practices in an economy. When the economy is viewed in this way, the importance of the public media (and public space) becomes apparent. For example, we can start to think about the role of advertising more intelligently, considering its influence on society.

Why is that important for economics? Because there is a social context in which humans live and act. Game theorists and experimental economists are coming to realize that context matters. Focal points are being studied in game theory (Schelling 1960; Kreps 1984; Shubik 1985; Myerson 1986) in order to see how context determines which of several equilibria may be chosen. In experimental economics, Alvin Roth (1986, p. 254) has found that attention focus explains more than risk aversion, in concert with the findings of March and Shapira (1987). Preference-reversal phenomena (see, for example, Tversky *et al*. 1988) also show that questions of risk aversion cannot be taken out of context.

We are studying situated rationality – intelligent agents engaged in the world. What economics often studies is economists engaged in the world. Here Arrow (1986, p. 207) writes: 'We have the curious situation that scientific analysis imputes scientific behavior to its subjects.' The possibilities for infinite regress are apparent. Economic agents are assumed to use the latest econometric techniques in learning about the objects in the economy. We must study economic agents attending to their worlds, not economists.

IMPLICATIONS FOR ECONOMIC ANALYSIS

The question inevitably arises as to how economic analysis would be done differently if attention were taken seriously. There have been some instances (for example, Radner and Rothschild 1975; Winter 1982) where economic models have been developed which explicitly detail the attention-allocation process, but it cannot be explained as the result of optimizing behaviour with respect to 'given' objects such as utility and cost functions. For how is the allocation of attention to expected utility maximization itself to be explained? Economic analysis cannot reduce the movement of attention to the result of calculated choice, for this movement emanates from the intersubjective realm – the context in which atomistic action takes place.

Now it is argued that people do not actually go through expected utility calculations prior to every action; they just act as if they do. Economic models are metaphors which select the most important aspects of human action and thus enable insight into an otherwise hopelessly complex world. Good enough. We must ask, however, with Mirowski (1987), a key question – how good is the metaphor? Consider Friedman's (1953) billiard player. He acts as if he knows the appropriate laws of physics, and his activity could be described by way of sophisticated mathematical operations. But this billiard player is an expert who has invested years of high-intensity attention into the game. How would we describe the play of the novice? He may be no less rational than the expert, but he has responded over the course of his life to other demands on his attention. The metaphor does not work so well here. It is always necessary to look to the attentional deployment of the agents in order to determine goodness of fit.

Herbert Simon has been asking economists to pay attention seriously for years. He has recently (1984) argued that economic models invariably rely on auxiliary assumptions when they are applied to particular settings (see also Arrow 1986, and Mirowski 1987). These models implicitly assume that agents attend to all relevant variables, no matter how many. This may be acceptable if the number of variables is small, and if they do not change without being noticed; but the point is that 'attentional mechanisms are critical to the quality of . . . rationality' (Simon 1984, p. 48). Simon calls for an empirical study of attention and shifts of focus in order to develop a theory of individual and social determinants of attentional deployment.

The economics profession has obviously not taken Simon's advice to heart. Nevertheless, it is possible – by using what is already known about attention – to judge the adequacy of model assumptions in various applications, and to favour one approach over another. Given the underdetermination of theories by 'the data', this would provide another perspective for assessment. Although attention allocation cannot be explained by the standard tools of economic analysis, it is possible to assume a particular attentional deployment and then apply the most appropriate tools so long as the realm is sufficiently delimited for atomistic analysis to apply. In the spirit of general equilibrium analysis, the total nexus of demands on attention should be taken into consideration.

Consider for example, economic theories of advertising. Milgrom and Roberts (1986) have explained the existence of advertising which appears to have little or no information content by way of a model in which both price and advertising expenditures serve as signals of quality. They conclude that under some cost structures the existence of the advertising signalling alternative results in a Pareto-improvement. Consumers are assumed to know which regions of price and advertising space correspond to credible signals on the part of high-quality producers. For Schmalensee (1978), on the other hand, consumers behave adaptively, and relative advertising expenditures determine the probabilities that they will switch products. Perverse outcomes may result in which the poorest quality firms advertise the most and are the most successful, due to consumers' lack of awareness of firms' incentives. Policy recommendations clearly differ with the two approaches. An understanding of attentional realities may provide some insight here.

Milgrom and Roberts (1986) give the example of the advertising campaign introducing Diet Coca-Cola, in which the clearest message (in their eyes) is 'We are spending an astronomical amount of money on this ad campaign'. All that matters is the level of advertising expenditures. Consumers infer quality from price and advertising levels, with the supposed minimal information requirement that they know which regions of price-advertising space correspond to credible signals of high quality. But it must be asked how such knowledge is to be acquired. Is an intuition developed as a result of exposure to many similar such situations? Milgrom and Roberts show how complex the relationship is between price-advertising signals and underlying cost structures. Do consumers acquire a sense for a correlation between certain cost structures and products, and therefore the price-advertising regions associated with those products?

The potential applicability of such a metaphor cannot be completely dismissed out of hand. In order to make a judgement, it is necessary to investigate the attentional deployment of consumers watching Diet Coke commercials. Suppose consumers were all well trained in economic theory and were therefore interested in firms' incentives. Of course, if this was post-Nelson (1974) but pre-Milgrom and Roberts (1986), they might only be focusing on the level of advertising expenditures. So let us assume that some theory – such as that of Milgrom and Roberts – has induced consumers to focus on both price and advertising levels, and that firms act as if they believe consumers are doing so and therefore provide the appropriate price-advertising signals. Then, after long years of careful attention to many products and their associated prices, advertising expenditures, and quality levels, it could very well be the case that consumers develop the corresponding intuitions if firms act all along as if they believe consumers have already developed them.

Notice that it is necessary to make auxiliary assumptions such as these in order to justify the application of the model. Implausible as they are in today's situation, it cannot be asserted that they would never be satisfied. Who knows what sorts of fads can capture the attention of the public and turn its fickle interest in such a direction? This is the very realm of the inter-subjective, the social context which cannot be explained by standard atomistic economic analysis, but must be assumed as the historical situation.

With respect to the applicability of the model to today's consumers, we must ask what sort of attention consumers actually pay to Diet Coke commercials. The situation is quite different from that of the billiard player. There it is clear that the focus should be on the balls, pockets, available cue strokes, and the context of the game at hand. The consumer, on the other hand, is attending to a social reality open to a wide range of perspectives. The choice of price-advertising signals as the unambiguous salient object is far from evident. This first phase in the choice process in which decisions are 'framed' (Tversky and Kahneman 1981) is crucial; it determines the agent's perspective and resultant interpretation of the situation. The academic observer's focus on price-advertising variables is no reason to assume that real-world agents will or should do so.

The question remains, how indeed is the attention of the typical consumer deployed while watching the Diet Coke commercial? Advertisers are interested in this question. In fact, most, if not all, of the content which Milgrom and Roberts claim is pointless is devoted to attracting the viewer's attention in order to ensure the highest degree of effectiveness per advertising dollar. It is fair to assume that given the other demands in their lives, most consumers pay little critical attention to the presentation. They are passively relaxing at home after spending a long day attending to their particular area of expertise at the job. Advertisers, on the other hand, pay a great deal of attention to the design of the commercial. It is hardly irrational that these firms hire psychologists well trained in the intricacies of attention attraction. The dancers and celebrities in the Diet Coke commercial all function to capture the attention of the viewer, with the eventual aim that a favourable feeling, quite unarticulated, will be evoked with respect to the product in a potential purchasing situation.

If Milgrom and Roberts' view of the world is correct, only the level of expenditure on the advertisement is important. If this is the case, then there surely are better ways to inform the public as to the exact amount spent. After all, if there is some uncertainty in this regard, the high-quality firm may lose some customers who underestimate expenditures. One approach would be to have a representative from Arthur Andersen announce the amount spent during the actual presentation of the advertisement, while the attention of the viewer is still engaged. This would ensure full credibility. Of course, if consumers were as sophisticated as Milgrom and Roberts would like them to be, these 'dissipative signals' would seem to be irrational; why not demonstrate through the appropriate experts and channels of communication the attributes which ensure that the product is of the highest quality?

Just as Milgrom and Roberts overestimate the attention that consumers pay to commercials, they underestimate the intelligence of the advertisers in designing them. Schmalensee's (1978) model, on the other hand, has the right balance in modelling sophisticated firms and adaptive consumers. By way of this sort of analysis it is possible to gain insight into firms' strategies and market outcomes. It allows an approach to the question of the social desirability of various forms of advertising. Is it possible that some advertisers may be guilty of polluting the social environment?

In the above analysis it was not possible to reject Milgrom and Roberts' assumptions on *a priori* grounds. However, there are some instances in modern economic theory in which the assumptions stretch credibility to such extremes that it is virtually impossible to imagine any conditions in which they could be justified. Consider Robert Townsend's (1987) study of economic organization and limited communication. Townsend conducts a 'formal, stylized' study of how communication matters in economic systems. Agents transmit privately observed information by way of communication-accounting systems which are varied in order to study how incentive compatibility constraints and resultant outcomes are affected.

Townsend assumes that each agent's preferences are characterized by stochastic utility functions. This in itself might be defensible in some applications, given the vagaries of the winds of social influence. However, he goes on to assume that the range of values which these utility functions may take on, along with the associated probabilities, are common knowledge to all agents! Only the specific realizations are private information which is to be transmitted to all other agents. The probabilities must be known in order to construct the incentive-compatibility constraints which ensure truthful announcements of the privately observed shocks to preferences. It seems strange that all agents have somehow learned the probabilities associated with these unobservables – which allow the construction of the incentive-compatibility constraints, which allow agents to learn the true values of the unobservables, which would in turn allow them to estimate the probabilities necessary to construct the incentive-compatibility constraints. Could it be that Townsend is in a hermeneutical circle?

Perhaps everyone is born knowing the distribution of all other agents' utility functions. Or perhaps this is just a metaphor – social realities are such that people act as if they have such knowledge. In order to assess the metaphor, it is necessary to inquire into the requirements on the associated attentional deployment which would lend it credibility. Putting aside for the moment Townsend's assumption that the utility-function realizations are not 'publicly observable', what would lead agents to focus on these events? How would the events change as a result of such a public shift of focus? Questions such as these must have been addressed before the model could ever be applied in a real-world situation and could yield some insight into how communication matters. Townsend gives an example in which the values of the utility function correspond to times when the agent is more or less 'patient' or 'urgent'. It is most difficult to imagine any circumstances in which all agents could agree on the 'true, objective probability' of such events taking place. What Townsend does not understand is that there are no brute data in social realities; for all observations must be interpreted through the medium of attention/language. Since they are partly constituted by articulation, states of patience and urgency are not subject to neutral observation by disinterested observers. It is difficult to imagine that one could have a fair estimate of one's own proclivity to fall into such emotional states, let alone that all could agree to such estimates.

The image underlying Townsend's model is that of scientific investigators separately performing experiments and replicating each other's findings. It is assumed that any objective observer will come to the same knowledge of the structure of the situation. There is no recognition of limited fields of vision (frames, interpretations) and knowledge of particular circumstances of place and time (see Hayek 1945). The fact that the subject matter is historical in nature, and affected by the actions of the 'observers', is ignored. But shocks to utility functions do not follow the timeless laws of physics to which billiard balls are subject. In order for there to be agreement on the distribution of shocks to preferences, there must be some communicative process by which agents come to a consensus of opinion (Lehrer and Wagner 1981). The distribution is not in plain sight for all to see. Townsend claims to explain how communication matters in economic systems, but he really does not take seriously the primacy of the intersubjective. Is common knowledge a metaphor for Taylor's common meanings, the focal points which constitute the public space? If so, then we need to know more about the development of professional integrity, trust, and values that transcend self, and less about the design of incentives to control isolated, self-interested individuals (March and Olsen 1987).

Satterthwaite (1979) provides an example of a model which takes communication seriously by making explicit assumptions about the social context and attentional deployment of consumers. He studies the demand structures which arise in markets where quality can be determined only after lengthy experience with the product. Information about producers is transmitted in the normal course of social life as consumers occasionally tell stories about their experiences. Since detailed reputations exist only when there are a small number of producers (due to limits on attentional capacity), entry can result in a decline in elasticity of demand and a higher equilibrium price. A model such as this is well grounded in intersubjective reality and provides interesting insights into potential market outcomes.

HERMENEUTICAL EXPECTATIONS

The models constructed by Milgrom and Roberts (1986) and Townsend (1987) bear little resemblance to real-world economic systems. They assume that the context is a game such as billiards, whose rules and possible strategies are known to all agents in advance. Laboratory experiments in which the rules are evident to all also ignore the problem. Hayek (1945) railed against the idea of 'given' knowledge which corresponds to the 'objective facts' of the situation. An explanation must be provided for the existence of such knowledge in order for the application of these models to be justified.

Of course, these theorists are not alone in positing economic structures which are known to all, for this is the essence of the rational-expectations 'revolution'. It has been argued in justifying the rational-expectations assumption that, although there is no reason to expect all individuals to have the same model in mind at any given point in time, gradually over time agents will learn about the underlying situation, and expectations will converge to the rational-expectations equilibrium. Roman Frydman (1982) has detailed some of the difficulties involved in convergence to such an equilibrium. Frydman (following the literature) assumes the situation is as follows: Each firm is characterized by a stochastic cost function, and the firm observes realizations of random variables (representing 'general' and 'local' conditions) which are components of the cost function in an effort to estimate the 'true' objective-probability distributions which generate the variables. Thus the firm is characterized by a cost function, and at the same time it is learning about itself. There is some fixed, objective reality which the firm is, but at the same time it is learning about what the objective reality is. This is a question of self-understanding. But the question is, does the self change when it comes to an understanding of itself? And what is the nature of these 'external conditions' which are so important in the cost function? Do they not reflect the results of the joint interaction of rational agents, such as price movements in the markets for the firm's inputs? If this is the case, then a change in understanding on the part of the firm implies a change in optimal behaviour, which means a change in the outcome which is embodied in the cost function.

In order to see this more clearly, consider the following. In Frydman's (1982) article, firm i's cost function is $C(y_i) = y_i^2/2s + k_iy_i + c_F$, where s is a scale parameter, c_F is a fixed-cost parameter, and $k_i = \alpha + \varepsilon_i$ is a random variable with $\alpha \sim N(\bar{\alpha}, \sigma_\alpha^2)$ and $\varepsilon_i \sim N(0, \sigma_\varepsilon^2)$. The random variable k_i

represents general and local conditions which affect the cost function. During the process of convergence, supply is given by

$$y_i = s \left(\frac{\hat{a}}{1+\hat{b}} + \frac{\hat{b}(1-\hat{\gamma})\hat{\bar{\alpha}}}{(1+\hat{b})(1+\hat{b}\hat{\gamma})} - \frac{k_i}{1+\hat{b}\hat{\gamma}} \right)$$

where $\hat{a}$ and $\hat{b}$ are estimated parameters in market demand and $\hat{\gamma}$ is a function of the estimated variables of α and ε_i. Expected supply is $Ey_i = s(\hat{a} - \hat{\bar{\alpha}})/(1+\hat{b})$. But a change in the estimated parameters implies a change in expected supply, and thus expected demand in the market for the firm's inputs – which implies a change in the distribution of k_i. In addition, a change in the estimated parameters could mean that a change in technology is called for, either in the short run by way of change in input mix or in the long run by way of capital expenditures. The process of estimation may also result in a redeployment of resources either into or out of the market-place in which the firm is currently selling its output. Thus there is no solid ground lying under the feet of these rational players, no underlying situation to which all expectations will gradually converge. A general equilibrium solution is called for, but again the solution must be provided in advance. Some underlying, pre-given, unchanging situation must exist to which the system converges.

As an example of a general-equilibrium model, consider Martin Hellwig's (1980) model of the aggregation of information. The random variables in the system are assumed to be independently normally distributed. The hypothesis of rational expectations is then 'imposed', requiring all agents to know 'the actual joint distribution' of variables dependent on the original distribution. But was the joint distribution primordially given to agents before there were agents? Clearly not; agents are included in the system. Then if this is not the case, how is it that all agents happen to learn this particular distribution if it is not there first waiting to be learned? Did God create rational-expectations equilibria? Perhaps the situation may be likened to that of a class of Ph.D. students studying economic theory together for a semester. The professor presents a series of models to be learned, and the incentives are high to learn them accurately. Even in this case it may have been noted that final examinations do not always reveal rational expectations. Real-world agents are not faced with such a felicitous situation as pre-existing models. As soon as they start learning about the primordial model, it changes – because they are included in the situation. The understanding of the agents is constitutive of the situation itself.

But perhaps it will be argued that the random variables represent sources of 'primitive uncertainty' which are completely exogenous to the system. For this to work, the forces must be exogenous to the entire social system – such as the weather, or the distribution of mineral wealth. These must be the only sources of uncertainty. But is it the weather, or is it the unknown thoughts and actions of others which present the greatest difficulties in our lives (see, for example, Smith *et al.* 1988)? Is the uncertainty natural or social? Of course, both sources are present, but it would clearly be a very different world if there were no social uncertainty. It is strange to suggest that the 'variation' in the results of social interaction is solely due to forces exogenous to the social system.

Rather, the question is how the Supreme Court will interpret a certain piece of legislation, or how the referees will interpret any given paper, or Keynes's question of the nature of the political system in the not-too-distant future; and it is hardly appropriate to model this sort of (Knightian) uncertainty by way of objectively pre-given probability distributions which do not change as they are jointly learned by all participants in the social system. These uncertainties concern the unfolding of a social, historical process, not the workings of a static, mechanical model. Frydman and Phelps (1983) have shown the importance of institutions and social norms external to the market for convergence to a rational-expectations equilibrium. They have convincingly argued that all agents are groping for the best model. The situation is one in which agents with different interpretations of the situation interact with one another, resulting in models meeting models which are constantly shifting and being shaped by the very interaction with others. There is no guarantee that over time they will converge to the 'real model'; it is not at all certain they will come to a common understanding with one another. The question of the actual status of communication between economic agents cannot be ignored.

CONCLUSION

Economics must come to grips with the questions of communication, community, and public space. The focal matters selected for concern in the public space lie at the heart of human action. The study of communication in economic systems cannot bypass this realm by way of rational-expectations assumptions. These assumptions of common knowledge of external structures cannot withstand the historical, self-interpretive movement of attention and language. So long as self-ignorance remains, it seems ridiculous to posit mechanical economic environments with outcomes known up to a probability distribution. Economics must turn its attention instead to self-interpretation; for it is constitutive of the object of concern, which is the economic environment itself.

NOTES

1 This essay originally appeared under the title 'Economics and hermeneutics', in the October 1989 issue of *Economics and Philosophy*. It has been revised for inclusion in this volume.
2 See Messer *et al.* (1988) for a discussion of the implications for psychology.
3 In explaining the 'bootstrapping' phenomenon, Bowman (1963, p. 316) wrote: 'Man seems to respond to selective cues in his environment — particular things

seem to catch his attention at times (the last telephone call), while at other times it is a different set of stimuli.' Linear decision rules might outperform the managers themselves due to detachment from the particulars of the situation at critical times.

4 Emotion is very powerful in determining what the agents focus on, and it is contagious. Here is where cultural and social influences may be admitted into economic discourse. Emotion reflects the significance of a situation, which in turn takes its meaning from the social–cultural matrix in which we are embedded. Emotion does not just 'colour' a situation, but is, rather, a fundamental factor in its constitution. There is a different focus, a different atmosphere in, for example, a bull market – where euphoria predominates. In a bear market on the other hand, there is panic and depression. These clearly have emotional meanings. Markets have moods, and they matter for market outcomes.

REFERENCES

Arrow, Kenneth A. (1986) 'Rationality of self and others in an economic system', in R.M. Hogarth and M.W. Reder (eds) *Rational Choice*, Chicago: University of Chicago Press, pp. 201–16.

Bowman, E.H. (1963) 'Consistency and optimality in managerial decision making', *Management Science* 9, pp. 310–21.

Chance, M.R.A. (1967) 'Attention structure as the basis of primate rank orders', *Man* 2, pp. 503–18.

—— and Larsen, R.R. (eds) (1976) *The Social Structure of Attention*. London: Wiley.

Clarke, Margaret S. and Fiske, Susan T. (eds) (1982) *Affect and Cognition*, London: Wiley.

Douglas, Mary and Wildavsky, Aaron (1982) *Risk and Culture*, Berkeley: University of California Press.

Eysenck, Michael W. (1982) *Attention and Arousal*, Berlin: Springer-Verlag.

Frankfurt, H. (1971) 'Freedom of the will and the concept of a person', *Journal of Philosophy* 67, pp. 5–20.

Friedman, Milton (1953) *Essays in Positive Economics*, Chicago: University of Chicago Press.

Frydman, Roman (1982) 'Towards an understanding of market processes: individual expectations, learning, and convergence to rational expectations equilibrium', *American Economic Review* 72, pp. 652–68.

—— and Phelps, Edmund (1983) *Individual Forecasting and Aggregate Outcomes*, Cambridge: Cambridge University Press.

Gadamer, Hans-Georg (1975) *Truth and Method*, New York: Crossroad.

Guttentag, J. and Herring, R. (1984) 'Credit rationing and financial disorder', *Journal of Finance* 34, pp. 1359–82.

Hands, D. Wade (1987) 'Charles Taylor's *Human Agency and Language: Philosophical Papers I* and *Philosophy and the Human Sciences: Philosophical Papers II*', *Economics and Philosophy* 3, pp. 172–5.

Hayek, F.A. von (1945) 'The use of knowledge in society', *American Economic Review* 35, pp. 519–30.

Hellwig, Martin F. (1980) 'On the aggregation of information in competitive markets', *Journal of Economic Theory* 22, pp. 477–98.

Hirschman, Albert O. (1984) 'Against parsimony: three easy ways of complicating some categories of economic discourse', *American Economic Review Proceedings* 74, pp. 89–96.

Izard, Carroll E. (1977) *Human Emotions*, New York: Plenum Press.

Kahneman, Daniel (1973) *Attention and Effort*, Englewood Cliffs: Prentice-Hall.

Knight, Frank H. (1935) *The Ethics of Competition*, New York: Harper.

Kreps, David (1984) 'Corporate culture and economic theory', mimeo, Stanford University.

Lehrer, K. and Wagner, C. (1981) *Rational Consensus in Society*, London: Reidel.

McCloskey, Donald (1985) *The Rhetorical of Economics*, Madison: University of Wisconsin Press.

March, James (1982) 'Theories of choice and making decisions', *Society* 20, pp. 29–39.

—— (1988) *Decisions and Organization*, London: Basil Blackwell.

—— and Olsen, J. (eds) (1976) *Ambiguity and Choice in Organizations*, Bergen, Norway: Universitetsforlaget.

—— and —— (1987) 'Popular sovereignty and the search for appropriate institutions', *Journal of Public Policy* 6, pp. 341–70.

—— and Shapira, Zur (1987) 'Managerial perspectives on risk and risk taking', *Management Science* 33, pp. 1404–18.

Messer, S., Sass, A., and Woolfolk, R. (eds) (1988) *Hermeneutics and Psychological Theory*, New Brunswick: Rutgers University Press.

Milgrom, P. and Roberts, J. (1986) 'Price and advertising signals of product quality', *Journal of Political Economy* 94, pp. 796–821.

Minsky, Hyman P. (1975) *John Maynard Keynes*, New York: Columbia.

Mirowski, Phillip (1987) 'Shall I compare thee to a Minkowski–Ricardo–Leontief–Metzler matrix of the Mosak–Hicks type? Or, rhetoric, mathematics, and the nature of neoclassical economic theory', *Economics and Philosophy* 3, pp. 67–95.

Myerson, R. (1986) 'Negotiations in games: a theoretical overview', in W. Heller, Starr, R.M., and Starrett, D.A. (eds) *Uncertainty, Information and Communication, Essays in Honor of Kenneth J. Arrow, Volume III*, New York: Cambridge University Press, pp. 3–24.

Nelson, P. (1974) 'Advertising as information', *Journal of Political Economy* 81, pp. 729–54.

Radner, Roy and Rothschild, Michael (1975) 'On the allocation of effort', *Journal of Economic Theory* 10, pp. 358–76.

Rommetveit, Ragnar (1987) 'Meaning, context, and control: convergent trends and controversial issues in current social-scientific research on human cognition and communication', *Inquiry* 30, pp. 77–99.

Roth, Alvin E. (1986) 'Laboratory experimentation in economics', *Economics and Philosophy* 2, pp. 245–74.

Satterthwaite, M. (1979) 'Consumer information, equilibrium industry price, and the number of sellers', *Bell Journal of Economics* 10, pp. 483–502.

Schelling, Thomas C. (1960) *The Strategy of Conflict*, Cambridge: Harvard.

Schmalensee, Richard (1978) 'A model of advertising and product quality', *Journal of Political Economy* 86, pp. 485–503.

Shiller, Robert J. (1984) 'Stock prices and social dynamics', in W.C. Brainard and G.L. Perry (eds) *Brookings Papers on Economic Activity*, pp. 457–98.

Shubik, Martin (1985) 'The use of simple games to illustrate concepts and to provide experimental evidence', Cowles Foundation Discussion Paper No. 744, Yale University.

Simon, Herbert A. (1965) 'Decision making as an economic resource', in L.H. Seltzer (ed.) *New Horizons of Economic Progress*, Detroit: Wayne State University, pp. 71–95.

—— (1978) 'Rationality as process and as product of thought', *American Economic Review Proceedings* 68, pp. 1–16.

—— (1984) 'On the behavioral and rational foundations of economic dynamics', *Journal of Economic Behavior and Organization* 5, pp. 35–55.

Smith, V., Suchanek, G., and Williams, A. (1988) 'Bubbles, crashes and endogenous expectations in experimental spot asset markets', *Econometrica* 56, pp. 1119–53.

Taylor, Charles (1985) *Human Agency and Language: Philosophical Papers I*, Cambridge: Cambridge University Press.

—— (1985) *Philosophy and the Human Sciences: Philosophical Papers II*, Cambridge: Cambridge University Press.

—— (1987) 'Overcoming epistemology', in K. Baynes, J. Bohman, and T. McCarthy (eds) *After Philosophy*, Cambridge, Mass.: MIT Press, pp. 464–88.

Townsend, Robert (1987) 'Economic organization and limited communication', *American Economic Review* 77, pp. 954–71.

Tversky, A. and Kahneman, D. (1981) 'The framing of decisions and the psychology of choice', *Science* 211, pp. 453–8.

Tversky, A., Sattah, S., and Slovic, P. (1988) 'Contingent weighting in judgement and choice', *Psychological Review* 95, pp. 371–84.

Winter, Sidney (1982) 'Attention allocation and input proportions', *Journal of Economic Behavior and Organization* 2, pp. 31–46.

—— (1986) 'Comments on Arrow and Lucas', in R.M. Hogarth and M.W. Reder (eds) *Rational Choice*, Chicago: University of Chicago Press, pp. 243–50.

13 What a non-Paretian welfare economics would have to look like

Tyler Cowen

INTRODUCTION

Although non-Paretian approaches to welfare economics receive considerable attention outside of mainstream economics, they have not received much critical scrutiny. Non-Paretian welfare frameworks, while not necessarily wrong in their present form, are seriously incomplete. I will discuss whether a non-Paretian welfare economics can avoid collapsing into Paretianism, and still serve as a promising model for policy analysis. I warn the reader in advance that no definitive conclusions will be offered.

HOW DO NON-PARETIAN APPROACHES DIFFER?

The search for an alternative welfare standard is motivated by the deficiencies of Paretianism. On a theoretical level, Paretian welfare theory simply stipulates that we should prefer all moves which make some individuals better off and none the worse off. The absence of unanimity over most policy changes, however, implies that purely theoretical Paretianism must be supplemented with some empirical procedure for aggregating values across individuals with conflicting desires (e.g. applied cost–benefit analysis).

The difficulties with applied cost–benefit analysis are well known. Outside of general equilibrium, prices will not accurately reflect the value of resources. Preferences can be aggregated across different consumers only under fairly restrictive conditions (i.e. quasi-homotheticity). Furthermore, the rankings generated by cost–benefit analysis depend upon whether we use *ex ante* or *ex post* levels of wealth, and may not be transitive. In short, attempts to apply Paretian theory to actual policy evaluation often leave a significant gap between the rough-and-ready policy analysis and the precisely refined theoretical underpinnings.

Non-Paretian frameworks replace Pareto optimality with some other standard, or set of standards, for evaluating an economic system or economic policies.[1] Typical suggestions for standards include co-ordination, responsiveness to change, innovation, discovery, and complexity. Under such standards, a desirable policy is associated with an increase in the relevant standard. A co-ordination standard, for instance, would give the highest ranking to the policy that did the most to further the mutual co-ordination of individual plans.

The particular choice of non-Paretian standard, however, is difficult. Welfare theory is concerned with the ranking of outcomes and must therefore focus upon the maximization of some attribute or set of attributes. These attributes should correspond to what our ultimate, most philosophic judgements consider a 'good result'. But our notion of a 'good result' is complex and may not correspond to the maximization of any particular quality or set of qualities. The welfare theorist must then find a set of attributes or qualities that serve as a proxy for our idea of a good result.

Non-Paretian approaches may thus differ from Paretian theory in two different respects: either they contain a different notion of what a 'good result' is, or they attempt to find a better proxy for good results than the Paretian notion of maximizing gains from trade. For the purposes of this essay, I will accept the vaue judgement underlying Paretianism that 'preference sovereignty', however defined, is our ultimate basis for judging a good result.[2] Whether preference sovereignty can be more accurately captured by some standard other than cost–benefit analysis is thus an important issue.

A central problem

A non-Paretian approach to welfare economics must outline a satisfactory notion of consumer welfare which does not collapse into the Paretian standard. This task has not yet been accomplished. Any attempt to invoke the concepts of co-ordination, complexity, discovery, etc. as normative standards, encounters the issue of whether these qualities are considered good *per se* or not; answering this question can lead to untenable results.

Regarding any of these qualities (or any mix) as good *per se* leads to the following problem: an economy may be comparatively rich in the attribute(s) we have selected, but still not fulfil our intuitive criteria for a good result. With respect to co-ordination, for instance, we can imagine a perfectly or highly co-ordinated economy existing on a low level of subsistence or with a low level of progress. (Ancient China may be an example here.) Similarly, one can imagine economies with enormous amounts of discovery or complexity in limited spheres of activity which have no significant impact upon the general standard of living. Maintaining a strict *per se* advocacy of the chosen standard might result in unwanted endorsements of such situations.

Escaping this problem is not easy. If our chosen standard is not considered desirable *per se*, its presence must be evaluated with respect to some other criterion or criteria. Such evaluations tend to undercut the newly-erected welfare standard. If complexity is good only when it increases wealth, for example, then we really have a wealth standard, not a complexity standard.

Our initial standard may even tend to slip away into applied Paretianism. There is a strong and understandable tendency to evaluate our non-Paretian standard in accord with its ability to satisfy consumer preferences. This judgement may in turn be represented by 'willingness to pay/be paid' criteria, which returns us to applied Paretianism and cost–benefit analysis. The central task of any non-Paretian welfare economics is to incorporate non-Paretian standards into welfare analysis while avoiding the dilemma discussed above.

SIDESTEPPING THE DILEMMA WITH ECONOMIC HISTORY

Alternative welfare approaches might choose to ground their standards in economic history. The chosen standard would not be considered good *per se*, but the probability of encountering outlying cases where satisfaction of the standard generates a 'bad result' may be small. I will first discuss the nature of value judgements in this approach, and then consider applying these value judgements to actual policy analysis.

A history-based approach to welfare theory contains no theoretical 'first step', and is instead empirical in nature. One starts with a number of historical examples which are generally considered instances of 'economic success'. Such examples may involve nations, cities, firms, specific policies and other economic entities. Possible examples might include Japanese post-war economic growth, the history of IBM, or the economic development of Europe. The relevant qualities which characterize these examples of success become our welfare standards.

It is unclear whether non-Paretian approaches involve more question-begging than Paretianism. The initial claim that success is defined relative to a consensual view of examples is controversial. This step, however, may be a necessary part of any policy-analysis process. If economics is viewed as an important rhetorical device in an ongoing dialogue of persuasion (McCloskey 1985), it must ultimately make reference to instances and examples which are consensually considered examples of success. Furthermore, the process of persuasion must attempt to relate the policy choices at hand to the prior notions of good shared by the policy audience.

The process of consensus-building around examples of 'success' is not necessarily more arbitrary than other approaches to welfare economics. For instance, starting with Paretian optimality as a welfare standard presumably reflects the intuition that exhausting all possible benefits from trade corresponds to a desirable economic system. This may sound uncontroversial, but in fact the presuppositions of Paretian theory have come under heavy fire from many welfare economists and philosophers (Sen 1982 is perhaps the best known critic).

A more important point remains, however. Even if the initial premises of Paretianism are less controversial than a history-based approach, the movement from initial premises to policy conclusions may be more controversial. Uncontroversial premises may not get us far in evaluating a controversial world. For instance, the simple premise of exhausting all possible gains from trade may not much help us evaluate policies in a complex world. Further ethical judgements need to be introduced at each step, through measurement techniques and aggregation rules for costs and benefits.

The value judgements behind non-Paretian standards directly reflect the complexity of economic phenomena by making a greater set of intial value judgements than Paretian theory does. The non-Paretian approach makes economic history – rather than measurement techniques and aggregation rules – the relevant field for normative presuppositions. While the initial normative presuppositions may be greater in non-Paretian theory, these presuppositions bring us closer to our final goal of policy evaluation. There may be less need for further normative presuppositions when we apply non-Paretian standards.

Developing a standard

The chosen examples of economic success are not used directly as normative benchmarks but instead for uncovering a number of underlying principles behind economic success. Through the use of contrast and comparison, the welfare theorist can attempt to discover common features behind each of the historical examples which were vital to the desirability of the outcome. These common features would be used as our 'standards' for judging economic policies or systems. We might decide, for instance, that co-ordination and innovation are critical features behind the economic success of nations.

The chosen features can be regarded as the result of the study of economic history and current economic institutions. This leaves three different levels at which disputes over welfare economics can be conducted. Such disputes may involve the choice of examples of success, their important common underlying characteristics, and the extent to which these characteristics will result from current economic policy choices. At no point is there a purely theoretical level of discourse which generates abstract propositions – each of these levels of argumentation is strongly empirical in nature. This method, however, need not be anti-theoretical – economic theory is necessary to discover the common underlying characteristics of success and to estimate the effects of current policy options upon these characteristics.

It might be argued that this method of policy evaluation is open to the dilemma discussed earlier. What is to prevent such a standard from approving of a policy that maximized the presence of the chosen characteristics at the expense of generating an intuitively undesirable outcome?

Adherence to, or rejection of, non-Paretian welfare criteria is based on empirical criteria. For the purposes of the following discussion, let us assume that one of the standards yielded is innovation, or discovery. One of the empirical presuppositions behind our use of discovery for welfare economics might be the following: economic systems are incapable of generating considerable amounts of predominantly useless discoveries over a long period of time. In other words, the only systems capable of sustaining a significant discovery process through time are also the systems that successfully utilize these discoveries. Without a 'healthy' discovery process, the capabilities of the system will tend to shrink on almost all fronts, thus curtailing discoveries. It may be possible to conceive of an intuitively undesirable system which can continually generate new discoveries in a few sectors. (The military establishment of the Soviet Union may be an example here.) Such systems, however, are incapable of generating significant discoveries across a wide range of sectors for a considerable period of time.

Empirical reasons might suggest that the discovery standard would not necessarily approve a misguided policy which subsidized discovery *per se*. Systems that do not pursue such policies will outdo (with respect to discovery, among other factors) systems that do. Of course, if this empirical claim were false, discovery would be a poor choice for a welfare standard. In this case, an alternative standard(s) should be chosen that does not suffer from this problem.

Using history to choose a good standard attempts to avoid the dilemma of either collapsing into Paretian theory or approving of our welfare standards *per se*. Our standards are chosen, not because they are always good, but because empirical analysis indicates that systems which are very successful with respect to the standard(s) are not likely to violate our intuitions concerning what a 'good result' would be.

Aggregation

Historically based non-Paretian approaches to welfare theory take a different view of the aggregation difficulties which have beset a number of other forms of welfare theory. Paretian welfare economics, for instance, insists that all propositions about societal welfare be derivable from the underlying individual preference functions. Aggregation can only proceed when such constructs as the representative consumer are applicable. Needless to say, this implies that rigorous aggregation is, in practice, almost always impossible.

A number of non-Paretian alternatives also insist upon foundational approaches to aggregation which imply that all statements concerning 'societal welfare' must be unambiguously derivable from a set of underlying postulates. Kirzner (1986, pp. 2 and 19), for instance, chooses the underlying postulates of subjectivism, methodological individualism and an emphasis on dynamic processes. These postulates impose stringent requirements upon the task of the welfare theorist. Kirzner notes that:

> we shall refuse to recognize meaning in statements concerning the 'welfare of society' that cannot, in principle, be translated into statements concerning the individuals in society (in a manner which does not do violence to their individuality) . . . we shall not be satisfied with statements that perceive the economic well-being of society as expressible in terms (such as physical output) that are unrelated to the valuations and choices made by individuals.

(Kirzner 1986, p. 19)

Such requirements, of course, would make welfare economics impossible in all but the most trivial circumstances where a number of persons benefit and no one is hurt. Using strict forms of subjectivism and methodological individualism as our foundational postulates implies that aggregation will *never* be possible.

'So much the worse for welfare economics' is a tempting reply, but such a reply ignores the necessity of normative comparisons between different states of economic affairs. Claiming that such comparisons are outside the realm of scientific discourse is a dubious escape from the problem at hand. Even in the unlikely event that a demarcation criterion for science could be found, the scope of our endeavour would simply be accordingly redefined. The enterprise of welfare economics would then be concerned with making sense of our 'non-scientific' conversations about economic well-being. Under this set of circumstances, 'non-science' would be a richer realm of exploration for welfare economics than the domain of 'science', and our endeavour could be accordingly relabelled with no necessary stigma. Terminologically excluding or including our sins from the realm of science cannot alter their perniciousness.

Aggregation is a different type of problem within the non-Paretian approaches examined here. Welfare economics is not seen as a science which must build from the bottom up and excoriate all judgements of well-being which cannot be derived from the underlying foundations. Instead, a welfare framework may consist of a web of interwoven propositions, each with a significant empirical (and aggregative) content. The decision concerning which propositions we decide to accept and use will contain our aggregative judgements. In many cases, these propositions will contain elements of economic intuition that cannot be reduced to any further micro-justification.

WHAT AN ACTUAL STANDARD MIGHT LOOK LIKE

I now wish to outline briefly some details of what a non-foundationalist normative approach would look like. In doing so, I will examine a hypothetical tripartite standard based upon discovery/innovation, complexity, and provision of consumer goods. I will discuss the question of which empirical propositions would have to be true to make this tripartite standard a good one. I will not, however, argue that these propositions are actually true; this discussion intends only to flesh out the structure of one possible approach – not to advocate a specific approach. The following discussion is thus heuristic in nature.

Under the tripartite standard, policies would be evaluated with respect to the degree to which they furthered innovation, complexity, and provision of consumer goods. The policy which fared best in these regards would receive the highest ranking.[3] We now examine each standard in turn, with a particular eye upon which empirical propositions would have to be true for the choice of standard to be a good one. For purposes of simplicity, I shall not phrase these statements in the subjunctive, although they should be read as 'if-then' statements rather than actual claims about reality.

Discovery and innovation

The discovery problem has a number of separate, though interrelated aspects, which include incentives for discovery, implementation of the discovery, and dissemination of the discovery. The last two features may also be expressed under the heading of innovation. In general, discovery refers to the expansion of the opportunity set occasioned by changes in the state of knowledge. Discovery is not restricted to the unveiling of unknown variables from a given distribution but also includes changes in the parameters of choice and the maximization problem which the individual faces (see Nelson and Winter 1982 for analyses of discovery).

One desirable property of a discovery standard is the incentive-driven nature of discovery. Such incentives may include money, fame, prestige, and altruism. Social systems that do not provide proper incentives for economic activity will perform poorly with respect to discoveries. Looking at discoveries thus gives an indirect handle on the kind of incentive system in the economy. Economies which allow participants to reap the benefits of welfare-improving activity will also generate significant quantities of innovation.

Another suitable property of discovery is that it cannot easily be forced upon an economic system beyond a certain limit. Attempts to increase the amount of resources devoted to discovery beyond some plausible limit will usually backfire. Let us imagine, for instance, that the government conscripted half of America's manpower resources for the service of scientific innovation. The empirical history of entrepreneurship and the creative process indicates that such a policy would yield fewer discoveries than current American policy. Other economic policies, however, such as the relaxation of anti-trust laws for joint research and development ventures, would be approved under this standard if they increased innovation.

The possibility of such policies leading to an 'overinvestment' in discovery is given little weight under this standard. This judgement is based upon the significance of the uninternalized externalities which attend most discoveries; the underlying empirical claim is that the greatest attainable (and sustainable) amount of discovery is likely to be the optimal amount. The best standards can be described as those whose practical maximum equals, or approximates, their normative optimum.

A final desirable property of discovery is the fact that unbalanced, single-sector spurts of discovery are unlikely to possess long-run sustainability. Economies with many varied and diverse sources of discovery, on the other hand, will be able to sustain this pattern for discovery for long periods of time. We are thus saved from having to make potentially difficult comparisons between economies which produce a great number of discoveries in a few limited areas and economies which produce a more varied and well-balanced pattern of discovery. Another way of stating this point is as follows: the best method of achieving growth in a specialized area is to adopt the policy which leads to the healthiest all-round pattern of growth. This view is based upon such factors as the importance of cross-fertilization between businesses, industries, scientific disciplines, etc. in the process of economic growth.

Complexity

A well-known concept in general systems theory, the issue of complexity is gaining increasing attention within the economics profession. Complexity is generally considered to be a 'cluster concept' which consists of a number of interrelated features (see Warsh 1984). These features include the number of different parts in a system, the number of interrelationships between these parts, the number of types of parts, the definiteness of function of each part (specialization and division of labour), the 'redundancy' of a system, and the functional interdependencies between parts of an order.[4] Perhaps complexity can be best visualized as the ability of a system to combine co-ordination and growth.[5] Herbert Spencer has offered the following useful comment on complexity:

> At the same time that evolution [of all sorts, including social] is a change from the homogeneous to the heterogeneous, it is a change from the indefinite to the definite. Along until an advance from simplicity to complexity, there is an advance from confusion to order – from undetermined arrangement to determined arrangement. Development, no matter of what kind, exhibits not only a multiplication of unlike parts, but an increase in the clauses with which these parts are marked off from one another.
>
> (Spencer 1930, p. 293)

Policies which increase complexity are identified with the progressive development of an economic system, as empirical evidence indicates that successful economies are generally characterized by an extraordinarily high degree of complexity. Complexity has several properties which make it a desirable welfare standard. Like discovery, the greatest possible amount of complexity may also be the optimal amount of complexity. Additional 'inefficient' doses of complexity are difficult to sustain for a number of reasons. Perhaps, most importantly, marginal increments of complexity must always survive a profit-and-loss test.[6] Additional complexity always involves a resource cost, and if it does not yield corresponding benefits it is likely to disappear.

The above argument may appear to beg the question by assuming an identity between the private and social costs of complexity. Is it not possible that individuals may invest in increasing complexity for the purpose of seeking rents? At least in the proximity of the first-best solution, this danger may not be significant. Societies possessing large amounts of rent-seeking-generated complexity will (*ceteris paribus*) be less complex than societies that do not permit such activities. Societies with less rent-seeking will have more wealth and be able to sustain complex patterns of organization considerably better than the societies with more rent-seeking. If this were true, then complexity would possess the desirable property of having its practical maximum coincide with its normative optimum.

Another advantage of the complexity standard is its close relationship with innovation and discovery. Complexity and innovation are two co-existing forces which supplement and encourage each other's development. Complexity helps innovation by giving potential innovators a highly developed network of ideas, resources and support to draw upon. Likewise, innovation encourages complexity by providing a continual stream of new ideas, resources and support to be incorporated into existing economic relationships. This not only increases the number of parts in the system but allows for new and previously unseen ways of rearranging old components and resources.

The complementary nature of complexity and innovation implies a strong presumption that the first-best outcome or policy will dominate in both areas. This does not imply, however, that only one of these standards is needed. Both characteristics are complementary pieces of information concerning the desirability of a given policy alternative. Demonstration that a particular alternative is superior in both spheres offers considerable evidence that we are at, or approaching, the first-best solution, information which is not yielded by any single attribute.

Provision of consumer goods

Perhaps our strongest intuitive judgement with respect to the success of economic systems is that provision of consumer goods is a mark of fundamental success. Systems which do not manage to procure consumer goods for citizens must be judged as failures, regardless of any other virtues the system may have. Policies which increase the number or availability of consumer goods receive a positive evaluation, while policies which do the opposite receive a negative evaluation.

Apart from its intuitive appeal, using consumer goods as one of the three welfare standards may fit well with the other two standards of innovation and complexity. Both of these features play a critical role in the mechanism which delivers consumer goods to those who value them. Discovery provides for a continual stream of new goods as well as new ways of making these goods available and new ways of enjoying existing goods. Complexity allows an economy to sustain the sophisticated network of co-ordination between the first steps taken in producing the good and the final consumption of the good. In contrast, relatively non-complex economies experience great difficulties in developing mature networks for the production and distribution of consumer goods.

Although consumption (and not discovery or complexity) is the ultimate goal of economic activity, the tripartite standard does not necessarily reduce to a consumption-goods standard. The effects of many policies upon consumption opportunities are not always immediately clear, but if they increase discovery and complexity, a long-run favourable impact upon the provision of consumer goods may result. A more fundamental reason why a consumption-opportunities standard is not self-sufficient is that what individuals value (i.e. what is defined as a desirable consumption opportunity) is itself a function of discovery and complexity, among other features (see Elster 1982). Using complexity and innovation as joint standards with consumption goods represents an attempt to come to terms with the problem of doing welfare theory when it is recognized that preferences are endogenous.

SECOND-BEST CONSIDERATIONS

A final issue for non-Paretian approaches I shall discuss is the problem of second best. Well known in Paretian theory, second-best theory suggests that local optimization may move us further away from the global optimum if the optimum conditions are not met in all others markets. An analogous problem exists in the non-Paretian framework discussed in this chapter.

As in Paretian welfare economics, the problem of second best does not arise when no constraints prevent the choice of the best possible policy for all sectors of the economy. In Paretian theory this can be proven *a priori* – in a non-Paretian framework it can be considered an empirical truth. The best outcome should receive the highest ranking from all the standards that we have chosen. If no such dominant outcome exists, this may suggest that we have chosen our standards poorly. It is possible, of course, that no choice of standards will assign dominant rankings to any of the outcomes and that we are always trading one attribute off against the other. This would imply that non-Paretian approaches are incapable of yielding determinant rankings.

If a strictly dominant alternative cannot be found or simply does not exist, a non-Paretian welfare economics will experience its own problem of the second best, which can prevent an unambiguous ranking of the policy alternatives. If the dominant alternative exists but is not available, improvements with respect to one of our standards may make matters worse in other directions. Increasing complexity may stifle innovation, for instance.

Our inability to obtain or find a dominant solution may require us to weigh one of our standards off against another in some fashion. The above discussion, however, implies that this cannot be done without our weighting scheme collapsing into some other welfare standard. Like Paretian theory, non-Paretian approaches experience serious problems when confronted with second-best analysis.

A NON-FOUNDATIONALIST APPROACH

Current interpretations of Paretian theory are foundationalist in nature. One starts with certain propositions from consumer theory and the theory of production, and deduces their implications. Policies are evaluated on the basis of how accurately their results correspond to the results stipulated by the theory's building blocks. The result which comes closest to a competitive general equilibrium receives the highest ranking (second-best problems aside). If we want to adopt a foundationalist approach, Paretian theory is most likely to offer the best foundations available.

An alternative approach to policy evaluation must therefore look to another method. The method we have examined has similarities with the concept of 'reflective equilibrium' outlined in John Rawls's *Theory of Justice* (1971). Rawls's concept of 'reflective equilibrium' establishes a congruence between the results yielded by our theory, our moral intuitions, and our understanding of the principles of economic and social theory. Both the framework and its results should justify certain intuitions and not violate others, while possessing an overall concordance with our understanding of social reality. Reflective equilibrium is an equilibrium of understanding, not the sort of mechanical equilibrium postulated by classical physics.

The end result of a process of reflective equilibrium will not possess any definite starting point or foundations but will instead consist of a web of interrelated propositions which focus around certain critical issues. For our purposes, comparisons between different frameworks (or 'webs of propositions') should be made on the basis of usefulness – to what extent does the approach further our understanding of the world or help us evaluate attempts to change the world?

An excellent summary of this approach can be illustrated by the following extended quotation from the final section of *Theory of Justice*, 'Concluding remarks on justification':

> Sometimes they [philosophers] attempt to find self-evident principles from which a sufficient body of standards and precepts can be derived to account for our considered judgments. . . . I have not adopted [this] conception[s] of justification. . . . There is no set of conditions of first principles that can be plausibly claimed to be necessary or definitive of morality and thereby especially suited to carry the burden of justification . . . justification rests upon the entire conception and how it fits in with and organizes our considered judgments in reflective equilibrium . . . justification is a matter of the mutual support of many considerations, of everything fitting together into one coherent view. . . . The aim throughout was to show that the theory matches the fixed points of our considered convictions better than other familiar doctrines, and that it leads us to revise and extrapolate our judgments in what seem on reflection to be more satisfactory ways. First principles and particular judgments appear on balance to hang together reasonably well, at least in comparison with alternative theories.
>
> (Rawls 1971, p. 579)

As Rawls notes, this concept of justification comes from the works of Willard Quine. Rawls, however, does not emphasize Quine's argument that all statements contain a significant empirical element, and that we do not have access to any body of purely theoretical propositions which are independent of experience. Quine's insight is consistent with the emphasis upon economic history offered above. If it can be said that Paretian welfare economics is based upon the theory of general equilibrium, it could be noted in contrast that a non-Paretian approach would have to be based upon economic history.

A non-Paretian approach offers a view of welfare economics which is simultaneously more modest and more ambitious than Paretianism. It is more modest because it is not able to generate any large class of abstract propositions comparable to the body of theoretical Paretian welfare economics. Due to the non-formalistic nature of this alternative non-Paretian enterprise, the development of such abstract propositions is neither possible nor relevant. The non-Paretian enterprise is more ambitious in the sense that it attempts to bring us closer to useful policy evaluations.

CONCLUDING COMMENTS

One of the most striking features of the non-foundationalist approach outlined above is its resemblance to 'ordinary language' conversations concerning the desirability of different economic policies. Arguments are based upon historical examples (either recent or old) and directed at a certain consensual view of what a good result would look like. Whereas Paretian theory attempts to reform our ordinary language practice of policy evaluation, a non-foundationalist alternative studies and reflects it.[7]

On the plus side, non-Paretian approaches to welfare economics avoid the obsession with rigour at the expense of relevance. Dynamic considerations involving change and discovery often fit poorly into the equilibrium models upon which Paretian theory is based. Furthermore, the type of non-Paretian approach examined here provides interesting insights into aggregation problems and might even suggest new approaches to the analysis of endogenous preferences.

On the negative side, non-Paretian approaches experience serious difficulties in dealing with second-best problems. We cannot even be sure that a non-Paretian method is capable of producing policy rankings at all. Those rankings which might be produced seem heavily dependent upon a large number of empirical propositions whose degree of truth is very difficult to discover. Using economic history as a basis for welfare economics should thus be viewed as an interesting idea, although one which still has serious difficulties.

ACKNOWLEDGEMENTS

The author wishes to thank Peter Boettke, Randy Kroszner, Don Lavoie and Ralph Rector for useful comments.

NOTES

1 Nelson and Winter (1982) and Kirzner (1986) offer two examples of non-Paretian approaches.
2 Cowen (1990) examines the strengths and weaknesses of preference sovereignty.
3 The possibility that no alternative will be unambiguously superior in all three capacities will be discussed below.
4 The notion of 'redundancy' was first developed by John von Neumann, and characterizes the ability of a system to cope with failure by utilizing alternate methods of communication, co-ordination, etc. After hypothesizing that failure is an essential property of complex systems, von Neumann argued that the critical issue was whether the system in question possessed enough redundancy to minimize the effects of failures of particular parts.
5 Some of the discussion of complexity reflects developments in systems analysis. See Checkland (1981) and Sahal (1982) for overviews on this approach.
6 This holds true under or near first-best conditions. The problem of the second best which can arise in this framework will be discussed below.
7 This mirrors the well-known tension between analytic and 'ordinary language' approaches to philosophy. However, it would be worthwhile to develop a non-foundationalist interpretation of Paretianism. Paretian theory could then be used primarily as a foil that gave us insight into the logical structure of normative propositions, rather than as a means of unambiguously ranking competing alternatives.

REFERENCES

Checkland, P.B. (1981) 'Science and the systems movement' in Open Systems Group (ed.) *Systems Behavior*, London: Harper & Row.

Cowen, Tyler (1990) 'The scope and limits of preference sovereignty', unpublished manuscript.

Elster, Jon (1982) 'Sour grapes – utilitarianism and the genesis of wants', in A. Sen and B. Williams (eds) *Utilitarianism and Beyond*, Cambridge: Cambridge University Press.

Kirzner, Israel (1986) 'Welfare economics: a modern Austrian perspective', unpublished manuscript.

McCloskey, Donald (1985) *The Rhetoric of Economics*, Wisconsin: University of Wisconsin Press.

Nelson, Richard and Winter, Sidney (1982) *An Evolutionary Theory of Economic Change,* Cambridge, Mass.: Harvard University Press.

Rawls, John (1971) *Theory of Justice*, Cambridge, Mass.: Harvard University Press.

Sahal, Devendra (1982) 'Structure and self-organization', *Behavioral Science* 27, July, pp. 249–58.

Sen, Amartya (1982) *Choice, Welfare and Measurement*, Cambridge, Mass.: MIT Press.

Spencer, Herbert (1930) *First Principles*, New York: D. Appleton & Co.

Warsh, David (1984) *The Idea of Economic Complexity*, New York: Viking Press.

14 The hermeneutical view of freedom
Implications of Gadamerian understanding for economic policy

Tom G. Palmer

Ludwig Wittgenstein (1968, p. 69) has remarked that philosophy 'leaves everything as it is'. The implication of this view is that philosophy does not change the world. This theme is also present, in a somewhat different way, in Hans-Georg Gadamer's view of his own philosophical hermeneutics. As Gadamer writes in *Truth and Method*:

> The hermeneutics developed here is not . . . a methodology of the human sciences, but an attempt to understand what the human sciences truly are, beyond their methodological self-consciousness, and what connects them with the totality of our experience of the world . . . it is not my intention to make prescriptions for the sciences or the conduct of life, but to try to correct false thinking about what they are.
>
> (Gadamer 1982, p. xii)

While Gadamer has indeed deepened our understanding of the event that understanding is, his claims may have been in some ways too modest (cf. Hekman 1986, pp. 139−59).[1] To understand what we do when we experience is inevitably to say something about the conduct of life, and to lay the ground for criticism of science and of life. It will be my claim that Gadamer offers us some very important hints for the proper conduct of economic science, and for the proper conduct of economic life.

As other contributors have explored the implications of a hermeneutical approach for economic science, I will offer only a few comments on the significance for economics of hermeneutic philosophy; the rest of this essay will address itself to some implications of this approach for economic policy.

WE LIVE IN A WORLD OF SIGNIFICANCE

It is a mainstay of modernist thought that one of the main problems of philosophical thinking is to show how things 'out there' are mirrored 'in here', i.e. how is it that the Cartesian dualities of 'thinking substance' and 'extended substance' can interact, or how the former can know the latter. A corollary of this question is the question of how the things 'out there', apprehended as they are by means of the senses, can have non-perceptual characteristics like 'utility', 'meaning', 'desirability', 'goodness', and so forth. This seems such an obvious way of thinking about these problems that we often overlook the fact that this is a very recent way of looking at the world, and would not be at all obvious to a thinker like Aristotle, for example.

One of the major motivations of the philosopher Edmund Husserl was to overcome such dichotomies, to show that the chasm between subject and object was not necessary, and that the two could properly be understood only within an overarching unity. To ask the typical question of how subjects and objects can be related not only entails degrading the subject to the status of an object – just one more thing among others – it also rests on questionable but unjustified philosophical assumptions. In contrast, Husserl's phenomenological (or descriptive) philosophy seeks to describe the phenomena just as they present themselves, without importing philosophical preconceptions about what they have to be. His project was to present a scientific philosophy, one that was true to the phenomena in all their richness, and not merely another 'nothing but' philosophy – according to which there are 'nothing but' impressions (David Hume), justice is 'nothing but' the greatest satisfaction of the greatest number (John Stuart Mill), and so forth.

Heidegger takes up Husserl's task in *Being and Time*, albeit in more dramatic and often more obscure language. Rather than attempting to show how inert objects can acquire significance, Heidegger shows, through his temporal analytic of everydayness, that they are *already* significant; merely to speak of objects is already to be in a relationship with them (see Heidegger 1962, especially pp. 95–107). We do not have to 'get to' objects, for we are already at home among them, and the task of the philosopher is to describe where we already are, and not to figure out how to get there.

The parallels with subjectivist schools of thought in economics should be clear. The world of the economic actor is a world of significance. The job of the economist, then, must be to explicate the phenomena of the social world in terms of the meaning structures at work,[2] and not merely to search for correlations among 'data' against which one tests theories pulled from philosophical hats. (This is not to say that such searches – or such tests of theories against observations – are pointless, but that they must ultimately be placed within plausible and meaningful accounts of human conduct.) The very worldliness of the world is a structure of significance, and can best be understood in such terms.[3]

THE 'IS' WITHIN THE 'OUGHT'

Are we left, however, with a merely descriptive science – one which can help us understand what *is*, but has nothing to say about what *should* be? Since Hume's philosophical interpreters have drawn the is/ought dichotomy (or, more precisely, chasm) out of the philosopher's writings, economists and other social scientists have been vexed by the problem of whether and what they can say about what should be. The allegedly scientific approach of the Pareto criterion has come under a great deal of criticism in recent years, and rightly so (see Cowen, this volume, Ch. 13). Not only does it lead to often repugnant conclusions, but it rests on assumptions that are highly suspect. Can philosophical hermeneutics offer an answer to this conundrum for the social scientist who wishes to participate in the community in a more important way than merely offering predictions about the likely outcomes of this or that policy? The latter approach has been clearly formulated by one of the profession's leading members, Milton Friedman: 'The economist's value judgements doubtless influence the subjects he works on and perhaps also at times the conclusions he reaches . . . [but] this does not alter the fundamental point that, in principle, there are no value judgements in economics' (Friedman 1967, p. 86; cf. Stubblebine 1975, pp. 11–22).[4]

I would like to approach this problem and offer an alternative to Friedman's position, but in a somewhat roundabout fashion. I will begin by explicating Gadamer's phenomenological description of what goes on in a conversation, and then draw implications for our understanding (as social scientists) of the market process, and for our evaluation of the moral status of various economic arrangements and of the institutions on which they rest. Gadamer is interested in conversation primarily because of the model it provides for the confrontation with a text; I will put it to use in a somewhat different context.[5]

First, however, it will be appropriate to consider the question – raised by the neo-Marxist Jürgen Habermas – of whether Gadamer offers us any criteria for social critique at all. Gadamer has gone to great lengths in his *Truth and Method* to argue that tradition, prejudice, language, and habit can be sources of truth, as well as of error. Does Gadamer offer any principle of criticism by which we can distinguish between true and false prejudices, the liberating and the enslaving? Just as the question can be asked of F.A. Hayek's evolutionary understanding of markets and morality (see Gray 1980, especially pp. 119–37), Habermas asks whether Gadamer has done more than merely offer a conservative defence of the *status quo*.[6] Much of my present essay can be interpreted as an implicit critique of the Habermasian enterprise, which proceeds – like this essay – from the discourse to ethics, but rests on a latent objectivism, a misunderstanding of economic processes, and an exaggerated elitism.[7]

In seeking for such a critical principle in Gadamer, Habermas overlooks Gadamer's insistence that, in overcoming the 'prejudice against prejudices' (a theme also found in Hayek's later work on social institutions), Gadamer stresses that authority (including that of tradition) rests ultimately on 'recognition and knowledge . . . and hence on an act of reason itself' (Gadamer 1982, p. 248).[8] Authority and reason are not polar opposites, but complementary elements of the same human rationality.

Not only are authority and reason already allied under the banner of rationality, but the authority of tradition is ineluctable. Man cannot escape living through one tradition or another – traditions which live through their incessant, creative and free appropriation by the men and women who live within them. Man's finitude rests in the inability to raise himself to the status of absolute consciousness – or consciousness without presuppositions (in the Hegelian sense).

Consistent with his stress on the role of reason in tradition and on the finitude of human existence, Gadamer shows that the appropriate way to treat a text is not to attempt to recreate the intention or meaning that was, one might say, 'in the author's head' but to try to learn from or listen to the text. The point is not to recreate the mental contents of an author, but to understand what the author has to say to us about a topic of common concern. If one reads Aristotle on politics merely to find out what Aristotle thought, one does a disservice to Aristotle; one should read Aristotle's *Politics* to learn about politics, to open oneself to a dialogue with the author and the text about a topic of common concern, and not simply to say, 'Such was Aristotle's view' and then return the volume to the shelf. Gadamer uses as his model of how to approach a text (in a way, a 'dead' thing) the way in which we approach a living interlocutor.

In approaching a tradition, Gadamer tells us, we should realize that tradition: 'is language, i.e., it expresses itself like a "Thou". A "Thou" is not an object, but stands in a relationship with us . . . tradition is a genuine partner in communication, with which we have fellowship as does the "I" with a "Thou" ' (Gadamer 1982, p. 321).[9] Gadamer models the confrontation between reader and text on the dialogical model of a conversation, with the reciprocal recognition appropriate to it:

> In human relationships the important thing is, as we have seen, to experience the 'Thou' truly as a 'Thou', i.e., not to overlook his claim and to listen to what he has to say to us. To this end, openness is necessary. But this openness exists ultimately not only for the person to whom one listens, but rather anyone who listens is fundamentally open. Without this kind of openness to one another there is no genuine human relationship. Belonging together always means being able to listen to one another. When two people understand each other, this does not mean that one person 'understands' the other in the sense of surveying him. Similarly, to hear and obey someone does not mean simply that we do blindly what the other desires. We call such a person a slave.
>
> (Gadamer 1982, p. 324)

Thus (as Habermas is also known for arguing), the model of conversation provides a norm for social intercourse. It is persuasion – not coercion, domination and manipulation – which characterizes the proper relationship of one human life to another.[10] What can we glean from this for the understanding of economic life and the guidance of economic policy?[11]

REASON, SPEECH AND PRICES

I propose, first, that we use this insight to recast radically our understanding of the market-price system. That prices transmit information has long been known, and acknowledged by both friends and foes of the market economy. The significance of this fact, however, is not widely agreed upon. Do prices serve merely as parametric guidelines for the appropriate reconciliation of human preferences in the allocation of goods?[12] Do they serve as indicators of opportunities for profit and loss, and thereby as a mechanism for plan co-ordination?[13] While I am most sympathetic to the 'plan co-ordination' view of Mises, Hayek and Kirzner – principally because it leaves room for the real-world *activity* of competition – I believe that this view can be enriched by a return to the conception of price held by Adam Smith. The implications of this for our understanding of the spontaneous emergence of order – as well as for such topics as property rights, advertising, competition and other topics – should be made clear shortly.

In a famous and oft-quoted passage from *The Wealth of Nations*, Adam Smith identifies the source of the general opulence attendant upon the division of labour:

> This division of labour, from which so many advantages are derived, is not originally the effect of any human wisdom, which foresees and intends that general opulence to which it gives occasion. It is the necessary, though very slow and gradual consequence of a certain propensity in human nature which has in view no such extensive utility: the propensity to truck, barter, and exchange one thing for another.
>
> (Smith 1978a [1776], p. 25)

The following paragraph, however, asks a much deeper question, which Smith puts off as inappropriate to the occasion:

> Whether this propensity be one of those original principles in human nature, of which no further account can be given; or whether, as seems more probable, it be the necessary consequence of the faculties of reason and speech, it belongs not to our present subject to enquire.
>
> (Smith 1978a [1776], p. 25)

Had Smith taken the time to spell out some of his thinking on this subject in his book, it might have avoided many subsequent misunderstandings in the science of economics. That he had thought about the matter is clear, however, as his lecture of March 30, 1763 shows:

> If we should enquire into the principle in the human mind on which this disposition of trucking is founded, it is clearly on the natural inclination every one has to persuade. The offering of a schilling, which to us appears to have so plain and simple a meaning, is in reality offering an argument to persuade one to do so and so as it is for his interest. Men

always endeavour to persuade others to be of their opinion even when the
matter is of no consequence to them.

(Smith 1978b [1896], p. 352)

That 'reason and speech' are necessary for the emergence of a market,
and therefore for our adequate understanding of it, has been shown by the
fact that animals do not trade (something which Smith noted). The mere
presence of well-ordered preferences, uncertainty, scarcity or property (in
the form of possession, or of territoriality) is not sufficient to generate trade
(see also Levy 1986). That is because trade requires reason and speech – i.e.
persuasion.[14] When we read in our translations of Aristotle that man is the
rational animal, what is brought to our modern minds is rationality in the
narrow sense of calculation, of fitting means to ends.[15] The phrase used by
Aristotle is *zoon logon*, which might better be translated as 'the animal that
talks'.

The market should be seen, then, not merely as a vast mechanism for the
efficient exchange of information, as it is often considered by neoclassical
economists, but as a forum for *persuasion*.[16] It is not simply an information-
collating system. Persuasion should be an integral part of our understanding
of the market process because the preferences of suppliers and consumers
are not *data* – merely the Latin term for 'givens' – to be fed into a vast calculating mechanism, thereby yielding a fully determinate result that was
implicit in the initial conditions. Instead, the market exchange process is
better illumined in the light cast by rhetoric, the art of persuasion (a constant
and recurrent theme in Gadamer's work). There was no 'given' demand for
portable computers, digital laser-guided music systems, video games, pet
rocks, or genetic engineering, to take but a few recent examples, before they
were developed by inventor-entrepreneurs who 'created' (i.e. persuaded) the
demand for them. In such cases, the end result could not have been implicit
in the 'initial' conditions, which did not include *any* demand for these goods
at all.

This approach has a number of implications. I will take the following in
order: (1) the charge that markets merely 'generate' wants to be fulfilled, and
that it is therefore no great feat to argue that they are superior to other,
coercive, arrangements at satisfying those wants; (2) the inseparability of
'process' and 'order'; (3) the hypostatization of preferences and the problem
of public goods; (4) the informative and persuasive dimensions of advertising; and (5) the role of legitimate property rights in facilitating conversation and opening a 'public place' for social intercourse.

THE SATISFACTION OF GENERATED WANTS

It is often raised as an objection to the market system that it 'creates' needs
and desires, 'forcing' us to want ever more 'things' and thereby making us
(1) greedy and miserable, and (2) pawns of those who 'create' these needs.

What this view fails to comprehend is that the process of civilization is, to a very large extent, precisely one of learning to 'demand' new things for which previous generations had no demand. As Hayek has remarked: 'If the fact that people would not feel the need for something if it were not produced did prove that such products are of small value, all those highest products of human endeavour would be of small value' (Hayek 1969, p. 315). That one acquires new desires through imitation of others, or through persuasion of one sort or another, should not be shocking.[17] The implicit premise of those who consider this obvious fact of social interaction and interdependence to be a damnation of the market is the assumption that the producers of new goods, fashions, or ideas somehow 'force' us to buy their products or adopt their ideas. This 'force', however, is the 'force' of persuasion – an altogether different kind of 'force' from that of the guillotine or the gun.

In line with this complaint, David Ingram laments:

> we find Gadamer arguing . . . that the rhetorical hegemony which corporate powers apparently exercise with respect to formation of public opinion is illusory because it is dialogically checked and countered by individual consumers whose scales of preference function as the decisive factor regulating production in the free market.
>
> (Ingram 1985, p. 46)

This is, of course, taken as evidence of the naïvety of Gadamer's philosophy.[18]

It would not be too strong to say that the emergence of civilization and the emergence of the market are largely the same process (Hayek 1988, pp. 38–47). It is this element of learning, not in the neoclassical sense of moving along a learning function, but in the sense of true novelty and surprise, which is indispensable for understanding the emergence of the market economy (what Adam Smith called 'The Great Society') and of civilization itself. This kind of learning is what Gadamer has in mind when he describes the openness of a conversation; in a true conversation I must be open to being convinced by my interlocutor. A conversation, properly so called, has no determinate conclusion. Analogously, the market process has no determinate conclusion.

PROCESS AND ORDER

In standard economic analysis, equilibrium is conceived as a state of the market, a state toward which the market is ever tending. Setting aside for the moment the conceptual difficulties (if not impossibilities) in treating a dynamic process like the market solely in static terms, there is a philosophical problem which vitiates the entire project. As James Buchanan has stated the matter:

the 'order' of the market emerges *only* from the *process* of voluntary exchange among the participating individuals. The 'order' is, itself, defined as the outcome of the *process* that defines it. The 'it', the allocation-distribution result, does not, and cannot, exist independently of the trading process. Absent this process, there is and can be no 'order'.

(Buchanan 1985, pp. 73–4)[19]

The act of choice is not the response of an automaton to stimuli, but a free and creative act, incorporating the moment of creative *application* so strongly stressed by Gadamer in his description of understanding (see Gadamer 1982, especially pp. 274–8).[20]

The understanding of the relationship between preference and choice can be better understood by recourse to Husserl's distinction between two different kinds of 'parts': 'pieces' are potentially independent parts of a whole (like my finger, which may be separated from me) while 'moments' are non-independent parts of a whole (like the brightness of a surface) (see Husserl 1970, pp. 435–89). The neoclassical equilibrium approach hypostatizes preference; it 'thingifies' it, and in such a way that choice is altogether obliterated. As Buchanan further explains:

Individuals do not act so as to maximize utilities described in *independently-existing functions*. They confront genuine choices, and the sequence of decisions taken may be conceptualized, *ex post* (after the choice), in terms of 'as if' functions that are maximized. But these 'as if' functions are themselves generated in the choosing process, not separately from such process. If viewed in this perspective, there is no means by which even the most idealized omniscient designer could duplicate the results of voluntary interchange. The potential participants *do not know until they enter the process* what their own choices will be. From this it follows that it is *logically impossible* for an omniscient designer to know, unless, of course, we are to preclude individual freedom of the will. . . . In economics, even among many of those who remain strong advocates of market and market-like organization, the 'efficiency' that such market arrangements produce is independently conceptualized. Market arrangements then become 'means', which may or may not be relatively best. Until and unless this teleological element is fully exorcised from basic economic theory, economists are likely to remain confused and their discourse confusing.

(Buchanan 1985, pp. 73–4)

The order of the market cannot be achieved without the voluntary process of exchange among multiple property owners which constitutes the market. Nor, as the model of openness offered by Gadamer implies, can state officials 'help' the market through indicative planning, 'targeted industrial policy', 'trends analysis', or any of the various other schemes recently placed on the policy agenda, for the very reason that the future that the planners claim to divine does not exist, and will not exist until the choices which will constitute it are made. As Karl Popper has shown, it is logically incoherent to claim to predict the knowledge that we will have in the future: 'For he who could so predict today by scientific means our discoveries of tomorrow could make them today; which would mean that there would be an end to the growth of knowledge' (Popper 1972, p. 298).[21]

The implications for the attempts of technocratic planners to 'plan' the economy, or even to 'direct' it on a piecemeal basis, are clear. They cannot justify their use of coercion on the standard welfare-economics grounds typically offered for such intervention.

PUBLIC GOODS AND THE HYPOSTATIZATION OF PREFERENCES

A similar difficulty faces the standard neoclassical account of public goods and their generation. As William Baumol puts the matter:

> if we assume the role of government to be that of assisting the members of the community to attain their own aims with maximum efficiency, then in a case such as we have just considered [military preparedness] it becomes the task of government to override the decisions of the market. This is not because the government believes, on some peculiar ground, that the people are not competent to judge, but rather because the market fails to provide machinery for these *decisions* to be given effect.
>
> (Baumol 1969, pp. 55–6, my italics)

This approach suffers from the very same problem discussed in the previous section of this chapter. It takes preferences (or even, more strongly, *decisions*) as existing independently of the choices made by market participants. After hypostatizing these preferences, it finds that the existence of transactions costs pre-empts their realization, requiring a shift to a level of 'meta-choice' in which we all agree to coerce each other.[22] Under voluntary exchange conditions, all of us have incentives to under-reveal our 'true' preferences or decisions.

Not only is this a hypostatization of preferences, and therefore subject to the same cricitisms as those found above, but an argument for *provision* of certain goods is framed in terms that require those goods already to exist – an inconsistency that undercuts the entire research programme. *Given* the existence of a good, for which the marginal cost of making it available to one more person is zero (or less than the cost of exclusion at the margin), it is inefficient to expend resources to exclude non-puchasers. This begs the question. Since we live in a world where goods are not *given*, but have to be produced, the problem is how best to produce these goods. An argument for state *provision* that assumes that the goods are already produced is no argument at all.[23]

This is not to discount the problem of preference revelation altogether.

It is a real problem. The point is to understand how people interact in real-world markets to overcome co-ordination problems, including the problem of co-ordinating their productive activities so as to satisfy their demand for goods often associated with characteristics of publicness (non-rivalrous consumption or non-excludability of non-payers). Such mechanisms as the definition of property rights,[24] bundling 'private' with 'public' goods,[25] fencing (exclusion devices),[26] and conditional contracts (also known as pre-contract excludability)[27] offer examples of how people actually voluntarily provide goods which, orthodox economists tell them, they cannot provide.

FINITUDE AND ECONOMIC POLICY: SOME PARTICULARS

Advertising

Advertising, as intimated earlier, should be rehabilitated in terms of voluntary persuasive behaviour. It is inappropriate to consider advertising as a wasteful expenditure of resources merely added on top of those expenditures necessary to produce the product. As Kirzner has pointed out:

> It is not sufficient . . . to make the product available; consumers must be aware of its availability. If the opportunity to buy is not perceived by the consumer, it is as if the opportunity to produce had not been perceived by the entrepreneur. It is not enough to grow food consumers do not know how to obtain; consumers must know that the food has in fact been grown!
>
> (Kirzner 1979, p. 10)

Those who ascribe coercive power to advertising typically underestimate the ratiocinative powers of the 'masses' and overestimate their own. Ultimately, the act of consumption – undertaken by the consumer alone – is the test of the quality of the product. As Coase points out: 'Any advertisement that induces people to consume a product conveys information, since the act of consumption gives more information about the properties of a product or service than could be communicated by the advertisement itself' (Coase 1977, p. 8).

More is at stake, however, than merely making the *availability* of a product known to its potential consumers. They must also be *persuaded* that they will find it useful, enjoyable, pleasurable, enlightening, elevating, and so on. In many cases, this will entail convincing the consumer that something previously unwanted should be wanted.[29]

The persuasive aspect of advertising is made more understandable when the 'openness' of processes of human interaction is considered. Market demand is not a 'given', something independent of the choices of flesh-and-blood human beings. The writer of a recent history of the video-cassette recorder writes of 'the idea of "educating the market" to the virtues of a product born of intuition rather than market research'. Writes James

Lardner of Sony chairman Akio Morita: 'Over the years Morita would often be asked, "Where is your market research?" He would point to his forehead and proclaim, "Here!" ' (Lardner 1987, p. 51).

To explain adequately the phenomena of the market and of exchange and co-operation, the science of economics must address itself to the rhetorical or persuasive aspects of advertising, and therefore to the dynamic self-creation involved in actual choice.

Property rights

Presupposed in all discussions of the market process is the notion of property – more specifically, of property *rights*. Given the ineluctability of both scarcity of resources and the law of the excluded middle, it is inevitable that there will be some system for deciding which, among the indefinite array of possible employments of a good, will in fact be actualized. That a variety of such systems is possible has long been known. What of the system of property rights underlying the market system? It should be obvious that not simply any assignment of property rights constitutes a market (e.g. assigning all rights to a dictator). Which system does define a market?

As there already exists a large (and expanding) literature on the economics of property rights, I will confine my remarks on this score to just a few observations. First, a market is a self-regulating system, one that does not require any participant to have access to a God-like perspective (the basic objection to the socialist conception of state planning in the service of human needs). That means that property assignments must emerge spontaneously from the voluntary interaction of market participants themselves; they cannot simply be imposed exogenously.[30]

The system of 'mine and thine' which we call property has not been with the human species since the 'beginning of time'. It emerged from the attempts of our ancestors to live together in community, to co-operate and co-ordinate their actions in pursuit of life.[31] The emergence of institutions, such as property law, is not a case of rational maximization (or maximizing choice among finite and known alternatives) but the product of our finitude. 'Rule-following behavior is the product . . . not of knowledge or omniscience but of ignorance' (O'Driscoll and Rizzo 1985, p. 119).[32]

At stake in this conception of property and law is a different conception of just what welfare economics, or the use of economic science to evaluate various possible economic arrangements, is to be. Gadamer has given us good reasons to eschew the 'infinite' perspective offered, for example, by Hegel. But that God-like perspective is typically the very perch chosen by many economists, who then propose schemes to rearrange the results of voluntary human interaction in accordance with principles of welfare maximization of their own concoction. Robert Sugden (1986, p. 7) characterizes this view as the 'US Cavalry model' of government and economic policy-making.

An alternative view, more in line with the finitude revealed by philosophical hermeneutics, would be to examine the spontaneous emergence of norms such as property and law out of the localized interactions of finite human beings. As Sugden has shown, utilizing a game-theoretic approach:

> some of our ideas of rights, entitlements and justice may be rooted in conventions that have never been consciously designed by anyone. They have merely evolved. A society that conducts its affairs in accordance with such standards of justice may not maximize its welfare in any sense that would be recognized by an impartial observer. To put this the other way round, a benevolent government may find that it cannot maximize social welfare, evaluated from some impartial viewpoint, without violating conventions that its citizens regard as principles of justice.
>
> (Sugden 1986, p. 8)

Our understanding of the role and development of individual rights, including the right to property, can be enriched by use of the notion of 'prominence' shown to be so important by Schelling (1960) in his work on co-ordination games.[33] In the kinds of games analysed by Sugden, the prominence of one's own self (i.e. my 'possession' of my self) offers a firm point for the playing of asymmetrical games, within which stable conventions can emerge. This lends strong support to the understanding of property rights offered in John Locke's *Second Treatise on Civil Government*, in which the right to alienable goods is rooted in a person's self-evident right to 'self-ownership'. (In Gadamerian terms, such rights can function much as prejudices do in human conversation, providing points of reference and possibilities for understanding and mutually beneficial interaction.) These rights are necessary for the conversation definitive of civil intercourse for the 'internalization of externalities' often cited as the central beneficial characteristic of property rights is but the emergence of a public place where interacting parties can voluntarily reach mutually satisfactory agreements.[34]

'Externalities', or third-party effects, are the effects of the actions of one or more persons on others, whether negative or positive. For example, sending out a music broadcast might generate positive externalities for those who enjoy the music; sending out a rival broadcast on the same wavelength, thus interfering with the first broadcast, would create negative externalities for the original broadcaster and her listeners. As Demsetz writes:

> What converts a harmful or beneficial effect into an externality is that the cost of bringing the effect to bear on the decisions of one or more of the interacting parties is too high to make it worthwhile. . . . 'Internalizing' such effects refers to a process, usually a change in property rights, that enables these effects to bear (in greater degree) on all interacting persons.
>
> (Demsetz 1974, p. 32)

Thus, the existence of property rights makes possible voluntary processes of interaction that would be impossible without them. 'Internalization' in this context refers to the process by which a 'public space' is opened up for people, within which they are able to engage in negotiation and contract.

CONCLUSION: COMPETITION AND LIBERTY

The voluntary competition of a free market, in which human beings are freed of domination by coercive elites, is not limited simply to the competition of ideas as expressed in speeches ('the marketplace of ideas'). In addition, it encompasses all of the voluntarily expressed forms of life, each of which can be seen as an 'entry' in the competition for adherents.

Habermas has charged Gadamer with the error of reducing 'the objective framework of social action' to 'the dimension of intersubjectively intended and symbolically transmitted meaning' (Habermas 1977, p. 361). In contrast, Habermas claims to incorporate the 'constraint of reality' in the form of labour and social power relations, which 'behind the back of language . . . affect the very grammatical rules according to which we interpret the world'. Yet, as noted above, it is the Habermasian project that typically ignores other forms of communication (e.g. market bids), empowering the intellectuals – the dealers in words – and privileging the spoken over the unspoken.

In his response to Habermas's charge, Gadamer argued that 'it is absolutely absurd to regard the concrete factors of work and politics as outside the scope of hermeneutics (Gadamer 1976, p. 31). Asks Gadamer: 'Where do [prejudices] come from? Merely out of "cultural tradition"? Surely they do, in part, but what is tradition from?' Tradition is in fact formed from experience, from – among other things – work and politics. Work and politics can indeed change tradition, but that does not earn them a status outside of the hermeneutical experience.

The discourse of society extends beyond the spoken, to encompass the exchanges of the market as well as the choice of 'styles of life' and forms of community. A revealing comparison for political economy would be to contrast the libertarian 'framework for utopia' in Robert Nozick's *Anarchy, State and Utopia* (see, especially, Ch. 10), in which communities and forms of life compete for human acceptance within a framework of uncoerced choice, with the forced 'consensus' of socialism described by Robert Heilbroner, in which:

> Dissents, disagreements, and departures from norms . . . assume a far more threatening aspect than under bourgeois society, for they hold out the possibility of destroying the very commitment to a moral consensus by which socialist society differs from capitalist.
>
> (Heilbroner 1978, p. 347)

The uncoerced competition of ideas, forms of life, and communities is the defining characteristic of the free society. But this competition and, indeed, the market process itself, can be adequately understood only as discovery procedures. Discovery does not mean, in this context, the simple 'uncovering' of already existent entities, but the introduction of true novelty, surprise, and innovation into the world. It is because man is capable of becoming other than he is that the liberty which lies at the base of the market process is so important. The orthodox utilitarian calculus of rational maximization is inadequate – either as an explanation or a defence of the market system: As Buchanan states:

Man wants liberty to become the man he wants to become. He does so precisely because he does not know what man he will want to become in time. Let us remove once and for all the instrumental defense of liberty, the only one that can possibly be derived directly from orthodox analysis. Man does not want liberty in order to maximize his utility, or that of the society of which he is a part. *He wants liberty to become the man he wants to become.*

(Buchanan 1979, p. 112)

NOTES

1 Susan Hekman (1986, pp. 139–59) argues that, while Gadamer offers us no methodology of the social sciences, his philosophy has implications for the method and practice of social science.
2 It is Ludwig Lachmann's view that:

in the study of human action we are able to achieve something which must for ever remain beyond the purview of the natural sciences, viz. to make events *intelligible* by explaining them in terms of the plans which guide our action.

(Lachmann 1977, p. 152)

For other approaches consistent with such a subjective orientation, but placed on a different philosophical footing, compare Carl Menger's empathetic approach, in which he contrasts the subjects of social sciences to the theoretical entities of the natural sciences ('atoms' and 'forces'), and concludes: 'Here the human *individuals* and their *efforts*, the final element of our analysis, are of empirical nature, and thus the exact theoretical social sciences have a great advantage over the exact natural sciences' (see Menger 1985 [1883], p. 142). Compare also Ludwig von Mises' neo-Kantian approach, within which 'action' is a category, or pure concept of the understanding, which allows us to combine the manifold of impressions into the unity of a judgement, i.e. of knowledge (see Mises 1978).
3 For an exposition of the philosophical background in Aristotle, Hegel, Husserl, and Heidegger involved in Gadamer's philosophical hermeneutics, see Palmer (1987).
4 Stubblebine summed it up in this way:

As a scientist, the social scientist has no basis on which to commend one criterion over another. Put another way, the social scientist is hopelessly lost as a *scientific* ranker of outcomes – whatever be his competence as a generator of theories of outcomes.

(Stubblebine 1975, p. 14)

UNIVERSITY OF BRISTOL

Department of Philosophy

9 Woodland Road
Bristol
BS8 1TB

5 Cf. Richard Ebeling (1986) on prices as texts requiring interpretation.

6 See Habermas's criticisms in his 'Review of Gadamer's *Truth and Method*', in Dallmayr and McCarthy (eds) (1977). Gadamer's response can be found in 'On the scope and functions of hermeneutical reflection', in his *Philosophical Hermeneutics* (trans. and ed. Linge 1976). Habermas defends his criticism in 'Summation and response', in *Continuum* 8, 1970.

7 Habermas's objective positing of what people 'really' want, independent of their actual choices, is subject to the same critique offered in this essay – of both Galbraithian 'dependency effects' and orthodox public-goods theory. Habermas's view is analogous to a static 'equilibrium' (or 'end state') approach, in contrast to Gadamer's dynamic (or 'process oriented') approach – exemplified in his discussion of language offered in Part III of *Truth and Method*.

8 Gadamer explicitly links tradition and reason, in a way that complements the Hayekian criticism of forms of 'constructivist rationalism', including coercive economic 'planning':

> there is no such unconditional antithesis between tradition and reason . . . tradition is constantly an element of freedom and of history itself. Even the most genuine and solid tradition does not persist by nature because of the inertia of what once existed. It needs to be affirmed, embraced, cultivated. It is, essentially, preservation, such as is active in all historical change. But preservation is an act of reason, though an inconspicuous one. For this reason, only what is new, or what is planned, appears as the result of reason. But this is an illusion.
>
> (Gadamer 1982, p. 250)

9 'Thou' is merely the now archaic form of the English 'You'; in German this is expressed as 'Du'.

10 An approach similar to mine is taken by Frank Van Dun (1986) in his essay 'Economics and the limits of value-free science'. Van Dun argues that the very pursuit of economics as a rational endeavour involves the scientist in a set of ethical commitments – that is, to the ethics of conversation, and thus to a transcendence of any claim to a complete divorce from ethical commitments.

11 Interestingly, many Habermas-inspired attempts to apply this model of unrestricted conversation typically confine themselves to the 'conversation' found in a journal article, a political speech, a committee hearing, or a planning-commission meeting! Not only does this reveal the class biases of the intellectuals who have written on this topic (and whose stock-in-trade is made up of just such products), but it reveals an extraordinarily cramped view of the human conversation. Cf., for example, the following essays: Fred R. Dallmayr's 'Public policy and critical discourse' (pp. 161–91 in Dallmayr 1984); Ray Kemp's 'Planning, public hearings, and the politics of discourse' (pp. 177–201 in Forester 1985); and Forester's 'Critical theory and planning practice' (pp. 202–7 in Forester 1985).

12 See, for example, Oskar Lange's 'On the economic theory of socialism':

> each individual separately regards the actual market prices as given data to which he must adjust himself. Market prices are thus parameters determining the behavior of the individuals.
>
> (Lange and Taylor 1964, p. 70)

13 Compare F.A. von Hayek's 'Competition as a discovery procedure':

> Utilisation of knowledge widely dispersed in a society with extensive division of labor cannot rest on individuals knowing the particular uses to which well-known things in their individual environments might be put. Prices direct their

attention to what is worth finding out about market offers for various things and services.

(Hayek 1978, p. 181)

14 Or, as Donald McCloskey (1985, p. 118) put it: 'Rhetoric in the sense used here . . . is reason writ large.'

15 On this, see Hume (1978 [1739–40], p. 415): 'Reason is and ought only to be the slave of passions, and can never pretend to any other office than to serve and obey them.'

16 To assert that the analogy of conversation can help us to understand the market exchange process is not to assert an isomorphism between the two phenomena in every dimension. In some ways, perhaps, the analogy is more illuminating when shined in the other direction – with the traditional model of exchange helping us to understand better what goes on in a conversation. Cf. Donald McCloskey (1985, pp. 76–8) on the use and limitations of metaphor in economics: for example, the conceptual treatment of children as 'durable goods' in Gary Becker's economic theory of the family.

17 Such activity, i.e. real learning, is typically banned from neoclassical equilibrium and perfect-competition models, which assume (in one way or another) perfect information and perfect foresight for all market participants. Such assumptions naturally 'set up' economics for the kind of 'miss-the-point' criticism offered recently by Amitai Etzioni (for example, see Etzioni 1986a and b). A better approach, reformulating equilibrium without becoming entangled in Etzioni's conceptual confusion, can be found in O'Driscoll and Rizzo (1985).

18 I do not mean to imply that no 'Galbraithian' criticisms of advertising can be found in some of Gadamer's writings, but only that to the extent that they are present they represent a departure from Gadamer's central themes.

19 Buchanan's essay, 'Order defined in the process of its emergence', was originally published in *Literature of Liberty* (Winter 1982).

20 For an example of a revealing treatment of choice which keeps this distinction in mind, see Sokolowski (1985). See also Aristotle's *Nichomachean Ethics* 1112b35: 'we do not deliberate about ends but about means (the "toward-the-ends")'. The translation 'means' is completely inadequate to capture Aristotle's point, which is to reveal the kind of part/whole relationship appropriate to 'means' and 'ends' without treating them as independently-existing pieces. This is another version of the same problem being treated by Buchanan (1985) and at greater length by O'Driscoll and Rizzo (1985, pp. 130–59).

21 See also Popper (1950). On the logical impossibility of predicting our future choices, see Schick (1979).

22 This public-goods-based contractarian theory of the state has been subjected to withering criticism on wholly internal grounds by Joseph Kalt (1981). The status of the state's very existence as a public good would itself require coercion for its creation, thus effectively undercutting any contractarian basis for the genesis of the state.

23 For a fuller exposition of this issue, with some empirical examples of public goods, see Palmer (1983). See also Palmer (1989) for a treatment of markets for intellectual goods without patents or copyrights. A criticism of orthodox public-goods theory which focuses on institutions can be found in Cowen (1985).

24 For the case of natural resources (including treatments of pollution externalities), see Stroup and Baden (1983); see also Anderson and Hill (1975). For the case of property right and the magnetic spectrum, see Mueller (1983).

25 See, for example, Klein (1987). For a discussion of the bundling of non-complementary goods, see Olson (1965), especially pp. 132–67.

26 For a discussion of exclusion devices, see Goldin (1977):

The evidence suggests that we are *not* faced with a set of goods and services which have the inherent characteristics of public goods. Rather, we are faced with an unavoidable choice regarding every good or service: shall everyone have *equal access* to that service (in which case the service will be similar to a public good) or shall the service be available *selectively*, to some, but not to others? In practice, public goods theory is often used in such a way that one overlooks this important choice problem.

(Goldin 1977)

See also de Jasay (1989) for a dynamic treatment of public goods.

27 See, for example, Brubaker (1975) and Schmidtz (1987).

28 Coase's point is that persuasion can also be seen as a form of information: this is complementary to, but not the same as, the thrust of my argument.

29 As Littlechild has put it:

[the manufacturer] has to help the consumer to act *entrepreneurially*. For this purpose, advertising may well have to be persuasive, even accompanied by a catchy jingle, because it is necessary to attract the consumer's attention, and persuade him that it will be worthwhile to take an interest.

(Littlechild 1986, p. 34)

30 Legitimate property rights, like law, emerge spontaneously from the interaction of the interested parties. As Bruno Leoni has pointed out, law is a 'horizontal' rather than a 'vertical' creation: 'The legal process always traces back in the end to the individual claim. Individuals make the law, insofar as they make claims' (see Leoni 1963).

31 For a discussion of the emergence of law as defining salient points for strategic interaction, and the normative status such rules can attain, see Postema (1982). For a game-theoretic approach to the spontaneous emergence of property rights, see Sugden (1986). For a juristic approach to the spontaneous emergence of law, see Leoni (1972). For a legal historical approach, see Trakman (1983).

32 For a brief discussion of the kinds of ignorance ('optimal' versus 'sheer' ignorance) relevant to discussion of the market process, see Thomsen (1987) who notes that:

the market system is, at any time, full of regrettable inefficiencies and mistakes (many of which will be in the process of being entrepreneurially discovered and corrected). But it is scientifically invalid simply to assume the existence of a government authority in possession of all the knowledge necessary for their solution. The analysis should, more appropriately, consider which social arrangement has the means for the discovery of such knowledge. Viewed in the light of such a standard, the market has at least one major advantage over other systems: through its translation of innumerable inefficiencies and mistakes into opportunities for pecuniary profit it alone seems to have the power to awaken and mobilize the entrepreneurial alertness of market participants and thus to promote the discovery of these inefficiencies and their solutions.

(Thomsen 1987, p. 1–17)

33 Schelling found consistently uniform responses to simple questions asked in various co-ordination games played by experimental subjects. The games played included asking two isolated respondents to name a number, such that if they name the same number, they would receive a prize. A remarkable number (given the infinite choice set) chose the same number, i.e. 1. The number one has a kind of natural prominence, as has, for example, the choice of Grand Central Station at noon as a meeting place and time for two people to meet in New York. As Sugden (1986) shows, such prominent points can provide the foundation for the spontaneous emergence of conventions.

34 On the significance of private property and contract for the creation of a public sphere, see Grace Goodell's (1980) anthropological study.

REFERENCES

Anderson, Terry L. and Hill, P.J. (1975) 'The evolution of property rights: a study of the American West', *Journal of Law and Economics* 18 (April), pp. 163–79.

Baumol, William (1969) *Welfare Economics and the Theory of the State*, Cambridge, Mass.: Harvard University Press.

Brubaker, Earl (1975) 'Free ride, free revelation, or golden rule?', *Journal of Law Economics* XVIII (April), pp. 147–61.

Buchanan, James (1979) 'Natural and artefacted man', in Buchanan, *What Should Economists Do?*, Indianapolis: Liberty Press.

—— (1985) 'Order defined in the process of its emergence', in Buchanan, *Liberty, Market and State: Political Economy in the 1980s*, New York: New York University Press, pp. 73–4.

Coase, R.H. (1977) 'Advertising and free speech', in Allen Hyman and M. Bruce Johnson (eds) *Advertising and Free Speech*, Lexington: Lexington Books.

Cowen, Tyler (1985) 'Public goods definitions and their institutional context: a critique of public goods theory', *Review of Social Economy* XLII (April).

Dallmayr, Fred R. (1984) 'Public policy and critical discourse', in Dallmayr, *Polis and Praxis: Exercises in Contemporary Political Theory*, Cambridge, Mass.: MIT Press.

—— and McCarthy, Thomas, A. (eds) (1977) *Understanding and Social Inquiry*, Notre Dame, Indiana: University of Notre Dame Press.

Demsetz, Harold (1974) 'Toward a theory of property rights', in Erik G. Furubotn and Svetozar Pejovich (eds) *The Economics of Property Rights*, Cambridge, Mass.: Ballinger Publishing Co.

Ebeling, Richard (1986) 'Toward a hermeneutical economics: expectations, prices, and the role of interpretation in a theory of the market process', in Israel M. Kirzner (ed.) *Subjectivism, Intelligibility and the Economic Understanding: Essays in Honor of Ludwig M. Lachmann*, New York: New York University Press.

Engelhardt, H. Tristram, Jr. (1986) *The Foundations of Bioethics*, New York: Oxford University Press.

Etzioni, Amitai (1986a) 'The case for a multiple-utility conception', *Economics and Philosophy* 2 (2) October, pp. 159–83.

—— (1986b) 'Founding a new socioeconomics', *Challenge* Nov.–Dec., pp. 13–17.

Forester, John (ed.) (1985) *Critical Theory and Public Life*, Cambridge, Mass.: MIT Press.

Friedman, Milton (1967) 'Value judgements in economics', in Sidney Hook (ed.) *Human Values and Economic Policy*, New York: New York University Press, pp. 85–93.

Gadamer, Hans-Georg (1976) 'On the scope and function of hermeneutical reflection', in Gadamer, *Philosophical Hermeneutics*, trans. and ed. by David Linge, Berkeley: University of California Press.

—— (1982) *Truth and Method*, New York: Crossroad.

Goldin, Kenneth (1977) 'Equal access vs. selective access: a critique of public goods theory', *Public Choice* XXIX (Spring), pp. 53–71.

Goodell, Grace (1980) 'From status to contract: the significance of agrarian relations of production in the west, Japan, and in "Asiatic" Persia', *European Journal of Sociology*, XXI, pp. 285–325.

Gray, John (1980) 'F.A. Hayek on liberty and tradition', *Journal of Libertarian Studies* 4 (Spring) pp. 119–37.

Habermas, Jürgen (1977) 'A review of Gadamer's *Truth and Method*', in Fred Dallmayr and Thomas McCarthy (eds) *Understanding and Social Inquiry*, Notre Dame, Indiana: University of Notre Dame Press.

―― (1970) 'Summation and response', *Continuum* 8, pp. 123–33.

Hayek, F.A. von (1969) 'The non sequitur of the dependence effect', in Hayek, *Studies in Philosophy, Politics and Economics*, New York: Simon & Schuster.

―― (1978) *New Studies in Philosophy, Politics, Economics and the History of Ideas*, Chicago: University of Chicago Press.

―― (1988) *The Fatal Conceit: The Errors of Socialism*, Chicago: University of Chicago Press.

Heidegger, Martin (1962) *Being and Time*, New York: Harper & Row.

Heilbroner, Robert (1978) 'What is socialism?', *Dissent*, Summer, pp. 341–8.

Hekman, Susan J. (1986) *Hermeneutics and the Sociology of Knowledge*, Notre Dame, Indiana: University of Notre Dame Press.

Hume, David (1978) [1739–40] *A Treatise of Human Nature*, ed. by L.A. Selby-Brigge, rev. by P.H. Nidditch, New York: Oxford University Press.

Husserl, Edmund (1970) 'On the theory of wholes and parts', in Husserl, *Logical Investigations*, translated by J.N. Findlay, New York: Humanities Press, vol. II, pp. 435–89.

Ingram, David (1985) 'Hermeneutics and truth', in Robert Hollinger (ed.) *Hermeneutics and Praxis*, Notre Dame, Indiana: University of Notre Dame Press, pp. 32–53.

de Jasay, Anthony (1989) *Social Contract, Free Ride: A Study of the Public Goods Problem*, New York: Oxford University Press.

Kalt, Joseph (1981) 'Public goods and the theory of government', *Cato Journal* 1 (2), Fall, pp. 565–84.

Kemp, Ray (1985) 'Planning, public hearings, and the politics of discourse', in John Forester (ed.) *Critical Theory and Public Life*, Cambridge, Mass.: MIT Press, pp. 177–201.

Kirzner, Israel (1979) 'Equilibrium versus market process', in Kirzner, *Perception, Opportunity and Profit*, Chicago: University of Chicago Press.

Klein, Daniel (1987) 'Tie-ins and the market provision of collective goods', *Harvard Journal of Law and Public Policy* X (2) Spring, pp. 452–74.

Lachmann, Ludwig (1977) 'Methodological individualism and the market economy', in Walter Grinder (ed.) *Capital, Expectations, and the Market Process: Essays on the Theory of the Market Economy*, Kansas City: Sheed Andrews & McMeel.

Lange, Oskar (1964) 'On the economic theory of socialism', in Oskar Lange and Fred Taylor *On the Economic Theory of Socialism*, ed. by Benjamin E. Lippincott, New York: McGraw-Hill.

Lardner, James (1987) *Fast Forward: Hollywood, the Japanese and the VCR Wars*, New York: W.W. Norton & Co.

Leoni, Bruno (1963) Lectures given at the Freedom School Phrontistery, Colorado Springs, Colorado, December 2–6.

―― (1972) *Freedom and the Law*, Los Angeles: Nash Publishing.

Levy, David (1986) 'Can we trade if we do not talk? Adam Smith and the Texas A&M Rats', unpublished manuscript, Fairfax: Center for Study of Public Choice, George Mason University.

Littlechild, S.C. (1986) *The Fallacy of the Mixed Economy*, 2nd edn, London: Institute of Economic Affairs.

McCloskey, Donald (1985) *The Rhetoric of Economics*, Madison: University of Wisconsin Press.

Menger, Carl (1985 [1883]) *Investigations into the Method of the Social Sciences with Special Reference to Economics*, New York: New York University Press.

Mises, Ludwig von (1978 [1962]) *The Ultimate Foundations of Economc Science*, Kansas City: Sheed Andrews & McMeel.

Mueller, Milton (1983) 'Reforming telecommunications regulation', in Edwin Diamond, Norman Sandler, and Milton Mueller (eds) *Telecommunications in Crisis: The First Amendment, Technology and Deregulation*, Washington, D.C.: Cato Institute.

Nozick, Robert (1974) *Anarchy, State and Utopia*, New York: Basic Books.

O'Driscoll, Gerald and Rizzo, Mario (1985) *The Economics of Time and Ignorance*, New York: Basil Blackwell.

Olson, Mancur (1965) *The Logic of Collective Action*, Cambridge, Mass.: Harvard University Press.

Palmer, Tom G. (1983) 'Infrastructure: public or public?', *Policy Report* V (5) May.

—— (1987) 'Gadamer's hermeneutics and social theory', *Critical Review* I (3) Summer, pp. 1–11.

—— (1989) 'Intellectual property rights: a non-Posnerian law and economics approach', *Hamline Law Review* 12, no. 2, pp. 261–304.

—— (1990) 'Are patents and copyrights morally justified? The philosophy of property rights and ideal objects', *Harvard Journal of Law and Public Policy*, vol. 13, no. 3.

Popper, Karl (1950) 'Indeterminism in quantum physics and classical physics', *British Journal for the Philosophy of Science* 1, pp. 113–73.

—— (1972) *Objective Knowledge: An Evolutionary Approach*, Oxford: Oxford University Press.

Postema, Gerald L. (1982) 'Co-ordination and convention at the foundation of law', *Journal of Legal Studies* XI (January), pp. 165–203.

Schelling, Thomas (1960) *The Strategy of Conflict*, Cambridge, Mass.: Harvard University Press.

Schick, F. (1979) 'Self knowledge, uncertainty and choice', *British Journal for the Philosophy of Science*, 30.

Schmidtz, David (1987) 'Contracts and public goods', *Harvard Journal of Law and Public Policy* X (2) Spring, pp. 475–503.

Smith, Adam (1978a [1776]) *An Inquiry into the Nature and Causes of the Wealth of Nations*, New York: Oxford University Press.

—— (1978b [1896]) *Lectures on Jurisprudence*, New York: Oxford University Press.

Sokolowski, Robert (1985) *Moral Action: A Phenomenological Study*, Bloomington: Indiana University Press.

Stroup, Richard L. and Baden, John A. (1983) *Natural Resources: Bureaucratic Myths and Environmental Management*, Cambridge, Mass.: Ballinger.

Stubblebine, William Craig (1975) 'On property rights and institutions', in Henry Manne (ed.) *The Economics of Legal Relationships*, New York: West Publishing Co., pp. 11–22.

Sugden, Robert (1986) *The Economics of Rights, Co-operation and Welfare*, Oxford: Basil Blackwell.

Thomsen, Esteban F. (1987) 'Knowledge, discovery and prices', *Humane Studies Review* V (1), Fall.

Trakman, Leon (1983) *The Law Merchant: The Evolution of Commercial Law*, Littleton, Colorado: Fred B. Rothman & Co.

Van Dun, Frank (1986) 'Economics and the limits of value-free science', *Reason Papers* no. 11 (Spring), pp. 17–32.

Wittgenstein, Ludwig (1968) *Philosophical Investigations*, vol. I, Oxford: Basil Blackwell.

Index